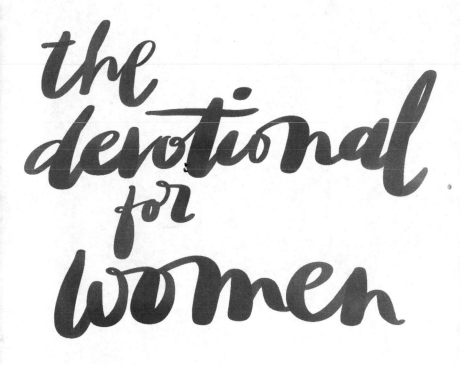

the
devotional
for
women

PUBLISHING GROUP

NASHVILLE, TENNESSEE

the devotional for women

edited by

Rhonda | Dorothy
Harrington | Kelley
Kelley | Patterson

978-1-5359-2833-5

Published by B&H Publishing Group
Nashville, Tennessee

Dewey Decimal Classification: 242.2
Subject Heading: WOMEN \ SPIRITUAL LIFE \ DEVOTIONAL LITERATURE

1 2 3 4 5 6 7 8 9 10 • 22 21 20 19 18

Contents

Introduction

What does God say to a woman in the twenty-first century? God's Word provides all you need for living life to the fullest and honoring the Lord Jesus in the process. This *Devotional for Women* is prepared directly from the text of Scripture by a multi-generational team of God-honoring, spiritually-gifted women. This inspirational tool follows the Thread of Biblical Womanhood found in the *The Study Bible for Women* and will guide your study and meditation throughout the Bible.

The *Devotional for Women* features relevant discussions on various topics relating to God's design for the woman as well as profiles of both named and unnamed women of the Bible. Each day's message includes application and encouragement for you as the Lord writes His truths on your heart, molding you into His image, and using you as a conduit for glorifying Him in every aspect of your life.

The single and married women who have written these daily commentaries come from different seasons of life and various geographical areas. We have several generational groups—a mother, daughter, and pair of granddaughters from one family; several mother-daughter duos; and a mother-in-love and daughter-in-love. We have teens in high school, college and seminary students, young mothers, and grandmothers. Their names are found with the devotionals, together with brief information about each in the list of contributors. All are committed to woman-to-woman ministries.

The *Devotional for Women* has a reading for every day but is undated. You can pick it up and begin your spiritual journey any day of the year. You can turn to the numbered day of your annual calendar or start with "Day 1" on any day you choose to begin. Each devotional stands alone. You can read the extended passage, or you can simply read the focus verse(s), printed for you as the devotional unfolds. The brevity of the passage enables you to savor its words and meditate upon its message, perhaps even memorizing the verse(s).

Use the guided prayer pattern to approach the throne of grace with your own petition and praise. Make your personal notes in the space for "Personal Reflection." Perhaps you will note somewhere on the day's page the date (day/month/year)—make your own "stones of help" along the way as reminders in days and years to come of what God has been doing in your life. This *Devotional* is not planned as a one-time experience; rather, we think you will want to come back, whether in successive years or return after skipping a year or two, and work through its pages again, seeing what God has already done in time past and looking afresh for His Word to you.

Let this journey through the thread of biblical womanhood be personal. Whether you are looking for answers to challenging questions, inspiration for spiritual nurture, direction for your life journey, renewal in your heart and spirit, or just conversation with the Lord—this *Devotional for Women* is prepared to be your companion and guide. Packed with insights from Scripture and practical applications, each day's reading will touch your life, perhaps speaking to your heart's deepest needs, your family challenges, or your service for Christ.

When you come to God's Word with an open heart, ready to hear God speak, willing to respond to Him in obedience, you will find yourself in His story—your place in His master plan. He will teach you; He will conform you to His image; He will then use you in ways you could never have imagined except that you have spent time with Him!

Dorothy Kelley Patterson

A Pattern of Personal Quiet Time

The commitment to building spiritual intimacy with the Lord Jesus is personal—not something anyone else can build into your life. Whether a child, teenager, young adult, or mature woman—whether you are new in your faith journey or spiritually strong and disciplined in your faith, **you** must initiate genuine, heart-felt communication with the Lord and establish your own pattern for sustaining the relationship you have established with the Lord Jesus.

Women throughout history—from Bible times to the current generation—have been marked by such a commitment. The maidservant of Naaman's wife was taken from her parents into captivity at a young age (2 Kin. 5:1–3); yet she had already developed a relationship with the living God. She kept her faith; she shared it. Her strength did not come because of many years of spiritual training but because she started at a young age and refused to let earthly circumstances destroy a heavenly commitment.

The Moabitess Ruth had no witness to the true God until after she married, but she observed her mother-in-law Naomi and learned spiritual disciplines, which brought her into a relationship with the living God and introduced her to the joys of serving Him. Mary of Nazareth, the mother of our Lord, as a young woman had been introduced to *Yahweh* God and taught His Word through her childhood years so that when she was faced with what seemed humanly impossible, she humbly bowed herself before God the Father and willingly accepted His assignment.

These "spiritual sisters" were characterized by a commitment to hearing and knowing God's Word, then living it out in practical ways (see Matt. 7:24). That commitment thrives and blooms in the presence of the Lord—reading His Word, listening for His voice, sharing innermost fears and petitions, spending quality as well as quantity time with Him.

Women more than anything else need a word from God. The written Word of God was prepared in "the fullness of time" (Gal. 4:4) and continues to speak to women in this generation with the same authority and clarity as it did in centuries gone by, and that Word will continue to speak to generations to come. Scripture does not speak in detail to every situation in life, but the Bible records timeless principles that continue to be timely solutions to all of life's challenges.

Let this volume be a tool for you to return to **Bethel** (Hb. "house of God"). Pursue with purpose and passion, putting yourself in the presence of the Lord for a time of prayer and reading His Word. Let these woman-to-woman devotionals add an inspirational thought or instructive moment to your time with the Lord.

In addition to the devotionals, you will find a Bible Reading Plan, which follows this Thread of Biblical Womanhood, prepared by Rhonda Kelley. Nothing will enrich your life so much as systematic and purposeful reading of the Word of God. She has also prepared an article that sets forth clearly how you can come to know Jesus Christ as your personal Savior.

Join me in a "Bethel" year. May you and I make our way, not merely on a whim of urgent need or as a perfunctory happenstance or even a passing fad, into the presence of the living Lord—sitting at His feet, reading His Word, meditating on its application to life, pouring out our praise and petition to Him! Do this every day, and consider making a commitment to work through the entire year with a pattern of personal quiet time devoted to pursuing the Lord—not through an ordinary ritual but rather establishing an extraordinary life discipline that will carry you through life with purpose and praise.

This time for personal intimacy with the Lord is yours to establish. The psalmist speaks of calling out to the Lord "morning, noon, and night." Surely you can select one time—even brief minutes—during the 24-hour cycle you are given to devote uninterrupted and focused minutes to the Lord. Start today!

Dorothy Kelley Patterson

The Christian Life

Are you a Christian? A Christian is anyone who has received by faith the salvation God has provided in Jesus Christ. **Salvation** is necessary because all have sinned against God (Rom. 3:23). Salvation begins with **repentance**—turning away from sin and turning toward God, who alone has the power to save. You cannot earn salvation by doing good works for it is a gift of grace from God, accomplished through the death of His Son, Jesus Christ (Eph. 2:8–9). When Jesus died on the cross, He paid the price to forgive all sin (John 3:16; Rom. 5:8; 1 John 2:2). Romans 6:23 says, "For the wages of sin is death, but the gift of God is eternal life in Christ Jesus our Lord." God's free gift of salvation—the exchange of your sin for His righteousness—must be accepted by faith (Rom. 10:9–10). When you accept God's gift of salvation, you become a new creation (2 Cor. 5:17). Salvation changes everything—your past, your present, and your future:

- **Justification** may be considered the past tense of salvation. Justification is God's declaration that you are righteous through the blood of Christ (Rom. 4:3–25).
- **Sanctification** is the present tense of salvation, the process of growing in faith and in holiness since you are set apart by and for God (1 Cor. 6:11).
- **Glorification** is the future tense of salvation. Glorification is the perfection of God's image and character in you when you enter His presence in heaven (2 Cor. 3:18).

If you are a Christian, you are promised security in your salvation, but what is your present "new creation" life supposed to look like? What responsibilities do you have in maintaining a vibrant relationship with your Savior?

The Beginning. Your Christian life begins the moment you turn away from sin and, by faith, receive the salvation God has provided in the crucifixion and resurrection of His Son Jesus Christ. At that moment, the Holy Spirit makes Himself at home in your life, immediately beginning the remodeling process necessary for Christ to be seen in every aspect. Just as the Christian life does not begin when you are born, when you become a church member, or when you mistakenly think you have earned God's approval for doing good, so it does not continue on the basis of who you are, whom you know, where you go to church, or what you do. Just as there is nothing you can do to get rid of your sin and restore your relationship with God—Jesus sacrificed Himself to provide the forgiveness needed, so you cannot "live the Christian life" on your own terms. Relinquishing ownership and control of your life to Christ is just the beginning of the total life makeover.

The Ongoing Story. From that point on, your salvation is secure. Regardless of how sin-stained or sin-wrecked your life is when you entrust it to Christ, all is forgiven. However, you have a ruthless enemy who is determined to thwart God's renovation plans for your life by any means possible and keep you from telling anyone else the Good News. In Christ you have freedom from the addiction to sin and from consequent death (i.e., eternal separation from God). No longer are you the enemy's slave to do his bidding, but he strives to convince you otherwise. Scripture often talks about this war in terms of light and darkness. Christ's message is that "God is light, and there is absolutely no darkness in Him" (1 John 1:5). Speaking to authentic Christians about their changed status, Ephesians 5:8 says, "For you were once darkness, but now *you are* light in the Lord" and commands, "Walk as children of light."

The power to "walk in the light as He [Jesus Christ] Himself is in the light" (1 John 1:7a) is available in the Holy Spirit who is always with the Christian. Living the Christian life—walking in the light—is only possible by continually agreeing with the truth He reveals and letting Him exchange, change, and rear-range however He sees fit. The truth is found in the Bible. The power to obey the truth is in the Holy Spirit. The Christian whose mind is Scripture-saturated and whose will is Spirit-directed is equipped to grow in Christlikeness, but this growth also requires staying connected to the body of Christ, the local church. The Christian life is nurtured in your personal devotional life of Bible study and prayer but expressed in your relationships—both with your brothers and sisters in Christ and with non-Christians.

In the End. Until Jesus returns, the physical lives of Christians will end but not without hope. Jesus' resurrection validates His promise of eternal life to those who follow Him. The Christian life is best lived with the end (as described in Scripture) in mind (see 2 Pet. 3), not only looking forward to God's justice and the rewards of endurance but also looking for opportunities to proclaim the gospel (see 1 Pet. 4). From confession of faith into eternity, the Christian life is a reflection of Christ Himself, an extension of His work in the world, and a witness of salvation to those who are unsaved.

Blessings,
Rhonda Kelly

God's Crowning Touch to the Creation Order

Genesis 1:26–31

"Then God said, 'Let Us make man in Our image, according to Our likeness; . . .
So God created man in His own image; in the image of God He created him;
male and female He created them.'" (vv. 26–27)

In the first chapter of Genesis, the Book of Beginnings, the woman is not an afterthought. The man and the woman were both created in the image and likeness of God Himself. The man was created first because God planned for him to be the provider, protector, and leader (2:15–17); but from the beginning he was designed and created physically, emotionally, socially, and spiritually to receive the woman as his helper and partner in the great work God planned for them to do.

The woman, according to God's design, is equal to but not the same as the man; she is equal to and different than the man. There is no inferiority or superiority. The woman and the man are equal in their personhood, equally clothed in His glory, equally joint-heirs (1 Pet. 3:7). Their divinely assigned role distinctions are carefully foretold in the creation of each and then faithfully affirmed in their respective role assignments.

Adam was created and placed in the garden to tend and guard it, to name the animals, to provide responsible leadership in the home—God's first institution and the one described here in Genesis—and later in the church. Balancing decision-making leadership with self-sacrificing love is exemplified in the Lord Himself. The woman is created from a part of the man's side. She is to be a full spiritual partner, assisting the man in the stewardship of guiding and caring for God's creation and performing spiritual service to the Lord. Even the Hebrew words used by Adam reflect the unique unity of the man (Hb. *'ish*) and woman (Hb. *'ishshah*). So the woman corresponds to the man as the same bone and flesh as well as in bearing the image of God—equal in every way (Gen. 1:27). Her worth and value are clearly confirmed (2:22–23), and the way is prepared for the man and woman to link their lives in accomplishing the Creator's plan for extending the generations and exercising dominion over creation.

The world tries to mar and destroy God's beautiful plan. Efforts continue to distort the perfectly balanced harmony God wove into this unique relationship of reciprocity—loving headship matched with gracious submission; godly leadership paired with faithful helping. Yet this clear picture runs consistently throughout Scripture without contradiction in every instructive passage. And the interwoven narratives illustrate the tragedy of disobedience as well as the joy of obedience.

Dorothy Kelley Patterson

Prayer: *Ask the Lord to give you a heart like His with a determination to be obedient to the Father, to line up under His commands, to accept His plan. Consider the life of Christ as the pattern for your submission just as His life is the model for your husband's headship.*

Personal Reflection: ....

....

....

....

....

....

Beautiful House or House Beautiful?

Genesis 2:8–15

"The Lord God planted a garden eastward in Eden, and there He put the man whom He had formed. And out of the ground the Lord God made every tree grow that is pleasant to the sight and good for food. The tree of life was also in the midst of the garden, and the tree of the knowledge of good and evil." (vv. 8–9)

The garden of Eden has become a euphemism for perfection of dwelling and lifestyle. Unfortunately, for most women home is a dream dwelling with a prestigious location, picturesque structure, exquisite furnishings, helpful neighbors, and a loving family. What happens to the "beautiful house"?

The Creator's plan begins with a clear statement that He—"the Lord God"—plants you where He wants you to be geographically, which often is not where you want to be This divinely appointed "garden" (Hb. *gan,* "a place hedged around" or "protected") is a wonderful metaphor for what the Creator designed as home. Gardens set apart a particular space; they suggest beauty—whether flowers or fruit trees or just a touch of green and some natural stones; some produce food and sustenance; they often create a sense of peace and quiet rest and provide a perfect setting for conversation and building relationships (vv. 9–10, 16, 21–23).

How fitting that God decided to name this garden "Eden" (a Persian loan word meaning "delight"). Here then is the challenge: Can you create a home of "delight" for those whom you love the most and for the strangers who pass your way? I truly have happy memories from all the dwellings in which I have lived—some more than others, several that demanded far less creativity and energy to pull together, none that I was privileged to design or even decorate exactly as I wanted. But I am grateful that this challenge to create "delight" in my home found me early in my journey! Understanding the Creator's plan and opening my heart to dream of "House Beautiful," a place of delight for me and my family, I have found the Lord faithful to provide creativity and energy in the journey.

How can you make your house beautiful? Regardless of the neighborhood in which you are living, whatever the age or size of your home, despite the quality of your furnishings and accessories—you can create "house beautiful" using your own creative energies and developing an attitude of faithful service to those whom you love the most.

Dorothy Kelley Patterson

Prayer: *Ask the Lord to give to you a sense of contentment with where He has placed you. Make your petitions to Him for ways you envision making your home* Eden, *a place of "Delight." Then consider the words of Amy Carmichael: "Wait and See" what He will do!*

Personal Reflection: ....

....

....

....

....

....

....

A Helper I Will Be

Genesis 2:18–23

*"And the LORD God said, 'It is not good that man should be alone;
I will make him a helper comparable to him.'" (v. 18)*

My young children and I did chores together. First the tasks were harder and more time-intensive as I included them in the work; but as they gained experience, I shared my burdens with their youthful energies and profited from their working alongside me. The heart of helping is not merely the fellowship of working together as delightful as that can be. Rather, greater productivity and sometimes even more efficiency are also in play.

In the work God has given me to do as First Lady at Southwestern Baptist Theological Seminary, I am blessed with "helpers." I have no technology skills, but a college student can rescue me and get me back on track. The size of the president's home and the extent of its hospitality are beyond what I am physically able to do. Students with far less experience can contribute creativity and fresh energies and help me serve our guests. Their new ideas sometimes surpass my old ways of doing the task.

In God's economy, a helper is one who provides what is lacking, doing what another cannot do alone. Yet every effective helper must be sensitive to the one she is helping. The recipient of help has a certain authority over the helper. So "helper" (Hb. *'ēzer*) does not suggest a servile role. Rather the helper may be better trained and equipped than the one she is helping in certain tasks.

For example, someone driving me to a church engagement is better at directions than I am. My husband says that even the dogs have a better guidance system than I do! God describes Himself as a ready "helper" for His children (Ex. 18:4; Deut. 33:7; Ps. 20:2); yet He is not beneath us or of less value. When we call Him, He brings something more to enable us to do the task.

So clearly God gives to me as a wife the role of being a "helper." Yet this phrase in Genesis includes another part—"his complement" (Hb. *kenegdo*) or one corresponding to what is in front of him. Here then is God's creative purpose for the woman wrapped up in a poignant and precious phrase that includes our common equality (like or corresponding to the man) as well as our unique function (helping or assisting him in the great work God has given to both the man and the woman)!

Dorothy Kelley Patterson

Prayer: *Ask the Lord to give you a vision of how this dynamic relationship—of equal status before God while embracing God-given differences in function—should work in your life and marriage. Rest in the equality you share before the Father, but rejoice in the unique role He has given to you.*

Personal Reflection: ....

....

....

....

....

....

....

....

God's Plan for Marriage

Genesis 2:24–25

∽

*"Therefore a man shall leave his father and mother
and be joined to his wife, and they shall become one flesh." (v. 24)*

Have you ever stopped to consider the origin of weddings and the roots of life's most basic human relationship, which we call marriage? Look no further than Genesis 2 where God Himself at the dawn of creation became the Father of the bride and presented the woman to the man. Then for all the generations to follow, God's plan is recorded in Holy Scripture—first in Genesis 2:24 but also in Matthew 19:5, Mark 10:6–8, and Ephesians 5:31 in the New Testament. Marriage was established in perfection with one man and one woman in a lifetime commitment. Their physical and emotional needs were to be met in this union, and they together were to glorify God, worship Him, and do His work.

Presented at the beginning of creation in the garden of Eden, this plan for marriage is meant to continue as God's standard through every succeeding generation. Although no parents were present, the Lord begins unfolding His plan as if they were! Here are his requirements for this unique union that surpasses all other human relationships:

- **Leave . . . father and mother,** overriding all other human commitments and replacing previous loyalties as well as a personal lifestyle marked by your own goals and plans;
- **Be joined** (Hb. *davaq,* "hold fast, cling to") as husband and wife in unconditional love and faithful commitment;
- **Become one flesh** in physical and emotional union—the most exclusive human intimacy.

No human bond—not with parent or even with child—is to supersede this union between husband and wife. Vows exchanged are not merely on the human level between husband and wife, but are witnessed and received by God Himself.

The same language describing this commitment is used elsewhere in Scripture as descriptive of covenant relationships (e.g., Deut. 11:22–23). Most definitely a new unit is formed, but there will still be extended family ties, including the responsibility to honor parents and to minister to others in the family circle. Yet the marriage between a man and a woman, according to God's design, is an intimate bond that is unbreakable, permanent, and complete in itself.

Ultimately a Christian woman marries because she senses that by linking her life to the man God has brought into her life, she and her husband together will be much stronger and be able to serve the Lord more effectively together than either could do alone. The potential is for their effectiveness as a couple to be multiplied and their burdens divided!

Dorothy Kelley Patterson

Prayer: *Spend time with the Lord praying for your marriage. Consider His blueprint and put alongside the ways you have followed the plan so simply and perfectly unfolded in Genesis. Focus on seeking His help to make your marriage strong and enduring.*

Personal Reflection: ....

....

....

....

....

....

Satan's Battle Plan

Genesis 3:1–6

"So when the woman saw that the tree was good for food, that it was pleasant to the eyes, and a tree desirable to make one wise, she took of its fruit and ate." (v. 6a)

God has given us the battle plan of Satan. No temptation to be drawn into disobedience and sin falls outside what is detailed in Genesis 3. Satan chose to disguise himself as a "serpent . . . cunning" ("crafty, shrewd," suggesting a well-planned and sensible attack on the prey).

Why did Satan approach Eve? Adam was created first. Perhaps Satan approached Eve since she, unlike Adam, had not received directly from God the prohibition concerning "the fruit of the tree."

Satan makes his approach in the same general way—whatever the test may be. You can stop at any point and refuse to be drawn into disobedience—until you reach the final step. Here is the adversary's battle plan:

- **Has God indeed said . . . ?** (v. 1). Did God really say that? Questioning God is the beginning of every slippery slope in your life.
- **You shall not eat it, nor shall you touch it, lest you die** (v. 3). Eve adds her own interpretation to God's words. Whether she was trying to make God's words more restrictive and thus unjust or simply carelessly exaggerating the words of God, she erred in putting her personal words in the mouth of the Creator God.
- **You will not surely die** (v. 4). The devil contradicted God, twisting the words coming directly from God.
- **You will be like God, knowing good and evil** (v. 5). At the root of every temptation is the desire to go your own way instead of God's way. Satan moves to surpass God—offering you more! He uses a half-truth; Eve's knowledge would be increased through experience. She would now "know" evil by doing it.

- **She took of its fruit and ate** (v. 6). Eve chose to disobey God. She saw, appealing to appetite, beauty, and ambition (see 1 John 2:16); she took and drew into her own heart; she ate. But she did not stop there—she also gave to her husband, extending the sphere of her disobedience.

Paul warned his protégé Timothy, "Flee also youthful lusts" (2 Tim. 2:22). Eve engaged in conversation with her adversary, lingered in his presence, then allowed herself to be drawn into his net of deceit. Refuse to allow Satan to pull you into disobedience lest you, too, are guilty of disobedience and a conduit for the ravages of your sinful choices to extend to any with whom you have influence.

Dorothy Kelley Patterson

Pray: *This battle begins on your knees. Ask the Lord to give you wisdom and discernment in the choices you are making. Remember the plan of Satan and heed the warning of Paul—flee to the presence of Jesus Himself for refuge.*

Personal Reflection: ....

....

....

....

....

....

The Dawning of the Gospel

Genesis 3:7–15

"And I will put enmity
Between you and the woman,
And between your seed and her Seed;
He shall bruise your head,
And you shall bruise His heel." (v. 15)

Eve chose to believe Satan rather than God; she turned her back on obedience to God's clear directive and chose to embrace Satan's lie. She not only marred her relationship with her Creator, but she also used her influence to draw Adam into disobedience. Yet our heavenly Father is ultimately, above all, the God of redemption. If you seek Him, you will find Him—His mercy and forgiveness. You can be reconciled to Him through Jesus' atonement on the cross.

Despite what many say in accusing God of considering women as second-class citizens, the Bible has a different message. Although the woman was approached by Satan and deceived by him to the point of her choosing his way over God's way, God did not give up on her. In fact, Eve is called "the mother of all living" (3:20), and God decreed that through her the Savior of the world would come (Gal. 4:4). In the human reproduction process, the sperm of the man is delivered to the womb of the woman. She becomes the nurturer of that life in the womb until the child is delivered, and then by God's design she continues to sustain that life. However, in God's plan for the incarnation of His Son Jesus, the Seed came to the woman through the overshadowing of the Holy Spirit, making her the divine conduit for the Son's incarnation.

This verse, labeled the *protevangelium* (Latin, lit. "the first preaching of gospel") points to the "good news" of Christ's coming to accomplish redemption. The serpent will be defeated by the Anointed One, who came into the world through the womb of His mother Mary. His conception was miraculous (Luke 1:35). The striking of "His heel" refers to the sufferings endured by Christ on the cross, which became the prelude to His ultimate victory and resurrection.

On the other hand, the striking of the serpent's head was a mortal wound, a prophetic announcement of his ultimate defeat.

Satan did not identify the woman for her role in redemption. In fact, he did everything he could to prevent it. She has that place in the drama of redemption because God Himself planned for her womb to bring His Son into the world to accomplish redemption. Jesus the Messiah came as a man—born of Mary—but without losing His deity so that He also lived a perfect life as the Son of God.

Dorothy Kelley Patterson

Prayer: *Remind yourself of God's love for you and of His purpose to use you in reaching out to your own children and family and even beyond with the wonderful good news of His redemption! Pray that those whom you love the most will open their hearts to the gospel and respond in obedience.*

Personal Reflection: ....

....

....

....

....

....

....

The Consequences of Disobedience

Genesis 3:16–19

"To the woman He said:
'I will greatly multiply your sorrow and your conception;
In pain you shall bring forth children;
Your desire shall be for your husband,
And he shall rule over you.'" (v. 16)

Every decision you make has consequences—whether good or bad. Yet God not only punishes for disobedience; He also pours out mercy and grace because of His unconditional love. His judgments are both loving and just. Despite the woman's sin, she still has the blessing of producing children and continuing the generations. Her role in God's plan of redemption is not taken away. However, God's judgment adds suffering—and that with pain—to the woman's joy of bearing a child.

The woman will still have a desire to dominate or rule over the man, for such is the essence, character, and result of all sin against God. She will have the strong desire to be with the man. Sin corrupted the willing submission of the wife and the loving headship of the husband. However, these distortions of the divine plan are not the result of God's judgment but rather the natural consequence of sin, arising out of our own rebellious hearts.

God began with His curse on the serpent who would be destined to move on his "belly" (3:14). Satan would receive a death blow because the woman's "Seed" would crush his "head" (v. 15). The woman would experience pain in her task of childbearing; and her submission, just as her husband's headship, would be tainted by their own respective selfishness (v. 16). The man would meet difficulty in his work of cultivating "the ground" so that it would bear fruit (vv. 17–19). What would have been easy and joyous in the garden before sin entered the picture now would be challenging and often full of sorrow.

Disobedience comes with a high cost. The man and woman did not nullify or change God's creation order, including His perfect plan for their union in marriage. However, their refusal of God's way did make the future more difficult and marred their fellowship with Him and between themselves. Work was always part of God's plan for the man (1:26–30; 2:15), but now living in a sinful world would make that work more difficult (3:17–19). Childbearing and bringing in the next generation would continue as God's plan for the woman (1:28; 2:24; 3:20), but conceiving and bearing and rearing a child would now be accompanied by pain and challenges (3:16). Disobedience and its inevitable consequences have continued through the generations to distort and make the pursuit of God's plan more difficult.

Dorothy Kelley Patterson

Pray: *Examine your own heart. Are you looking for ways to obey God? Do you long to pattern your life after His way? Focus on the task God has given you with the determination to seek His way and to follow it with an obedient heart.*

Personal Reflection: ....

....

....

....

....

....

....

Eve—Mother of All Living

Genesis 3:20–24

*"And Adam called his wife's name Eve,
because she was the mother of all living." (v. 20)*

As the first woman of God's creation, Eve represents the principal picture of God's design for women. God made her second, but she was in no way an afterthought. Rather, Eve was created in the image of God and with a specific purpose. God continues to create women as bearers of His likeness and for a unique purpose! The most important way that you fulfill God's purpose for your life is through relationships—first, a relationship with Him and then relationships with others. Let's look to the life of Eve for an example.

One aspect of Eve's creation in God's image was her possession of a will. God gave her freedom of choice as well as boundaries of protection. When she lived within His plan, the balance was maintained in perfect harmony. There was no disharmony in the relationship between Eve and God or between Eve and her husband. However, Eve chose to put her own will above God's will and everything changed. Her sin separated her from those she loved. You have the choice whether to follow God's will or your will. The choice to go your own way often causes personal pain and separation in relationships.

I am a strong woman and have many plans for my own life. In fact, I have many plans for the lives of other people as well. As a child of God, made in His image, He has a perfect plan for me. I must choose daily to obey His will or to disobey and follow my personal desire. If I obey, I receive the blessings of God. If I disobey, I must suffer the consequences. Eve was created by God in His image and to be "the mother of all living" (v. 20). However, she disobeyed God and suffered the consequences for her sin. What about you?

Eve's legacy is not just one of sin and consequences. She also gives us a beautiful picture of God's redemptive plan for the world. Although she experienced greater suffering in childbirth and the pain of losing her sons—Abel by death and Cain by exile—God also gave her a way to return to Him. Eve gave birth to a third son, Seth, from whose lineage the Messiah would come! Eve experienced God's grace and demonstrates to us His offer of hope of redemption to women who have been disobedient, separating themselves from God. What will your legacy be?

Rhonda Harrington Kelley

Prayer: *Thank God that you are not an afterthought but rather a beautiful reflection of His image. Ask Him to help you fulfill His purpose in your life. Choose today to obey God, not follow your own desires.*

Personal Reflection: ....

....

....

....

....

....

....

Hagar—Abused but Not Abandoned

Genesis 16:1–16

"Then she called the name of the LORD who spoke to her, You-Are-the-God-Who-Sees; for she said, 'Have I also here seen Him who sees me?'" (v. 13)

Hagar's life was heartbreaking. The innocent maidservant of Sarah had no personal rights or physical protection. When Sarah was unable to conceive a child, she conceived a plan for Hagar to bear Abraham's child. Sarah's plot violated God's perfect plan for marriage and for her life.

Soon Ishmael was born to Hagar, and her problems intensified. Hagar despised her mistress, and Sarah dealt harshly with her maid. Because of abuse and mistreatment, Hagar fled and later gave birth to her child. Alone and afraid in the desert, this innocent victim realized she was not abandoned.

The angel of the Lord spoke to Hagar at her time of despair. She responded in faith to the God-Who-Sees: "Have I also seen Him who sees me?" (v. 13). Despite her difficult circumstances and human injustices, Hagar experienced the protection and provision of a just, loving God.

Innocent victims are abused people, often shunned by society today. However, God has not abandoned them. He loves them and wants to care for them. Are there hurting women in your family or your church? Have they suffered mentally and emotionally due to mistreatment? Are there abused women in your community who have been exploited or battered? Have their rights been violated and their freedom been withheld? Are there impoverished women in the world? Have they been mutilated or massacred unjustly? Yes. There are hundreds of thousands of wounded women in our world.

In New Orleans, the Baptist Friendship House provides shelter and protection for homeless women and their children. It is a biblically-based ministry providing physical, emotional, and spiritual support to women in their times of greatest need. Whether exploited by others or battered by husbands, they receive help and hope from a loving staff. Many also receive job training and assistance with transitional living arrangements. It is a wonderful ministry to wounded women.

There are similar ministries in this country and around the world for women who are hurting. The God-Who-Sees them loves them and offers them protection. He notices their needs and provides for them. He sees their loneliness and comforts them. He recognizes their bondage and offers them freedom in Christ.

You as a child of God must see those who are hurting around you. Do not allow your own problems or the fast pace of your life to blind your eyes to the extreme needs around you. You can give hope to others when you introduce them to the God-Who-Sees.

Rhonda Harrington Kelley

Prayer: *Pray that women today who are abused will realize they are not abandoned. Let God work through you to give them help and hope.*

Personal Reflection: ....

....

....

....

....

....

Sarah—Barren but Blessed

Genesis 17:15–21

"I will bless her, and she shall be a mother of nations;
kings of peoples shall be from her." (v. 6b)

More Scripture is devoted to Sarah than any other woman in the Bible. Her life unfolds in the Old Testament as the wife of the patriarch Abraham. She is also mentioned in the New Testament to contrast the bondage of the law and freedom through Christ (Gal. 4:21–31). She was commended for her obedience to God and Abraham in 1 Peter 3:5–6. And, Sarah was included with the heroes of the faith (Heb. 11:11). Sarah was a woman of faith, but she was not faultless.

Sarai is first introduced in the Bible when she marries Abraham: "Then Abram and Nahor took wives: the name of Abram's wife *was* Sarai" (Gen. 11:29). She is immediately described in the next verse as barren and with no child. She was deeply loved by her husband, who received the blessing of God and the promise to become the father of a great nation (12:1–3). While Sarai was also a faithful follower of the Lord, her faith was quickly tested after marriage when she was unable to conceive a desired child. She took matters into her own hands and tried to have a baby through her maidservant Hagar (16:1–4). The surrogate mother and her son Ishmael were soon rejected by Abram and Sarai.

Many women today face infertility. I learned only a few years into our marriage that I was unable to conceive a child. I, as Sarai, was tempted to take control of the situation. However, my husband and I prayed fervently, seeking God's plan for our family. God promised us children, not of my womb or adopted into our home. Instead, He has given us many spiritual children, not only nieces and nephews, but children in the ministry. I have been barren but blessed.

Abraham and Sarai were in their 90s when God made a new covenant with them. First, God gave Sarah a new name; then He promised her a son. God's covenant was fulfilled and Isaac was born (21:2–3). Sarah lived by faith and became the mother of nations. She was 127 years old when she died. Hebrews 11:11 says, "By faith Sarah herself also received strength to conceive seed, and she bore a child when she was past the age, because she judged him faithful who had promised." Sarah was barren but blessed. You too will be blessed by God!

Rhonda Harrington Kelley

Prayer: *Has God made a promise to you? Have faith that the covenant God always keeps His promises. Trust Him in your physical or spiritual barrenness and wait patiently for His blessings.*

Personal Reflection: ....

....

....

....

....

....

....

....

Lot's Wife—The Dangers of Looking Back

Genesis 19:15–26

"So He overthrew those cities, all the plain, all the inhabitants of the cities,
and what grew on the ground. But his wife looked back behind him,
and she became a pillar of salt." (vv. 25–26)

What comes to mind when you think of Sodom and Gomorrah? For most, the names of these cities evoke thoughts of complete moral depravity. I recall the sick feeling in the pit of my stomach as I prayer-walked through the red light districts of Bangkok, Thailand. On these neon-lit streets, malicious men roam and darkness reigns. In Genesis 19, we read the story of when God said "Enough!" to the wickedness of Sodom and Gomorrah. He sent His angels to erase them from the map. God saw the people for who they truly were and found righteousness in the heart of just one man—Lot.

Lot offered hospitality and protection to two men who entered the city, not realizing that they were God's angels. Because of this, God provided a way of escape for Lot and his family. Even though Lot hesitated, the Lord had compassion on him! The angels delivered Lot and his family outside the city and gave them their instructions. They were to run for their lives and not look back. God rained sulfur down on Sodom and Gomorrah, thoroughly demolishing the cities. However, even after God's display of compassion and control, Lot's wife did not trust Him and disobeyed the instructions of the angels. She looked back.

As Lot's wife glanced back over her shoulder in the direction of Sodom, her action represented something much deeper. She had allowed the perversion of Sodom to invade her heart, and she did not want to leave her people. Perhaps she was longing for her home and her possessions, or she felt pity for those being destroyed. The Lord had just rescued her from utter depravity, and she had the hope of a new future in Him! Yet her heart longed for what she had back in Sodom.

While the text does not reveal all the details of exactly what took place that day, one thing is certain: A woman of God cannot follow after her Father's plans when her heart longs for the past. Maybe God called you out of darkness into the light as He did Lot's wife, but you still struggle to relinquish one sin from your past. Perhaps God has just brought you to a new place and you wrestle with stepping outside of your comfort zone. You may have endured a deeply painful loss that still keeps you from fixing your eyes fully on Him. The Lord has compassion on the righteous and offers grace and the hope of a future in Him. All you have to do is trust Him and choose not to look back.

Laura Landry

Prayer: *Thank God for His compassion today. Remind yourself of the powerful God who rescued you from your past and make a commitment not to look back.*

Personal Reflection: ....

....

....

....

....

....

....

Rebekah—A Chosen Wife

Genesis 24:1–67

*"Here is Rebekah before you; take her and go, and let her be
your master's son's wife, as the Lord has spoken." (v. 51)*

Rebekah is one of the most beloved women in Scripture. The daughter of
Bethuel and great-niece of Abraham, who lived in Haran. She is described in
the Bible as "very beautiful to behold, a virgin; no man had known her" (v. 16).
While the young maiden was going about her daily chores of drawing water for
her family at the nearby spring, God had a much greater purpose for her life.
During an ordinary day, God intervened with an extraordinary plan. She was
chosen by God to be Isaac's wife.

Earlier in the account, Abraham sent his servant Eliezer back to his
homeland of Mesopotamia to find a wife for his son Isaac. He promised that
the angel of the Lord would go before him to fulfill God's plan (v. 7). At a spring
near Haran, the servant waited for the appointed bride to arrive to draw water.
Immediately, Rebekah appeared and offered water, then lodging, to the servant
of a distant relative. Rebekah's kindness was the sign that she was Isaac's chosen one.

My husband shares a similar story about our first encounter at church one
Sunday morning during our first year of college. It was an ordinary Sunday but
God had an extraordinary plan for our lives. As the worship service concluded, I
joined the church by membership. Chuck was in the balcony and says he felt led
by the Lord to join the same church that night. He knew then, and I knew soon
after, that I was his chosen one. God's plan for us was to be husband and wife.
God's plan is always the best plan.

Rebekah married Isaac, who loved her dearly. They enjoyed the blessings of Abraham's influence though not the blessing of children. After years
of barrenness, Rebekah finally gave birth to twins who were named Esau and
Jacob (25:24–28). Her faith faltered and tension developed in her home as Isaac
favored Esau and Rebekah favored Jacob. Esau sold his birthright to Jacob. Then

Rebekah conceived a plot to trick Isaac into blessing Jacob, whom Isaac thought was Esau (27:1–29). Though her deceit worked, Rebekah suffered the consequences of her sin. She lived out her later years in broken fellowship with her husband and separation from her favored son. The chosen one made bad choices and found herself sad and lonely. In Genesis 27:46, Rebekah complained, "I am weary of my life." What a warning to believers today who are chosen by God and then disobey Him!

Rhonda Harrington Kelley

Prayer: *Ask God who has chosen you to clearly direct your paths. Trust God for your future. Do not manipulate others to achieve your personal desires.*

Personal Reflection: ....

....

....

....

....

....

....

....

Leah—An Unloved Wife

Genesis 29:16–35

"When the LORD saw that Leah was unloved,
He opened her womb; but Rachel was barren." (v. 31)

The most fundamental human desire for women, i.e., to connect with other humans, reflects God's design for us as relational beings. We want to be fully known by another and then accepted and loved. We live our lives in little villages of other people. We seek out new friendships and join small groups for "community." We long to find husbands who will want to know our most secret thoughts and who will love us when they are revealed. In contrast, our greatest fear is that when our true self is revealed, the response will be rejection.

In this passage, Leah is wrestling with this very desire. She married a man who did not want her, but she was hopeful that once he knew her his heart would change. The morning after the wedding, Jacob awoke infuriated to find her in his bed instead of Rachel. Can you imagine her pain? She was vulnerable and exposed before him, and his actions told her, "I do not want you!" Of course, Jacob had every right to be angry. Laban intentionally deceived him after seven years of hard labor, and Jacob's dreams were dashed in an instant. Yet the reality of the situation probably did not soften the blow to Leah's heart.

As weeks turned into years, Leah remained the unloved wife. Jacob's heart did not change toward her as he grew to know her more. The Lord saw Leah's pain and began to bless her with children. With the birth of each son, Leah's hope swelled—perhaps the husband who did not love her would finally "become attached to" her (v. 34). But the story stayed the same. Jacob loved Rachel, and Leah felt rejected. Not until she truly found contentment in her relationship with her Lord did she cease striving for Jacob's affection. In her wisdom, Leah knew that God cared for her and that His love for her was endless. Even if her circumstances never changed, she always had a reason to praise the Lord!

Our desire for a loving husband-wife relationship reflects our need for the only One who could ever truly fill our hearts. Ultimately, nothing can satisfy our need to be known and loved like an intimate walk with Jesus. Leah was able to find contentment and rest in her heavenly Father's love even in the absence of earthly love. When we look to relationships with other people to meet our deepest need, we will always find ourselves disappointed. God knows even the deepest, darkest parts of our hearts, and yet His love for us remains unchanged and unending. Let us never cease to sing His praises!

Rhonda Harrington Kelley

Prayer: *Thank Jesus that you are His desired daughter—not an unloved bride. Ask Him to show you how to seek intimacy with Him above fulfillment from others. Praise Him for fulfilling your greatest need in relationship with Him.*

Personal Reflection: ....

....

....

....

....

....

....

....

Rachel—A Beloved Wife

Genesis 30:1–24

*"Then God remembered Rachel, and God listened
to her and opened her womb." (v. 22)*

For Jacob it was love at first sight when he saw Rachel with her father's sheep at the watering hole. He had returned to the homeland of his father Isaac to find a wife. And he found a trophy wife, a woman "beautiful of form and appearance" (Gen. 29:17). Jacob promised Rachel's father Laban that he would work seven years to marry her. The years seemed to Jacob only a few days because of the love he had for Rachel (30:20).

On the wedding night, Jacob was deceived by Laban, who sent his older daughter Leah into the marital tent. Deceived but determined, Jacob worked for seven more years to marry the woman he loved. Jacob fulfilled the covenant with Laban in order to marry his daughter. Covenants in Scripture are not only agreements between two parties; they are symbolic of God's covenant relationship with His children. God always keeps His covenants. Jacob kept his covenant with Laban and worked seven more years to marry Rachel.

Jacob was married to two sisters, but loved only Rachel who was unable to conceive (v. 31). Can you imagine the jealousy of Rachel who watched her sister Leah have son after son? Jealousy is an emotion that produces negative thoughts and feelings when someone else has what you want. It can cause tension in relationships and result in bitterness. It changes a heart of love to a heart of hate.

Rachel, who once loved her sister, shunned her. Her heart became hardened toward her husband and his God. Jealousy is a real emotion experienced by women today. It can sever relationships and divide families. Beware of jealousy in your own life. Don't let your love for someone become hate when they have what you want. Rejoice with others who are blessed by God and wait patiently for Him to bless you.

In God's time, He remembered Rachel, and she conceived (v. 22–24). She gave birth to Joseph, who was dearly loved by his father. Jacob gave a coat of many colors to his favored son Joseph (37:3). Rachel later gave birth to a second son, Benjamin, though she died in childbirth (35:16–20). She was remembered later in Scripture as a mother who loved her children, weeping for them and for all of Israel (Ruth 4:11; Jer. 31:15).

Rhonda Harrington Kelley

Prayer: *Thank the Lord for His love and the love of your family. Ask Him to help you avoid feelings jealousy when they enter your heart. Be confident that the Lord always remembers you!*

Personal Reflection: ....

....

....

....

....

....

....

....

Dinah—The Tragedy of Rape

Genesis 34:1–31

"Now Dinah the daughter of Leah, whom she had borne to Jacob, went out to see the daughters of the land. And when Shechem the son of Hamor the Hivite, prince of the country, saw her, he took her and lay with her, and violated her." (vv. 1–2)

Have you or someone you loved ever had to walk through the tragedy of rape? In this passage in Genesis 34, we see the heartbreaking results of living in a fallen world, when sinful people act according to what seems right in their own eyes instead of living according to God's perfect plan. Just as we grieve what happens to Dinah in this text, it is important to remember that God knows and hurts with every woman who has ever been the victim of sexual violence. God calls rape a sin and the victim of rape to be faultless in the crime committed against her (Deut. 22:25–27).

Dinah's was the only daughter of Jacob and Leah who settled with her family in the land of Shechem. One day as she went to find other young women in the land, she was seized and raped by Shechem, a prince of that region. The reaction of a father whose daughter has just been raped is generally outrage and grief. Jacob's silent reaction is quite shocking (Gen. 34:5). When Dinah's brothers arrived home, they were deeply angry by the incident and devised a plan to enact revenge for the outrage committed against Dinah. After tricking the men of Shechem into being circumcised, Dinah's brothers Simeon and Levi went into the city while the men were still in pain and killed every male (vv. 25–26).

Reading this account, many people may be tempted to cheer on the brothers' reaction. However, the problem with the brothers' response is that while sin has natural consequences, the judgment against sinners belongs to God. Dinah's brothers put themselves on the same level as the Hivites through their violence instead of reacting in a way that would bring glory to God. They became detestable to the people of the land (v. 30), and their witness to the Canaanites was ruined due to their violent actions. Just as believers are to be "the fragrance of Christ" to those around them (2 Cor. 2:15), the Israelites were to be a pleasing aroma to the surrounding inhabitants to draw them to Yahweh God. However, that opportunity had been lost in a moment of vengeance.

Candi Finch

Prayer: *Ask the Holy Spirit to be the comforter to those who have suffered through the tragedy of sexual assault so that they will find healing and hope and restored joy. Pray for the families of the victims that will have wisdom as they seek to comfort and minister to their loved one and that they will not act out in revenge against the perpetrators as did Dinah's brothers, worsening an already tragic situation. Pray also for those guilty of sexual assault that they will come to know Christ and repent of their sins.*

Personal Reflection: ....

....

....

....

....

....

....

Tamar—A Determined Widow

Genesis 38:6–26

"So Judah acknowledged them and said, 'She has been more righteous than I, because I did not give her to Shelah my son.' And he never knew her again." (v. 26)

Have you ever been treated unfairly by someone in authority over you? It is painful and wrong when others do not honor our inherent human rights or deal with us justly. The temptation stirs within us to disrespect them in return or even seek retribution. Our sense of justice comes directly from God because He bestows value on His creation. To allow others to take advantage of us does not honor God, but to repay evil for evil would be sinful. Is it possible to stand up for yourself and honor God at the same time? Tamar's life tells the story of an astute woman who demanded the rights that were refused her.

Tamar was married to Er, the son of Judah, whom the Lord "put to death" because of his evil ways (v. 7). In those days, the second-born son had the duty of taking his brother's widow and providing her with a son. The widow's son would then receive the inheritance intended for her first husband, providing for the needs of the widow throughout the rest of her life. However, Er's brother Onan did not want to fulfill his duty because he knew that any son born to Tamar would outrank him and receive more inheritance than he. Onan used dishonest methods to prevent Tamar from conceiving, and the Lord punished his greed by putting him to death as well (v. 10).

After the death of her second husband, Tamar's father-in-law Judah treated her dishonestly and disrespectfully by sending her back to live with her father, although it was her right to marry his third son, Shelah. Judah desired to prevent the marriage of Tamar and Shelah, perhaps because he held her responsible for the deaths of his sons rather than acknowledging their evil deeds. Tamar was at risk of being left with no one to care for her. Feeling cast aside and concerned for her future, she decided she must do something to solve her predicament.

Tamar could have resigned herself to remain a childless widow, but she acted according to the laws and customs of her time to hold Judah responsible for his actions. Although Tamar's motives were good, clearly her method was dishonorable by biblical standards. However, Scripture does add that Judah "never knew her again" (v. 26). The sin of others does come to light in God's timing.

Rhonda Harrington Kelley

Prayer: *Ask God to make clear to you the boundary between standing up for your rights and waiting on His timing and action. Thank the Lord that His standard of justice is perfectly balanced with His mercy and love for us.*

Personal Reflection: ....

....

....

....

....

....

....

Midwifery

Exodus 1:15–17

*"But the midwives feared God, and did not do as the king of Egypt
commanded them, but saved the male children alive." (v. 17)*

Women have been helping other women through the beautiful and challenging journey of motherhood from the beginning of recorded history. In many parts of the world, the role of a midwife is still primarily to support a woman through labor and safe delivery of her baby. The traditional and modern-day practice of midwifery reflects a belief that God designed a woman's body to carry and birth a baby. During pregnancy, the womb grows from the size of a pear to that of a watermelon and, when fully stretched, is strong enough to push and squeeze a baby into the world. As the baby is born, a complex array of hormones is shared between mother and baby, providing life-support and facilitating bonding between mother and child. Childbirth is hard work, but God's fingerprints are all over the amazing process.

Midwives in ancient Egypt were often depicted in artwork working in teams. These teams likely consisted of two midwives and a third helper called a *doula* (Greek for "helper"), whose primary role is emotional support. These teams were trained and skilled professionals laboring alongside women as servants to their communities. The Hebrew midwives did not merely watch women give birth; they provided medical care to the baby, such as cutting the umbilical cord, washing with water, and rubbing with salt (Ezek. 16:4).

Shiphrah and Puah may have operated as a team, but more likely they were the directors of a larger group of midwives. Due to his fear of an uprising, Pharaoh summoned the Hebrew midwives and instructed them to kill any boys born to Hebrew mothers. Likely Shiphrah and Puah knew that to defy Pharaoh's orders was to risk their own lives. However, these women believed in God's plan for mothers and babies. They knew the devastation a mother would feel if her child was killed and that God was sovereign over the lives of those yet to be born. Shiphrah and Puah courageously protected the lives of the baby boys and did not follow through on the tyrant's decree.

Shiphrah and Puah as professionals performed their duties in a way that honored God. They literally put the lives of their patients before their own in their pursuit of God's glory. They worked with compassion and trusted God's design in caring for mothers and babies. In today's world, to put more faith in modern medicine, science, and culture than in God's plan for our bodies, our families, and our vocation is easy. Challenge yourself to ask the hard questions about God's plan for your life. Actively seek ways to glorify God in your "duties," whether at home or at work, even when others may persecute you.

Laura Landry

Prayer: *Ask the Lord to help you trust His plan in all areas of your life. Thank Him that He has cared for you even since before you were born!*

Personal Reflection: ....

....

....

....

....

....

....

Shiphrah and Puah—Courageous Midwives

Exodus 1:18–21

*"And so it was, because the midwives feared God,
that He provided households for them." (v. 21)*

The previous passage of Scripture introduced Shiphrah and Puah, two courageous Hebrew midwives. Pharaoh gave the midwives strict instructions to kill baby boys born to the mothers in their care because he was afraid that the Israelites would grow in number and over-run the Egyptians. Nevertheless, Shiprah and Puah *feared God* and they preserved the lives of the baby boys. The Hebrew word used in this passage for "fear" is *yarē*, meaning to have reverence for or stand in awe of God. Shiphrah and Puah had more honor and respect for the Lord than any earthly source of authority, and they refused to defy God's view on the sanctity of life by participating in infanticide.

When Pharaoh found out that the midwives had failed to carry out his orders, he demanded answers for their defiance. These two servants of the Hebrew community must have felt a different kind of fear standing before the king who held God's people in slavery. Yet God gave them discernment and wisdom, allowing them to see through Pharaoh's plot and respond to his own fear. Pharaoh had noticed the strength of the Hebrew men, and it was for this reason that he had ordered the midwives to kill their male offspring in the first place. The midwives answered that Hebrew women were more "lively" or vigorous than the Egyptians, often giving birth before the midwives could reach them. Pharaoh's insecurity made this excuse believable in his eyes, and the women were released without consequence.

Because of their obedience to uphold His standard, God demonstrated His sovereignty over life and death in their own lives. The Lord removed the obstacle preventing them from conceiving, blessing them with children of their own. Whether this blessing came through providing husbands for them or healing infertility is unclear. The text merely tells us that God "dealt well" with them (v. 20). Our obedience to live righteously opens the door for His goodness to flow into our lives! When we compromise on His values, we rob ourselves of God's provision.

When Pharaoh's plot failed, he came up with a new plan to have all Hebrew baby boys thrown into the Nile. Despite the best efforts of the Pharaoh, a Hebrew woman still gave birth to a son who would one day lead the Israelites out of Egypt. Ironically, that very man would grow up in Pharaoh's own household! We serve a great God, and no human plan can undermine His will. When we obey God, we demonstrate that we fear Him far more than the disapproval of man. God blesses those who live righteously and seek first His kingdom (Matt. 6:33)!

Laura Landry

Prayer: *Thank the Lord for His goodness in your life. Ask Him to give you the courage to uphold His standard even when men may ridicule you.*

Personal Reflection: ....

....

....

....

....

....

....

Jochebed—A Devoted Mother

Exodus 2:1–11

"So the woman took the child and nursed him." (v. 9)

Jochebed was a Levite woman, married to Amram and the mother of Miriam, Aaron, and Moses (Ex. 6:20; Num. 26:59). She lived during a tumultuous time in Egypt. The new king was concerned that the Israelites were growing in number and power in Egypt. Worried about a rebellion, the king oppressed them and ordered the midwives to kill any male baby born to an Israelite. Afraid of God's wrath, the Hebrew midwives ignored the king's edict.

In the next years, Hebrew people multiplied and became stronger in Egypt. Enraged, Pharaoh ordered every Hebrew son thrown into the Nile and allowed only daughters to live (Ex. 1:22). Jochebed's story picks up here. Already the mother of a daughter and son, she gave birth to another baby, a boy. She successfully hid him for three months, then later placed him in a basket in the Nile River. God protected the baby, who was rescued by Pharaoh's daughter.

God had a great plan for that baby boy. He would be nursed by his biological mother, then raised by the princess in the palace. While bathing in the Nile, the princess saw the baby in the basket and sought help for the child (vv. 5–6). The baby's sister Miriam was nearby and offered to find a nurse. Of course, she went straight to her mother who had the privilege of nursing her own child. Moses spent his earliest formative years within his own ethnic and religious culture, learning the language and values of God's people.

Jochebed was a devoted mother. She loved God and her family. She knew that God had a divine plan for each of their lives. She nurtured her children physically and spiritually, leaving a lasting legacy of faith. Jochebed is remembered in Hebrews 11:23–29 for her faith in God and courageous obedience. All three of her children learned from her godly instruction. Moses became a great leader of his people and wrote the first five books of the Bible. Aaron was the first priest of Israel who, with Moses, led the Hebrews out of captivity. Miriam was a gifted poetess and prophetess. Though their lives were not perfect, they obviously were strengthened by the love and devotion of their faithful mother.

A devoted mother has a profound influence on her children. If you have been blessed with children, nurture them as did Jochebed. Provide for their physical growth but also invest in them spiritually. Teach them the ways of the Lord, then see God's perfect plan revealed in their lives. Jochebed is a wonderful example in the Bible of a devoted mother.

Rhonda Harrington Kelley

Prayer: *Ask the Lord to empower you to be a devoted mother. Commit your children to the Lord and pray for them daily. Keep your family as the primary responsibility in your life.*

Personal Reflection: ....

....

....

....

....

....

....

Birth and Adoption

Exodus 2:1–10

*"And the child grew, and she brought him to Pharaoh's daughter,
and he became her son. So she called his name Moses, saying,
'Because I drew him out of the water.'" (v. 10)*

Moses is one of the most prominent characters in Scripture, but he had a very precarious start in life. Before Moses had parted the Red Sea or written the first five books of the Bible, his mother hid him in a basket in the Nile, hoping that he had some chance for survival. According to God's plan, Moses was discovered and then given a new chance at life through adoption. The story of Moses' early life is a beautiful parallel of adoption in modern times.

Scripture tells us that Jochebed saw her son as "beautiful," and she desired to keep him in her household (v. 2). God allowed her special time with him after his birth, and then again after he was found by Pharaoh's daughter. She was able to nurse her son, forming an irrevocable bond with him. Jochebed undoubtedly loved Moses deeply and wished that she could raise him and always be recognized as his mother. Yet, due to circumstances beyond her control, she was unable to keep her son. She knew that if Moses continued to live in her home and was discovered, Pharaoh would kill him. Jochebed wanted her son to have safety; and as painful as it must have been for her, she sent Moses to live with Pharaoh's daughter.

Pharaoh's daughter decided to adopt Moses when she found him hidden and crying in a basket where she went to bathe. Perhaps Jochebed knew that the princess went regularly to that spot in the Nile and hoped that the heart of this woman would be moved by her helpless baby. Indeed, Pharaoh's daughter "had compassion on him," despite realizing immediately that this was one of the baby boys whom her father intended to kill (v. 6). She knew that if she did not do something, he had little hope for a future. So the princess adopted the Hebrew babe, naming him Moses and calling him her son (v. 10).

In today's broken and desperate world, many children are born into difficult situations; they desperately need safe homes where they can be raised. Sometimes their birth parents long to keep them, but their circumstances make this impossible. Just as compassion moved Pharaoh's daughter to action, God calls His people to do something to help orphans today (James 1:27). If God has not burdened you personally to adopt, there are many ways in which you can be involved to support adoptive families, birth families, and their children. Extend prayers and understanding to families who cannot keep their babies, love their children, and offer tangible support to families who adopt them.

Laura Landry

Prayer: *Ask the Lord to show you how you can be involved in caring for orphans, whether it be to support adoptive families or even to adopt yourself. Thank God for heavenly adoption and for calling you His daughter!*

Personal Reflection: ....

....

....

....

....

....

....

Zipporah—A Wife with Attitude

Exodus 2:16–22; 4:20–26; 18:2–6

"Surely you are a husband of blood to me!" (4:25)

Moses was a great leader of the Jews. He was nursed by his own mother, though raised in the Egyptian palace after Pharaoh ordered all sons born to Israelite women be killed. The Bible story of the basket in the bulrushes is taught to young children in church as a symbol of God's protection. As Moses grew, he became concerned about the Egyptian treatment of his own people. He fled from Pharaoh who had raised him and from his own people (2:11–15).

Jethro, a Midianite priest who had seven daughters, met Moses at a well. Moses was offered hospitality and housing and later married Jethro's oldest daughter, Zipporah. He cared for the sheep and began his family while living among Jethro and his tribe.

Zipporah did not share the spiritual values of her husband Moses. She did not understand what God meant when He spoke to Moses through an angel in a burning bush (3:1–4:17). She hesitantly accompanied him when returning to his people in Egypt (4:18–23). She begrudgingly performed the circumcision on their son to fulfill the covenant with God identifying him as a "son of Israel" (4:24–26). She and her sons were sent back to Midian (18:2–3). She was a wife with an attitude, primarily because she lacked a personal relationship with the living God.

Moses was used by God to free his people from slavery in Egypt (13:17—14:4) and to miraculously part the waters of the Red Sea for the Israelites to cross safely into freedom (14:15–31). He led his people through the wilderness (15:22—18:27) and received the Ten Commandments from God on Mount Sinai (19:1—20:26). He built the tabernacle (26:1–37) and renewed the covenant with the Lord (34:10–28). He established a pattern for offerings (Lev. 1:1—7:21), laws for God's people (Lev. 9:1—22:33), and feasts for the Lord (Lev. 23:1–44). Moses accomplished many great works for the Lord. However, he did not have a supportive, spiritual wife. Also, he was denied by God the privilege of entering the Promised Land.

Let Zipporah be a warning to you to seek God's will and follow His chosen leaders. Her story would have been much different if she had put her faith in God and had respected her husband's godly leadership. So don't let a bad attitude hurt your influence or hinder the work of others. Have the mind of Christ (Phil. 2:5)—have a good attitude toward others.

Rhonda Harrington Kelley

Prayer: *Take a few moments to examine your attitude. Do you have bad feelings toward others? Is so, confess your sin and ask God to improve your attitude. A woman's attitude influences others for good or bad.*

Personal Reflection: ....

....

....

....

....

....

The *Ketubah*—Documenting Marital Commitment

Exodus 24:1–8

◡◠◡

*"Then he took the Book of the Covenant and
read in the hearing of the people." (v. 7a)*

The Jewish marriage contract is a document (Hb. *Ketubah*, "her writing") required from the groom to be read aloud during the marriage ceremony. This carefully prepared, one-sided, contractual document is not a romantic sentiment but details a husband's responsibilities to his wife during their life together.

The Old Testament was explicit in its requirements for food, clothing, and even conjugal rights (Ex. 21:10); and the rabbis added to the document the necessity for a husband to respect his wife. Some documents even added the commitment that a husband would not make his wife cry! Underlying all is the necessity for a husband to deny himself in order to provide for the needs of his wife. Although prepared by the husband, the wife had the responsibility of preserving the document.

Even though the *Ketubah,* dating back at least to the third century B.C., originated in an era in which women were not valued and often suffered from injustices, this document emerged as one of the ways God used to protect the rights of women. Although the bride is not required to sign the document, the groom—together with official witnesses—must sign this binding contract.

My *Ketubah* was designed and created as an aesthetically beautiful work of art by one of the few female Jewish scribes. The creativity in its Second Temple design and skill in the elaborate calligraphy applied to a high-quality parchment truly set this work of art apart. My traditional document is penned in the Aramaic language. Although I did not know about the *Ketubah* at the time of our wedding, my husband later gave me an exquisite one as part of an anniversary celebration. It hangs in our home next to my wedding portrait.

A copy of the *Ketubah* document is found in the front matter of *The Study Bible for Women*. You have an excellent pattern for developing your own contract of commitment. You should include the date and location for your wedding, the names of the groom and of his father, the names of the bride and of her father. The heart of the document is the groom's pledge to his bride of what he will do to provide for, protect, and give guidance to their family. Beyond this you may want to add a challenge from Scripture—a life verse for your marriage. The essential signatures of the groom and witnesses may be augmented by the bride's optional signing of this important document.

Dorothy Kelley Patterson

Prayer: *Ask the Lord to guide you in finding a way to create a testimony to your marriage. Rethink the commitments your husband—and you—bring to your union. Never cease to pray that the Lord will hold you close to those commitments since your marriage is a metaphor the Lord has chosen to use in unveiling His unconditional love and unfailing faithfulness.*

Personal Reflection: ....

....

....

....

....

....

....

The Laws of Purification

Leviticus 12:1–8

*"She shall then continue in the blood of
her purification thirty-three days...." (v. 4)*

What in the world can we glean from this Scripture? While it might seem like an obscure, ancient law, these verses are rich with significance and meaning. First, we see God's care for a woman who has just given birth. She was not allowed to go to the sanctuary during her time of purification, which allowed her to stay at home to rest and care for her newborn. The only interruption for her time of purification was when her male child was circumcised at eight days of age. Rather than be separated from her newborn son during this event, she was able to be with him when he would need her tender care. Thousands of years before modern government policy, God created mandatory maternity leave! This law demonstrates His care for mothers at a time when they most need physical and emotional rest.

Second, the time of purification reinforced the sacredness of life to the family. The reason for her purification was that, during labor, she lost blood. Throughout the Law, blood is regarded with great reverence. As Leviticus 17:11 says, "The life of the flesh *is* in the blood." All life and all blood are sacred to God. When blood is shed, as in a sacrifice, or discharged, as in giving birth, the response of God's people was never casual, but rather reverent. Therefore, after a woman had discharged blood during labor, she acknowledged the sacredness of life by observing the days of purification.

Third, this law had great significance for the community of God's chosen people. Through this law, and others involving the presence of blood, God prepared His people for the blood sacrifice of His Son, "The Lamb of God who takes away the sin of the world!" (John 1:29). These laws reinforced the promise of the coming Messiah and looked forward to all He would accomplish through the shedding of His blood (Eph. 1:7).

While we are no longer required to practice the laws of purification after childbirth, we are reminded that all of God's laws are not only good but also for our good. His laws reflect His character and enable us to value what He values. These verses demonstrate God's constant care and concern for women, as well as His relentless revealing of the redemption we have in His Messiah.

What comes to mind when you think of God's Law? It is easy to see it as an ancient set of codes that no longer apply to us. (How often do we **want** to read Leviticus?) However, we have an opportunity for rich discovery when we study His laws, especially those pertaining to women.

Katie McCoy

Prayer: *Are you willing to devote more time to studying these less familiar passages of Scripture? Ask the Lord to reveal His character and His heart for women through His Law.*

Personal Reflection: ....

....

....

....

....

....

....

Sexual Prohibitions

Leviticus 18:1–30

⌒

"You shall observe My judgments and keep My ordinances,
to walk in them: I am the LORD your God." (v. 4)

God calls His people to be holy as He is holy. Sexual immorality was rampant among Israel's surrounding nations, both where they came from (Egypt) and where they were going (Canaan, v. 4). Being holy, or set apart, in one's sexual behavior was, and still is, a biblical mandate.

Throughout Scripture, sexual sin is especially offensive to God and damaging to humanity. God created sexuality to display His own relationship to His people. He calls the nation of Israel His wife, beckons her to return to Him and reveals that marriage was made to portray Christ's unbreakable union to the Church (Eph. 5:22–33). All sexual activity between a man and a woman outside the covenant of marriage is a distortion of the reality it was created to display. As with all of God's laws, to disobey them brings spiritual, psychological, and even physical consequences upon ourselves, consequences God wants to protect us from bearing (see 1 Cor. 6:18).

Leviticus 18 is explicit in its prohibition of all forms of incest, as well as homosexuality, cultic prostitution, and bestiality. Some of the most shocking sexual sins are included in this list. Despite our culture's changing definitions of morality, *"there is* nothing new under the sun" (Eccl. 1:9). If any among God's people committed one of these sexual sins, they were excluded from the covenant community, and by extension, from a relationship with the Lord.

The severity of this law is not the end. The blood of Jesus has the power to redeem every lawbreaker and to purify from every sexual sin. In addition, the Spirit of Christ who indwells God's children has the power to break every chain caused by even the most deplorable distortion of sexuality. The Lord fully knew the depths of human depravity when He died to rescue us from the grips of sexual sin.

You may be surprised that within Jesus' own family tree are two people who violated one of these commandments. Judah had sexual relations with his daughter-in-law, Tamar (Gen. 22:15). The bloodline of the sinless Savior includes immorality. Our God never runs away from the defiled in order to shun them; He runs to the defiled in order to purify them. No matter what you have done or what has been done to you, Jesus will never shame or shun you when you come to Him in repentance. Just as in his physical genealogy, Jesus identifies Himself with the woman who comes to Him for purity, forgiveness, and healing. He will always claim you as His own.

Katie McCoy

Prayer: *Do you have the same perspective of sexual purity as God? Remember that no sin is hidden from Him, but all sin can be forgiven (Prov. 28:13). Seek forgiveness from the Savior and commit yourself to sexual purity.*

Personal Reflection: ....

....

....

....

....

....

....

The Path to Holiness

Leviticus 19:1–2 and 1 Peter 1:15–16

"You shall be holy, for I the LORD your God am holy." (Lev. 19:2b)

Is it more difficult to live a holy life in the twenty-first century than it was in the first century A.D. or in the 1890s? Many Christians think so. The assumption seems to be that our century is rife with new pitfalls. Despite the fact that holiness entails a certain amount of attention to particulars, which can vary enormously from one era or culture to another, two foundational underpinnings hold true for every century: Trust and Obey. Holiness means loving God and doing what He says. The first-century heart is the same as the twenty-first-century heart—desperately in need of saving, stubbornly selfish, and fairly disinclined to trust and obey God.

Here we are, weltering in a plethora of choices, overloaded with information, stymied by our energy-saving devices, with too many places to go, too many things to do, too many choices all the time. It's easy to see why we believe our path to holiness is more difficult than that of earlier or simpler Christians.

Too many choices, too little time—but the same human heart reaching up to the same God who says "Be holy, because I am holy" (1 Pet. 1:16). Peter is addressing Christians, those who bear the name of Christ, and he is backing up his imperative (do it!) by quoting the book of Leviticus. Jesus Christ is the same yesterday and today and forever. He sees everything in your world and He wants you to listen to Him, trust Him, obey what He tells you to do.

Is there a way of life, a manner of serving the Lord, that will deliver you from the temptations and distractions around you? Life in a convent or monastery looks to many on the outside as though it would almost guarantee a degree of holiness that is far beyond the rest of us. But a letter from a friend who is a nun showed me that there is no such guarantee. For her, as for me, to walk with God is to walk by faith, to trust and obey one day at a time, recognizing our never-ending need for grace.

Even in this complicated century, the path to holiness remains the same as it was in the first century after Jesus was born:

- **Prayer and meditation** (quiet time apart with God, listening to Him, thinking about what He tells us, learning to trust Him), followed by
- **Simple obedience** to what He has said.

Elisabeth Elliot

Prayer: *Ask the Lord to help you identify areas where you are conforming to the world's standards rather than to God's standard of holiness. Then, ask Him to help you to trust that His way is better and fully obey Him.*

Personal Reflection: ....

....

....

....

....

....

....

An excerpt from Elisabeth Elliot's *Be Still My Soul* (pages 71–73, 78).

Sabbath—God's Plan for Rest

Leviticus 25:1–7, 18–23

"And the LORD spoke to Moses on Mount Sinai, saying, 'Speak to the children of Israel, and say to them: 'When you come into the land which I give you, then the land shall keep a sabbath to the LORD.'" (vv. 1–2)

God established the principle of Sabbath rest from the beginning: "He **rested** on the seventh day from all His work" of creation (Gen. 2:2). He also "blessed the seventh day and sanctified it, because in it He **rested** from all His work" (Gen. 2:3). The fourth of the Ten Commandments—"Remember the Sabbath day, to keep it holy"—is so fundamental that not only does explanation immediately follow the command, but also the rationale for the law is reiterated right away: "For *in* six days the LORD made the heavens and the earth, the sea, and all that *is* in them, and **rested** the seventh day" (Ex. 20:11).

In Leviticus 25:2, God commands His people to apply the same principle of Sabbath rest to "the land." This instruction would go into effect when the Israelites entered the promised land, where they were supposed to exemplify living abundantly under God's rule. If they were obedient, the Israelites—people who belonged to the Lord—would keep the seventh day holy by resting and honoring the Lord. Likewise, they would enforce a sabbath year "of solemn rest for the land, a sabbath to the LORD" (v. 4).

To observe the Sabbath (day or year)—whether as individuals, families, or farming communities—required the Israelites to exercise faith in the Lord to keep His promises. At face value, these Sabbath commands make no sense to sinful minds. "What shall we eat in the seventh year?" the Israelites wondered, as though God would command them to stop cultivating and harvesting for an entire year only to let His people starve (v. 20). He promised them bumper crops for the sixth year and crops continuing to grow on their own during the seventh. They would have plenty to eat even during the eighth year of planting crops anew (vv. 21–22).

Observing the Sabbath as a day of rest hardly makes sense to twenty-first-century women, does it? We all know, "A woman's work is never done." Whatever the work is— housework or office work, home-based work or homework, volunteer work or busy work—how often we wear ourselves out trying to do it all our own way (using all seven days of the week) instead of living God's Sabbath way. Is it time to exercise your faith in the Lord to keep His promises (like Matt. 11:28) so you can set apart "the seventh day" for worship and real rest?

Tamra Hernandez

Prayer: *Ask the Lord to make you aware of at least one change you can make* **today** *to enable you to establish God's principle of Sabbath rest in your life. Commit to obeying Him in making that change.*

Personal Reflection: ....

....

....

....

....

....

The Beauty of God as Our Father

Numbers 1:1–46

"These were chosen from the congregation, leaders of their fathers' tribes, heads of the divisions of Israel." (v. 16)

It's not fair!!! Have you ever uttered that phrase? Maybe a sibling growing up got more privileges than you. Or, maybe you have even felt that way when you read some of the biblical passages that indicate that God has some distinct roles for men and women—that fathers, and not mothers, are the "heads" of families (possibly you even start humming "I Can Do Anything You Can Do Better!" from the musical *Annie Get Your Gun* . . .).

In Numbers 1:16, God instructs particular **men** to help Moses and Aaron with a census and calls out a man from each tribe (literally the "head of the household of his father, head of his father's house"). Why are men called heads of the household? Was God just accommodating the culture of the ancient Israelites? The language used in this passage about the heads of families and fathers is precise, significant, and very important in the overall understanding of the God-ordained creation order.

The importance of the father's role is fully developed throughout Scripture as the father blesses (Gen. 27:14), loves (Gen. 37:4), rebukes (Gen. 37:10), grieves (Gen. 37:35), pities (Ps. 103:13), and rejoices (Prov. 10:1). The father is also clearly the object of honor as well as of obedience and love (Gen. 28:7). This metaphor becomes more important because God chooses to identify Himself as the "Father" of Israel (Is. 63:16), and His fatherhood is very much a part of the way He relates to His people (Ex. 4:22; Jer. 31:9). God also expresses particular concern for the poor and suffering (Prov. 22:22–23) and those who are fatherless (Ps. 68:5). The Lord's role toward those who fear Him is that of a father (Ps. 103:13). He describes His guidance and correction of believers in the language of father and children (Prov. 3:12).

Some women stumble over the "Fatherhood" of God because they had a really bad earthly father—absentee, abusive, or deadbeat. However, our God is not any of those things! He is the epitome of the caring Father, knowing what exactly is best for His children. He is not abusive but compassionate; He is not absentee but ever-present; He is not a deadbeat but provides for the needs of His children. God is not being misogynistic or unfair when He refers to Himself as Father; He is communicating a significant truth about the way He relates to each of us.

Candi Finch

Prayer: *Thank God for His loving care of His children. Take a moment to pray that your own father or fathers you know would lead their families well, demonstrating the kind and compassionate qualities of the heavenly Father as they interact with their own children.*

Personal Reflection: ....

....

....

....

....

....

....

....

A Special Vow to the Lord

Numbers 6:1–21

"All the days of his separation he shall be holy to the Lord." (v. 8)

God has always been interested in drawing men and women closer to His heart and His purpose for their lives. Just prior to the beginning of their journey from Mt. Sinai toward the land of Canaan, God gave a specific word to Moses to give to His people concerning a very special personal vow. The taking of this "Nazirite" vow was voluntary, not required. However, anyone who entered into the vow automatically bound themselves to fulfill it. Taking a vow is a very serious commitment in the eyes of God.

The Nazirite vow did not mean you came from Nazareth. Rather than describing a geographical location, this Hebrew word *nēzer* means "separation." The person taking the Nazirite vow was making a personal decision to "separate" himself in distinctive ways for a period of time in order to walk more closely with God in an observable lifestyle of holiness.

Three "no touch" requirements were to be observed by the Nazirite: No Razors. No Dead Bodies. No Grapes. Nazirites wore long hair untouched by a razor. Their physical appearance was unique. They were willing to appear differently in public. Nazirites refrained from the immediate defilement incurred with touching a dead body. They desired to remain eligible, fully qualified worshippers. Contact with dead bodies excluded individuals from worship for a time and required a special ceremony of cleansing. Nazirites refused to enjoy the fruit of the grapevine in any form. They chose to find their joy completely in the Lord, not in physical pleasure. Outward deeds gave testimony to their inward commitment.

According to Numbers 6:2, the opportunity to enter into the Nazirite vow was offered to both men and women. Biblical examples include Samson the judge (Judg. 13), Samuel the prophet (1 Sam. 1), John the Baptist (Luke 1) and Paul the apostle (Acts 18:21).

Perhaps you desire a closer walk with God. On this side of the Cross of Calvary, please know that the key to understanding this passage of Scripture is not found in the keeping of requirements. Jesus died to set us free to live as willing, faithful, daily bondservants of His Father. The true definition of a modern-day Nazirite is discovered in a phrase that is repeated over 10 times in Numbers 6—". . . to the Lord." Turning our backs on things that bring sorrow to God will immediately focus the eyes of our hearts toward Him. Lives that lean toward God will begin to look more like Jesus. The goal of every believer should be holy living in an unholy world.

Becky Brown

Prayer: *Upon completion of the Nazirite vow, locks of hair were shaved and burned as a sacrifice to God. What needs to be removed from your life as an offering to God? Ask the Lord to forgive you and recommit to a life of holiness.*

Personal Reflection: ....

....

....

....

....

....

....

Miriam—A Life Lesson in Focus

Numbers 12:1–16

"Then Miriam and Aaron spoke against Moses because of the Ethiopian woman whom he had married; for he had married an Ethiopian woman." (v. 1)

The criticism of Moses targeted his wife, apparently because she was "Ethiopian" (Hb. *Kushite*, possibly another name for "Midianite"). The woman may have been Zipporah or perhaps a second wife, married after Zipporah's death (which Scripture does not record). The point of contention may simply have been that Moses had married a non-Israelite. From the Lord's perspective, however, the ethnicity of Moses' wife was a non-issue. He did not even mention it. Instead, the Lord called Miriam and Aaron to account specifically for speaking against Moses (v. 8).

As the chapter unfolds, the reason Miriam and Aaron found themselves in such serious trouble (vv. 4, 9) becomes apparent. In verse 2, they promoted themselves in a bid either to share Moses' leadership or to replace him: "Has the Lord indeed spoken only through Moses? Has He not spoken through us also?" They asked these questions, failing to see Moses' position and theirs from God's point of view. The Lord had chosen not only to speak through Moses but also to put Moses in charge of His people. God made very clear that Miriam and Aaron's disregard for Moses betrayed a lack of reverence for the Lord Himself, and they should have known better. The Lord's closing question to them demanded, "Why then were you not afraid to speak against My servant Moses?" (v. 8).

Moses' brother and sister seem to have lost their focus on the Lord even as He was leading the people to the promised land (Num. 10:11–13, 33). A little over a year before this incident, Miriam—identified as "the prophetess, the sister of Aaron"—had led the women of Israel in celebrating God's triumph over the Egyptians (Ex. 15:20–21). Aaron had served as Moses' spokesman during their confrontations with the pharaoh (Ex. 4:14, 27–30). In recent months, Aaron and his sons had been consecrated as priests (Ex. 29:44). Both Miriam and Aaron had been entrusted with their own responsibilities and opportunities for influence.

Like Miriam and Aaron, even mature Christians can be distracted by petty concerns and lose their focus on what the Lord is doing. Have you ever been like Miriam in Numbers 12, your attention so firmly fixed on a point of disagreement with a ministry leader or fellow Christ-follower that your focus on the Lord was compromised? Are you more disgruntled with that person or with the Lord Himself? Focus on God when you are tempted to disagree, and encourage those who are appointed by God to lead.

Tamra Hernandez

Prayer: *If the Holy Spirit convicts you about being an instigator of criticism (like Miriam), repent and seek to serve and pray for the other person(s). Ask the Lord to remind you of this lesson from Miriam's life whenever your focus is being drawn away from Him.*

Personal Reflection: ....

....

....

....

....

....

....

The Daughters of Zelophehad—Faithful and Wise

Numbers 36:1–13

*"Just as the LORD commanded Moses,
so did the daughters of Zelophehad." (v. 10)*

As the Israelites prepared to enter the Promised Land, Moses and the leaders of the community began planning how they would divide the land among the various Hebrew clans. The Israelite custom was to transfer a father's land to his sons when he died. The daughters did not receive an inheritance because the male heirs supported them until they married and were given a dowry. Then they were to nurture the family. A generation of Israelites had died in the wilderness, and the Promised Land would be divided fairly among their living sons as an inheritance.

One of the leaders of the tribe of Manasseh, Zelophehad, died in the wilderness but did not have any sons. In a minor oversight, his family was completely forgotten from the registry. Zelophehad's five daughters realized that they would have no one to care for them and no place to call home in their new land, so they spoke up for the rights to their inheritance. The daughters did not seek an inheritance out of selfish motives or in a deceitful manner. Rather, they respected the authority and structure of the time, correctly submitting their petition to Moses, Eleazar, and the leaders of the community. They asked to receive their land, although they had no male representative through whom to receive it (Num. 27:4).

As a result of their request, the Lord actually instructed Moses to change the custom. Moving forward, the daughters of men who died without sons would receive their father's inheritance. Because Zelophehad's daughters handled their situation with wisdom, the Lord provided for them and Moses affirmed them. They followed the legal guidelines for marriage and inheritance, and in return they were allowed to choose their husbands from within their clan (36:6). These women understood God's priorities and honored Him in their pursuit of justice.

The beauty of this story lies in the fact that God did not overlook the needs of women in Hebrew society, just as He sees the needs of women today. Mahlah, Noah, Hoglah, Milcah, and Tirzah were not punished for presenting their needs, and they are mentioned by name in the Bible (27:1)! God knew them, He saw their need, and He provided for them. Even if they had not received an inheritance of land, God still would have provided for them because they were first His daughters and He is a good God.

When you are faced with an unjust situation and you fear that your needs are not heard, bring them to your Father. He knows your name, and He cares for you! Receive the blessings that come with persistent faith in the provision of the Almighty.

Rhonda Harrington Kelley

Prayer: *Thank the Lord that He knows your name and sees your need. Ask Him to help you honor His priorities and provide you with the wisdom to rightly handle difficult situations.*

Personal Reflection: ....

....

....

....

....

....

Remember God, Teach Your Children

Deuteronomy 4:1–10

"Only take heed to yourself, and diligently keep yourself, lest you forget the things your eyes have seen, and lest they depart from your heart all the days of your life. And teach them to your children and your grandchildren." (v. 9)

One day, when I was being particularly forgetful, my son, aware of my health issues, asked, "Mom, why are you forgetting? Is your thyroid acting up?" If only my mind could hold all of the names, numbers, appointments, and lists that I need to know. Yet, even though our minds are limited, God gives us a specific command to remember His Words and to teach them to our children and grandchildren.

Scientists are fascinated by the workings of the mind. Memory studies have suggested that we forget due to **decay** because of the lack of reviewing and reinforcing the memory or **displacement**, i.e., by replacing the memory with a new one. God, our Creator, understands the working of the mind. His command in Deuteronomy 4 tells us to guard the memories of God's presence and instruction. In this passage, a word meaning "guard, keep, obey" is used in these instructions: "keep the commandments" (v. 2); "be careful to observe" (v. 6); "take heed to yourself"; and "keep yourself" (v. 9). The emphasis is to remember purposefully and to obey actively, so that our knowledge of God will not decay or be displaced.

Not only are we to guard these words from God, but we are also to teach them to our children and grandchildren. God's commands, statutes, and judgments teach us about who He is. God is pleased when you obey Him. He promises that He is near and that you can call upon Him. By teaching your children these spiritual truths, you are giving them wisdom and understanding for their lives.

While rocking my infant son as he nestled on my shoulder, I remember praying: "Lord, please help me never forget this precious moment." My desire to preserve the memory was based on a connection to my heart—my love for my son. God wants you to remember His presence and His love for you, memories connected to the heart. He wants you to remember His words of instruction that you might live for Him with wisdom and understanding, obedience out of love from Him and for Him. By teaching your children and grandchildren, you introduce them to the loving, heavenly Father.

Do you know about the love of the Lord for you? Have you committed to remember all He has done for you and to obey His commands? What is one practical way that you can teach the children you influence about God and His Word?

Karen Yarnell

Prayer: *Ask the Lord to help you be aware of all He has done for you. Pray that God will help you make teaching His words to the children in your life the greatest priority.*

Personal Reflection: ....

....

....

....

....

....

....

The Lord's Commandments

Deuteronomy 5:1–21

*"I am the LORD your God who brought you out of
the land of Egypt, out of the house of bondage." (v. 6)*

Have you ever heard this accusatory statement: "You took my words out of context"? When words are disconnected from the context in which they were spoken, they are easily misunderstood. Modern communication through emails and texts lends itself to miscommunication since facial expressions, voice inflections, and body language are lacking. In the same way, God's words can be misunderstood when disconnected from the One who spoke them.

What comes to mind when you read the Ten Commandments? Do you interpret rules and restrictions to be followed ritualistically? God did not give His instruction to regulate us, but that we might relate to Him as His children.

In this passage of Scripture, the One who is speaking is "the LORD your God." When "LORD" (Hb. *Yahweh*) is written in this way, with all capital letters, the reference is to God's personal name—the covenant name used by God of Himself. *Yahweh* means "I am" or "the existing One." God is the One "who is and who was and who is to come" (Rev. 1:4). You are here today but may not be tomorrow; God is eternal. In Hebrew thought, your actions reveal who you are. "I *am* the LORD . . . who brought you out of the house of bondage." The One who speaks is the God who has set you free.

Yahweh, the living God, has set you free from sin. His commandments teach you how to live as one who belongs to God. They are given that you might live as people in relationship with God and others.

The Ten Commandments are divided into two categories—the first relating to God and the second relating to others. Jesus spoke of the commands this way: "You shall love the LORD your God with all your heart . . . and love your neighbor as yourself" (Matt. 22:37–39). The greatest command is to "love the Lord" with all of your being. The second is to love others as yourself. In fact, Jesus included "all the Law and the Prophets" under these headings

(Matt. 22:40). The first four commandments are directed toward God and our worship of Him. The other six commandments instruct us in our relationships to others.

God's commandments are good because they are a reflection of God: He is the Lord who has set us free, and we are blessed when we obey. "Blessed *are* the undefiled in the way, Who walk in the law of the LORD" (Ps. 119:1).

Karen Yarnell

Prayer: *Meditate on the goodness of the Lord. What words can you use to describe Him? Ask Him to convict you of sin and to help you obey His words. Thank Him for setting you free from the sin.*

Personal Reflection: ....

....

....

....

....

....

....

....

How Do You Teach Your Children to Obey?

Deuteronomy 6:4–9

"You shall teach them diligently to your children." (v. 7a)

In the fifteenth century, artists began to paint more realistic paintings using a technique called "perspective." By creating depth and using light, the artist directed the viewer's eye to a certain focal point in the painting. As Israel was entering the Promised Land, God provided the focal point for His people; they were to worship Him alone. He chose the family as the venue for His instruction, teaching them to be His people among the nations that worshipped other gods.

This passage, also known as the *Shema*, became the Jewish prayer spoken morning and night, the first one learned by a child. It can be divided into three sections. First, "the Lord *is* one" (v. 4) is not only a statement of the unity of Father, Son, and Spirit, but it is also a recording of the fact that God is the only God and the only God Israel is to worship. The second section describes complete personal devotion, which is the only proper response to the Lord (vv. 5–6). Love for God includes all of the person: heart, soul, and strength.

The third division of this passage describes the place of God's words in the home. We are commanded to teach the children purposefully and repeatedly. Every activity of the home affords the opportunity to teach about God in the daytime, evening, and morning. God's words direct the work of the hands and the direction of the eyes. The entryway to the home declares the focus of the home to be the word of God.

Busyness of life can steal away precious time spent teaching children about God. When all activity is seen as an opportunity to teach, time is not wasted. Every circumstance, every celebration, and every crisis teaches our children how we respond to life. If God is the One we worship, will He not then be a part of all that we do?

Certain activities specifically teach God's Word. Memorizing verses of Scripture together as a family is an eternal investment. Spending time together, reading the Bible, singing, and praying, unifies the family in the Lord. Even times of correction and discipline can teach biblical principles. Parents use their energy and creativity purposefully to teach their children the truths of God. Obeying God's command takes prioritizing and often eliminating some other commitments in order to focus the family on activities of lasting value.

The goal of teaching your children should be that they would have a relationship with God. As they mature, we want them to worship the one true God with all of their hearts, souls, and strength. May we listen to the instruction of the Lord and be diligent in the task!

Karen Yarnell

Prayer: *Ask the Lord to help you teach the children you influence to worship Him. Ask for diligence and wisdom as you teach.*

Personal Reflection: ....

....

....

....

....

....

....

Let Him . . . Return to His House

Deuteronomy 20:1–8

"And what man is there who is betrothed to a woman
and has not married her? Let him go and return to his house,
lest he die in the battle and another man marry her." (v. 7)

Imagine being a young woman among the Israelites who have recently settled in the promised land. You, and even your parents, were born during the 40 years of wilderness wandering. The Lord has driven out the idol-worshipping people who previously occupied the village where your family has now settled, but news arrives of enemies rapidly approaching. Soon every able-bodied man has assembled for military action. Among them is the man to whom you have been betrothed. Perhaps when the priest speaks words of assurance to the people, as prescribed in the Torah, you trust his reminder that God Himself will "fight for you against your enemies, to save you" (v. 4). There is no promise, however, that war will bring no casualties, no assurance that your fiancé will return alive. If he dies before the marriage is consummated, your life, at best, will be drastically different than expected.

In the Deuteronomy chapter that instructs the priest to counsel the people against fear when they are "on the verge of battle," the Lord instructs the military officers also to address the people. Verses 5–7 identify three categories of men for the officers to exclude from service in the army—men (1) who have "built a new house . . . [but] not dedicated it," (2) who have "planted a vineyard . . . [but] not eaten of it"; or (3) who are "betrothed to a woman . . . [but have] not married her." If you were the fiancée of one of these men allowed to "return to his house," can you imagine the relief this provision would bring to you and your respective families?

In giving these instructions, the Lord demonstrated His commitment to bless His people for their continued obedience in the promised land (see Deut. 7:12–14 and 28:30, in which the loss of these same blessings is listed among the curses that would result from disobedience). The Lord protected the particular investments being made—dedicating homes newly established in the land, cultivating newly planted vineyards, and consummating marriages. He also affirmed the enjoyment of these family-building endeavors (see also Deut. 24:5).

A number of young families were spared the difficulties and disruption of a man's death. Furthermore, God compassionately spared young brides-to-be from the possibility of early widowhood as the result of war. Assured by the priest that God would defeat their enemies and grant the return of their betrothed, these women enjoyed a unique expression of God's favor.

Tamra Hernandez

Prayer: *Praise the Lord for at least one specific way that He has blessed you because of your obedience. Thank Him for this evidence of His taking pleasure in you.*

Personal Reflection: ....

....

....

....

....

....

....

Divorce and Hard Hearts

Deuteronomy 24:1–4

*"When a man takes a wife and marries her, and it happens that she finds no favor
in his eyes because he has found some uncleanness in her, and he writes her
a certificate of divorce, puts it in her hand, and sends her out of this house...." (v. 1)*

Divorce is widespread in our society; today over a million marriages end in divorce every year. In fact, you or someone close to you has probably been impacted by divorce. Whenever something has become so pervasive, you must make sure you are taking God's perspective on the issue instead of letting conventional wisdom determine your thinking on the matter.

The Bible has several important passages to consider in order to understand God's view about divorce (Mal. 2:16; Matt. 5:31–32; 19:1–12; Mark 10:1–12; Luke 16:18; and 1 Cor. 7:10–16, 39. See the devotions on days 213, 222, 226, and 270 for more information). Divorce is first mentioned in the Bible in today's passage. Moses tried to regulate divorce in Israel in order to protect abuses that in all likelihood were predominately adversely impacting women. Moses allowed a husband to give his wife a divorce certificate, but the stipulation about "uncleanness" implies that a wife could not simply be thrown out whenever her husband was unhappy with her.

The husband needed a compelling reason; "uncleanness" in this passage refers to indecent conduct. This stipulation was actually a protective measure for women so that a husband could not just divorce his wife on a whim. Nevertheless, just because Moses puts some regulations in place regarding divorce, he **never** mandates that a husband or wife must get a divorce. Consider the book of Hosea when God actually tells Hosea to stay with his unfaithful wife Gomer in order to show the Israelite people the Lord would never abandon them despite their repeated unfaithfulness to Him.

In Matthew 19, Jesus refers to this passage in Deuteronomy, stating that Moses allowed divorce only because of the hardness of men's hearts. While Deuteronomy 24 was an effort to curb abusive practices, Jesus points people back to God's original design for marriage as the ideal (Gen. 2:24). Marriage according to God is to be a lifelong, faithful union of one man and one woman. God uses strong language to underscore His opposition to treating marriage as something less than a sacred union (Matt. 19:6). He wants us to pursue His high standard and not conform to the culture's low view of marriage.

Candi Finch

Prayer: *Pray that married couples you know would view marriage as a lifelong, faithful union. Thank God that He is a faithful husband to His people, despite our unfaithfulness to Him. Search your heart to see if you have any attitudes regarding marriage and divorce that may reflect cultural ideas rather than biblical truths.*

Personal Reflection: ....

....

....

....

....

....

....

Rahab—A Courageous Canaanite

Joshua 2:1–24

*". . . for the LORD your God, He is God in heaven
above and on earth beneath." (v. 11b)*

Rahab lived along the city wall of Jericho, which made it easy for people to come and go discretely. She lived her life by the standards of the land of Cana, not by following God's law. How did a sinful woman come to find her name listed alongside heroes of the faith in the book of Hebrews (v. 31)?

Word of what the Lord was doing for His people had traveled across the land and reached Rahab's ears. She knew that the Lord had used Moses to part the Red Sea and destroy the Egyptian army. She had heard that God helped the Israelites completely destroy the Amorites, and she knew that Jericho was next on the list. The Canaanites were a powerful people who had terrified the Israelites just a generation before, and now they were the ones in a panic. Rahab must have believed that her people were scared for a good reason. Perhaps the God of the Israelites was more powerful than her city's walls. She was on the precipice of faith.

That night in Jericho, the men knocking on her door were not the people she expected. They had been sent by Joshua and, therefore, by God Himself. She faced a choice. She could defend her way of life and turn the Israelite spies over to her king, or she could courageously stop running from the true God.

Rahab wisely chose the latter. When Rahab aligned herself with God's values, she became a part of God's plan for the Israelites to conquer the Promised Land. She hid the spies, and devised a plan to keep them safe after their escape. In return, the Israelites promised that they would not kill her or her family when God gave them Jericho. Rahab professed her faith—she believed that God was the true God, who had authority over heaven and earth (v. 11). The result of her faith was kindness and faithfulness from the Israelites. Rahab was welcomed into God's family and given a new identity.

When Rahab's fear of the Lord became faith, her life changed forever. Rahab's story serves to remind us of what God can do with even the most sinful life. When you have faith in the Lord, He can use you as a part of His plan. He blesses you with a new identity through your relationship with Him, and desires to change your life for His glory. No matter what has happened in your past, God can make you a courageous woman who fears Him alone. Imagine the amazing ways that He could use YOU as a part of His plan!

Rhonda Harrington Kelley

Prayer: *Thank God for rescuing you from a sinful life and making His values your values. Ask the Lord to reveal any part of your heart that lacks the fear of the Lord.*

Personal Reflection: ....

....

....

....

....

....

....

Memorial Stones

Joshua 4:1–24

*"And these stones shall be for a memorial to
the children of Israel forever." (v. 7b)*

God sends a "Special Delivery" sympathy card to Joshua after the death of his mentor Moses, the man of God. Joshua was the servant of Moses from his youth. Together, they led the Jewish nation out of their four-century-long bondage in Egypt to the freedom God had promised to Abraham in Genesis 15. This "card" of comfort and condolence, which read: "Be strong and courageous for I am with you" was also a challenge.

Exodus records the story of the 10 plagues and the intense conflict with Pharaoh. After crossing the Red Sea, the people camped at Mount Sinai for approximately one year. God presented them with His Ten Commandments. He gave His blueprints for the tabernacle, establishing the priesthood and the sacrificial system. God taught them how to live and how to worship. After a 40-year journey through their wilderness of disobedience, they were now camped at the eastern edge of Canaan.

Deuteronomy ends with the death of Moses. Joshua had been commissioned and ordained. He was well prepared to lead the people westward across the Jordan River into the covenant land promised to Abraham, Isaac, Jacob and their descendants.

Moses recorded a message concerning stone memorials in Deuteronomy 27 for Joshua and the leaders of Israel. They were to gather and to stack stones that would stand as visual reminders of the presence and power of God. They were to coat some of the stones with lime and record the commands of God, encouraging national and personal accountability. All stones pointed to God, the Rock-Maker.

Two poignant stone memorials were constructed the day the Israelites crossed the Jordan. The Lord stopped the river waters at Adam, a town north of the crossing place. The whole nation (approximately two million people, by some estimates) walked across on dry land. Joshua selected 12 tribal leaders to take up a stone from the riverbed as they crossed. Each leader was to carry his tribal identity stone on his shoulder. These 12 stones were stacked as a memorial at their first camp in Gilgal, in the shadow of that walled city of Jericho as their first stone memorial in Canaan.

While the priests were standing in the riverbed holding the ark of the covenant, 12 additional stones were selected and placed at their feet. When the priests stepped onto the land, the waters of the Jordan were released by the hand of God and the 12 stones were covered completely. The stones would remain underwater as a valuable teaching tool for the next generation. Even though you can't SEE God, you know He is there. God is your ROCK!

Becky Brown

Prayer: *Ask God to help you leave spiritual reminders of His goodness for the continued growth of your own children. Thank Him for the rocks of remembrance in your life!*

Personal Reflection: ....

....

....

....

....

....

God's Provision

Joshua 7:10–26

*"Now Joshua said to Achan, 'My son, I beg you, give glory to
the LORD God of Israel, and make confession to Him, and tell me now
what you have done; do not hide it from me.'" (v. 19)*

The first challenge for Joshua and the Israelites in the land of Canaan was to conquer the impregnable walled city of Jericho. The Lord of Hosts commanded a seven-day march of faith around the city to be concluded with trumpet blasts and a great shout of victory. The walls literally fell down flat.

Like Moses, Joshua led the people to trust God and walk in full obedience to Him. Part of that obedience was to dedicate all of the spoils of this initial battle to the Lord. As they charged into the city, Joshua reminded them to stay away from anything dedicated to God. In the meanwhile, there was a man whose name was Achan, which means "trouble," from the tribe of Judah in the camp. Initially prophetic, his name remains as a warning for us against anything less than full obedience to God.

The dust of Jericho had barely settled when Joshua sent spies to the next battleground, a town called Ai, which means "wickedness." Spies reported that only a few soldiers would be needed for this battle. Instead of inquiring of the Lord, Joshua dispatched the soldiers. Within moments, 3,000 warriors were in full retreat with 36 Jewish casualties. Joshua and the leaders were stunned. In despair, they grieved in prayer before the ark of the covenant. At evening, the Lord revealed their defeat occurred because of sin in the camp. Items dedicated to Him were stolen. God called for consecrated cleansing.

Through a very amazing God-orchestrated selection process laced with several opportunities for immediate confession, "Mister Trouble" was revealed to be the looter. Found guilty, realizing he had no way out of the situation, Achan essentially said, "I have sinned against the Lord. I saw the items. I coveted them. I took them. I hid them in the ground underneath my tent." His actions implicated his whole family. God destroyed them all in the sight of all Israel in the "Valley of Trouble."

Starkly contrasted with the troubling choice of Achan, today's title is "God's Provision." True provision of God is found in His Word. God is holy. God will not tolerate sin. God taught us how to live. Disobedience, even partial obedience, will never be pleasing to God. When we DO commit sin, He provides a way out of that sin through conviction by His Holy Spirit. As we respond, we are offered an opportunity to confess sin, allowing God to cleanse and restore us. God sacrificed Jesus on Calvary to purchase our forgiveness.

Becky Brown

Prayer: *Ask God to help you remember these truths: Obedience is victory. Disobedience is defeat. Prayer comes before, not after, battle. Personal confession wipes the slate of sin clean.*

Personal Reflection: ....

....

....

....

....

....

....

Achsah—A Clever Daughter

Joshua 15:13–19

*"Now it was so, when she came to him, that she persuaded him to ask her father
for a field. . . . and Caleb said to her, 'What do you wish?' She answered, 'Give me
a blessing; since you have given me land in the South, give me also springs
of water.' So he gave her the upper springs and the lower springs." (vv. 18–19)*

After 40 years of wandering in the desert, the Israelites finally moved into the Promised Land. God led them to conquer their land, victory by victory, teaching them to trust Him along the way. Joshua (the military leader) and Eleazar the priest were to distribute the land to God's people. First, the Israelite leaders allotted land to the heads of the families of the various Israelite tribes.

As Joshua was dividing the land, he was approached by his friend, Caleb, the faithful spy who trusted God's promise to give the Israelites the Promised Land. Because of his faith, Moses had promised to give him the land of Hebron as his inheritance. The time had come for Caleb to request his inheritance, and Joshua honored Moses' promise.

Caleb began driving the remaining Canaanites from the land and offered to give his daughter's hand in marriage to the man who could conquer the last little piece along the Jordan. His nephew Othniel accomplished the task, and so he married Caleb's daughter, Achsah.

Later, Othniel became one of the judges of Israel, and Achsah asked him for his permission to approach her father to ask for a "blessing." Likely Achsah was asking Caleb for her dowry, which was given to daughters in place of an inheritance. Scripture says that when Achsah approached Caleb, she "dismounted from *her* donkey," showing respect to her father. Achsah asked humbly, thanking him for what he had already given her, and specifically, for the upper and lower springs. Caleb gave her what she wished.

Sometimes you and I need a blessing, and yet we do not ask our Father. Maybe you are afraid to ask, or you are concerned that you do not deserve the Lord's blessing. Achsah provides a beautiful example of how to approach the

Father. First, she waited for the right time. Then, she respected her authorities and sought counsel. She was humble, grateful, and specific. The Lord answers our prayers. We should ask Him specifically for what we need. Finally, Achsah was open to whatever answer Caleb gave her. A "no" from the Lord does not threaten your relationship with Him. You can still trust Him to provide for your needs, and He graciously answers you according to His eternal perspective and plan for you.

Rhonda Harrington Kelley

Prayer: *Pray over what you are lacking when it comes to serving the Lord. Ask the Lord for a specific blessing in your life. Have faith that he will answer your prayer and trust that His answer is best.*

Personal Reflection: ....

....

....

....

....

....

....

Female Diplomacy

Joshua 17:1–6

*"They came near before Eleazar the priest, before Joshua the son of Nun,
and before the rulers, saying, 'The LORD commanded Moses to give us
an inheritance among our brothers.' Therefore, according to the commandment
of the LORD, he gave them an inheritance among their father's brothers." (v. 4)*

The five daughters of Zelophehad are mentioned several times in the Old Testament. In Numbers 26:33 and 27:1–11, these faithful and wise daughters received from their father their rightful inheritance, which previously was given only to sons until God intervened to provide for the needs of female offspring (see Num. 36). In Numbers 36:10–13, they obeyed God's command by marrying within the tribe in order to keep their father's inheritance within the family. Now, in Joshua 17:1–6, these godly women teach another important lesson.

How do you approach individuals in authority with a personal request? Questions or needs may arise in your life. Human nature often prevails and you demand that your rights be granted. Defensiveness and arrogance take charge. However, God has a different plan for diplomacy. The daughters of Zelophehad followed His plan perfectly. They humbly went before the leaders to request their inheritance, and they patiently waited for the judgment of the authorities. They went directly to Eleazar the priest; to Joshua the leader of the Israelites; and to other leaders (v. 4). In essence, they worked through the chain-of-command to present their case in a spirit of submission and respect.

There is a difference between an arrogant demand and an assertive request! Many people, even Christian women, become overbearing and forceful when they want their way. Such an emotional approach is not biblical. While the Bible often encourages us to make petitions, there are parameters. Ask in God's name and according to His will (Matt. 7:7; John 14:13–14). Humble yourself before God and seek His guidance (2 Chr. 34:27; Mic. 6:8). When you have a request, go to God first; then approach those in authority over you.

Have you ever needed to approach someone in authority about a concern in your life? What was your attitude? Did you aggressively approach the one in charge with your personal demands? Or did you humbly seek his counsel to handle the situation? Consider this biblical example the next time you have such a challenge. Follow the example of the daughters of Zelophehad—approach humbly then wait patiently.

Rhonda Harrington Kelley

Prayer: *Ask the Lord to give you humility and wisdom when you approach an authority with a personal request. Seek to follow God's commands and leave the results to Him.*

Personal Reflection: ....

....

....

....

....

....

....

God's Promises, God's Faithfulness

Joshua 23:5, 10, 14

*"Behold, this day I am going the way of all the earth. And you know in all
your hearts and in all your souls that not one thing has failed of all
the good things which the LORD your God spoke concerning you.
All have come to pass for you; not one word of them has failed." (v. 14)*

God's promises fill the Bible . . . promises to His people, to His daughters. Some promises come with an "if you do this, then I will do that" stipulation.

In Joshua 23, Joshua is saying goodbye to the Israelites as he has grown old and close to death. He had completed his mission. Now he wanted the people to know more than anything how faithful God had been and would continue to be as they followed Him in obedience. He reminds them that God will continue to force their enemies out of the land as He had promised.

Joshua tells them that if they continue to follow and love God without wavering, then God would continue to fight for them. If they failed to do this, the enemy would overtake them as God would withdraw His strength from the battle. Joshua reminds them that God has never failed in keeping His promises: "All have come to pass for you; not one word of them has failed" (v. 14).

Do you believe that? Do you know how much God loves you and desires to show his strength in and through you? When I am faced with a new challenge, I reflect on His past faithfulness. I have walked long enough with God, seeing His work in difficult, hopeless situations. I know Him to be totally true and faithful.

While I was out of town, a loved one faced a terrible temptation. The enemy attacked at the weakest place, and I was helpless to do anything except pray and trust that God would bring good. I experienced peace as I waited. How could I do that? I had seen what God had done before in a seemingly hopeless situation.

As God's people, we should never lose hope and give up (2 Cor. 4:1)! Instead, we remember His promises and His faithful love as Jeremiah did (Lam. 3:19–26). He called to mind God's love and "therefore I have hope." That same hope is ours.

Do you need to lay down your fears, frustrations, failures, and pain to allow God's loving promises and faithfulness to wash over you? List what is on your heart, submit it to Him, let Him handle it, then experience His power, peace and love as He guides you each step in your journey.

Chris Adams

Prayer: *Ask God to show you areas you have not given Him complete control. Pray for a willing heart. Ask Him to strengthen your faith because HE is faithful to ALL his promises. Believe He will bring good as you love Him and heed His call according to His purposes (Rom. 8:28).*

Personal Reflection: ....

....

....

....

....

....

....

Teaching the Next Generation

Judges 2:7–15

"When all that generation had been gathered to their fathers, another generation arose after them who did not know the Lord *nor the work which He had done for Israel." (v. 10)*

Upon first reading this verse, I wondered what happened between the time Moses taught Joshua to follow God and the time Joshua failed to pass it on to those who came behind him. No leaders like Joshua were raised up when Moses commissioned him to take the people into the Promised Land.

The occasion of this verse follows the time when Joshua and the elders—those who had seen what the Lord had done for Israel—lived (v. 8). The generation that came after Joshua "did not know the Lord" or the works He had done (v. 10). Where was the break in passing down the legacy of leadership?

Throughout Psalms, one generation is told to teach the next, instilling in them the truths of Scripture (see Pss. 22:30–31; 71:18; 102:18; 145:4–7). Parents were the primary teachers of truth to their children. Women, in general, have been given a mandate to teach younger women (see Titus 2:3–5). We are to be reverent, not slanders, not addicted to wine, and we are to teach what is good, encouraging women to love their families, have self control, be pure, homemakers, kind and submitting to their husbands. Women are to teach women to be women! Most important, teach them to be godly women.

What if the chain of faith had not been broken after Joshua died? What if the truths of God had been entrusted and strengthened within the following generations rather than the distortions that led to following false gods? What if we do not faithfully raise up the next generation of women? What if we fail to entrust them with the truths of God's Word and with leadership skills? Consider the consequences. We must invest in eternal things that will last not only throughout the generations on earth but into eternity, as we share our faith with those who do not know Jesus.

The best way to teach others is to keep learning yourself—studying Scripture, asking God to reveal His truths, and seeking to live out those truths. Do you spend time in prayer and Bible study, seeking Him daily for His direction in your life?

As you continually follow those faithful women who have gone before you and as you faithfully lead those coming behind you, you continue the chain of faith so that a future generation will know the Lord and His works!

Chris Adams

Prayer: *Ask God to show you His truths. Ask Him with whom He wants you to share those truths. Seek His forgiveness for your lack of diligence in learning and teaching others about Him. Who is He asking you to mentor? Pray and ask Him to identify a woman who needs your wisdom, then ask Him to show you someone to learn from as well.*

Personal Reflection: ....

....

....

....

....

....

....

What Defines a Woman?

Judges 4:1–4

~~~

"Now Deborah, a prophetess, the wife of Lapidoth,
was judging Israel at that time." (v. 4)

Deborah, whose name in Hebrew means "honeybee," is identified as "a prophetess, the wife of Lapidoth, . . . judging Israel at that time" (v. 4), and later as "a mother in Israel" (5:7). These were tragic days in the history of Israel. Disobeying God's commands, intermarrying with the pagan people in the land, and neglecting to teach the truths of God's word to the next generation led to the decline of the nation and apostasy of its people. The book of Judges details the tragic cycle of sin and disobedience, followed by the cries of the people for a deliverer, and then God's merciful deliverance only to see the people return to their own way of disobedience, beginning the destructive cycle again.

The judges often functioned administratively, but they were not kings ascending to power through family lines. Primarily they were military leaders who arose at a time of crisis—often because of personal charisma or simply being in the right place at a propitious time to deliver the people from an oppressor. These leaders raised up by God were empowered by the Spirit for a particular task. The only bright spot in the midst of these years of tragedy, suffering, and unbelievable wickedness is the unwavering faithfulness of God, whose unconditional love awakened His pity and caused Him to pour out His mercy on an undeserving and rebellious people.

As a prophetess, Deborah was called upon to speak the truth of God. She had no message of her own, nor did she try to explain God's message—she simply delivered the word from God. In this book of Judges, among the judges, Deborah is portrayed in the best light.

There are many lessons to be found by women who want to study Deborah's legacy. First, observe her sharing wise judgments, upon request, under a "palm tree" in her own yard. There is no suggestion that she circulated fliers or even put out a sign, but she went outside her own home and made herself available.

She lived in Ephraim, although her influence extended far beyond the southern region in which she lived.

Second, Deborah put aside personal ambitions. She called for Barak, who lived in the north, to lead the Israelites into battle even though other judges had assumed this role themselves. When Barak wavered, she only agreed to go with him. She refused to take command of the armies even in the wake of Barak's cowardice. God blessed her obedience and used her for His purposes.

Dorothy Kelley Patterson

Prayer: *If you sometimes feel that your role as a wife or mother is not significant in the kingdom, remember that the Lord has used women like you in a myriad of ways. Make yourself available to the Lord, beginning in your own household. Be willing to serve him with a humble and teachable heart.*

Personal Reflection: ....

....

....

....

....

....

....

An Example of Feminine Leadership

Judges 4:5–16

"And she would sit under the palm tree of Deborah between Ramah and Bethel in the mountains of Ephraim. And the children of Israel came up to her for judgment." (v. 5)

Leadership is sometimes complicated by the indifference or lack of understanding of those you are assigned to lead. There may also be awkward circumstances and even puzzling situations as you look for biblical guidelines. Deborah experienced this frustration as, under God's instructions, she asked Barak to act on what the Lord has "commanded" (v. 6), even to the point of specifically noting how many men from each tribe, where they were to go, what God would do on their behalf, and how the battle would turn out (vv. 6–7). Yet Barak hesitated to follow the Lord's instructions; in fact, he refused to go on this mission without Deborah. The text does not give a reason—whether he doubted his own expertise to command the army or lacked faith in God's power to deliver the people from their oppressor.

Deborah did not dismiss Barak, as she well might have done under the circumstances, nor did she take over his job as the commander of the army. However, she remained faithful as God's prophetess, warning Barak that there would "be no glory" for him (v. 9). She did not make any effort to grab that glory for herself, but she declared to Barak that "the Lord will sell Sisera into the hand of a woman" (v. 9). With no concern about her own interests and recognition, she then "went up with him" (v. 10).

As a godly leader, Deborah was wise and discerning, courageous and confident, obedient and committed to God-control in her life. She was strong and prepared for the battles of life. Deborah showed her sense of divine priorities in her life:

- She listened to God (v. 5).
- She had a servant's heart (v. 9).

- She motivated others by delegating tasks appropriately (vv. 6–7, 14).
- She gave the credit for any success to God (5:2).

On one hand, Deborah's importance is not limited to the nation of Israel. However, neither should her accomplishments be elevated beyond what the text records. She seemed an ordinary woman in the beginning, but she did an extraordinary service to the Lord because of her obedience. Every woman has the opportunity to offer herself to the Lord and then to be obedient to His plan. It is amazing what you can accomplish when you are not concerned with who gets the credit!

Dorothy Kelley Patterson

Prayer: *Examine your own life and open your eyes to where God has placed you. Be willing to serve Him regardless of who gets the credit.*

Personal Reflection: ....

Deborah—A Mother in Israel

Judges 5:1–23

"Village life ceased, it ceased in Israel,
Until I, Deborah, arose,
Arose a mother in Israel." (v. 7)

The song of Deborah and Barak immortalized the destruction of the Canaanites in Hebrew poetry. They described the events leading to a mighty victory for Israel in a beautifully crafted song of praise recorded in Judges 5. Deborah began as a homemaker in Israel. She was a wife and a mother—at least in the sense of exercising nurturing sensitivity. Although no children are attributed specifically to her womb, she chose to identify herself as "a mother in Israel" (v. 7). Undoubtedly she was troubled by the atrocities her people were experiencing as they were overrun by pagan nations and abandoned by godless leaders. Her compassions for her people and her commitment to the God of Israel caused her to step forward and make herself available. Not only did she trust God herself, but she was also able to inspire her people to turn to the Lord for their deliverance.

Indeed Deborah used extraordinary decision-making skills, but one must not overlook that her greatest strength was her total commitment to the Lord and to His purposes for her life. She determined to be obedient to Him in every decision of life. This commitment gave her tools for uniquely effective leadership in the sphere in which the Lord placed her.

For a woman, nurturing is not confined to her offspring as the baby in the womb or even to his years of childhood. That nurturing sensitivity—often referenced as maternity—extends to the broadest arena of influence. Although Deborah identifies herself as "a mother in Israel," no children are mentioned in the text. Deborah's influence stretched beyond the family circle, extending first to those who came to her as she sat under the palm tree in her yard, then to those whom she summoned in order to deliver prophecies from the Lord, and finally to the nation of Israel.

Even mothers—or perhaps especially mothers—must take upon themselves the mantle of courage, not merely to sustain themselves but in order to help sustain others. History has been marked by women whose courage has been responsible for deliverance from oppression, for endurance in the midst of overwhelming difficulties, and for wise discernment beyond their own understandings. Deborah inspires us to present ourselves to the Lord, to humble ourselves before Him, and to arise as women in obedience to whatever task the Lord may assign to each of us.

Dorothy Kelley Patterson

Prayer: *Ask the Lord to awaken that nurturing sensitivity in your heart—whether for your own children or for others who need maternal encouragement. Be willing to take that stewardship of influence seriously and invest in the lives of those whom God brings into your lie.*

Personal Reflection: ....

....

....

....

....

....

....

Jael—An Artful Assassin

Judges 4:17–24; 5:24–27

～

"Most blessed among women is Jael." (5:24)

What an honor to be noted in Scripture as "most blessed among women!" Jael received that commendation in the Song of Deborah in Judges 5. Why was she blessed by God and praised by Deborah? It is a complicated story. Jael was an artful assassin used by God to slay the Canaanite leader Sisera, who had defeated the Israelites. Let's examine that account and apply its lesson to our lives today.

Jael was the wife of Heber the Kenite (4:17). They were a part of a semi-nomadic desert tribe of farmers and medal workers, who since the time of Moses were in close contact with the Israelites. During the time that Deborah was a judge in Israel, the Canaanite King Jabin was threatening the Israelites. Jael chose to side with the Israelites and oppose the Canaanites, the allies of her husband. He had alerted Sisera that the Israelites were gathering at Mount Tabor (4:11–12). Her action suggests that she placed her commitment to God even above her allegiance to her husband.

When Sisera gathered 900 iron chariots and all his men in the Jezreel Valley (4:13), the military leader Barak led 10,000 Israelites to defeat them. The entire Canaanite army was slain with the exception of Sisera who fled by foot to the tent of Jael (4:16–17). She gave him a place to stay and milk to drink, then lulled him to sleep. Although asked to stand guard at the tent to protect Sisera from attack, Jael herself "took a tent peg and took a hammer in her hand, and went softly to him and drove the peg into his temple . . . so he died" (4:21). Through this gruesome act God brought victory for His people over the hated Sisera (4:9, 23–24). From that point on, the Israelites grew stronger in their opposition to Jabin, King of Canaan.

The song of Deborah and Barak in Judges 5 praises God for His victory over the enemy. In beautiful poetic form, the battle is recounted and their deliverance is remembered. While Deborah is clearly the central figure in the Song, recognition is given to others for their contributions. Jael is praised for being an instrument of God's victory. The Song of Deborah concludes with a petition for God to defeat all His enemies.

The life lesson of Jael is that God will work out His purposes through whom He chooses. His plan is not always clear at first but is revealed in His time and way. Every woman can choose to make herself available to God as did Jael. Will you follow His leadership even when the results are unclear?

Rhonda Harrington Kelley

Prayer: *Offer yourself to God for His purposes and seek to see His plan. Commit yourself to the Lord and ask for His guidance.*

Personal Reflection: ....

....

....

....

....

....

....

An Honorable Daughter

Judges 11:29–40

"So she said to him, 'My father, if you have given your word to the LORD, do to me according to what has gone out of your mouth, because the LORD has avenged you of your enemies....'" (v. 36)

During the period of Judges, with no king in Israel, everybody did what was right in their own eyes (Judg. 17:6; 21:25). Israel regularly ignored and disobeyed God's laws, resulting in oppression. Flawed judges delivered Israel while demonstrating the need for a perfect Savior.

Jephthah, the eighth judge over Israel, freed Israel from the Ammonites and is listed as one of the heroes of the faith (Heb. 11:32). However, he is remembered for a foolish vow, which resulted in personal heartache for his daughter and him.

Jephthah vowed, "If you will indeed deliver the people of Ammon into my hands, . . . whatever comes out of the doors of my house to meet me . . . shall be the LORD's, and I will offer it up as a burnt offering" (Judg. 11:30–31). Upon his victorious return his daughter, his one and only child, came out to meet him with tambourines and dancing, celebrating her father's victory (v. 34). Devastated, Jephthah tore his clothes, regretting his rash vow.

This young girl, loving and trusting her father, declared, "My father, *if* you have given your word to the LORD, do to me according to what has gone out of your mouth, because the LORD has avenged you of your enemies, the people of Ammon" (v. 36). She requested that he allow her to go into the mountains for two months to weep for her virginity (v. 37). Her father granted her request. After two months, he carried out his vow, and, "She knew no man" (v. 39).

The text never definitively states what happened to this honorable daughter. Some believe that Jephthah offered her as a burnt sacrifice, which would have been against the law (Lev. 18:21; 20:1–5; Deut. 12:29–32; 18:9–12). Others believe that Jephthah dedicated his daughter to perpetual virginity, which would have been a form of sacrifice since she was his only heir, ending his lineage. Whatever the case, this young girl had a heart to honor both her earthly father and her heavenly Father.

What is your heart attitude toward your earthly father? Has a poor decision he made caused you heartache? If so, will you seek to forgive him? As a parent, are you seeking to make wise decisions to avoid inflicting heartache on your children?

What is your heart attitude toward your heavenly Father? Unlike earthly fathers, our heavenly Father makes no mistakes. He is worthy of our trust, adoration, and worship. You can rest in the fact that God loves you and has a perfect plan for your life. Will you trust Him?

Joy Martin White

Prayer: *Ask God to help you develop a right relationship with your earthly father. Then spend some time in prayer, thanking God for being the perfect heavenly Father.*

Personal Reflection: ....

....

....

....

....

....

....

The Nazirite Vow

Judges 13:3–7

⁓

"For behold, you shall conceive and bear a son. And no razor shall come
upon his head, for the child shall be a Nazirite to God from the womb;
and he shall begin to deliver Israel out of the hand of the Philistines." (v. 5)

The announcement from "the Angel of the LORD" consists of three main elements. First, the Angel of the Lord announces the woman's barrenness (v. 3). Obviously, this announcement was no great revelation to the woman. She knew that she had no child. Unlike the story of Hannah (1 Sam. 1:8–18), the text does not reveal any appeals from Manoah's wife to God or any suggestion that she longed to have a child. However, the woman's barrenness had not gone unnoticed by God.

Second, the Angel of the Lord came with the proclamation of great news. Manoah's wife would conceive and bear a son (Judg. 13:5). Along with the privilege of bearing a child, came great responsibilities and specific instructions (v. 5). The Nazirite vow was a tool to set one apart for service and complete dedication to the Lord. The Nazirite vow was also a voluntary act. *Nazir* (Hb.) derives from a root word meaning "to dedicate or consecrate oneself" solely to the Lord. This vow was usually temporary. However, Samson's vow was to be permanent (v. 7). In Samson's case, the Lord called him out from the moment of his conception for the purpose of complete dedication to Himself. According to Israelite Law, a person under the Nazirite vow committed himself to abstain from three things: (1) wine or intoxicating drink, (2) the razor, and (3) contact with dead bodies (Num. 6:1–21).

Third, in Judges 13:6–7, Manoah's wife immediately reports to her husband what the Angel of the Lord revealed to her. Although she may have had many questions concerning what she had just heard, the message was clear—she would bear a son. Immediately after hearing his wife's account of this divine appointment, Manoah addresses God directly (v. 8). He pleads with God to send "the Man of God" a second time in order to teach him and his wife how to raise their son.

God has called you, as a woman, for a specific purpose. Whether you are a student, a stay-at-home mom, or a grandmother, God has called you to seek Him in all that you do. In seeking Him, you are to act differently and look differently than the world.

Jessica Pigg

Prayer: *Ask the Lord to show you what your specific purpose is within your walk with the Lord. If you have children, take time to commit your children to the Lord. If you do not have children, ask the Lord to give you spiritual children that you can pour into daily.*

Personal Reflection: ....

....

....

....

....

....

....

A Wise Woman of Faith

Judges 13:8–24

"But his wife said to him, 'If the LORD had desired to kill us,
He would not have accepted a burnt offering and a grain
offering from our hands, nor would He have shown us all these things,
nor would He have told us such things as these at this time.'" (v. 23)

Judges 13 unveils a great example of a wise woman of faith even though her name is unknown. The wife of Manoah, who would become the mother of Samson, experienced barrenness like other women in Scripture such as Sarah, Rebekah, Hannah, and Elizabeth. All of these women ultimately had children, after receiving a divine announcement. God also had significant plans in Israel's history for the sons whom they bore.

Judges 13 describes the visit from "the Angel of the LORD," who appeared twice to this wise woman of faith, both times basically conveying the same information. Once she received news from the Angel of the Lord that she would have a son, she told her husband. Manoah had questions his wife was unable to answer, so he prayed that "the Man of God" would come again and "teach" them what they needed to do for their son (v. 8). They were a wise couple, with teachable spirits, yearning to be obedient to God.

When the Angel of the Lord appeared to her a second time, she "ran in haste" and told her husband (v. 10). She knew the heart of her husband and that he greatly desired to meet the Angel of the Lord, so she did everything she could to make that happen.

After the encounter with the Angel of the Lord, Manoah thought they would die because they had "seen God" (v. 22). His wife sensibly said, "If the Lord had desired to kill us, He would not have accepted a burnt offering and a grain offering from our hands, nor would he have . . . told us *such things* as these at this time" (v. 23). She was a woman of faith. She believed God's words would come to pass. She knew they would not die because she knew that she had to live so that God's Word could be fulfilled.

How is your faith? Would you be described as a wise woman of faith? We need to be women of faith. We can trust God and we can trust God's Word. Do you have a teachable spirit? Are you yearning to be obedient to God? Like Manoah and his wife, we need to be seeking God daily in His Word. We need to be hiding God's Word in our heart, seeking to obey Him, running in haste toward whatever God has for us.

Joy Martin White

Prayer: *Ask God to speak to you each day as you spend time with Him in His Word. Pray that you will become a wise woman of faith, who runs in haste towards whatever plans God has for you.*

Personal Reflection: ....

....

....

....

....

....

....

....

Parenting a Strong-Willed Child

Judges 14:1–2

*"So he went up and told his father and mother, saying,
'I have seen a woman in Timnah of the daughters of the Philistines;
now therefore, get her for me as a wife.'" (v. 2)*

How difficult it must have been for Samson's parents! Samson was called of God as a Nazirite and given strength beyond human ability. But, Samson also possessed a strong will and was disobedient to the law of God, even as a judge for Israel.

God has a plan and purpose for each person He creates (Eph. 2:10). He designs not only the physical and mental characteristics but also the personality. He equips strong-willed people to do hard things when others have lost strength and vision. They are determined to accomplish a task without being dependent on the praise or support of others. God can use them to do great things for His glory! What a privilege it is to train one with such strength of character.

Yet, parenting a strong-willed child can feel like canoeing upstream with only one paddle. Though all children have a will that must be trained, a strong-willed child pushes against authority to find his or her way. Instead of accepting guidance, she demands that situations conform to her desires. A parent can feel constant resistance and become weary or angry. The weary give up, while the angry domineer, trying to "break the will." Neither approach brings about the desired outcome: a child maturing into an adult who knows and obeys the Lord.

Every child needs her parents' prayers, which can bring eternal change. Philippians 4:6 instructs us to pray about everything: "Let your requests be made known to God." One must identify the specific request for the child. Is the child defiant? Then the request would be that he would humble himself before the Lord. Is the child unusually gifted? Then the request would be that he would always use his gifts for God's glory. Praying Scripture is another effective form of prayer.

Patience and kindness are a must in parenting a willful child. If a parent is angry when dealing with the child, then angry behavior is being modeled and the child will imitate the negative actions. James 1:20 reminds us that "The wrath of man does not produce the righteousness of God." The fruit of the Spirit in Galatians 5:22–23 includes "love, joy, peace, longsuffering, kindness, goodness, faithfulness, gentleness, self-control." Only by the Spirit of God is one able to remain firm yet gentle when strongly challenged.

For the parent, training a child whom God has gifted with a strong will, **prayer**, **patience**, and remembering the **potential** of the child will help in this challenging role.

Karen Yarnell

Prayer: *What Bible passages can you pray specifically for your strong-willed child? Pray for yourself as a parent, that God would give you understanding and wisdom for your child's particular needs.*

Personal Reflection: ....

....

....

....

....

....

A Marriage Doomed from the Start

Judges 14:3–20

‿

"And Samson said to his father, 'Get her for me,
for she pleases me well.'" (v. 3b)

Samson, a Nazirite from birth and a judge in Israel, had wrong priorities. His marriage, built on a flawed foundation of superficial looks and violations of God's standard, had little chance of succeeding. Although attraction can play an important role, destruction awaits a marriage based solely on fleeting beauty.

Samson's godly parents disapproved of this union. They preferred that he take a wife from among the Israelites rather than "the uncircumcised Philistines" (v. 3). His parents had a spiritual issue with this union because they knew that Mosaic Law prohibited marriage to a non-Israelite (Deut. 7:3). Ignoring his parent's advice, Samson married her, seeking only to please himself (Judg. 14:4). His selfish desire continued throughout his life until his final moments.

At his wedding feast, Samson proposed a riddle that no one could answer. Due to a threat on her family, Samson's new bride used tears and manipulation to get him to explain the riddle. Samson did not want to unveil it to her because he had not even explained it to his parents. Both elevated loyalty to their respective families over each other. God's plan for marriage is that "A man shall leave his father and mother and be joined to his wife, and they shall become one flesh" (Gen. 2:24). In marriage, your spouse should be more important than any other person and thing in your life other than God. Neither Samson nor his new bride lived this out.

Because "Samson's wife wept on him" (Judg. 14:16), "pressed him so much" (v. 17), and claimed that he hated her (v. 16), Samson gave in and explained the riddle to his new bride. This manipulative bride immediately told the men of the city the answer, ultimately betraying her husband. Her betrayal made Samson furious. He walked 23 miles to Ashkelon, killed 30 men, walked back 23 miles, and went back to his father's home angry (v. 19). As a result, Samson's wife was given to his companion (v. 20). Thus, Samson's first marriage was over, 30 people were dead, and then the Philistines burned Samson's bride and her father anyway (Judg. 15). From beginning to end, this marriage was doomed.

Samson and his Philistine bride provide a negative example for marriage. Marriage should not be selfish, but selfless. Marriage should not be self-centered, but God-centered. Their stillborn marriage never found life or displayed the gospel but only the sinfulness of humanity. Let their unbiblical union be a warning to you.

Joy Martin White

Prayer: *Pray that God would help your marriage be built upon the strongest foundation—the Word of God. Examine your heart and confess areas where you have been selfish in your marriage. If you are single and desire to be married, examine the characteristics you would like in a spouse and whether they fit with God's Word.*

Personal Reflection: ....

....

....

....

....

....

....

Delilah—A Heartless, Manipulative, and Conniving Woman

Judges 16:4–21

"Then she lulled him to sleep on her knees, and called for a man and had him shave off the seven locks of his head. Then she began to torment him, and his strength left him." (v. 19)

The first mention of love in Samson's life was not directed toward his parents or his wife. Instead, he directed it toward a woman named Delilah, the only woman whose name is provided in this biblical account.

Aware of Samson and Delilah's relationship, the Philistine leaders approached Delilah, offering her over 500 times the annual wage if she could discover the source of Samson's strength. Accepting their offer, she set out to find the answer by asking him directly. Obviously not in love and not even caring about him, Delilah knew the Philistine's intent to harm Samson. She valued money far more than Samson's life.

When Delilah asked Samson how he could be bound, he lied to her—three times. With the false information Delilah got from Samson, she sought in vain to subdue him (vv. 8, 12–13). His lies demonstrated that although he claimed to love her, he did not trust her. True biblical love has a foundation of trust. Samson did not understand love.

After three attempts to subdue him, Delilah asked Samson, "How can you say, 'I love you,' when your heart *is* not with me? You have mocked me these three times, and have not told me where your great strength *lies*" (v. 15). Using manipulation, Delilah "pestered him daily with her words and pressed him, so that his soul was vexed to death" (v. 16). She illustrates the contentious and angry woman mentioned in Proverbs 21:19.

Succumbing to her pestering, Samson finally told her the truth. He was a Nazirite and no razor had ever come to his head (v. 17). This portion of the Nazirite vow was the only one Samson had not broken. Delilah was just finding out that he was a Nazirite. Samson should have valued this important part of his life, but the text never indicates that he shared his commitment or that God was truly the source of his strength.

With Samson's confession, Delilah collected her money from the Philistines, then lulled Samson to sleep. She summoned someone to shave his head, then "she began to torment him" (v. 19). Delilah proved to be a greedy, manipulative, heartless, and conniving woman—the very epitome of what not to be.

Are there any ways in which you are like Delilah? Is there a price at which you can be bought? What is more important to you—your friends and family or money? Do you seek to manipulate or encourage? Seek to be the opposite of Delilah. Be gracious and compassionate to others and exhibit the fruit of the Spirit in your life.

Joy Martin White

Prayer: *Pray and ask God to show you any areas of your life in which you may be acting like Delilah. Ask God to change you and help you become more like Christ instead.*

Personal Reflection: ....

....

....

....

....

....

Micah's Mother—One Who Led Her Son Astray

Judges 17:1–6

"In those days there was *no king in Israel;*
everyone did what was *right in his own eyes" (v. 6).*

The last chapters of Judges serve to illustrate Israel's spiritual depravity during this time period. Micah was a man from the mountains of Ephraim, an area of idolatrous worship (Judg. 17—18). His name actually means "Who is like Yahweh?" to which the implied answer is "No one is like Him." This man Micah was definitely not like God because he worshipped other gods. Numerous men named Micah (Micha or Michaiah) are mentioned in the Old Testament (v. 1; 2 Sam. 9:12; 2 Kin. 22:12; 1 Chr. 8:34–35). The book of Micah was written by a prophet bearing the same name in eighth century B.C. What can Micah and his mother teach Christians today?

Judges 17 describes the idolatry of Micah and reports his mother's loss of 1,100 pieces of silver. In her anger, Micah's mother put a curse on the stolen money (v. 2). Curses bore serious consequences in the pagan culture of the ancient Near East. Her dishonest son returned the money and confused his sin (v. 2). His mother forgave him, reversed the curse, and dedicated the money to the Lord (vv. 3–4).

A dishonest woman herself, Micah's mother gave the 200 shekels of silver promised to God to a silversmith to mold into household idols (v. 4). She gave the carved images to her son who anointed one of his sons as priest of their false religion. No wonder Samuel, the ascribed author of the book of Judges, spoke the chilling words about that idolatrous time: "Everyone did what was right in his own eyes" (v. 6). Micah and his mother were both guilty of that pronouncement.

Unfortunately, this bad apple didn't fall far from the tree. Micah was dishonest like his mother. He deceived her when he took the money. Micah's mother tried to deceive God when she used the money that she had promised God to make an idol. Because mothers have much influence on their children, the offspring often follow in their footsteps, becoming like them for good or bad.

What about you? Have you followed in the godly footsteps of another or have you been led astray? Have you influenced others to live a good life or a bad one? Let the negative example of Micah's mother inspire you to be a positive influence.

The challenge for Christian women today is to do what is right in God's eyes, not your own. Keep your eyes focused on God. Repent of your sinfulness and return to Him with renewed commitment. Seek His guidance so you won't lead others astray.

Rhonda Harrington Kelley

Prayer: *Spend some time in prayer reflecting on those who have influenced you. Commit to living a godly life and being a positive influence on your family and others.*

Personal Reflection: ....

....

....

....

....

....

....

Naomi—A Woman of Persevering Faith

Ruth 1:1–5

". . . So the woman survived her two sons and her husband." (v. 5b)

During a time of famine in Israel in approximately 1200 B.C., a man named Elimelech took his wife and sons to Moab, a fertile land to the east of the Dead Sea. He was an Ephrathite from Bethlehem in Judah. His wife was Naomi and their sons were Mahlon and Chilion (v. 2). Unfortunately, Elimelech died and left Naomi as a widow (v. 3). The sons married the Moabite women Orpah and Ruth and lived happily together for 10 years before they also died, leaving Naomi without her husband or children (vv. 4–6).

Naomi is known for the special relationship she had with her daughter-in-law Ruth and for being a woman of persevering faith. During the time she was alone as a widow, Naomi's faith in God was strengthened, though she believed God had dealt harshly with her (v. 20). Resolute in her faith, Naomi returned to her homeland and experienced the blessings of God.

Ruth, a pagan Moabitess, chose to follow her mother-in-law to Israel, and she had begun to worship Naomi's God. This passage of Scripture includes Ruth's words of commitment, which have been immortalized through the centuries (vv. 16–17). Often used in wedding ceremonies, a bride pledges her commitment to her husband. In this text, Ruth expresses her affection for Naomi and her new faith in the one true God. Naomi's unwavering faith influenced Ruth and others.

Despite her bitter experiences in Moab, Naomi was blessed during her return to Israel. God provided for Ruth and Naomi through a close relative, Boaz, who became their kinsman-redeemer (see Ruth 2 for this beautiful account). Through the union of Ruth and Boaz, Naomi was blessed with a grandson. She tenderly cared for Obed, who later became the father of Jesse and the grandfather of Israel's famous King David (4:13–17). Naomi's persevering faith yielded her abundant rewards on earth and in eternity.

I am so very grateful for the godly influences of my precious mother-in-love Doris Kelley. She had the same persevering faith of Naomi. While at times her life was difficult (orphaned as a child, infirmed as an adult, alone as a widow in her senior years), Mom Kelley received many rewards in life. She had a wonderful family including five children, eight grandchildren, and 12 great-grandchildren. She lived until the age of 91 and had a meaningful ministry of prayer and note writing until her death. She is now receiving her eternal rewards in heaven. Let Naomi and Mom Kelley be examples for us to persevere in our faith and leave a lasting legacy.

Rhonda Harrington Kelley

Prayer: *Ask God to strengthen your faith to face the challenges of life. Seek to persevere like Naomi to receive earthly and eternal rewards as you leave a lasting legacy.*

Personal Reflection: ....

....

....

....

....

....

....

Chesed—God's Lovingkindness

Ruth 1:6–13

〰

"And Naomi said to her two daughters-in-law, '... The Lord
deal kindly with you, as you have dealt with the dead and with me.'" (v. 8)

After living in Moab for 10 years, Naomi heard good news about her homeland. The famine, which had prompted her husband to move the family to Moab in the first place, had ended. However, the writer of the book of Ruth does not put it that way. Possibly recounting the way Naomi either heard or interpreted this news, the text says she heard that "the Lord had visited His people by giving them bread" (v. 6). Although Naomi denied having hope (v. 12), she actually stepped out in faith—"the substance of things hoped for, the evidence of things not seen" (Heb. 11:1). What gave her hope was hearing about evidence of the Lord's *chesed* (Hb.).

The English language has no perfect translation for the Hebrew word *chesed*. As a characteristic of God, *chesed* conveys His "covenant love," emphasizing the absolute fidelity and unwavering constancy of His love. During this period of the Israelites' history ("when the judges ruled," Ruth 1:1), famine in the Promised Land indicated their failure to obey the Lord (Deut. 28:15–18, 38–40). If, as Naomi heard, "the Lord had visited His people," she knew this meant He had intervened (cp. Ex. 3:16–18). Having loved His people enough to allow them to suffer the consequences (famine) of rejecting His provision, He remained devoted to their well-being, loving them enough to hear their prayers and finally to restore both their crops and the hope of the "empty" like Naomi (Ruth 1:21).

Naomi did not realize it at the time, but the Lord had already been demonstrating His *chesed* to her while she was in Moab—through His gift of two daughters-in-law who would not abandon her when their husbands, Naomi's sons, died. In this way, Naomi implied, they had dealt "kindly" (Hb. *chesed*) with their mother-in-law (v. 8). The Lord had also been demonstrating His *chesed* through Naomi to these young women. As she bid them farewell, Naomi not only was expressing her love for them but also was extending to them the Lord's covenant love: "The LORD deal kindly [Hb. *chesed*] with you . . . ." Sadly, Orpah went "back to her people and to her gods" (v. 15). Ruth, however, embraced Naomi's God and, thereby, His *chesed*—"your God, my God," Ruth insisted as she "clung to" Naomi (v. 14; cp. 2:12, 20).

How has the Lord demonstrated His "lovingkindness" to you recently? In what ways has He extended this gracious, faithful love to others through you?

Tamra Hernandez

Prayer: *Praise the Lord for specific ways by which He has demonstrated His* chesed—*His gracious, unmerited love and unwavering commitment—in your life. Ask Him to extend His love through you to someone specific today.*

Personal Reflection: ....

....

....

....

....

....

....

Ruth—Commitment from God's Perspective

Ruth 1:14–22

"But Ruth said:
   'Entreat me not to leave you,
   Or to turn back from following after you;
   For wherever you go, I will go;
   And wherever you lodge, I will lodge;
   Your people shall be my people,
   And your God, my God.'" (v. 16)

These words from the lips of Ruth the Moabitess have long been immortalized. They are appropriate as often used in wedding ceremonies to express the commitment of a bride to her husband. Perhaps the Lord chose what is often the most troublesome relationship (for example, between a mother-in-law and a daughter-in-law) in an extended family as the setting in which to record the commitment that He expects for our relationship to Him.

Every earthly or heavenly relationship depends upon the foundation of commitment. Ruth expresses her willingness to give up her family and the only home she has known and venture into the unknown in her search for the living God. She is willing to accept a different nation as her people, to live in a strange and distant land; and most important, she is determined to embrace a new faith—one totally foreign to her own experience, which she has seen lived out in the life of Naomi.

Ruth shows an understanding of the exclusivity of the new faith and the living God who is drawing her to Himself. She recognizes the serious nature of this covenant as a totally consuming and permanent commitment, but she also seems to grasp the enabling perseverance that would be hers even in the midst of difficulties and adversities.

Ruth's words of commitment to her mother-in-love Naomi are discerning or prophetic or perhaps both! The upcoming journey, challenging situations, and new relationships are all covered in her words of covenant commitment.

In fact, her use of God's covenant name *Yahweh* (note in your Bible the word "LORD" in all caps, which is how the translators designate the use of *Yahweh* in the Hebrew text, v. 17) rather than *Elohim* (the Hebrew word for "God" as used in v. 16). That change in the impersonal/generic way Ruth addressed the living God is a clear indication of the completion of her journey to His presence. Remember that Ruth's departure from Moab, the land of her birth, and from the ties with her family was a choice she made—with no human encourager and even discouragement from Naomi. Ultimately her heart was drawn to *Yahweh* God, and He welcomed her to come under the "wings" of His protection (2:12).

Dorothy Kelley Patterson

Prayer: *Examine the commitments in your life. Consider whether or not you have followed the pattern of Ruth in your commitment to the Lord? To your husband? To others who are important to you? Ask the Lord to teach you how to pursue that all-consuming commitment to Him as a foundation for all other relationships.*

Personal Reflection: ....

....

....

....

....

....

The Person Who Stands in the Gap

Ruth 2:19–23

"Then Naomi said to her daughter-in-law, 'Blessed be he of the LORD,
who has not forsaken His kindness to the living and the dead!' . . .
'This man is a relation of ours, one of our close relatives.'" (v. 20)

The importance of the family is noted throughout Scripture. God started in the garden of Eden with one man and one woman—a family. He continues to reveal Himself with a myriad of metaphors coming out of relationships within the family. In the book of Ruth, two important Hebrew concepts motivated by preserving the family line are combined with a special emphasis on continuing the generations. The first is a reference to the person who stands in the gap—"a relation of ours and one of our close relatives" (v. 20). The latter term (Hb. *go'ēl*) refers to a close family member assigned the responsibility to be the "redeemer" for the family business (see also Lev. 25:23–27, 47–55), working in behalf of another person to keep property within the family in a time of crisis. Boaz was eligible to be the kinsman who would redeem for the widow Naomi the inheritance Elimelech forfeited when he left Bethlehem for Moab.

The second concept is the law of levirate marriage (see Deut. 25:5–10), which added the care for the widow of the dead relative to the return of property. Although not compulsory, levirate marriage allowed for conjugal union to produce an heir for the deceased husband. The widow became the wife of her husband's brother or other close relative in order to conceive a child, who would then inherit her first husband's estate, thereby preserving his name and continuing his line of descendants.

The kinsman Boaz, willing to redeem without hesitation, paid the cost required for the one he loved—Ruth—just as Christ later redeemed mankind. Jesus Christ faithfully fulfills this responsibility for believers. Whatever your trial or difficulty, Jesus is standing by as your kinsman-redeemer. He dwells in your heart when you commit yourself to Him. He hears your prayers when you call out to Him. He guides your decision-making and life choices when you allow Him to do so. He goes before you to prepare the way; He walks beside you to encourage and sustain; He is the rear guard who follows to protect and deliver.

These family-centered concepts remind us of God's commitment to the family and His determination to continue the generations through godly seed. Jesus is our Redeemer, and He stands ready to offer His loving care when we come under His protection. As with Naomi and Ruth, such protection does not mean the absence of tragedy and difficulty or even death; rather His commitment is to take us through whatever may come, never leaving us without a redeemer!

Dorothy Kelley Patterson

Prayer: *Call upon the Lord to come to you as Kinsman-Redeemer. Find refuge under His wings. Allow Him to heal and protect your family.*

Personal Reflection: ....

....

....

....

....

....

....

A Relationship Focusing on Law or Love

Ruth 3:1–9

⌒

*"So she went down to the threshing floor and did according to
all that her mother-in-law instructed her." (v. 6)*

There are many relationships within the family unit—both those related by blood and those related by marriage (or law). According to Hebrew as well as other Middle Eastern cultures, the husband and wife were more closely related to the parents of the husband than to those of the bride. Essentially the bride left her family to enter the household of her husband's family, and there she assumed all the rights and responsibilities of a daughter (1:1–7). In a perfect world, these relationships that formed because of legal commitments would benefit all within the family so that each member of the household made every effort to help and encourage the others. Together they would impart the values and truths of their faith to succeeding generations (see Ps. 78:4–6). However, not every household mirrored the mutual love between Naomi and her daughters-in-law (Ruth 4:15; see also Gen. 26:34–35).

In the lives of Naomi and Ruth, both women committed themselves to each other (Ruth 1:7–8, 16–17). Naomi expressed her appreciation for the kindnesses extended to her (1:8–9), and Ruth reciprocated with affirming her loyalty to the family she had embraced (1:10). Naomi put the welfare of Ruth ahead of her own needs (1:11–13), and Ruth responded by risking all in order to provide for the needs of Naomi (2:14–18). Naomi became bitter toward God and sank into self-pity (1:20–21), and Ruth took the lead in finding a way for them to exist by seeking food (2:1–3). Naomi showed interest in Ruth's efforts to provide for their needs (2:19), and Ruth answered her questions with detailed information (2:19, 21, 23). Naomi offered to Ruth advice on how to move toward security (3:2–4, 18), and Ruth responded with a teachable spirit (vv. 5–6).

What, then, can we learn from Naomi and Ruth to help navigate what may be troubled waters and a challenging relationship? There are some clear lessons that move from legal requirements to loving service:

- The women must choose to move from legal codes to loving hearts in their mutual commitment to one another.
- The gratitude in the heart of one can awaken loyalty in the heart of the other.
- Selflessness on the part of one demands unselfishness from the other.
- Bitterness in one gives opportunity for creativity in the other.
- Interest from one may be rewarded by a warm response from the other.
- Counsel from one often bears fruit when honored and accepted by the other.

Dorothy Kelley Patterson

Prayer: *Examine any difficult relationships in your life. Consider ways you can apply the lessons learned from Naomi and Ruth to turn difficulties into ways for extending love and offering service. Ask the Lord to allow you to be His hands and feet to minister to all within your family circle.*

Personal Reflection:

What Can Ruth Teach Women Today about Dating?

Ruth 3:1–18

". . . All the people of my town know that you are *a virtuous woman." (v. 11b)*

Have you ever thought about trying to get a husband by picking up some leftover grain and finding a threshing floor or maybe even offering to water some man's camels? Hey, it worked for Ruth and Rachel in the Bible! Seriously, though, while we may not find cultural terms such as dating or courtship in the Bible, God has given us "all things that *pertain* to life and godliness" (2 Pet. 1:3), including timeless principles for God-honoring dating relationships.

Boaz and Ruth beautifully depict the dynamic of pre-marital romance between a man and a woman. Boaz was an honorable man (Ruth 2:1), who acted with integrity and respected authority (vv. 11–13; 4:1–10). He protected Ruth's reputation from potential harm (2:9), guarded her honor (v. 14), and provided for her overall well-being (2:8, 14–16).

Boaz respectfully pursued Ruth for the purpose of marriage and was capable of providing for a wife. Ruth was a virtuous woman who was concerned for the needs of others (2:2–3), hard-working and submissive (2:23; 3:5), and committed to her family (1:16–17). While Ruth made herself available to Boaz, she did not initiate their romantic relationship (vv. 1–11). Further, she received and followed the counsel of an older, godly woman (v. 5).

Both Ruth and Boaz were known for their noble character and devotion to God; each was described with the Hebrew word *chayil* ("strength, integrity, virtue, ability," Boaz in 2:1 and Ruth in 3:11). A person of great integrity and virtue is an ideal candidate for a potential spouse.

For Christian singles today, much can be learned from these two people of integrity. As you consider the significance of dating or courtship, several other principles in Scripture can serve as a guide. First, a believer should not date an unbeliever (2 Cor. 6:14). Your choices today determine your tomorrows so it is best to think of every date as a potential mate. If there is a character quality about someone you are dating that you would not want in a husband, then you have no business dating that person. Second, you should only date growing Christians who could be spiritual leaders, a man you can respect since the Bible says you should respect your husband (Eph. 5:33). Third, seek godly counsel and accountability (Eccl. 4:9–10). During this season, do not isolate yourself from people who can help you and your boyfriend be above reproach.

Candi Finch

Prayer: *Pray for single people you know to honor God in their dating relationships— that they would not awaken love before its time (Song 2:7) and that they would view their season of singleness as an opportunity to deepen their walk with the Lord (1 Cor. 7:32–34). Pray they would be men and women of character like Ruth and Boaz.*

Personal Reflection: ....

....

....

....

....

....

....

....

Individuals Matter in the Big Picture

Ruth 4:9–22

". . . and Boaz begot Obed; Obed begot Jesse,
and Jesse begot David." (vv. 21–22)

How would you answer this question: What is the book of Ruth about?

"Simple," you might say, "it's about Ruth." Good answer. She is obviously a central character in the story. You might suggest that the book is about Ruth's relationship with her mother-in-law or about the love story leading to her marriage to Boaz. True, both summaries highlight important aspects of this relatively small book wedged between Judges and 1 Samuel.

Taking another approach to the question, consider what this book contributes to "the big picture" of the whole Bible: What is the book of Ruth about in terms of the overarching story reaching from Genesis to Revelation? Asking the question this way may seem too expansive, but today, stretch your understanding of what Ruth is about from God's "big picture" perspective. And for now, let the brief 13-verse portion at the end of the book provide a glimpse of that more expansive view. In these few verses, 19 individuals—five women and 14 men—are mentioned by name. Although the narrative revolves around only three—Naomi, Ruth, and Boaz—the significance of their story emerges when you notice the way a bridge stretches from God's past promises to their future fulfillment.

Boaz publicly declared this significance of his marriage to Ruth. As the kinsman-redeemer, he assumed responsibility not only for preserving the inheritance of her deceased husband Mahlon but also for securing the entire inheritance of Naomi and Elimelech, including the part otherwise lost because Mahlon's brother Chilion had also died (see Ruth 1:1–5; 4:1–8; Deut. 25:5–10). The names and promised-land property of three Israelites consequently were **not** "cut off" (Ruth 4:10). The blessings proclaimed on Ruth and the house of Boaz directly linked this couple's future offspring with the names of five more individuals through whom the Lord had built "the house of Israel" (Rachel and

Leah) and preserved the tribe of Leah's son Judah (through Tamar and her son Perez; see Gen. 38). From this tribe's descendants would come the promised Messiah (Gen. 49:8–12; Matt. 1:1–3).

"The genealogy of Perez" (Ruth 4:18–21) further demonstrates that he was the ancestor of Boaz. It includes five more names of men in the lineage from Perez to Boaz. Verse 17 shows why Ruth and Boaz are so important in the "big picture" view of Israel's history, but the formal genealogy cinches it—they were the great-grandparents of King David. Fast-forward to the opening verse of the New Testament, to "the genealogy of Jesus Christ, the Son of David" (Matt. 1:1). Name by name Matthew recounts the Messiah's human ancestry, including Ruth in the list. In God's "big picture" view of history, individuals—like Ruth **and** like **you**—matter.

Tamra Hernandez

Prayer: *Ask God to help you see each person you encounter today as someone who matters to Him.*

Personal Reflection: ....

....

....

....

....

....

Struggling with Infertility

1 Samuel 1:10–18

"And she was *in bitterness of soul, and prayed to
the LORD and wept in anguish." (v. 10)*

Infertility. The very word is like a dagger in the heart of every woman. After months of testing, seeing three different doctors, and going through a year of emotional anguish, I heard what many women fear: "Amanda, you will probably never have children." I will never forget that day or the overwhelming feeling of sadness and despair that washed over me. I was a single, 27-year-old woman, and, now I was barren. Although I was not married, I had my own Peninnah—Satan—who "provoked . . . [me] severely, to make . . . [me] miserable" (v. 6). He taunted me with accusations. "What man would ever want to marry you? What did you do to deserve this punishment? You are now a broken, sad woman who cannot even fulfill a woman's basic purpose—having children." Sound familiar?

Many of you understand Hannah's situation, for her story is your story. Some of you may be in the midst of struggling with infertility, and the longing for a child has taken over every aspect of your life. Maybe you have tried every drug, every medical procedure, and every conception method available, yet God has chosen to close your womb. You have cried out to the Lord—the Giver of life—and begged Him to open your womb . . . but nothing. You wait, month after month, year after year, decade after decade, but God has provided no child. What are you to do? Hannah offers a wonderful example.

Scripture is not silent about Hannah's despair. God shows us a woman who is hurting, and, in the process, He validates our pain. But, Hannah does not simply stop and forever focus on her pain. At one time Hannah was bitter, but then she prayed. At one time she was angry, but then she prayed. At one time she was overcome with despair, but then she prayed. Out of her brokenness, she cried and poured out her soul to the Lord (v. 16). Then, she got up, ate food, and she refused to be sad (v. 18). She refused to allow her infertility to define her.

Dear friend, your Lord sees you, and He hears you. Do what you have done time and time again—pour out your soul to Him—and then GET UP. Yes, God created us with a desire to nurture children, but, more importantly, He created us for Himself. He has a plan and purpose for every woman and that includes you. God may choose to keep your womb closed, but He still loves you and looks upon you with favor. Will you trust Him?

Amanda Walker

Prayer: *If you are overcome with bitterness, pray and ask God to lift up your face. Ask God to help you be defined by His nature and not your infertility.*

Personal Reflection: ....

....

....

....

....

....

....

Dedicating Your Children to the Lord

1 Samuel 1:19—2:11

"For this child I prayed . . . Therefore I also have lent him to the Lᴏʀᴅ." (1:27–28)

After years of struggling with infertility, you can imagine the shock and joy Hannah experienced when she discovered the Lord answered her prayer for a child. However, motherhood was not what Hannah thought it would be—it never is. Motherhood is not **just** about experiencing joy and excitement—though children are a delight—but motherhood is also characterized by sacrifice. While worshipping the Lord in Shiloh, Hannah made a vow to God. She promised God, if He chose to give her a son, then she would dedicate him back to the Lord (1:11). And, that is exactly what she did!

Ladies, we, too, have a decision to make. Will we dedicate our children to the Lord or teach them to live for themselves? How we answer that question will determine how we choose to raise our children. It is our responsibility to nurture, train, and prepare them for the future. But, we must always remember that our children are on loan to us by God. He has a specific plan and purpose for them. Just like Hannah dedicated Samuel to the Lord, God wants us to dedicate our children to Him and let Him plan their lives. I can hear you asking: What if God leads them down a path we would not have chosen? What if God asks my child to be a missionary, and we had plans for him to be a doctor? What if God chooses a life of martyrdom instead of a life of security and comfort? And, the "what ifs" of our children's futures could go on indefinitely.

I will never forget the moment when I realized that God loves my children more than I do. Medically, I was not supposed to have children. But, God stepped in and provided my husband and me with two little girls. Immediately, my maternal instincts went into action and all I wanted to do was protect them from the world. Hannah must have had the same feelings. Instead, of pursuing her personal desires for her child, she obediently gave Samuel to the Lord. I assume this decision was not easy.

Eli was not the best father and his sons were definitely not godly examples for young Samuel to follow (2:12–17). However, if Hannah had not given Samuel to the Lord, then Israel would have suffered. Young Samuel turned out to be one of the greatest prophets in Israel. We, as mothers, do not know who God has entrusted to us. You could be raising the next great evangelist, president, or community leader. Will you entrust your precious child to the Lord and allow Him to determine his future? God has great things in store for your children.

Amanda Walker

Prayer: *Ask the Lord to help you see your children the way He sees them. Pray God will give you the courage to dedicate your children back to Him and His service.*

Personal Reflection: ....

....

....

....

....

....

....

The Glory of God's Presence

1 Samuel 4:1–22

*"And she said, 'The glory has departed from Israel,
for the ark of God has been captured.'" (v. 22)*

When Hannah took her son Samuel to Shiloh (chap. 2), he was only a toddler. When the Israelites went to war against the Philistines (chap. 4), Samuel was a young man recognized throughout Israel as "a prophet of the Lord" (3:20–21). Eli the priest still lived in Shiloh, but his sons, Phinehas and Hophni, were the priests on duty at the tabernacle. In stark contrast to Samuel, these two men were "corrupt; they did not know the Lord" (2:12). In fact, chapters 2–3 indicate that the Lord intended to kill Eli's sons because of their wickedness (2:25; 3:11–14). They had "made themselves vile" (3:13), showing contempt for "the offering of the Lord" (2:17) and openly promoting Canaanite-style religion through prostitution "at the door of the tabernacle" (2:22).

The woman who named her newborn son "Ichabod" was the wife of Eli's wicked son Phinehas. Her name is not given, but we know that she was already near childbirth when news of an unthinkable tragedy reached her—"news that the ark of God was captured" (4:19). Stricken with overwhelming grief, she went into labor and died after delivering her son. Verses 19 and 21 both mention "the deaths of her father-in-law and her husband" as news compounding the woman's grief. Yet she repeated, "The glory has departed from Israel," and immediately clarified what she meant—"for the ark of God has been captured" (v. 22).

Like Eli, her father-in-law (vv. 15–18), this woman was overwhelmed not because her loved ones had died but because she believed that with the ark's capture, all hope was lost. The women standing by tried to comfort her by pointing to the newborn son as a legacy of hope for the future, but she knew better. All hope for her son's future and for that of Israel lay in the presence of the living God—i.e., "His glory," represented by the ark of the covenant.

Ichabod's mother rightly feared the worst. If God had truly "departed," Israel was helpless. All hope for Israel's future lay in the presence of the living

God. Nevertheless, she underestimated God. His glory and power were neither contained in nor limited by the ark of the covenant, which the leaders of Israel had foolishly carried to the battle lines like a weapon they could manipulate (vv. 3–7). See 5:1—7:2 for the rest of the story.

What sort of tragedy or unfathomable loss might prompt you or your nation utterly to lose hope? Let the anguished words of Ichabod's mother challenge your value system. Although her perspective was limited, she recognized what is absolutely essential for life—the presence of God.

Tamra Hernandez

Prayer: *Relinquish to the Lord something or someone more precious to you than His presence in your life.*

Personal Reflection: ....

....

....

....

....

....

....

A Woman after God's Own Heart

1 Samuel 13:1–14

∽

"But now your kingdom shall not continue. The LORD has sought for Himself a man after His own heart, and the LORD has commanded him to be commander over His people, because you have not kept what the LORD commanded you." (v. 14)

Have you ever had to wait for God to act? King Saul found himself waiting in this story. Saul and his men were battling the Philistines. The battle was not going well. Saul's men were hiding in caves and behind rocks. Some of the troops were deserting. Saul was waiting for Samuel to come to Gilgal and offer a sacrifice to bless the battle. Often prophets of God would burn a sacrificed animal on an altar to ask God for a blessing. Samuel did not come at the appointed time. He became impatient and decided to take matters into his own hands. He offered the sacrifice of a burnt offering, instead of waiting for Samuel. Just as Saul finished, Samuel arrived. Samuel told Saul how foolish he had been. God had established Samuel as the prophet, not Saul. When Saul acted as the prophet, he disregarded God's command to him.

Here at Gilgal, where Saul once became king, Saul was now rejected as king by God. Saul thought he was doing something good, but he offered the sacrifice at the wrong time and in the wrong way. Saul was unwilling to wait. God wanted someone who had a heart to follow Him. Saul followed in his own way.

God has given us many commands that require us to wait on God's timing. Sometimes waiting is hard. Things are not going well, and we get discouraged. We want to fix the problem ourselves, instead of waiting on God's plan. Even something that is normally good is not good if we do not wait on God for the right time.

One example of waiting is in marriage. Marriage is a great gift of God to humanity. However, God wants us to wait for the right time and the right man before we marry. Many women wait years and years before God's plan unfolds for them. Some women decide the wait is too long and just go ahead and marry someone who they know is not following God. The marriage is less than what it could be because they did not wait on God's plan. God does forgive and ultimately work things out for good, but He does not spare us the pain of our wrong decisions.

What about you? In what ways are you waiting for God? Can you be loyal to God and wait even when the time is long and life is difficult?

Ann Iorg

Prayer: *Ask God to give you the grace and patience to wait on His plan and follow what He has said in His Word, the Bible. Seek not to go your own way, but to listen to what God wants and obey.*

Personal Reflection: ....

....

....

....

....

....

....

....

Beauty Is More Than Skin Deep

1 Samuel 16:1–13

~

"But the LORD said to Samuel, 'Do not look at his appearance or at his physical stature, because I have refused him. For the Lord does not see as man sees; for man looks at the outward appearance, but the LORD looks at the heart.'" (v. 7)

In the book of 1 Samuel, the prophet was tasked with choosing the next king of Israel. When Jesse brought all of his sons except David before the prophet, Samuel took one look at Eliab and assumed that he would be the next king based purely on his looks. God reminded Samuel that He was more concerned about the state of a person's heart, and He rejected Eliab (v. 7). David was the last one his father considered, but he was the Lord's first choice. David became known as a man after God's own heart (Acts 13:22). His character was what counted in God's eyes.

Unfortunately, today, external beauty is more important than character to many people. We are bombarded with advertisements about how to make ourselves more outwardly beautiful. Magazines, TV shows, movies, billboards, and commercials that emphasize the importance of appearance, pointing to the "Eliabs" of the world. The problem with the world's standards, though, is that they are constantly changing!

If you had been born in the Victorian Era, the standard of beauty reflected by a very pale and overweight woman represented her wealth and privilege. In the Roaring Twenties, women started dressing in shapeless gowns and getting bobbed hairstyles to be stylish. In the 1950s, Marilyn Monroe caught the eye of many men, but by today's standards she would be considered overweight with her hourglass figure. In the 1970s era of heroin-chic, models for the first time were severely underweight like the popular Lesley Lawson better known as Twiggy. Just a decade later, most models gracing the covers of magazines had a more athletic build. What's a woman to do when the world keeps changing its standards for beauty?

Remember that God's standard of beauty is unchanging. For God, what you are on the inside is of infinitely more value than any external feature. The most beautiful woman I have ever known was my 96-year-old grandmother. She may not have been beautiful in some people's eyes because of her age and wrinkles, but she exuded a kindness and grace that came from walking with the Lord for many years. Her beauty was internal and drew people to her. She had a gentle and quiet spirit that was precious to God (1 Pet. 3:4). A woman who fears the Lord is beautiful in His sight (Prov. 31:30).

Candi Finch

Prayer: *Do you find yourself more concerned with external beauty than developing your inner character by spending time with the Lord? Take some time to thank the Lord that His standard of beauty never changes.*

Personal Reflection: ....

....

....

....

....

....

....

The Danger of Comparison

1 Samuel 18:5–17

"Then Saul was very angry, and the saying displeased him; and he said, 'They have ascribed to David ten thousands, and to me they have ascribed only thousands. Now what more can he have but the kingdom.'" (v. 8)

This biblical account includes David, who is gifted and filled with God's Spirit, and Saul, who has lost favor with God. Saul had God's favor in the beginning but lost the blessing when he consistently disobeyed God (1 Sam. 13:14; 15:10–11). Even though David was successfully battling the Philistines, who were a constant source of trouble, Saul was not happy. Saul was not thinking about the good of the people of Israel. He was only thinking of himself. Saul wanted the praise of the people. He could not tolerate someone else receiving honor. In his displeasure, he tried twice to spear David to the wall, but David escaped. He also continued to put David in battle against the Philistines, hoping that eventually David would be killed in combat. As David became more and more successful, Saul became more and more jealous. Saul refused to repent and let David share the glory.

Though you may prefer to think that you could never be like Saul, you may find yourself in the same mode of jealousy. You compare yourself with women who are prettier, smarter, more accomplished, better mothers, better wives, and the list goes on and on. Why can't you just be happy for another's success? The root of the problem is putting your security in something other than God. If you are secure in God's love, then you can be happy when God blesses someone else. Your own sense of well-being is not threatened by someone else's success. The creator of the universe loves and cares for you. What more could you want?

Consider Eve who had everything good; yet she wanted more. Our minds can always imagine ourselves better in some way. The strengths of others are often a glaring reminder of our weaknesses. However, weaknesses are our friends. They humble us, causing us to depend on God and others.

Without this balance in our lives, we would be hopelessly arrogant, not needing God or anyone else. God made us with weakness on purpose, so that together we are whole, not separate. One person excels in one area, another in a different area. We should be inspired by the success of others and learn from them, not be angry with them. Paul boasted in his weakness, because he could depend on Christ's power to overcome (2 Cor. 12:9).

Ann Iorg

Prayer: *Ask the Lord to help you accept His love and unconditional acceptance by faith. Seek His help to see that His love is all you need. Rejoice in the success of others and learn from them, resisting the urge the urge to be jealous, comparing yourself to others.*

Personal Reflection: ....

....

....

....

....

....

....

....

Abigail—An Intelligent Beauty

1 Samuel 25:1–44

*"Blessed is the LORD God of Israel, who sent you this day to meet me!
And blessed is your advice and blessed are you...." (vv. 32b–33a)*

In our society today, great value is placed on outward appearance. Women may believe the idiom that "beauty is only skin deep," but they often compare their own appearances to those of others. While physical beauty is superficial, first impressions are based on what the eyes behold. The Bible teaches about the importance of the heart. True beauty comes from within and is manifested by pure motives and a loving spirit.

Abigail is one of many women in the Bible who are described as beautiful (see the description of Sarah in Gen. 12:11; Rebekah in Gen. 24:16; Rachel in Gen. 29:17; and Bathsheba in 2 Sam. 11:2). Esther was noted as beautiful, winning a beauty pageant held by King Ahasuerus, and she later became queen (Esth. 2). Abigail is introduced as "a woman of good understanding and beautiful appearance" (1 Sam. 25:3). She was beautiful inside and out!

Abigail, the daughter of Nahash, married a wealthy landowner and shepherd named Nabal. Unfortunately, Nabal was selfish, immoral, foolish, and inebriated (vv. 11, 17, 25, 36). When he refused David's request for food, his irresponsible behavior put his wife and household at risk (v. 10). In contrast to her husband's character, Abigail was wise and quickly gathered food for David, averting his plan to kill Nabal. Her gracious speech and generous gifts softened David's heart (v. 33).

David, who would later become King of Judah, was impressed with Abigail's intelligence and courage (vv. 32–33). When she returned home, Nabal was once again feasting and drinking. Wisely Abigail waited until later to tell her husband about David's plan to retaliate. Ten days later, he died—"the LORD struck Nabal dead" (v. 38). David remembered the beauty and brains of Abigail and sought her hand in marriage (vv. 39–42). Abigail responded to the proposal humbly: "Here is your maidservant, a servant to wash the feet of the servants of my lord" (v. 41). Of his eight wives, Abigail was certainly the most influential on his future leadership as king.

God desires you to be the woman He created inside and outside, with a heart for Him and wisdom from above. When faced with challenging circumstances, God will give you divine insight and supernatural courage to accomplish His will. Let Abigail be an example of a woman whose beauty is not simply skin deep. She had a beautiful heart and a lovely spirit. As a result, Abigail's influence began with a nation and continues today.

Rhonda Harrington Kelley

Prayer: *Spend time in prayer reflecting on your human tendency to judge others by their outward appearances. Seek forgiveness then recommit to a biblical basis for beauty, see the hearts of others.*

Personal Reflection: ....

....

....

....

....

....

....

A Woman's Influence

1 Samuel 25:1–42

⤜⤚

"Then David said to Abigail: 'Blessed is the LORD God of Israel, who sent you this day to meet me! And blessed is your advice and blessed are you.'" (vv. 32–33a)

My mother says, "The man may be the structure of the house, but the woman is the thermostat determining whether that home is cold and hostile or welcoming and safe." The power of a woman's influence in her home is great, and it is clearly seen in this story of Abigail.

Scripture introduces Abigail during a difficult time in her life. She was married to a very "foolish man" (v. 25). Nabal's negative reputation preceded him throughout his land (v. 17), and Abigail was the problem-solver, the one to whom their servants went when Nabal's anger could not be contained. She was the thermostat.

David, the upcoming king of her nation, is on her husband's vast property unbeknownst to her. He inquires after Nabal for some help with his sheep, but Nabal throws a fit and jumps into it! Nabal's refusal to help the king was a great offense to David, and David seeks retaliation for the snub (vv. 10–13). This is where we see the shining character of a woman who understands the power of influence she has, to "do her husband good and not evil" (Prov. 31:12).

Abigail is quick on her feet. She raids her pantry and sets off to show appropriate hospitality to their guests. Calling herself a servant multiple times (vv. 24–31), she openly respects and honors the authority of David. Abigail considers him to be God's man, and the honor that she gives him is not ego-centered but God-centered. When she greets him, she falls on her face, immediately showing humility as she submits to his authority and begs for grace to be shown to her, her husband, and their household. Abigail's outward display of an inward trait disarms the angered king, and he relents in his pursuit of Nabal. Her husband is saved and their household as well.

The ending is the best part of this story. After saving his life, Abigail did not return and explain to Nabal how she saved him from certain death. Instead, she waited until the next day, and God fought her battle for her (vv. 37–38).

When problems arise in your life, do you go into panic mode adjusting the thermostat in your home to an uncomfortable environment? Or do you seek the counsel of God and diffuse the situation with grace and dignity? Can it be said of you, "Blessed is your advice and blessed are you?"

Sarah Bubar

Prayer: *If your attitude in your home creates tension in your relationships, confess that to the Lord. Acknowledge God's presence and do not be blind to your influence in your home. Ask God for wisdom in being the thermostat in your home, making it warm and comfortable.*

Personal Reflection:

The Medium of En Dor—An Accomplice to Disobedience

1 Samuel 28:1–25

*"And his servants said to him, "In fact, there is
a woman who is a medium at En Dor." (v. 7b)*

In the Bible, mediums were people who consulted with the dead, especially for information about the future (Deut. 18:10–11). Very common in the pagan world, the practice of divination was strictly prohibited (Deut. 18:12–14). However, desperate circumstances for the children of Israel often drove people to desperate measures. Throughout history, human beings have sought advice from mystics, psychics, or spiritualists who profess supernatural ability to commune with the spirit world. Today people read horoscopes, visit palm readers, or consult professional mediums to learn about their future and hear from the dead. Television programs about mentalists and psychics are very popular. Children of God need not resort to channeling. Direct access to God is available through prayer and His Word.

King Saul was running from God and threatened by the Philistines when his desperation led him to consult a medium (v. 8). Rather than waiting for God to answer him, Saul sought inferior advice in a deceitful manner. He disguised himself and asked the medium to conjure up the spirit of the deceased prophet Samuel to give him a battle plan (v. 11). She complied after being reassured she would not be punished. The medium was frightened when she called up Samuel and recognized Saul (v. 12). She reportedly saw a spirit ascending out of the earth, an old man covered with a mantle (vv. 13–14). Shortly after Saul spoke to the spirit, he was wounded in battle and then took his own life to avoid capture (31:4–6).

The medium of En Dor was an accomplice to Saul's disobedience. While she practiced an illegal form of witchcraft, she demonstrated sincere concern for Saul when he fell to the ground in despair, preparing food to restore his strength (vv. 22–25). Her human kindness was still disobedience to God. The Bible teaches that spiritual needs are met totally by God.

I live in New Orleans, Louisiana, a unique city with many spiritual interests, including witchcraft and voodoo. Around Jackson Square in the French Quarter, palm readers sell their services to tourists who seek to know their future. These human predications are limited to their own experiences or psychic abilities not absolute truth. God is the only source of truth about the past, present, and future. His truth is available to all through prayer and the Word.

God's people then and now should turn to Him for counsel, not seek advice from other gods. Do you read your horoscope? Are you interested in palm reading? Are you intrigued by psychics? Remember that only God is all-knowing, and He has you in the palm of His hand. He knows the past, present, and future; and He will guide you as you faithfully ask Him. When in need of counsel, seek God!

Rhonda Harrington Kelley

Prayer: *Thank the Lord for His omniscience! Recommit yourself to let God and His Word be your guiding light (Ps. 119:105).*

Personal Reflection: ....

....

....

....

....

....

Michal—A Scornful Wife

2 Samuel 6:16–23

*"So David said to Michal, 'It was before the L*ORD*, who chose me instead of your father and all his house, to appoint me ruler over the people of the L*ORD*, over Israel. Therefore I will play music before the L*ORD*.'" (v. 21)*

Second Samuel, chapter six, tells the story of the ark of the covenant's joyful return to the city of Jerusalem. King David was the ruler God used to finally drive the Philistines out of Israel. The ark was to reside in the capital of Jerusalem to represent the restoration of a nation, both politically and spiritually. David was careful to listen to the Lord and wait on His timing in transporting the ark. When the priests approached the city, King David led the people in worship to welcome the ark.

King David danced and shouted before the Lord while wearing a linen ephod, a garment worn by priests specifically for times of worship. Worship was reverent and rituals marked the occasion. As David entered the city, his wife Michal saw him dancing in front of the people. She felt embarrassed. In fact, Scripture says that she "despised him in her heart" (v. 16). Interestingly, the text refers to Michal in this passage as "the daughter of Saul," suggesting that her heart reflected her father's legacy (v. 20). She was more concerned with royal dignity than spiritual authenticity.

After the ark was placed in the tent, David returned to his home. Expecting to receive a blessing, David was met instead with seething disgust. Michal spewed scorn on her husband, criticizing his behavior before the people. She was bitter and sarcastic, even accusing him of lewd behavior in front of the slave girls (v. 20). She was shallow, preoccupied with what others thought, showing jealously and hatred. David confronted her dishonorable conduct (vv. 21–22).

King David pointed out to Michal her misunderstanding of God's authority. God gave David authority, and, therefore, he worshipped God. As a wife, Michal's role was to encourage her husband to seek the Lord, not try to deter him. David had a pure heart of worship, but Michal was selfish and did not value God's glory. God punished Michal by preventing her from having a child (v. 23).

Your words have the power to build up or tear down. More important, they reveal the contents of your heart. Are you willing to worship God honestly, not caring about what others may think of you? Can you support others in their obedience to the Lord? Commit today to prioritize deepening your spiritual life over advancing your social life. Glorify God through encouraging others, and ask the Lord to make your heart a reflection of His.

Rhonda Harrington Kelley

Prayer: *Thank the Lord for His goodness and offer Him your worship this day. Ask Him to help you value what He, more than anyone else, thinks.*

Personal Reflection: ....

....

....

....

....

....

....

The Kindness of God

2 Samuel 9:1–13

⁓

*"Then the king said, 'Is there not still someone of the house of Saul,
to whom I may show the kindness of God?' And Ziba said to the king,
'There is still a son of Jonathan who is lame in his feet.'" (v. 3)*

After becoming king, David sought to honor any living descendants of Saul. He commissioned Ziba, a former servant of Saul, to find such a person. Earlier in 1 Samuel, David forged an agreement with Saul's son Jonathan (1 Sam. 20:14–17). As a condition of their agreement, David promised Jonathan never to withdraw his kindness from Jonathan's household. Jonathan requested this agreement knowing that David would soon replace his father as king and inherit the authority over everyone in Saul's household. During this period, a king would sometimes kill members of the previous king's dynasty in order to protect his throne and eliminate any viable threat. Because of this agreement with Jonathan, David desired to show kindness to Saul's household (v. 1). The Hebrew word for "kindness" (Hb. *chesed*, "constant favor, mercy, lovingkindness, loyalty, or faithfulness") is directly related to the Lord. Aside from being a key attribute of God's character, *chesed* is also used to describe the covenant relationship between God and His people.

In 2 Samuel 9:3, *chesed* refers to the merciful use of power and the great determination David uses in order to fulfill his agreement with Jonathan and ultimately show the Lord's favor on David's heir. Ziba was able to locate the son of Jonathan and grandson of Saul, Mephibosheth, in the town of Lo Debar (v. 4). As a descendant of Saul, Mephibosheth had every reason to be fearful as he approached David. However, David calmed his fears by assuring him that he wanted only to show him kindness due the agreement he had made earlier with Jonathan (v. 7). David was to restore to Mephibosheth all of the land that Saul had owned and even went beyond his agreement with Jonathan by extending an invitation for Mephibosheth to obtain a permanent place at the king's table (v. 7).

David's kindness towards Mephibosheth is a direct illustration of the kindness and the loving mercy God has bestowed upon us. Because we have received such kindness, we have a responsibility to share God's kindness with others. In doing so, we ultimately serve Him.

Jessica Pigg

Prayer: *Pray today that God will give you a heart that seeks to be kind to those around you. Thank the Lord for His abundant kindness, which He showed forth through His Son Jesus.*

Personal Reflection: ....

....

....

....

....

....

....

....

Bathsheba—Sexual Integrity

2 Samuel 11:1–27

"Then David sent messengers, and took her; and she came to him, and he lay with her, for she was cleansed from her impurity; and she returned to her house." (v. 4)

The name "Bathsheba" evokes the darkest time in the life of King David as he descended into sin—adultery, murder, and much more. Clouded by his power and privilege, the king thought he could have anything he desired and do anything he wanted. He did, but the consequences for his sin were great, for David and for those he involved in his sinful behavior.

Bathsheba was the daughter of Eliam and the wife of Uriah the Hittite. Both men were elite soldiers in the army of David (v. 3; 23:34, 39). While the army was away fighting battles, King David noticed the beautiful woman bathing on her rooftop nearby (11:2). He sent for her, then had his way with her (vv. 3–4). When she became pregnant, Bathsheba sent word to the king. She was an innocent victim of his sexual lusts. While Bathsheba acted with integrity, David continued his spiral of deceit.

David sent for Bathsheba's husband and tried to cover his sin. When the faithful soldier refused to comply with his plan, David arranged for Uriah's death (vv. 14–25). God held David accountable for the murder and grave consequences were experienced (11:27—12:19). The baby conceived by Bathsheba as a result of the adulterous affair died seven days after birth as prophesied by Nathan (12:15–19). The king did marry Bathsheba, and later they had a son, Solomon, who followed his father as king of Israel (12:24).

The years of David's reign were filled with tumult, politically and personally. As queen, Bathsheba was aware of the unrest with his leadership and the fighting among his sons who were vying for the throne. Bathsheba lovingly raised Solomon, preparing him for his future reign.

Throughout history and today, women have found themselves to be victims of people in powerful positions. God provides redemption and restoration for those who seek Him. His love covers the sin and forgives the sinner. Let this biblical account encourage you and others you know who have been wounded.

Bathsheba ultimately found grace and redemption. She served honorably as the wife of King David and the mother of King Solomon. By following the wise counsel of the prophet Nathan, Bathsheba played a key role in securing the throne for her son and continuing the Davidic lineage of Jesus the Messiah (1 Kin. 1:11–40; Matt. 1:6). While she may be remembered most as the victim of a king's lust, Bathsheba should also be revered as the queen mother who raised one of the wisest kings of Israel.

Rhonda Harrington Kelley

Prayer: *Go to the Lord in prayer asking Him to work in your life to redeem any hurt and restore new life. Then share His message of redemption with others.*

Personal Reflection: ....

....

....

....

....

....

....

Dealing with the Consequences of Sin

2 Samuel 12:1–23

*"But now he is dead; why should I fast? Can I bring him back again?
I shall go to him, but he shall not return to me." (v. 23)*

Approximately nine months passed between the illicit conception of Bathsheba's child and the day of his birth, but David presented no sign of repentance. When his cover-up plan failed, he had arranged the death of Bathsheba's husband and married her himself. Few knew the truth, and David kept his sins a secret. So he thought. Even when Nathan the prophet arrived, David seemed oblivious to the purpose for his visit. Perhaps he assumed Nathan had come to congratulate him on the birth of another son? In any case, David had already so carefully excused and justified himself that he failed to follow the trail of Nathan's parable until the prophet spelled out the parallels for him: "You *are* the man!" (v. 7).

The next words from Nathan's mouth introduce the scathing judgment of God that follows: "Thus says the LORD God of Israel. . . ." Read them aloud, if you can. Hear the intensity of the Lord's protest against David's betrayal. If David began the day believing that the birth of this son was gladly received evidence that God had come around to his way of thinking about the whole situation, that he had literally gotten away with murder, or that God freely forgives all when you're His handpicked king over His chosen people, then Nathan's delivery of God's verdict must have stung like an arrow through his right hand. All he could say was, "I have sinned against the LORD" (v. 13).

This stunned confession came too late. The Lord revealed to David what he had, up to that point, effectively ignored—that his sin "had given great occasion to the enemies of the LORD to blaspheme" (v. 14). Therefore, the son conceived in adultery would "surely die" (v. 14), and he did (vv. 15, 18). The facts alone are instructive.

However, verses 16–23 further record David's surprising response to the consequences of his sin. He did everything he could to plead with God for mercy. Then David accepted the fact and finality of the boy's death, released him to the Lord, and confidently expressed hope that the child was alive in the Lord's presence.

Because of Jesus' death and resurrection, the Lord offers forgiveness for any and every sin. He does not eliminate all consequences. Like David, however, you can pray through them, accept His answers, and move forward instead of arguing with God or indulging in anger against Him.

Tamra Hernandez

Prayer: *Accepting forgiveness in Christ, pray for wisdom to understand what to do and not to do regarding the consequences of your sins.*

Personal Reflection: ....

....

....

....

....

....

....

Tamar—A Violated Beauty

2 Samuel 13:1–14

"Absolom the son of David had a lovely sister, whose name was Tamar; and Amnon the son of David loved her. Amnon was so distressed over his sister Tamar that he became sick; for she was a virgin. And it was improper for Amnon to do anything to her." (vv. 1–2)

The story of Tamar rivals any Greek tragedy. A family is torn asunder by lust, revenge, and heartbreak. Tamar was a princess, the daughter of King David and the sister of Absalom and the half-sister of Amnon, who desired her. She desperately rejected Amnon's advances, while caring for him during his feigned illness (vv. 7–14). Yet he raped her and left her in humiliation (v. 17). Amnon's change in behavior demonstrated his lack of care and concern for his sister, indicating that he had only desired to gratify his lustful passions rather than to express true love for Tamar.

Tamar was cared for by Absalom in his home but lived as a "desolate woman" (v. 20), conveying her hopeless situation and also the fact that she never married. The heartrending summary of Tamar's life as "desolate" implies that she was bereft of what normally brought joy and hope to a woman's life—the opportunity to be a wife and mother. Compounding the tragedy, Absalom had Amnon killed in retribution for his vile treatment of Tamar (v. 32).

Tamar's innocence was protected under the law—only Amnon was guilty of a capital crime (Deut. 22:25–29). However, her virginity and, therefore, her eligibility for an honorable marriage had been lost because among the people of Israel her virginity was necessary for marriage (1 Sam. 13:11–14). Thus, Tamar suffered not only the physical and psychological trauma of rape but also the cultural shame of being still unmarried and bereft of her biological virginity. Nevertheless, do not miss that if a woman is raped, this account does not mandate a woman's ineligibility for marriage or deserving of shame.

What can be learned from this terrible episode? Tamar, as many women today, was a victim of rape by someone whom she trusted. Spiritual and emotional support was not available to her even within her family, adding to this heartbreak. The Lord considers rape to be a grievous sin and the victim of rape to be faultless in the crime committed against her (Deut. 22:25). God knows the hurting and broken hearts of every woman who has ever been forced to suffer sexual violence. No woman should feel shame for losing that which was stolen from her against her will. In God's eyes, the victim of rape is still pure. He has promised to restore all that was broken and to repay every wrong in perfect measure (Pss. 23:3; 147:3; Rom.12:19; Rev. 21:5).

Candi Finch

Prayer: *Pray for the modern-day "Tamars" who have suffered sexual abuse at the hand of someone they trusted. Pray for family members and friends to be true comforters to the victims.*

Personal Reflection: ....

....

....

....

....

....

....

Failure to Confront

2 Samuel 13:15–39

⸺

*"And Absalom her brother said to her, 'Has Amnon your brother been with you?
But now hold your peace, my sister. He is your brother; do not take this thing
to heart.' So Tamar remained desolate in her brother Absalom's house." (v. 20)*

Confrontation is never easy and most do not enjoy the uncomfortable experience, even when necessary for the well being of others. Failing to confront, however, can allow pain, bitterness, and resentment to build, as well as the destruction of lives and relationships.

The story in 2 Samuel is a difficult one. Tamar experienced one of the deepest shames and hurts a woman can endure. But, as horrible as was Amnon's violation of Tamar, the actions that followed had a more far-reaching and significant impact. No one confronted Amnon.

When King David heard what happened to Tamar, he did nothing. While not translated in the canon of Scripture, the Septuagint gives a glimpse of the reason: "But he would not punish his son Amnon, because he was his first born." We are unsure if Amnon was a favorite of David's or perhaps, after his own sin with Bathsheba, he saw a little too much of himself in his son. We do know that David did not confront his son for the evil deed Amnon had done.

Absalom, did not challenge his father's decision, speaking neither good nor bad to Amnon. Seemingly, he simply ignored his half-brother, allowing hatred to grow for Amnon because of the rape of his sister. That anger would intensify for two years when it would explode, resulting in murder and rebellion, causing a split in the family, and impacting a nation that never fully recovered.

And what of Tamar? Absalom directed her to be silent, to hold her peace and not take it to heart. To hold something so painful tightly to your soul, never to speak of it again, led to lifelong trauma.

The three people involved made the decision not to confront the sin for different reasons, and for each the consequence of failing to confront led to devastation. For David, he lost both Amnon and Absalom (2 Sam. 13:28–29;

18:14–15). For Absalom, the consequence of failing to confront was hatred so deep that he killed his half-brother and rebelled against his father. Tamar, led a life of desolation instead of finding restoration and healing.

God places us in the lives of others, and vice versa, to hold one another accountable. Part of accountability is caring enough about the other person to confront. Like the story in 2 Samuel, fear of confrontation or failure to confront can lead to devastating consequences where families are torn apart, relationships are broken, and those who are wounded never find healing.

Terri Stovall

Prayer: *Ask the Lord to give you the courage to confront in love when needed. Seek to have a heart that keeps your accounts short so that hatred does not take root.*

Personal Reflection: ....

....

....

....

....

....

....

The Wise Woman of Tekoa

2 Samuel 14:1–14

༄

"And Joab sent to Tekoa and brought from there a wise woman,
and said to her, 'Please pretend to be a mourner, and put on mourning
apparel; do not anoint yourself with oil, but act like a woman who
has been mourning a long time for the dead.'" (v. 2)

The tragic story of Tamar's rape continues in 2 Samuel 14. Amnon, the perpetrator, was David's oldest living son, making him heir to the throne. This fact, or perhaps his own history of sexual sin, prevented David from taking action to punish his son for his actions against his half-sister. For two years, the hurt and anger over Amnon's sin grew in the hearts of the family members. Absalom, a younger son and Tamar's brother, used the time to plot revenge against his half-brother. Soon he had the opportunity and used his servants to kill Amnon. Absalom then hid in Geshur, where he remained until this point in the story.

Joab, the commander of David's armies, recognized how the division in David's family was threatening the unity of his kingdom. He devised a plan to convince David to reconcile with Absalom, who was next in line to the throne. Joab's plan hinged on a wise woman from Tekoa, a farming town 10 miles south of Jerusalem. Joab gave her the script, and the woman used her quick wit to portray a story of brokenness that would mirror what was happening in David's own family (vv. 1–3).

The woman humbly opened her monologue before King David by asking for his help. In her story, one of Rizpah's sons had killed the other. The family called for the death of her remaining son as retribution for his crime. If her son was killed, there would be no male heir left to care for her or continue the family name. She pleaded with King David to defend her son and prevent her entire family from being extinguished. David was moved with compassion by the wise woman's persuasive presentation. When the king agreed, the woman asked if she might speak further (vv. 4–11).

With caution and intent, the woman noted the discrepancy between King David's mercy toward her and the lack of mercy toward his own son. She spoke wisely and respectfully, reminding him of the brevity of his own life (vv. 12–14). As a result, David agreed to allow Absalom to return home. God worked through this wise woman to bring restoration to David's family.

Aren't you grateful for wise people who speak words of truth into your life? Have there been times when God has spoken to you through someone else? The wisdom of God is available to all who seek to know Him and His will. Allow God to speak His truth wisely through you to others as you have opportunity. Be a good steward of your insights from God.

Rhonda Harrington Kelley

Prayer: *Seek to gain wisdom from the Lord and share His truth with others wisely.*

Personal Reflection:

Courage to Confront

2 Samuel 18:31—19:8

⟨∾⟩

*"Then Joab came into the house to the king, and said, 'Today you have
disgraced all your servants who today have saved your life, the lives of your sons
and daughters, the lives of your wives and the lives of your concubines.'" (19:5)*

In the Day 75 devotion, you read about the difficult events of Tamar's rape and
the consequences of failing to confront the offender. The story of David's family
continues in 2 Samuel 18—19, recording David's grief over the death of his son
Absalom. Continuing to feel the consequences of his previous actions, David's
grief was an unexpected reaction for those in his army. They expected the celebration of a successful mission. Instead, they retreated back into the shadows
of the city. Literally, they fled to their tents, burdened with a sense of shame.

David's grief over losing another son was painful, in a sense, punishing the
people for carrying out his directives. Someone needed to confront the king and
that was Joab's job. David listened to Joab when he spoke directly and bluntly,
reminding him that these people saved his life and the lives of his family, and
imploring him to go out and encourage the people.

David was at a critical juncture in his leadership. If he had chosen to wallow in his own grief, he very well could have lost his army. But Joab's courage
to confront, even if it meant condemnation by the king, returned him to his
position of leadership. Joab could have easily cowered in fear. Instead, he stood
courageously before David and held him accountable.

Loving confrontation can at times seem unloving. Most effective confrontation reminds the person about the journey she has walked, the decisions she
has made, the benefits she has received, and the effect her actions have had on
others. Then, the person is given an alternative for her current behavior. After
reprimanding David for his current response, Joab told him to "arise, go out and
speak comfort to your servants" (v. 7).

There may be times that you will need to stand firm, swallow hard, take a
deep breath, and then speak words of confrontation and accountability for the

sake of the many . . . or the one. There may also be times that God uses someone to confront you. You need to hear the words of loving confrontation. Whether on the giving end or the receiving end, confrontation always requires courage.

Terri Stovall

Prayer: *Ask the Lord to give you ears to hear and a heart to receive when He uses someone to confront you and hold you accountable. When you find yourself being called upon by the Lord to confront another, ask the Lord to give you strength, courage, and a heart that speaks truth with love.*

Personal Reflection: ....

....

....

....

....

....

....

....

Rizpah—A Protective Mother

2 Samuel 21:7–14

"Now Rizpah the daughter of Aiah took sackcloth and spread it for herself on the rock . . . she did not allow the birds of the air to rest on them by day nor the beasts of the field by night." (v. 10)

Important life lessons can be learned in surprising ways and at surprising times! Rizpah is mentioned only briefly in the Bible but teaches a profound lesson of courage and love. This protective mother is a positive example for mothers today.

Rizpah was the daughter of Aiah and concubine of Saul (v. 8). She bore two sons by Saul, Armoni and Mephibosheth. She lived during the final years of David's reign. When David inquired of the Lord about the famine in Israel, he learned that it was God's punishment for Saul's sin (v. 1). He and his family had murdered the Gibeonites and experienced the wrath of God. The Gibeonites were foreigners allowed to live in Israel following a special treaty with Joshua (Josh. 9:3–27). Saul was wrong to break the treaty, so God judged him and found him guilty of murder. The children of Saul suffered the consequences of their father's sin. They followed in his ungodly footsteps and received punishment from God (2 Sam. 21:1).

In retaliation, the Gibeonites demanded the lives of the sons of Saul: "Let seven men of his descendants be delivered to us, and we will hang them before the Lord" (v. 6). Saul's sons were delivered to the people he had wronged, and they were slain (vv. 7–9). What a tragedy for Saul! What a heartbreak for Rizpah! Can you imagine losing your sons at the hands of your enemy? The two sons of Rizpah were among the seven sons of Saul who were murdered.

Jewish custom demanded that the dead be buried the same day. However, no one immediately claimed the bodies of Saul's sons, who were hung by the Gibeonites. Rizpah's maternal instincts led her to care for her sons, protecting their corpses from wild animals. She watched over them from April or early

May, when barley was harvested, until rain fell again, probably in October or November. What a picture of a mother's love!

When David learned of Rizpah's loving actions, he gathered the bones of Saul and his sons to bury them (vv. 11–14). While she was unable to save her sons from death, Rizpah did protect her sons after death. Because of their protective mother, Armoni and Mephibosheth died in dignity not disgrace.

Rhonda Harrington Kelley

Prayer: *Do you have children? If so, spend some time praying for them, their godliness and protection. If not, pray for the children you love to grow in faith and follow the Lord.*

Personal Reflection: ....

....

....

....

....

....

....

A Wise and Understanding Heart

1 Kings 3:12; 4:29–31

*"And God gave Solomon wisdom and exceedingly great understanding,
and largeness of heart like the sand on the seashore." (4:29)*

If God spoke these words to you, and said, "Ask me for anything, and I will give it to you," what would be your answer? What would be the one thing that you asked from the Lord? That is exactly what happened to Solomon.

While he was sleeping, God appeared to Solomon in a dream with a question: "Ask! What shall I give you?" Solomon did not ask for material things or anything self-serving. He asked for an understanding heart and the wisdom to judge the people who had been entrusted to him.

God was so pleased with Solomon's request that he not only answered Solomon's request, but He also gave Solomon wisdom that "excelled the wisdom of all men" (4:30). Scripture is clear that God wishes to give wisdom to follow His plan and purposes. Like Solomon, though, we have to seek wisdom and ask God for what wisdom we lack. James writes: "If any of you lacks wisdom, let him ask of God, who gives to all liberally and without reproach, and it will be given to him" (James 1:5). Paul calls us to walk in wisdom, understanding the will of the Lord (Eph. 5:15–17).

Wisdom and understanding are not gifts that were reserved for Solomon alone. No, the Lord's desire is that you, too, have a wise and understanding heart. How do you receive wisdom like Solomon? Solomon tells us in Proverbs 2:

- Know the Word of God;
- Treasure the commands of the Lord; and
- Cry out to the God for understanding, discernment, and wisdom.

What did Solomon say about the rewards that come from seeking wisdom?

Happy *is* the man *who* finds wisdom,
And the man *who* gains understanding;
For her proceeds *are* better than the profits of silver,
And her gain than fine gold.
She *is* more precious than rubies,
And all the things you may desire cannot compare with her.
Length of days *is* in her right hand,
In her left hand riches and honor.
Her ways *are* ways of pleasantness,
And all her paths *are* peace.
She *is* a tree of life to those who take hold of her,
And happy *are all* who retain her. (Prov. 3:13–18)

These are evil days! You will be challenged on every side. Every step down the path that the Lord has put before you can seem treacherous. Know God's Word, treasure His commands, and cry out to God for understanding. Then, you, too, can ask for and receive wisdom and understanding just as Solomon did.

Terri Stovall

Prayer: *Ask the Lord to give you a wise and understanding heart. Seek after His wisdom that you may know His will.*

Personal Reflection: ....

....

....

....

Queen of Sheba—An Admirer of Wisdom

1 Kings 10:1–13

*"Blessed be the LORD your God, who delighted in you, setting you
on the throne of Israel! Because the LORD has loved Israel forever,
therefore He made you king, to do justice and righteousness." (v. 9)*

At the height of King Solomon's reign, word of the splendor of the kingdom spread throughout the nations of the day. Soon the queen of Sheba heard of King Solomon's wealth and decided she must see for herself if the rumors were true. She also wondered about the power of King Solomon's God (v. 1).

The land of Sheba, now eastern Yemen, was known for its own wealth because of its location on the Red Sea and its control over Arabian trade routes. As a woman of enormous riches, the queen filled her suitcases with evidence of her great position and influence, and then she journeyed to see the far-famed king. She even brought along the largest quantity of spices ever imported to Solomon's kingdom (v. 3).

The queen of Sheba traveled hundreds of miles through the desert to quench her curiosity. When she arrived in Jerusalem, what she discovered did not merely confirm the reports she had received but far exceeded her expectations. She praised King Solomon's wisdom and noted the prosperity of his nation and happiness of his subjects. She acknowledged that God Himself had given Solomon his authority as well as his purpose for administering justice and righteousness (vv. 4–9). The queen of Sheba also attributed the king's wealth and the success of his kingdom-building to the Lord's love for Israel, and she then praised God!

The queen of Sheba demonstrated respect for King Solomon, but more important she acknowledged the God of Israel. Even though the queen came from a land with a different religion, what God had done in Israel was undeniable. Her recognition of God's blessing in Israel foreshadowed the nation's impending demise, which ultimately came as a result of King Solomon's idolatry (1 Kin. 11:1–13).

Later, even Jesus commended the queen of Sheba for her disapproval of Israel's decision to turn away from their great God: "The queen of the South will rise up in the judgment with this generation and condemn it, for she came from the ends of the earth to hear the wisdom of Solomon; and indeed a greater than Solomon is here" (Matt. 12:42). While rebuking the Pharisees and scribes who wanted yet another sign from Jesus, Jesus recalled Jonah's delivery from the fish after three days and prophesied His death, burial, and resurrection on the third day. The wisdom of the queen of Sheba was mentioned in contrast to the lack of wisdom of the Jewish leaders.

Let the queen of Sheba be a role model for you today. Do not be blinded by the power or possessions of others. Seek the wisdom of God, not the follies of man.

Rhonda Harrington Kelley

Prayer: *Pray for wisdom from the Lord to understand Him, His ways, and His plans for your life.*

Personal Reflection: ....

....

....

....

....

....

Foreign Women and Pagan Gods

1 Kings 11:1–13

⌒

"But King Solomon loved many foreign women.... For it was so, when Solomon was old, that his wives turned his heart after other gods." (vv. 1a, 4a)

King Solomon of Israel had the good life! His father was King David: the Giant Slayer, the Shepherd Boy from the hills of Bethlehem, the Psalmist and Sweet Singer of Israel. Ascending the Jerusalem throne approximately 970 B.C., Solomon had a deep, personal relationship with the One True God, which was natural by birth and nurtured by choice.

Solomon prayed for wisdom not wealth. With great affirmation, God granted him both! His kingdom was extravagantly blessed. He was revered and respected by all people both at home and abroad. The Lord allowed Solomon to build the temple of God in Jerusalem. God personally appeared to Solomon twice (see 1 Kin. 3; 9). His name came from the Hebrew word *shalom* ("peace"), defined as "well blessed, prosperous, greatly favored, healthy and strong." God called him *Jedidiah*, meaning "beloved of Yahweh" (2 Sam. 12:25). Jesus, the Prince of Peace, would come through this kingly line of David of the tribe of Judah of which Solomon was a part (see genealogy list in Matt. 1).

Sadly, the three initial words of this chapter are powerful clues to the imminently certain downfall of David's beloved son: "But [however], King Solomon." A somber mood of foreboding demise is described with a deep, sorrowful sigh from this author of the book of 1 Kings. Destruction follows pride (Prov. 16:18). Having penned these words, Solomon knew better.

God warned all future earthly kings not to "multiply" for themselves wives who would subsequently turn (stretch, bend) their hearts away from God (Deut. 17:17). Solomon chose to ignore that command. He had "seven hundred wives, princesses, and three hundred concubines" (1 Kin.11:3). Few of them appear to be true God-fearers or Jewish in nationality. Naamah, mother of Solomon's son Rehoboam (who succeeded Solomon as first king of Judah), was an Ammonite descended from the daughters of Lot (Gen. 19).

One of Solomon's first acts as king was forming a marriage alliance with the daughter of Pharaoh, king of Egypt (1 Kin. 3:1). Military alliances with potentially threatening nations were disguised as "marriages." Of course, each of these king-ordered "brides" arrived with her own worship requirements. Solomon saw to it that they had full sway to worship exactly as they pleased. Verse 4 reveals the grievous result—his wives "turned [i.e., bent, swayed] his heart away to pursue other gods." Saying that Solomon left his first love would be an understatement.

God put His wisdom into Solomon's heart (1 Kin. 10:23–24). Solomon rejected and replaced the Lover of his soul and holy, godly wisdom with foreign LOVES. What foreign loves have you willingly married into the "God space" inside your heart?

Becky Brown

Prayer: *Seek forgiveness from God if other "loves" reign in your heart. Renew your commitment to love Him first.*

Personal Reflection: ....

....

....

....

....

....

An Evil Grandmother

1 Kings 15:9–14

"Also he removed Maachah his grandmother from being queen mother, because she had made an obscene image of Asherah. And Asa cut down her obscene image and burned it by the Brook Kidron." (v. 13)

Her name was Isabelle McCollough, but everyone called her Belle. I called her Grandma because I was the thirty-second of her thirty-six grandchildren, and every one of us loved her deeply. She was the quintessential grandmother who cooked wonderful meals, answered our endless questions, and took care of us. Most of all, I recall "catching" her reading her Bible, even on weekdays, at her kitchen table. We always knew to be quiet until she finished reading and praying, then we had her full attention. She had the most profound influence on my budding faith in Jesus and my commitment to Him. How I aspire to be a grandmother just like her!

However, this was not true, of the evil grandmother Maachah. This granddaughter of Absalom was married to Rehoboam, son of Solomon. He "walked in the way of David and Solomon for three years" (2 Chr. 11:17) and then took wives to himself. But, Rehoboam loved Maachah more than all of his 18 wives and 60 concubines. Sadly, the Scripture says: "And he did evil, because he did not prepare his heart to seek the Lord" (2 Chr. 12:14). Could she be the one who turned his heart from God?

Their son Abijam became king after Rehoboam, and the cycle of evil continued as "he walked in all the sins of his father . . . his heart was not loyal to the Lord his God" (1 Kin. 15:3). After only three years of reigning, he died; and his son Asa succeeded him. Things changed dramatically in that moment.

"Asa did *what was* right in the eyes of the Lord" (v. 11). After his coronation, Asa banished all male prostitutes connected to idol worship and destroyed all the idols erected previously. The cleansing extended to his family as he dethroned the idolatrous Maachah from her position as queen mother, a position she had held for two generations. She had personally erected a detestable, repulsive idol to Asherah, probably a long pole formed from a tree stripped of its branches. This Canaanite deity was considered a goddess of the moon and of fertility. Worship practices included prostitution, fortune telling, and divination—corrupt and immoral practices strictly forbidden by the Lord. Instead of trusting God, women were drawn to her, believing falsely she would help them conceive and bear children. Asa burned the idol publicly by the brook in Jerusalem's Kidron Valley. This grandmother's corrupting influence simply had to be stopped.

Janet Wicker

Prayer: *Remove any idol that is keeping you from loving God and being loyal to Him more than anyone or anything else! Ask the Father to cause you to see the power of your influence over the generations to come.*

Personal Reflection: ....
....
....
....
....
....
....

The Widow of Zarephath—More, and Then Some

1 Kings 17:8–24

*"And as she was going to get it, he called to her and said 'Please bring me
a morsel of bread in your hand.' So she said, 'As the LORD your God lives,
I do not have bread, only a handful of flour in a bin, and a little oil in a jar;
and see, I am gathering a couple of sticks that I may go in and prepare
it for myself and my son, that we may eat it, and die.'" (vv. 11–12)*

Even in their distractedness, inconsistency, and deficiency, I can be confident
that my prayers rise to Him like incense ("Let my prayer be set before You as
incense, the lifting up of my hands as the evening sacrifice!" Ps. 141:2). I will
offer Him my prayers, my sighs. I will pour out my heart to Him. He receives
my imperfect prayers like the mother receives the crushed dandelions, as gifts
made perfect in love. Besides, He Himself has been praying for **me** all along:
"Therefore He is also able to save to the uttermost those who come to God
through Him, since He always lives to make intercession for them" (Heb. 7:25).

What else can I offer Him? In the words of Isaac Watts' great hymn, "When
I Survey the Wondrous Cross":

Were the whole realm of nature mine,
That were an offering far too small;
Love so amazing, so divine,
Demands my soul, my life, my all.

The widow of Zarephath was destitute, even more desperate than the ordinary widow of the time because those were days of famine. Along comes Elijah,
who had been getting supplied with bread and meat morning and evening courtesy of divinely ordered ravens, but who had left when the brook dried up from
the drought. The ravens did not come with him to Zarephath. When he came
to the town gate, he saw the woman gathering sticks (read 1 Kin. 17:11–12).

The widow was a most unlikely prospect to provide for his needs. But the prophet Elijah prevailed upon her, and she believed him when he spoke, "For this is what the Lord the God of Israel, says: 'The jar of flour will not be used up and the jug of oil will not run dry until the day the Lord gives rain on the land'" (v. 14 NIV).

The nameless widow used up all her flour and oil and made him bread, giving her all, and the word came true. The same God who ordered for Elijah more than was on the menu will do the same for us, if we are listening when He asks us for some small, but usually very important, sacrifice.

Elisabeth Elliot

Prayer: *Give thanks to the Lord for how you have seen Him provide for you over the last year. Express your gratitude for how Christ sacrificed for you on the cross, giving His life as a sacrifice for sinners.*

Personal Reflection: ....

....

....

....

....

....

An excerpt from Elisabeth Elliot's *Be Still My Soul* (pages 24–26).

Jezebel—A Vicious Queen

1 Kings 18:30—19:2

"Then Jezebel sent a messenger to Elijah, saying,
'So let the gods do to me, and more also, if I do not make your life
as the life of one of them by tomorrow about this time.'" (19:2)

Jezebel's name carries a reputation of wickedness even into the twenty-first century. She is known for her vicious spirit and violent acts that antagonized the followers of God. A worshipper of Baal, she promoted worship of false gods among the people of Israel. Her very name meant "unchaste," and her marriage to King Ahab was itself considered an evil union (16:31). The marriage was arranged to promote an alliance between Israel and Tyre. Instead, it was a partnership of two evil people who caused evil outcomes for both their nations.

Jezebel often usurped power from her husband and even pushed him to commit sinful acts. God sent the prophet Elijah to confront King Ahab and the Baal worshippers in Israel for their belief in false gods. He warned that God would stop the rain, a direct challenge to their belief that a fertility god could send rain. Jezebel did not respond kindly to this threat (18:1–19).

The prophet Elijah learned quickly that one did not want to be on Jezebel's bad side! At Jezebel's order hundreds of prophets of the true God were murdered. Many others went into hiding, depending on smuggled food and water to survive while living in a cave. Elijah became the center of Jezebel's disdain, receiving death threats from her, which caused him to flee from Israel. Despite the fact that God used him mightily to ruin the prophets of Baal, Elijah was left discouraged and defeated by Jezebel's vendetta.

Jezebel's words demonstrated that she not only refused to acknowledge the authority of Israel's God, but she also actively determined to fight against Him (19:2). Yet, the true God was in no way threatened by the words of an arrogant woman. In fact, God inspired Elijah to prophesy that dogs would eat Jezebel's body (21:23). God's judgment was finally pronounced on the pair who died in disgrace.

Jezebel's hatred toward God led directly to her demise—a disgraceful and gruesome death. There are always consequences for rejecting the God of Israel. Jezebel personifies the principle of reaping what is sown (see Gal. 6:7). She lived a wicked life and died a horrifying death. She demonstrates that the power and influence of evil, although allowed by God for a limited time, ultimately never triumphs. God and good always win in the end!

Rhonda Harrington Kelley

Prayer: *Thank the Lord for being a just and fair God who is sovereign on His throne! Ask Him to guide your life and protect you from evil. Encourage those you love to sow good seeds for God and reap His blessings.*

Personal Reflection: ....

....

....

....

....

....

....

How Do We Overcome Spiritual Depression?

1 Kings 19:11, 15–17

~~~

"Then He said, 'Go out, and stand on the mountain before the LORD.'" (v. 11a)

I have a great job! One aspect of it is counseling. Counseling is often like getting a front-row seat to watch God work in someone's life. Many of the women I see suffer from spiritual depression. One of the first things I will address is their physical well-being. I know from my training, as well as personal experience, that a lack of sleep, poor eating habits, and too little exercise can exacerbate feelings of depression. Usually, attention to the physical condition is pretty simple. Then, we discuss their spiritual health. Are they spending time each day in God's Word and in prayer? Frequently, the answers are, "No, not like I used to." As counselor, I know that taking care of the physical and spiritual needs is a key to restoration.

Elijah experienced spiritual depression, too. In fact, he was so depressed that he prayed God would take his life (19:4). This is interesting since he recently had been used by God to display great miracles. There was an abundance of flour and oil provided to the widow of Zarephath (1 Kin. 17). Her dead son was brought back to life (1 Kin. 17). Elijah had victory over 450 prophets of Baal on Mt. Carmel (1 Kin. 18). Yet, Elijah's focus was on his present circumstances. Elijah thought he was the only worshipper of God left; not only that, Queen Jezebel wanted him dead!

Examine God's remedy for Elijah's spiritual depression. First, God understood his weakened physical state. He sent an angel to minister to Elijah's needs (1 Kin. 19:5–8). Then He addressed Elijah's spiritual needs and invited him to stand in His presence. Finally, the Lord graciously answered Elijah's fears by assuring him that he was not the only worshipper of God left. Then, rather than leaving him there, God gave him a mission (vv. 15–17).

People are often like Elijah when we forget who God is and what He has done in our lives. We allow the present circumstances to depress us spiritually rather than remember all we know to be true about God. Before you and I get to the point of spiritual depression, let us implement lessons learned from Elijah. Make sure you are getting enough rest and eating well, especially in times of intense ministry. Remember all the great things that the Lord has done for you. Seek His voice through the reading of His Word and prayer.

Denise O'Donoghue

Prayer: *Pray that God would help you be alert to signs of spiritual depression. Pray that He would help you to take your thoughts captive when you allow circumstances to rule your heart and mind. Close your prayer by recalling all the many ways you have seen God work. Offer thanksgiving.*

Personal Reflection: ....

....

....

....

....

....

....

....

An Evil Wife

1 Kings 21:1–26

~~

"But there was no one like Ahab who sold himself to do wickedness in the sight of the Lᴏʀᴅ, because Jezebel his wife stirred him up." (v. 25)

Have you ever heard of anyone naming their daughters after Jezebel? No person's name is more associated with such ruthless, murderous evil. To call another woman a "Jezebel" is to characterize her as completely immoral and corrupt. The wicked queen, daughter of the pagan Sidionian King Ethbaal ("with Baal") was married to King Ahab of Israel (v. 5). She quickly infiltrated Israel with false idols and influenced her husband to set up an altar to worship the false god Baal, considered by the Canaanites to be supreme deity of the sun and the storm. Loud, raucous orgies were part of the worship practices. Dedicated devotees tragically sacrificed their first-born child to Baal in the fire of his altar.

Jezebel also tried to murder all the prophets of God in the land to silence the messages from God, but Obadiah saved 100 from her hand. She vowed to kill the godly prophet Elijah after his victorious "god contest" on Mount Carmel (18:16–45). Her murderous rage and her evil schemes truly knew no bounds.

Jezebel's story is a window into her life and marriage to Ahab. One day, King Ahab decided he needed a vegetable garden and wanted the vineyard of his neighbor Naboth, who respectfully refused because the land was his family inheritance. When Jezebel learned Ahab was refusing to eat and depressed, she demanded to know why. When he whined about Naboth's refusal to sell, she caustically reminded him that he was King and should get whatever he wanted. She proceeded to handle it herself. The domineering schemer hatched a wicked plot that ended in Naboth's death. Jezebel thought, her husband could take the land, with Naboth out of the way—a life taken for a vegetable garden!

Through the prophet Elijah, the Lord pronounced judgment upon the weak Ahab and depraved Jezebel, telling her that dogs would one day eat her dead body (2 Kin. 9:10). It was a severe sentence for severe crimes. The master manipulator, vengeful murderess, wickedly idolatrous woman met a disastrous end. Ahab himself would be remembered as a "sell-out" and more wicked than any king before him because of her ungodly influence.

To every woman, Jezebel serves as a warning in large, flashing letters. She wasn't just the "power behind the throne," she took the throne! When you are tempted to take things into your own hands or to incite your husband to do the wrong thing, you should remember Jezebel and stop. God is clear; He will hold you accountable!

Janet Wicker

Prayer: *Are you hungry for power, control, and influence over your husband? Relinquish control to Christ alone. Ask God to protect you from a "Jezebel spirit" and use you to influence your husband for godliness and not for selfish ends.*

Personal Reflection: ....

....

....

....

....

....

....

The Prophet's Widow—A Desperate Woman

2 Kings 4:1–7

*"So she went from him and shut the door behind her and her sons,
who brought the vessels to her; and she poured it out. Now it came to pass,
when the vessels were full, that she said to her son, 'Bring me another vessel.'
And he said to her, 'There is not another vessel.' So the oil ceased." (vv. 5–6)*

Nestled in the middle of the historical account of a battle between Israel and the Moabites is the beautiful picture of God's concern for the personal needs of His children. The prophet Elisha was trying to lead the Israelites back to God, and yet his heart was moved from compassion to action on behalf of a widow. He stopped to listen to her story, and then he offered to help her find a solution (v. 2).

The woman's husband had died and left her with debts that she could not pay. Now, her creditor had come to collect, threatening to take her two sons as slaves, which was a common custom of the time. Many Jews in poverty found themselves facing the possibility of slavery. However, the culture also required that a woman live under the protection and provision of a male family member. Elisha understood the implications of the woman's loss of her sons. She would be utterly destitute with no one to provide for her needs.

The widow had already witnessed God's power working through Elisha; thus she approached him for help. When he gave her instructions, she followed them explicitly. Elisha told the woman to collect as many empty jars as she could find from her friends and neighbors. Then, she was to go into her house and pour her oil into the jars. So she poured, and she poured, and she poured! God multiplied her limited amount of oil until all the jars were full.

The widow then returned to Elisha for further instructions. The woman was able to sell the oil and use the money to pay off her debts. Then, she still had enough oil left over for herself and her sons. God's power was displayed in her life and before her community! He went above merely meeting her needs—He gave her hope for a future!

The widow had faith in the provision of God, and she sought guidance from the prophet—someone who had a relationship with God and a man she trusted. The widow's faith bore fruit, and God's multiplication of her resources was a testimony of His power for others. What resources has God given you? Is He asking you to trust Him to multiply those gifts for ministry? God desires to be actively involved in your life and to shape your future for His glory!

Rhonda Harrington Kelley

Prayer: *Ask the Lord to increase your faith in His resources for your life. Thank Him for His provision of your personal needs.*

Personal Reflection:

The Shunammite Woman—A Generous Hostess

2 Kings 4:8–37

"Now it happened one day that Elisha went to Shunem, where there was
a notable woman, and she persuaded him to eat some food." (v. 8)

A prominent woman, who was both wealthy and influential, lived in the town of Shunem during the time of the kings. She was also a wise woman with great faith. Shunem was in the southern Galilee area of Israel southeast of Mount Carmel. It was a place controlled by the Israelites under Joshua (Josh. 19:18) and the site where the Philistines fought Saul (1 Sam. 28:4). It was a significant place in history for a prominent woman to live.

Because Shunem was located on a main thoroughfare from north to south, the prophet Elisha often passed through the town during his travels. He was the frequent guest of a local couple who offered him food and lodging. They are introduced in 2 Kings 4:8–10: "Now it happened one day that Elisha went to Shunem, where there *was* a notable woman, and she persuaded him to eat some food" (v. 8). The Shunammite woman knew he was a man of God and wanted to serve him (v. 10). In return for her hospitality, Elisha blessed her.

Elisha's servant Gehazi told the prophet that the Shunammite woman had no child, a tragedy for an Israelite wife. The grateful prophet wanted to express appreciation for her kindness, so he announced that she would have a son by this time next year (v. 15). The Shunammite woman conceived a child, bore a son, and raised him lovingly (vv. 17–18). Years later, the child became ill and died in his heartbroken mother's arms (vv. 19–20).

The Shunammite woman remembered the man of God and immediately went to Elisha at Mount Carmel (v. 25). The grief-stricken mother trusted God and the prophet with her son's life. She followed the prophet back to Shunem and waited patiently as he ministered to the child (vv. 32–35). He prayed and God revived the dead child. Elisha called for the Shunammite woman saying, "Pick up your son" (v. 36). Again, this precious mother held in her arms the son who was prophesied by Elisha, then restored to life by God through the faithful prophet.

Do you think the woman questioned God when her promised child was taken from her? Was her faith all that God needed to perform the miracle? Did she totally trust the life of her son into the hands of the prophet? The Shunammite woman had faith in God and provided for the needs of His prophet. In her time of greatest need, God demonstrated His love for her through the prophet who was grateful for her hospitality. What a powerful lesson for Christian women today!

Rhonda Harrington Kelley

Prayer: *Spend some time in prayer seeking to hear from God. Listen carefully when He speaks and faithfully speak His words to others who need ministry or encouragement.*

Personal Reflection: ....

....

....

....

....

....

....

Naaman's Maidservant—A Faithful Witness

2 Kings 5:1–27

"And he returned to the man of God, he and all his aides,
and came and stood before him; and he said, 'Indeed, now I know that
there is no God in all the earth, except in Israel; now therefore,
please take a gift from your servant.'" (v. 15)

This historical account in the Old Testament depicts Israel in a battle to maintain control over their land and facing enslavement by their conquerors. Although many of Israel's defeats were a result of their unfaithfulness to God, there were some Hebrews who continued to worship God and serve Him even in their subjugation. The young Israelite slave girl in this passage was one of those faithful Hebrews.

Despite being captured and brought to Syria as a slave, the young girl knew that at her core she was first a servant of God. She became a missionary even in difficult circumstances, expressing her faith in God without hesitation to her pagan master Naaman. The girl was insignificant in the eyes of her captors, but God allowed her to have a significant impact on Naaman and his entire household.

The slave girl demonstrated genuine concern for Naaman's well-being as he suffered from a skin disease. She told her mistress that there was a prophet in Israel who could heal him by God's power. The mistress gave this message to Naaman, who then traveled in the company of his aides to Elisha's house. Elisha the prophet knew that this encounter was about much more than healing one man. The Lord had given him this opportunity to demonstrate the sovereignty of the true God to all the nations (v. 9).

Elisha instructed Naaman to go and wash in the Jordan seven times. At first, Naaman was infuriated. He expected Elisha to wave his hand over his skin immediately and heal him. He expected no personal task from the prophet. But Naaman's entourage encouraged him at least to give Elisha's solution a try. They expressed faith that Elisha was indeed a man of God. Naaman did as Elisha instructed and was healed. When he saw his skin "restored like the flesh of a little child," he declared that the God of Israel was God of all the earth (vv. 10–15).

One "insignificant" slave girl with faith in the power of God became an instrument to reach the lost in a foreign land. Although she was raised in a pagan nation, she revealed the superiority of Israel's God. She exercised her own simple faith and testified to God's power to heal leprosy. Her persevering testimony led her master Naaman to put his faith in the God of Israel. Let the faithfulness of this young maid be an example to follow God even in difficult circumstances and be available for His miracles. Naaman's maidservant was a faithful witness who brought glory to God!

Rhonda Harrington Kelley

Prayer: *Recommit yourself to the Lord as your Savior and renew a determination to follow Him in tough times. Be available for Him to work through you to lead others to a saving knowledge of Christ.*

Personal Reflection: ....

....

....

....

....

....

Athaliah—A Murdering Queen

2 Kings 8:16–29; 11:1–16

*"When Athaliah the mother of Ahaziah saw that her son was dead,
she arose and destroyed all the royal heirs." (11:1)*

As 2 Kings continues, the focus is more on the kings of Israel and Judah than the role of the prophet Elisha. Jehoram, who was the son of the godly King Jehoshaphat, replaced his father as king of Judah (8:16). He was 32 years old when he became king and reigned for eight years in Jerusalem. Jehoram married Athaliah, the daughter of Israel's King Ahab, and they brought Baal worship to Judah. The Bible says: "He did evil in the sight of the LORD" (8:18).

Athaliah was a wicked woman. She followed in the evil ways of Ahab and Jezebel (8:18, 26). She was a follower of Baal and an enemy of Israel's God. As queen, Athaliah led her husband and the people of Israel astray. Her son Ahaziah became king, and his mother continued her evil influence (2 Chr. 22:3). Ahaziah and his brothers were killed by the Philistines, so Athaliah murdered her own grandsons in order to rule over Judah herself for six years.

During the first century A.D., Agrippina was a Roman empress. She was the great-granddaughter of the emperor Augustus and the fourth wife of Emperor Claudius and a cunning and self-centered woman, desiring power for herself. She convinced Claudius to adopt her son Nero and make him the next emperor of Rome. She had all the women of the Roman court praised by Claudius murdered and poisoned her husband to put her son Nero on the throne. She became known as the Empress of Poison. Her legacy of evil in history is similar to Athaliah in the Old Testament.

Evil women like Athaliah and Agrippina are still in our world. Their selfish actions hurt their families. Their devious plotting complicates their own lives. Their ungodly behavior harms God and His Kingdom work. But, God is still on His throne in glory and at work in the lives of His people. He offers forgiveness and redemption to all who call on His name.

Athaliah exercised great political influence during her son's one-year reign as king (8:27–28). When he died of battle wounds, she seized the throne by having all male heirs killed (11:1–4). She was an illegitimate occupant of the throne and continued her idolatrous traditions. Jehoiada the priest led a revolt, crowning the child Joash who had been hidden safely from the wicked queen and calling for Athaliah's death (11:5–20). The murdering queen herself was killed in the coup. Her wickedness stains Israel's history and warns of the evil influence of an ungodly woman. Let the negative example of Athaliah be a warning to you today!

Rhonda Harrington Kelley

Prayer: *Spend some time in soul-searching to understand your own motives. Ask God to forgive your selfishness. Pray for those who have followed their own evil ways instead of God's perfect ways.*

Personal Reflection: ....

....

....

....

....

....

....

Did a Righteous Mother Make a Difference?

2 Kings 22:1–13

"Josiah was eight years old when he became king, and he reigned thirty-one years in Jerusalem. His mother's name was Jedidah the daughter of Adaiah of Bozkath. And he did what was right in the sight of the LORD, and walked in all the ways of his father David; he did not turn aside to the right hand or to the left." (vv. 1–2)

The eight-year-old King Josiah has always fascinated me. How did this young boy grow into a fine young leader, compared with King David? Someone significant had to influence his life for good. It was not his father King Amon, who died at 22 and was already evil (2 Kin. 21:19–24). It was not Amon's father King Manasseh, one of the worst kings in Judah's history (2 Kin. 21:6, 9, 16). The clue is in our key Scripture. The names and hometowns of Josiah's mother and mother's father are mentioned. Jedidah means "beloved," and Adaiah means "witness of Yahweh." Josiah had a beloved mother and a godly grandfather. The small unknown town Bozkath is also significant. When Amon was murdered by his own servants, the Bible says the common people executed the servants and made Josiah king. The common small-town people loved this family greatly, and they risked their lives to get Josiah on the throne.

Mothers do make a difference! This young boy had almost all the odds against him, yet he had a powerful influence in his favor. Jedidah was able to overcome the influence of her son's evil father Amon and of his grandfather Manasseh. She was able to help Josiah deal with loss and assume significant responsibility at a young age. She had made sure Josiah learned about God and how to follow Him so that this boy became one of the best kings in Judah's history.

If you are a young mother, be encouraged that the constant care and training you provide for your young children will reap benefits someday. A child of six years has already developed habits that will last a lifetime. You must be sure your young children develop good habits for relating to God and people, as well as daily living skills. They may not be able to remember verse numbers, but they can learn Scripture and Bible stories. These biblical principles will guide their lives forever. Now is the time to invest in your children to be sure they are ready when God calls them into leadership. Your offspring may not become an eight-year-old king, but prepare your children for whatever God calls them to do. As a mother, you can make the difference.

Ann Iorg

Prayer: *Ask God to help you train your children so they can be godly leaders. Remember that a mother's good influence can overcome bad influences in every way. Let God remind you that mothers make a difference.*

Personal Reflection: ....

....

....

....

....

....

....

....

Huldah—A Prophetess of Integrity

2 Kings 22:14–20

*"So Hilkiah the priest, Ahikam, Achbor, Shaphan,
and Asaiah went to Huldah the prophetess." (v. 14a)*

The Bible identifies several female prophets who spoke the words God gave them. Miriam was the first prophetess mentioned in Scripture (Ex. 15:20). Deborah was described as a prophetess and judge (Judg. 4:4). "The prophetess Noadiah," however, was numbered among Israel's enemies (Neh. 6:14). Then in the New Testament, Anna, who recognized Jesus as the promised Messiah, was known as a prophetess. In the book of Revelation, Jezebel claimed to be a prophetess (Rev. 2:20). A prophetess named Huldah also played a significant part in the history of Israel (2 Kin. 22:14–20).

During the Babylonian exile in the first century B.C., the Israelites enjoyed the blessings of God though they did not always obey Him. God raised up prophets to warn His people about His inevitable judgment for their sin. Huldah was a prophetess who lived in Jerusalem during the reign of King Josiah and after the reigns of David and Solomon. She spoke words from the Lord and lived a godly life.

Huldah was the wife of Shallum, the son of the keeper of the royal wardrobe (v. 14). Her wise counsel, rather than the advice of other more well-known prophets like Jeremiah and Zephaniah, was often sought by King Josiah and other leaders. In this passage, the king instructed the priests to inquire with Huldah about the meaning of the Book of the Law. She answered them over and over again with the exact words from God: "Thus says the LORD God of Israel . . . I will bring calamity on this place and on its inhabitants . . . because they have forsaken Me" (vv. 15–17). Huldah accurately proclaimed God's message; then the Lord fulfilled His promise to judge them for their unrighteousness. Huldah's faithfulness to God and her life of integrity were instrumental to the future of her nation.

Integrity refers to blameless character and exemplary behavior. The Old Testament uses the term integrity often to describe an attitude of the heart and a godly walk (see Gen. 20:5–6; 1 Kin. 9:4; Prov. 19:1; 20:7). The psalmist often described a person of integrity (Pss. 7:8; 25:21; 26:1; and 101:2). In the New Testament, integrity is encouraged as marking a godly life ("in doctrine *showing* integrity," Titus 2:7). Integrity is an important Christian virtue.

Are you a woman known for your faithfulness and integrity? Do others turn to you with their important questions? When you answer, do you speak the words of God? The prophetess Huldah is a role model for Christian women who desire to make a difference in the world today by proclaiming God' message to others. Live a life of integrity so the Lord can speak His truth through you.

Rhonda Harrington Kelley

Prayer: *Reflect on people you know who have lived with integrity and been witnesses for the Lord. Ask Him to speak to others through your life and words.*

Personal Reflection: ....

....

....

....

....

....

Satan—The Instigator of Sin

1 Chronicles 21:1–8

"Now Satan stood up against Israel, and moved David to number Israel. So David said to Joab and to the leaders of the people, 'Go, number Israel from Beersheba to Dan, and bring the number of them to me that I may know it.'" (vv. 1–2)

Only one sentence in this chapter—in fact, in all of 1–2 Chronicles—mentions Satan. Once is enough. No matter how successful King David had been in establishing Israel's national security (see 1 Chr. 22:18), this one arch-enemy kept coming back. All it took was one well-timed attack on one weak spot in David's character to set in motion a series of devastating consequences (vv. 14–30).

The events described in chapter 21 also appear in 2 Samuel 24, which opens with a different sentence: "Again the anger of the LORD was aroused against Israel, and He moved David against them to say, 'Go, number Israel and Judah.'" To read that the Lord's anger was "aroused against" His people or an individual (e.g., 1 Chr. 13:10) always signals deadly consequences. Details about Israel's sin in this instance are not provided, but this one sentence conveys that the nation was in big trouble.

Second Samuel also says that the Lord incited David against Israel. David was the Lord's instrument for punishing Israel, but David himself proved vulnerable to the enemy's schemes. He apparently did not inquire of the Lord (cp. 14:10, 14), and both accounts clearly depict him as the one responsible for the judgment that fell upon Israel. However, the Chronicler helpfully zeroes in on the real instigator of it all—Satan (Hb. "adversary, accuser, enemy").

Two actions are mentioned. First, Satan "stood up against Israel" (v. 1). The phrase implies that Satan had waited for an opportune moment to attack. When Israel, and David himself, let their guard down, Satan seized the moment and "stood up against" them. Whatever Israel was doing that had aroused the Lord's anger, Satan had instigated it.

Second, Satan persuaded David to impose the census. To number the "men who drew the sword" (v. 5) was not a clear violation of God's law (as were

David's adultery and murder, 2 Sam. 11), but it was clearly presumptuous on David's part. David was the earthly king, but he ruled Israel as a shepherd under the Lord's sovereign authority. Israel's strength and security rested not in the number of men ready to go to battle but in the Lord. David knew this better than anyone (read Ps. 33:16–22). Yet, despite Joab's protest and warning of the spiritual danger (1 Chr. 21:3), David insisted on having his way, and "God was displeased" (v. 7).

Tamra Hernandez

Prayer: *Inquire of the Lord, asking for awareness of your weak spots—areas vulnerable to temptation and situations in which you tend to let your guard down or insist on getting your way. Listen to and obey the Holy Spirit's warnings and correction.*

Personal Reflection: ....

....

....

....

....

....

....

How Should We Respond to God's Discipline?

1 Chronicles 21:17—22:1

"... I am the one who has sinned and done evil indeed ... I will not take what is yours for the LORD, nor offer burnt offerings with that which costs me nothing." (21:17, 24)

Rarely does anyone enjoy being told that she is wrong. It is humbling, exposing the fact that you aren't as good or as smart as you might have thought. I have four children—three girls and a baby boy. My girls keep life chaotic and colorful! Most days are drama-filled and joyful. However, there are days when they struggle to get along. After much investigation, we try to come to the place where each can say "I'm sorry for hurting you. I was wrong. Will you forgive me?" And then, the children hug and all is right with their little world!

King David had committed a sin before God when his pride led him to count all of the people of Israel. David was depending on the strength of his own forces and resources, taking personal credit for work that God had done. When his sin was confronted, all of Israel felt the wrath of God.

Pride often leads to sinful actions or harmful words. We never sin in a vacuum; our actions affect others. In that moment when your sin is confronted, how would God have you respond? David's heart changed, and his life is a good example to follow when receiving God's discipline.

Own your sin; take responsibility for your actions. It is always easy to explain *why* we did a certain thing. In following David's example, we learn not to blame others. "Was it not I who commanded the people to be numbered ... ?" (21:17). Our nature is to shift the blame to someone else, even in an apology to another: "I'm sorry if you were hurt, but if only you wouldn't. . . ." Don't blame your mistakes on others. Take responsibility for your own behavior. I had to learn that it's not my husband's fault, my children's fault, or my parents' fault. Yes, other things influence you, but ultimately you alone are responsible for your actions.

Offer your own sacrifice; feel the consequences of your actions. As the king, David could have demanded anything from anyone. He recognized that making things right was also his responsibility. He needed to feel the consequence of that prideful action of numbering the people. Painful consequences should keep us from walking down that path of pride again.

Kristin Yeldell

Prayer: *Your joy is found in the forgiveness of Christ, not in the perfection of your actions. Thank Him for making the ultimate sacrifice and taking the punishment you deserved. Ask God to expose any prideful attitude in your heart and reveal how your sin may be affecting others. Confess it as sin and make it right before Him and with those who have been offended.*

Personal Reflection:

True Wisdom and Wealth

2 Chronicles 1:1–17

◡◠◡

"Now give me wisdom and knowledge. . . ." (v. 10)

Miss Martha Johnson was my kindergarten Sunday school teacher. Every Sunday, she greeted each child at the door with a delightful smile and hug. If a Sunday was missed, a copy of the lesson was mailed to the homes along with sheets of stickers and a note. On each child's birthday, she would mail a birthday card and a one dollar bill. Miss Martha loved the children God had entrusted to her, for she had none of her own. Miss Martha was a single woman who cared for her disabled adult sister and supported the two of them by working as an elevator operator. She was a mighty prayer warrior who daily prayed for my family. She embodied grace and wisdom and was a woman of the most generous kind.

The Lord came to Solomon and said, "Ask! What shall I give you?" (v. 7). He could have asked for anything! What Solomon asked of God revealed what was truly in his heart.

Several key factors reveal what is truly in your heart. Others have said that if you want to know a person's priorities, simply look at her calendar and her checkbook. How you spend your time and money reveal what you really value. I would add that how you pray shows a great deal of what matters most. Is your time of prayer filled with requests for more money and resources, for a better job, house, or car? Do you ask God for the salvation of lost family members, pray for the gospel to go to the nations, for revival in our churches, or renewal in your own mind? What you ask of God in prayer reveals a great deal of what you truly value.

Solomon asked God for wisdom to lead the people of Israel. He had a heart that acknowledged the work of the Lord to his father David: "You have shown great mercy to David my father . . ." (v. 8). In his heart was a desire to lead the people well and to govern with wisdom and knowledge. James 1:5 says, "If any of you lacks wisdom, **let him ask of God,** who gives to all liberally and without reproach, and it will be given to him."

Each day you are confronted with difficulties that require you to think with a renewed mind (Rom. 12:1–2). Renewed thinking leads to revitalized living that results in the reality of Christ being seen!

Kristin Yeldell

Prayer: *In asking God for wisdom, you can be confident that He delights to answer this prayer! Ask God to give you wisdom and to help you to think with the mind of Christ. I don't know specifically about Miss Martha's prayers, but I know she lived a godly life and glorified the Lord. May you and I do the same today!*

Personal Reflection: ....

Hear My Heart

2 Chronicles 6:19–40

*"When Your people go out to battle against their enemies, wherever
You send them, and when they pray to You . . . then hear from heaven their
prayer and their supplication, and maintain their cause." (vv. 34–35)*

Several acts of worship were initiated prior to Solomon's prayer of dedication. The temple was complete after years of building. The ark of the covenant was relocated and properly placed in the "inner sanctuary of the temple," into the Most Holy Place. Harmony existed between the instruments and the singers praising and thanking God, declaring God is good, and His mercy endures forever. The house filled with a cloud, the glory of the Lord.

Solomon stood before the assembly of Israel, knelt, and spread his hands toward heaven, and made several requests, specifically for God's protection of Israel from her enemies. In response, the Lord appeared to Solomon declaring, "I have heard your prayer" (2 Chr. 7:12). The Lord made a request for the people to pray, stipulating the terms for answered prayer (2 Chr. 7:14).

The sincerity of prayer is clearly illustrated when it is non-scripted or mechanical but straight from the heart. Solomon witnessed the fulfillment of God's promise to his father David to build a temple. Now he prayed for God to watch the temple day and night and to forgive all manner of sin. Israel had a natural tendency toward sin and idolatry, just as all men and women have a sinful nature. Solomon clearly prayed to his God in heaven ("Hear from heaven," v. 21). Solomon requested God's forgiveness in spite of sin when the proper conditions of repentance were met.

The hymn "What a Friend We Have in Jesus" is a constant reminder to bring everything to God in prayer. I have spent far too many days in praying the same request over felt needs and personal concerns in my daily conversations with God. When the very act of praying and a habit of repentance infiltrated my days, daily peace followed. The frequency of answered prayer overwhelmed me as the proper conditions were met, over and over again. A request to pray for others increased.

The creation of a daily prayer log has kept me in touch with the petitions of many saints who have crossed my path. Their prayer requests are with me very early in the morning as I spend time with the God of heaven, who alone answers prayers. My personal blessing is a multitude of intercessors who have made it known that I am the recipient of their daily prayers. Greater then all intercessors is Jesus Christ, who is even at the right hand of God, who also makes intercession for us (Rom. 8:34).

Elizabeth W. Luter

Prayer: *If answered prayer is your desire, consider a devoted relationship with the God of heaven. Repent of any sin and return your focus to living out the desires of God by keeping His commandments (statutes and precepts).*

Personal Reflection: ....

....

....

....

....

....

....

The "If" That Keeps on Appearing

2 Chronicles 7:1–22

*". . . If My people who are called by My name will humble themselves,
and pray and seek My face, and turn from their wicked ways, then I will hear
from heaven, and will forgive their sin and heal their land." (vv. 13–14)*

In the midst of God's destruction of a people who had been immersed with their own self-sufficiency (v. 12), the Lord set forth conditions for answering the prayers of Solomon as well as the corporate prayer of the people (vv. 17–22). The Lord's judgment was on His "people who are called by [His] name"—those who belonged to Him and even publicly represented His **name**, while still disobeying His commands. This scenario has been occurring again and again throughout the generations. God has high expectations of His people; He demands obedience. Yet despite His unconditional love and the pouring out of His blessings upon them, those who belong to the Lord continue to reject Him.

As the Lord sought to pull His people away from trusting anyone or anything that would take His place in their hearts, His actions directly undermined their dependence on the land and even affected their physical health (v. 13). Yet despite their arrogant rejection of Him, the Lord still moved to keep His promise to "hear" them, "forgive their sin and heal their land" (v. 14). The Lord promised to answer Solomon's prayer for the Lord to receive and respond to the prayers of repentance from the people.

How do you seek the Lord's face when you have sinned and find yourself before Him guilty of disobedience?

- **Humble** yourself, voluntarily bend your knee, and open your heart to receive His mercy and obey Him.
- **Pray and seek [His] face**, requesting a face-to-face audience with the Lord and refusing to give up.
- **Turn**, an act of the will that suggests doing a complete about-face, returning to the starting point and changing direction.

What do you receive in return for this heart-felt repentance?

- The Lord will **hear**; He will not ignore such genuine repentance.
- He will **forgive**. God's forgiveness is as if it never happened—the complete restoration of fellowship with Him.
- He will **heal**. Even the land itself will experience healing and renewal.

Never has our nation needed this healing touch more than now! Never have so many of God's people been in need of the healing in His wings! May the Lord's appeal to Solomon take root in the hearts of this generation!

Dorothy Kelley Patterson

Prayer: *Call upon the Lord with a humble heart; seek His face; turn in repentance to Him. Ask the Lord to spare our nation and to restore what the locusts have eaten, reviving and renewing our hearts and calling us to repentance.*

Personal Reflection: ....

....

....

....

....

....

Jehoshabeath—A Courageous Wife

2 Chronicles 22:1–12

"But Jehoshabeath, the daughter of the king, took Joash the son of Ahaziah, and stole him away from among the king's sons who were being murdered, and put him and his nurse in a bedroom . . . so that she [Athaliah] did not kill him." (v. 11)

Jehoshabeath or Jehosheba was one of the women who played a key role in the dramatic events in Israel when the new king Jehu attempted to purge the country of Ahab's descendants, including Judah's king Ahaziah. She was the daughter of King Jehoram and his wicked wife Athaliah, the sister of Ahaziah the king of Judah and the wife of the priest Jehoiada (vv. 11–12; 2 Kin. 11:2). She and her husband rescued her young nephew Joash and protected him from Queen Athaliah's attempt to kill all male heirs to the throne to guarantee her own power (2 Chr. 22:10). They hid the baby boy and his nurse "in the house of God for six years, while Athaliah reigned over the land" (vv. 11–12). The courage of this woman was used by God to change the course of Israel's history.

Does this account remind you of the rescue of baby Moses when the king of Egypt ordered that all male babies of Hebrew descent be killed? God intervened in the evil plan through the Pharaoh's daughter who found baby Moses hidden in a small ark in the bulrushes of the river. Through divine providence, Moses was raised by his own mother in the Pharaoh's palace (Ex. 2:1–10). Jehoshabeath was also an instrument of God to protect Joash and fulfill His promise that a son of David would always be king and part of the lineage of Messiah.

Second Chronicles 23:1–11 records the rightful ascent of Joash to the throne of Judah. The priests and Levites, as well as all Israel, helped unseat the illegitimate queen and her priest by replacing the legitimate King Joash and his priest. Soon after, Athaliah was killed (2 Chr. 23:15), and Joash began his reign. While he was only seven years old when he became king, Joash reigned for 40 years in Jerusalem (2 Chr. 24:1). King Joash rebuilt the temple but failed to teach the people the Law of the Lord and instead led them to worship idols (2 Chr. 24:17–18). The prophet Zechariah spoke the words of the Lord to warn

Joash about his sin. Zechariah said to them, "Thus says God: 'Why do you transgress the commandments of the LORD, so that you cannot prosper? Because you have forsaken the LORD, He also has forsaken you'" (2 Chr. 24:20). What a tragic judgment!

While the rule of Joash did not end well, the courage of Jehoshabeath did protect the Davidic line of rulers, through whom the Messiah would come. One never knows the extent of blessing and influence that will come through simple obedience to the Lord.

Rhonda Harrington Kelley

Prayer: *Ask the Lord to give you courage to stand for Him and be an instrument of His divine work.*

Personal Reflection: ....

....

....

....

....

....

....

Seek, Do, Teach

Ezra 7:1–10

*"Ezra had prepared his heart to seek the Law of the Lord, and to do it,
and to teach statutes and ordinances in Israel." (v. 10)*

God used certain Bible characters to show us how NOT to live. Ezra did not fit in that category. He was a faithful servant of God.

First, consider some historical highlights. Just as God had plainly warned through his prophets, the people of God were sent into exile as a result of their continued disobedience. The northern kingdom of Israel was taken away by the Assyrians in 722 B.C. The southern kingdom of Judah was captured by the Babylonians in 586 B.C. Babylon was conquered by Persia around 539 B.C. As God had promised, Cyrus, the new leader of Persia, allowed some of the exiles to return to Jerusalem.

The first group of returnees left immediately. Then around 458 B.C., Ezra led a second group from Babylon back home to Jerusalem. He had been working on a major project. Ezra was a priest who had descended from the tribe of Levi. From Ezra 7:1–5, we see the biblical proof that he could trace his genealogy all the way to Aaron. The first high priest ordained by God in the book of Exodus was Aaron, the brother of Moses. Ezra was also a scribe, which meant that he was a teacher and a recorder of the Word of God. His area of concentrated study were the writings of Moses. Even the king of Persia recognized the value of this servant named Ezra.

Consider the testimony of the life of Ezra. The name "Ezra" means "help." He was indeed a great helper of his nation. He also knew that his own source of help rested in the hands of Almighty God. His threefold purpose was to SEEK the Law of the Lord, to DO the Law of the Lord, and to TEACH the Law of the Lord in Israel. He had faith to believe that God would keep His promises to free the people from exile, restoring them to their homeland. He spent his exile days in preparation for God's assignment for his life.

The key to meeting his threefold purpose was: Methodically and with full surrender, Ezra prepared his heart. He SET HIS HEART firmly on God and the study of His Word. He was resolute in his zeal to learn the law and then live the law in a way that was pleasing to God. Only then could he be ready to record the law and teach the law to others. Ezra, a dedicated Levite, became an arrow in the hand of God to point His people in the direction of holiness and purity.

Becky Brown

Prayer: *God put His HAND on Ezra's ministry when Ezra set his HEART fully on God. Ask God for a re-focused heart. As you pray, follow Ezra's example: Prepare. Seek. Do. Teach.*

Personal Reflection:

My Sin, Her Sin, Our Sin

Ezra 9:1–16

*"And I said: 'O my God, I am too ashamed and humiliated to lift up
my face to You, my God; for our iniquities have risen higher
than our heads, and our guilt has grown up to the heavens.'" (v. 6)*

Most people who are privileged to have access to dental care understand the importance of anesthetics—the "numbing medicines." Used properly, they prevent most of the pain that would otherwise prevent the dentist from doing whatever work has become necessary. If the numbness did not wear off, however, you would rightly conclude that something had gone wrong. Unlike the "numbing medicines" used in the dentist's office, the constant bombardment with all things shocking, sensational, and sordid is rapidly numbing our souls to the horrific consequences of sin.

When the first Jewish exiles returned to Jerusalem, they were surrounded not by digital social media and advertising but by idol-worshipping peoples with occultic and pornographic religious practices. By the time Ezra arrived about 80 years later, even the Jewish leaders—"the priests and the Levites"—in Jerusalem were compromising Israel's covenant with the Lord (vv. 1–2). The leaders who had just arrived with Ezra reported to him that God's people were intermarrying with the pagan peoples around them and referred to the practice as a "trespass" (v. 2). The Hebrew word denotes "an act of unfaithfulness." The first exiles to return to Israel knew better. God had allowed His people to be taken into exile because of their unfaithfulness to Him. Furthermore, these marriages to pagan wives directly violated the law (Deut. 7:1–4) and exemplified the grave danger of becoming numb to sin.

Thankfully, Ezra was shocked to hear what was happening and was willing to do something about it. Having come to Jerusalem with a strong sense of purpose as a "skilled scribe in the Law of Moses" and eager "to teach statutes and ordinances in Israel" (Ezra 7:6, 10), Ezra could have given up in despair. He could have condemned the guilty ones. Instead, he prayed for them.

The way he prayed not only "hit a nerve," prompting the sinners' repentance (10:1), but also exposes the "lack of nerve" of many Christians. Ezra himself had not committed the sins he was confessing, but he identified with and confessed them anyway. Instead of distinguishing between his sin and her sin, this one's sin and that one's sin, Ezra included himself with all the remnant of Israel in the confession, speaking of "our guilt" (9:6, 15) and "our iniquities" (v. 7). Do you have the nerve to pray that way for members of your church family whose lives look no different from those of the idol-worshippers around them (e.g., embracing views and exalting values that contradict God's Word)?

Tamra Hernandez

Prayer: *Commit to being available, as the Spirit leads, to pray with and for fellow Christians who seem unaware of becoming numb to sin (remembering to include yourself, as did Ezra).*

Personal Reflection:

Social Injustice

Nehemiah 5:1–13

*"And there was a great outcry of the people
and their wives against their Jewish brethren." (v. 1)*

As the people of Israel were attempting to rebuild their nation, many found themselves in dire financial circumstances. Yet unlike the economic hardship they experienced under their Babylonian captors, these Jewish families were in financial bondage to other Jews. Some mortgaged their property to buy food for their children. Others went into debt just to pay their taxes, which had been levied by their fellow Jews who had positions of authority. Not only were the people indebted, but they were also required to pay interest on the money borrowed, a practice that was forbidden in the Law (Deut. 23:19–20). Having nothing left, many sold their children into slavery.

After being released from foreign slavery, Jewish families devoted themselves to building the walls and building a new future for the next generation. Facing a mountain of debt during a time of national instability, the people were moving backward. Their children became indentured servants out of financial desperation. The Jewish nobility and rulers were taking advantage of national instability and economic crises for their own financial gain (v. 7). Their actions sharply contrast the later actions of believers in the early church, who gave to their spiritual family until everyone had what he needed (Acts 2:44–45; 4:34).

Nehemiah held the Jewish rulers and nobles accountable, commanding them to restore the property and the interest accrued to these impoverished families. He accused them of profiting from the plight of their Jewish brothers and taking advantage of desperate circumstances for their own personal gain. He even acknowledged his part in the problem and resolved to stop lending money (Neh. 5:10). The rulers absorbed the remaining debt and returned the property to the people. Nehemiah's response, and the course correction he led others to take, broke the cycle of poverty and enabled the families to have a new start.

The self-seeking practices of the Jewish rulers and nobles contrast the self-denying habits of Nehemiah (5:14–19). Although Nehemiah had the legal right to collect a tax from the people as a Jewish governor, he refused to receive any financial gain or even to purchase land. He also required his servants to work on the wall. For Nehemiah, leadership meant the responsibility to serve rather than the right to be served.

Injustice against the poor is still prevalent in many countries today. Nehemiah's solution should inform our response to this social issue. As we learn of social injustice in our communities and throughout the world, we must remember that our privileges are gifts for which we are stewards. We are responsible for the wellbeing and dignity of others as we use our resources and influence for their sakes.

Katie McCoy

Prayer: *Do you consider social justice to be your responsibility? Ask God to show you a practical way to serve others in need through them.*

Personal Reflection: ....

....

....

....

....

....

Keeping a Vow of Commitment

Nehemiah 10:30–39

⌒

". . . And we will not neglect the house of our God." (v. 39b)

Vows, commitments, and contracts are often violated at will. An assumption exists, or at least a sense, that one's word will be broken, even if certified with a signature. Likewise, vows made to ourselves (i.e., lose weight, spend less, exercise more) are easily broken and laughed at as too hard to do, too many changes to make. How many New Year's resolutions have been made and broken before the end of the first month? Perhaps that makes the significance of biblical vows difficult to grasp fully.

In Nehemiah 10, the people had read God's Word, responded by confessing their sins, and were making a commitment that would require making a change in their daily lives. They made a covenant with God, a binding agreement that signified their formal commitment to follow Him, writing it out and sealing it with the signatures of their leaders. Nehemiah was the first to place his seal on the document, followed by the priests, the Levites, and the brethren. The people committed to obey all of the Lord's commands and laws.

In the second half of chapter 10, the plan of the people to fulfill that vow is detailed. These concrete plans helped to guide their commitment. The plans addressed marriage and a commitment not to intermarry. They detailed financial commitments regarding offerings and support of the temple. The people committed to observing the Sabbath and to caring for God's house. The detailed listings describe how serious their commitment was and how strong their desire to keep all the requirements of the law, committing not to neglect the house of their God. These areas of their lives would be impacted the most by their commitments.

The lesson for us is not in the specific areas they addressed necessarily, but that the people were detailed and specific. As women, we hear the Word of the Lord, we repent, and we commit to obey. If we stop there and do not put our abstract words into concrete actions, we run the risk of breaking the commitment we just made. Our commitments to the Lord require more than lip service. They require actions that affect our daily lives, transforming us all the more into the likeness of Christ.

Terri Stovall

Prayer: *Is there a commitment you have made that you are struggling to keep? Have your responses and prayers to the Lord been merely words that have never been put into action? Do you desire to follow the commandments of the Lord, but do not know how to follow through? Start today by reconfirming with the Lord your commitment to Him. Ask Him to help you list in detail the ways you are going to put your words into actions.*

Personal Reflection: ....

....

....

....

....

....

....

....

Courageous, Uncompromising Leadership

Nehemiah 13:1–31

"Remember me, O my God, concerning this, and do not wipe out my good deeds that I have done for the house of my God, and for its services!" (v. 14)

Leadership requires courageous perseverance. In Kingdom work, leadership also requires abandonment to the will of God and refusal to compromise His Word, even in adversity. Nehemiah was that type of leader.

The final chapter in the book of Nehemiah summarizes the reforms instituted by Nehemiah along with some of the difficulties he faced in that process. The task that God set before him was not easy. He encountered many critics, difficult decisions, and challenges to the completion of the work. We can learn from Nehemiah how to navigate similar challenges as we have opportunities for influence.

Nehemiah was a man who could take bold, courageous action when necessary. He addressed the evil influence of Tobiah's presence in the temple courtyards, throwing him out and demanding the area be cleansed (vv. 7–9). Nehemiah confronted the rulers when he discovered they had stopped tithing and, consequently, providing for the Levities (vv. 10–13). In these instances and others written throughout the book of Nehemiah, a man who was willing to take bold, courageous action on behalf of the people and for the will of God arises.

Nehemiah was a man who did not compromise, remaining obedient to the Word of God. Discovering some of the people were violating the laws of the Sabbath, rather than turn a blind eye or rationalize it away as unimportant, Nehemiah confronted the people, accusing them of profaning the Sabbath. He then took steps to ensure that the commands of the Lord would not be violated (vv. 15–22). Similarly, he held the priests accountable for violating the Word of the Lord by intermarrying, reminding them that doing so was a transgression against God (vv. 23–28).

Nehemiah was a man of prayer. Repeatedly he prayed, "Remember me, O my God" (vv. 14, 22, 29, 31). Leadership can be lonely, but Nehemiah knew that God was always with him. Whether making difficult decisions to protect the house of God, seeking the Lord's mercy, or interceding for others, Nehemiah continually turned to the Lord. The pain and struggle of dealing with difficult people paled in comparison to the assurance that God would remember him.

You may never hold a formal position of leadership, but you will have opportunities to influence others. You may face a time when, as Nehemiah, the Lord calls upon you to make hard decisions or be challenged to compromise the truth. When that time comes, how will your leadership be evaluated?

Terri Stovall

Prayer: *As God gives you positions of leadership and opportunities for influence, ask Him to help you remain a woman who is obedient to the Word of God, without compromise. Ask Him to give you courage to take bold action when it is His will and to live a life abandoned to Him.*

Personal Reflection: ....

....

....

....

....

....

Vashti—A Deposed Queen

Esther 1:1–22

". . . Vashti shall come no more before King Ahasuerus; and let the king give her royal position to another who is better than she." (v. 19b)

King Ahasuerus (or Xerxes I) reigned over 127 provinces of Persia from 486 to 465 B.C. (v. 1). The powerful king hosted for all his officials and allies a feast that lasted for 180 days (v. 4). The extravagant celebration ended with a seven-day banquet for citizens of Shushan, the capital of Persia and site of the royal palace (vv. 5–8). The eating and drinking continued until the drunken king sent for his wife.

In the meanwhile, Queen Vashti hosted a feast for the women in the royal palace (v. 9). King Ahasuerus sent for the queen, planning to present the queen to his guests. The king commanded the eunuchs to "bring Queen Vashti before the king, *wearing* her royal crown, in order to show her beauty to the people and the officials" (vv. 10–11). The irritated queen refused the king's request, and thus her sad tale begins.

Defying the king was a serious offense even for the queen. Therefore, Ahasuerus called together his official advisors to determine the most appropriate action according to the law (vv. 13–19). Vashti was essentially tried for treason since her act of defiance was a public humiliation for her husband, the king. While the king acted inappropriately, her response not only challenged his authority but was also considered a bad influence on the women of the kingdom. The advisors were concerned that widespread disrespect for husbands and upheaval in the homes would result.

Interestingly, the decision of the pagan advisors affirms the divine creation order: "All wives will honor their husbands, both great and small" (v. 20). The plan of God from the beginning calls for the husband's loving headship and the wife's gracious submission (Gen. 2:15–18; Eph. 5:21–33). Before the time of Ahasuerus and the wise men of Persia, God had a perfect plan for man and woman to live in harmony. Unfortunately, they disobeyed God and experienced serious consequences.

Vashti received a harsh sentence: "Come no more before King Ahasuerus; and let the king give her royal position to another who is better than she" (Esth. 1:19). From the prominence of a royal throne, she was deposed to the unknown. The king's decree was a warning to all wives in Persia to honor their husbands: "Each man should be master in his own house, and speak in the language of his own people" (v. 22).

This tragic account in history was followed by one of the most endearing stories of the Old Testament, the selection of Esther as Queen of Persia. Both Vashti, who dared to challenge her husband and the royal law, as well as Esther, who courageously protected her people, were used to accomplish God's purposes. God's sovereignty will always reign victorious over man's will.

Rhonda Harrington Kelley

Prayer: *Reflect on times in your life when you have been tempted to defy God's commands. Ask Him to forgive you and commit to a life of obedience.*

Personal Reflection: ....

....

....

....

....

....

The Value of Submission

Esther 1:16—2:18

⌒

"For the queen's behavior will become known to all women,
so that they will despise their husbands in their eyes, . . .
Thus there will be *excessive contempt and wrath." (1:17–18)*

Queen Vashti of Persia was outwardly beautiful but inwardly vain and self-ruled. The king's command for one's presence was an order, not an invitation. Vashti not only refused to come before the king, but no explanation or apology is recorded in the text (1:12). She was hosting a banquet feast for the women (v. 9). Her refusal to obey the king's command would be costly. This foolish response cost Vashti her throne.

The advisors of King Ahasuerus interpreted Vashti's action as an act of rebellion against the king, and they warned the king of consequences throughout the kingdom. Vashti's dishonoring her husband, as well as her king, would have repercussions and create widespread upheaval in the homes of the nation, prompting wives to despise their husbands, resulting in the contempt of wives for their husbands and the outpouring of wrath on the part of husbands toward their wives (vv. 17–18).

A wife's submission to her husband is introduced in the Old Testament. The headship of the husband in the home is not only the law of God, established in the creation order, but honored, even if unknowingly, by the counselors to the king of Persia. Vashti dishonored her king and husband and ignored the law of God.

On the other hand, after Esther ascended to the throne, she responded to her pagan husband and king with humility and respect. She won the love and respect of her husband; and at a crucial time when the Lord called her out for a special task, she had the ear of her husband. God used Esther's beauty, intelligence, and creativity, coupled with her submission to and respect for her husband as well as her courageous faith, to accomplish His purposes.

What prepared Esther for the challenges that came to her in the pagan court of Ahasuerus? Esther made right choices that enabled her to be used of the Lord.

- She developed inner disciplines to complement her outer beauty.
- After she became the queen of Persia, she honored her cousin Mordecai, who had reared her since her parents' deaths.
- She disciplined her heart to be obedient to the authorities in her life.
- She was obedient to the Lord even when she did not understand His plans.

Wives in this generation have the same challenge that faced Vashti and Esther—whether to submit to their husbands or follow their personal desires. Perhaps a look at these women will help to decide whether to obey God or men.

Dorothy Kelley Patterson

Prayer: *Ask the Lord to help you examine your own heart. Are you willing to be obedient even when you cannot see how that obedience will help you? Can you trust the Lord's commitment to you even when you cannot see Him working?*

Personal Reflection: ....

....

....

....

....

Is Fasting a Spiritual Discipline?

Esther 4:1–4

*"And in every province where the king's command and decree arrived,
there was great mourning among the Jews, with fasting, weeping,
and wailing, and many lay in sackcloth and ashes." (v. 3)*

Genuine fasting, depriving the body of nourishment, was not merely a ritual on the calendar or for a regular cycle. Fasting meant denying personal needs because of an urgency to focus on God—pouring out your heart, hearing from Him, and obeying His word. The innermost emotion is often prompted by grief or tragedy and inevitably accompanied by humility, sorrow, confession of sin, and prayer. Fasting as an external ritual done to impress others or to gain spiritual rewards was a mockery, but genuine fasting put a pure and uninhibited focus on the Lord:

- To gain God's attention in behalf of someone's suffering;
- To aid in making critical decisions or pursuing an ominous course of action;
- To mourn sin or respond to being confronted with sin;
- To prepare for a special service to God.

Although fasting was often observed during the day and broken with a meal in the evening (1 Sam. 1:7–10). Esther specified that her fast would be night and day (Esth. 4:16). She knew that God had called her for special service to Him. Her choice was whether or not to obey Him. God will always honor one who turns away from the responsibilities and pleasures of life in order to present herself in humility before Him.

A sincere call to fast suggests that prayer is part of the package. Prayer is not mentioned in the book of Esther, but its omission is so conspicuous that one may assume the author may have chosen to avoid any religious language. Certainly the divine providence working throughout the book shows God's presence in going before to prepare for what is to come, shepherding through each crisis, and then claiming His glory as the book draws to a close.

In calling the fast, Esther affirmed that she needed the help of God as well as others. She found a powerful armor of protection to surround her in the important mission to which God had called her—the support from people who cared enough to join her in intercession and the ear of God who does indeed hear and answer when His people call upon Him for deliverance.

Dorothy Kelley Patterson

Prayer: *Perhaps you are in a time of crisis in your life. Your heart cries out to the Lord, and you have no thought for pursuing tasks or any desire for food. Such is the opportune time for reaching out to God and laying your burdens before Him.*

Personal Reflection: ....

....

....

....

....

....

....

Esther—Under Divine Appointment

Esther 4:5–17

༄

*". . . Yet who knows whether you have come to
the kingdom for such a time as this?" (v. 14)*

Queen Esther had a reasonable explanation for her cousin Mordecai when he asked her to go before the king and plead for the lives of her people. Her reticence may not have been cowardice as much as the assumption that she would not survive to make her appeal. Anyone coming before the king without an invitation would be put to death unless the king intervened. Her concern was well founded since she had not been summoned by the king for 30 days.

Yet Mordecai's response was straightforward and even blunt. His prophetic warning reminded Esther of the power resting in the providence of God. He was confident that if Esther failed to accept the challenge, God would bring forward another to deliver His people. What a powerful reminder to each of us: When God gives gifts or opportunities or strategic position to accomplish His purpose, one dare not refuse the heavenly assignment—whatever the personal cost! God does not waste His equipping or timing. He expects obedience from His children.

The phrase "who knows" is considered God language, reminding the reader that divine wisdom is superintending every event. Although God is not mentioned by name in the book of Esther, He is not hidden. His footprints are everywhere, orchestrating His will. There is the confidence that deliverance will come through the Lord's providence in working through life's circumstances to accomplish His purpose. The entire book of Esther is filled with natural occurrences that happen precisely at the right moment—so much so that one cannot dismiss lightly these "coincidences," such as the accession to the Persian throne of a Jewess, the timely discovery of a plot against the king's life by Mordecai and the delay in rewarding him, the king's extending his scepter to Esther when she approached him without invitation—all these and more become testimony to divine appointments through which God is working.

Divine appointments still happen to you and me. In the biblical schema, you are appointed for service to God—not according to what is in your heart to do but what God calls you to do for Him. Esther was not named Queen of Persia for her own advancement. She was placed in that position through the providence of God to become His instrument for delivering His people. The Lord will work your life circumstances together to accomplish His purposes for you and through you to glorify Himself.

Dorothy Kelley Patterson

Prayer: *Ask the Lord to make you open to divine appointment for whatever task He may have for you. Surrender your will to His direction with no thought for personal cost or inconvenience. Take joy in being brought to the kingdom for a time when you can serve the Lord in a special way.*

Personal Reflection:

Why Do Bad Things Happen to Good People?

Esther 5:1–14

~

*"So Haman went out that day joyful and with a glad heart; but when
Haman saw Mordecai in the king's gate, and that he did not stand
or tremble before him, he was filled with indignation against Mordecai." (v. 9)*

Indeed, those who follow the Lord will have enemies; they will suffer persecution in varying degrees; some will seal their commitment to the Lord with their lives. Mordecai was a thorn in the flesh of Haman. Because this Jew refused to bow down and worship him, Haman was determined to seek his destruction (v. 14). In fact, Haman thought he had managed to get rid of all the Jews in Persia through a plan for genocide of the nation (Esth. 3:13).

God's timing is always perfect. He often waits for wickedness to grow to its full measure so that the wicked fall into the trap they themselves have designed. So it was with Haman. Despite his powerful position in the court of Ahasuerus, he was not beyond the reach of God. Mordecai the Jew in his own strength was helpless before this high-ranking court official. His righteous life and good standing among the Jews did not protect him from experiencing persecution. In fact, both characteristics probably made him a target.

The adversities of life will come as surely as do the blessings to God's children. Yet nothing happens without God's permission. Ultimately He is sovereign over every decision you make and every action you take; and He will guide all to accomplish His purposes. The "co-incidence" or human happenstance in reality is "God-incidence" or divine providence. Just as in the lives of Esther and the Jewish people in ancient Persia, God's providence even now overrules tragedy and poor judgment to bring good from evil. He arranges even the smallest detail in order to preserve His people and to reward those who are obedient to Him.

Tragedy will strike, suffering will come, crisis will appear at the most inopportune moment. However, in the midst of whatever evil or hurtful circumstance you face, as a child of God, you only need to wait for God's providence to guide you with His perfect knowledge, matchless wisdom, and unconditional love. He will not cease to work in your behalf to bring about what is ultimately best for you. God never works against you; He is always working for you (see Rom. 8:28–32).

Dorothy Kelley Patterson

Prayer: *When you are in the valley and suffering injustice or some other sorrow, call upon the Lord. He will come to your side and walk with you. He will not waste your suffering but will use it in ways you cannot imagine. Ask the Lord for the healing balm from Gilead for your wound.*

Personal Reflection: ....

....

....

....

....

....

....

....

The Tragedy of Ungodly Counsel

Esther 6:1–14

~

". . . And his wife Zeresh said to him, 'If Mordecai, before whom you have begun to fall, is of Jewish descent, you will not prevail against him but will surely fall before him.'" (v. 13)

The prophetic words of Zeresh, the wife of Haman, are too little, too late! Before Haman knew that he would be instructed by the king to honor the Jew Mordecai, Zeresh had given Haman her counsel to build a gallows, have Mordecai "hanged on it; then go merrily with the king to the banquet" (Esth. 5:14). Of course, this earlier advice based only upon her knowledge of her husband's hatred of the Jew, had pleased Haman and was an easy suggestion from his wife based on Haman's favor with the king. Zeresh knew of his hatred for Mordecai but made no effort to consider the matter with any care before blurting out her ungodly and inappropriate advice. Rather than thoughtful contemplation of the matter and consideration of the inevitable fickleness and intrigue of palace relationships, she simply gave Haman the words he wanted to hear.

A history lesson might have tempered her remarks. Haman, the Agagite, was a marked man since a conflict between his ancestors the Amalekites and Israel had long been raging. In fact, the Lord declared that He would wage war against every generation of Amalekites (Ex. 17:16). For Haman to lift up his hand against the Jews ultimately would mean nothing but defeat. The words of Zeresh were similar to the advice Jezebel gave her wicked husband Ahab, suggesting that he kill Naboth and take possession of Naboth's vineyard, which he coveted, and then have this innocent man killed (1 Kin. 21). That, too, had a disastrous outcome, and Zeresh was headed the same way. Both Jezebel and Zeresh focused on removing the obstacles to their respective husbands' happiness rather than on determining what would be the most righteous and best solution to the problem.

The wife who wants to give godly counsel to her husband must nurture her personal walk with the Lord, for He is the source of genuine wisdom. She must also add to her wisdom a discerning spirit, which will enable her to use the wisdom she acquires most effectively. She must be willing to do her homework, examining every situation carefully and reaching widely to gather her information. History from the past, detailed information from the present, and discerning analysis of the future is important in order for her to use the mind and heart God has given her. God created the wife to be a helper to her husband, and offering godly counsel is one of the ways she can fulfill this important assignment.

Dorothy Kelley Patterson

Prayer: *Seek the Lord's face as you prepare to offer counsel for making important decisions for your family. Ask the Lord to give you a discerning spirit to sift through all to be considered in a decision.*

Personal Reflection: ....

....

....

....

....

....

....

God's Signature in Your Life

Esther 8:1–17

༒

*"On that day King Ahasuerus gave Queen Esther the house
of Haman, the enemy of the Jews." (v. 1a)*

God's signature in your life is His providential care of you and all of His creation. He sustains and directs the world and everything in it. How comforting
to know that God continually orders your life events. He helps you to fulfill His
purpose, and he guides His world according to His perfect plan. Providence—
both the seen and the unseen—is the umbrella under which your life journey
is made. Take comfort in knowing that the Lord is compassionate, gracious,
longsuffering, and always faithful (Ps. 16:9–11).

Clearly inscribed in my mind are the circumstances surrounding the
home-going of my mother. She became an orphan in her childhood. She was
faithful to my father during his lengthy illness. I wanted someone with her
when she stepped out of this world and into the court of heaven. The gracious
providence of God came to my mother, me, and our family:

- The night before she died, her only son decided to deliver her medicine
  himself several days early and have a special visit.
- My sisters and I had telephone conversations with her; my call was
  longer than usual and full of happy interchange.
- She wrote notes (one of her most precious ministries), addressed and
  stamped and left for mailing.
- She went to bed and slept through the night, awakening early in the
  morning with coughing and respiratory distress. In the past she would
  have not called for help; but this time she did.
- As she transitioned from this life into the arms of Jesus, two atten-
  dants, whom she knew and loved, came and were with her until my
  brother and sister-in-love arrived.

Such a minor thing in the overall schema, but these events were a reminder to me of the gracious providences of our Lord. The least important things for the world are not beyond His reach. The Lord does not grant every desire, but He is faithful—just when I need a reminder—to make Himself known!

In the book of Esther, God placed His agents in fitting places to do His work (2:5–6), balancing opportunity with responsibility. You are a free agent, choosing whether or not to obey.

Dorothy Kelley Patterson

Prayer: *What challenge is in your life? Seek the face of the Lord before you try to fix it. Wait on the Lord even when all seems to be lost. Ask Him for patience to give Him time to work. Ask Him to give you perseverance to keep working toward whatever assignment He has given you.*

Personal Reflection: ....

....

....

....

....

....

....

Job's Wife—A Foolish Woman

Job 1:1—2:10

*"Then his wife said to him, 'Do you still hold fast
to your integrity? Curse God and die!'" (2:9)*

The book of Job is part of the wisdom literature of the Bible and the first of the books of poetry in the Old Testament. The focal character is Job himself who "was blameless and upright, and one who feared God and shunned evil" (1:1; 2:2–3). While he lived a good life, bad things always seemed to happen to Job. His intense grief and pain prompt the question: Why do the righteous suffer? The book of Job demonstrates that suffering cannot always be directly attributed to personal sin and that God sometimes allows even those who love Him to suffer for reasons He may or may not explain (Jon. 9:1–3). Throughout history, Job has been known as the suffering servant.

Job and his wife had seven sons and three daughters as well as large herds of sheep, camels, oxen, and donkeys. He was prominent and wealthy, "the greatest of all the people of the East" (Job 1:2–4). Job's wife led a life of privilege until adversity began. Hardship revealed the faith of Job in contrast to his wife's lack of faith. When Job suffers, Satan attacks God's servant through his wife. When he was struck with painful boils, Job's wife challenged him to "curse God and die!" (2:9). Sometimes Satan works through loved ones or close friends to discourage and distract God's children from their faith.

Despite his extreme suffering, Job's faith did not waiver. He called his faithless wife "foolish," one who did not accept adversity as well as good from God. But, "In all this Job did not sin with his lips" (2:10). Job's wife has been called by some "the helpmeet of the devil" since she added salt to the wounds caused by Satan. Job always responded to her in love. Job's wife failed him when he most needed her support. Instead of comfort and compassion, she gave him discouragement and doubt.

From a human perspective, Job's wife had reason to curse God. She endured her husband's affliction, lost her children, and lost her earthly possessions.

However, she could have followed the leadership of her wise husband instead of resorting to her own foolish nature. When you face trials, choose to be faithful not foolish. You may have reason to give up hope. Trust the Lord in the bad times as well as the good, knowing that He has your best interest at heart. You can depend on Him to care for you. When you are faithful, God will bless you as He did Job: "Now the LORD blessed the latter *days* of Job more than his beginning; . . . So Job died, old and full of days" (42:12–17).

Rhonda Harrington Kelley

Prayer: *Ask the Lord to give you wisdom to trust Him even in your suffering. Seek to be faithful and not foolish all the days of your life.*

Personal Reflection: ....

....

....

....

....

....

....

....

Faithfulness in the Midst of Suffering

Job 2:1–10

"Then his wife said to him, 'Do you still hold fast to your integrity?
Curse God and die!' But he said to her, 'You speak as one of
the foolish women speaks. Shall we indeed accept good
from God, and shall we not accept adversity?' In all this Job
did not sin with his lips." (vv. 9–10)

Sometimes the state of our souls seems as hopeless as the state of trees in wintertime. Nothing can possibly be happening, God has forgotten us, the idea of springtime is preposterous. The naked wood, bare and brittle and dry, is as much a part of the tree's life as the sap's rising in spring. The Lord is still in charge, still moving in mysterious ways even when He gives the enemy of our souls permission to trouble us. Permission was given in the case of Job, a man who in no way deserved the calamities that befell him.

Note that Job never denies God's existence, never imagines that his troubles come by pure chance. God surely has something to do with it, and he has a thousand questions. Unknown to Job was a strange encounter that had taken place in the court of heaven. The members, we read, had taken their places in the presence of the Lord, and the Adversary was there among them.

Satan leaves the Lord's presence, and everything Job possesses is taken away—oxen, donkeys, herdsmen, sheep, shepherds, sons, and daughters. Not once in all this did Job sin or charge God with unreasonableness.

Then . . . Job is smitten with running sores, loses his health, his position (he went from executive suite to an ash heap), and the confidence of his wife. A woman with a thorough-going secular mind-set, Job's wife advises him to curse God and die. "If we accept good from God, shall we not accept evil?" says Job, and he "did not utter one sinful word." Job passes the test. His manifesto is "Though He slay me, yet will I trust Him" (13:15).

Take heart from the suffering of Job. Suffering was the necessary proof of the reality of his faith—to us, as to his contemporaries and the enemy Satan (his and ours). The suffering of our Savior proved the reality of His love for His Father. The world still needs to be shown that there are those who, no matter what the circumstances, for love of Him, will do exactly what God commands. The end He has in view is a glorious one. You can fully count on that, as you can count on the naked woods one day exploding into a glory of blossom.

Elisabeth Elliot

Prayer: *Ask the Lord to give you strength like Job to be a faithful witness for Him during your times of suffering and take time to pray by name for any believers whom you know are going through a difficult time right now.*

Personal Reflection: ....

....

....

....

....

....

....

An excerpt from Elisabeth Elliot's *Be Still My Soul* (pages 47–53).

Will God Bless My Life If I Am Obedient to Him?

Job 3:1–26

"May the day perish on which I was born,
And the night in which *it was said,*
'A male child is conceived.'" (v. 3)

Can you imagine losing your children, your health, your possessions, having your own spouse tell you to curse God and die? For Job, this pain and sorrow became a reality. In this chapter, Job took out his frustration by cursing the day of his birth and wishing the night that he was conceived would perish (vv. 1–10). In the Hebrew, the term "perish" literally means "cease from existence" or to "be utterly destroyed." Considering how Job had lost everything, one can imagine why Job would question the misfortune of his birth. Job spoke of darkness as equivalent to nothingness in referring to the day of his birth. "Darkness" (Hb. *choshek*, "absence of light" or "separation from light") often is a metaphor for death or destruction.

Job asks a series of "why" questions of God hoping that the answers would somehow ease his pain (vv. 11–23). Unfortunately, Job has to wait until chapter 38 to receive an audience with God. Despite the outpouring of "why" questions and extreme frustration with his current situation, Job never once cursed God. In the meantime, through a series of dialogue with his friends, Job received bad advice (chaps. 4—37). The discussions between Job and each of his three friends begin with the premise that good comes to those who are righteous and evil comes to those who are sinful. Suffering is due to the sin in a person's life. The theological term for this is "retribution theology" or what is found in Buddhism.

Job describes how his afflictions are affecting him and how the very thing Job feared has come upon him (vv. 24–26). Despite losing everything, Job's biggest fear is feeling like God has left him to suffer alone.

There is great encouragement from this passage. Here are five truths reminding you that we serve a God who is in control:

- Obedience unto the Lord has its own reward.
- Godly wisdom is submitting to God regardless of temporary rewards or suffering.
- Personal sin is not the only reason for human suffering.
- Humans are unable fully to grasp God's work and purposes.
- The Lord is over all things.

Jessica Pigg

Prayer: *When you pray, ask God to help you receive help from Him for any trial or difficulty that you might be going through. Tell God that you trust Him because you know that everything is according to His plan and purpose. Finally, read and pray to God Romans 8:28–29 to confirm in your heart that you believe that God wants to use everything in your life to make you more like His Son, Jesus Christ.*

Personal Reflection: ....

....

....

....

....

....

....

Pressing the "Pause" Button

Psalms 3:1–8; 4:1–8

"I cried to the LORD with my voice,
And He heard me from His holy hill. Selah" *(3:4)*

"Selah."

No one knows for sure what it means. The best guess is that it indicates a pause in the psalm's performance, either for silence or a musical interlude. Simply pronouncing the word aloud suggests taking a deep breath: *"Selah."*

Next time you read these two psalms, when you get to the word *"selah,"* substitute "Stop here for awhile and think about this." Then, do that—stop reading for awhile and reflect on the portion just read. Before reading further, anticipate what might be said next, if anything. When you read other psalms, with or without a *"selah,"* try the same approach. This technique is most helpful after you have read the entire psalm more than once.

Taking time to listen to the Lord speak through His Word requires being intentional. Your daily "quiet time" or devotion and prayer time will be most consistent when you establish a routine around it. Like any necessary discipline, to build the habit of spending time with the Lord every day, you must make the appointment with Him on purpose and keep it on purpose.

If you have played a team sport, you know that your team's performance depends largely on time spent with a good coach. Players spend time not only in training or at practice sessions but also listening to the coach's directions before and during the game. Depending on the sport, the coach calls a "time out" at strategic points in the game. Whether the team wins or loses, the team's perspectives and attitudes are built during time spent after the game with an insightful coach who gives both honest evaluations and expert guidance for doing better next time or for pursuing another goal.

Life resembles being "in the game." As a follower of Jesus, you are on His team, along with all the other disciples. Your performance—both yours and that of your team—depends on intentionally spending time with the Lord, stopping to listen to Him. In some sports, training includes watching video footage of you and your team playing the game. Either you or the coach intentionally presses the "pause" button to review a play, analyze technique, or simply to take a break. Spending time with the Lord also requires "pressing the 'pause' button" on your life.

Both Psalms 3 and 4 are prayers voiced in the midst of distress—both the life-threatening kind and the sort involving the inner turmoil of trying to make sense of grievous circumstances. Maybe that's why the word *"selah"* appears five times in this pair. At such times you need, more than ever, to pause for prayer. David did (3:5; 4:4, 8).

Tamra Hernandez

Prayer: *Press the "pause" button right now instead of rushing to the next thing in your life. Be still and talk with the Lord. He hears and responds.*

Personal Reflection:

Trusting God in the Waiting Room Times of Life

Psalm 13:1–6

"How long, O Lord? Will you forget me forever?
How long will You hide Your face from me?" (v. 1)

Sometimes it is hardest to accept the **waiting** parts of life. I think of the story told by Amy Carmichael in her first year of missionary work in Japan. She and a missionary couple were delayed on a journey because of a boat that did not arrive. Not just hours but days went by, and the young missionary began to fret because of the time lost and the consequences to others who counted on them. The older missionary said calmly, "God knows all about the boats." It became a maxim of faith for the rest of her life.

Many times in my life God has asked me to wait when I wanted to move forward. He has kept me in the dark when I asked for light. I like to see progress. I look for evidence that God is at least doing something. If the Shepherd leads us beside still waters when we were hoping for whitewater excitement, it is hard to believe anything really vital is taking place. God is silent. The house is silent. The phone doesn't ring. The mailbox is empty. The stillness is hard to bear—and God knows that. He knows our frame and remembers we are made of dust. He is very patient with us when we are trying to be patient with Him. Of course for most of us this test of waiting does not take place in a silent and empty house, but in the course of regular work and appointments and taxpaying and grocery buying and trying to have the car fixed and get the storm windows up; daily decisions have to go on being made, responsibilities fulfilled, families provided for, employers satisfied. Can we accept the patience-taxing ordinary things alongside the four-alarm fires of our lives?

Psalm 16:5 is one of my life verses now: "Lord, you have assigned me my portion and my cup; you have made my lot secure" (NIV, 1984). My "lot" is what happens to me—my share of that which comes by the will of the Power that rules my destiny. My lot includes the circumstances of my birth, my upbringing, my job, my hardships, the people I work with, my marital status, hindrances, obstacles, accidents, and opportunities. Everything constitutes my lot. Nothing excepted. If I can accept that fact at every turn in the road, I have indeed stepped into everlasting arms even more securely, and there I will find peace and joy.

Elisabeth Elliot

Prayer: *Ask the Lord to help you trust Him in those "waiting room" times in your life (Ps. 13:5). Pray that you will have perseverance and diligence in seeking His wisdom and not lose heart if the answer isn't clear immediately.*

Personal Reflection: ....

....

....

....

....

....

....

....

An excerpt from Elisabeth Elliot's *Be Still My Soul* (pages 33–35).

The Practice of Praying Through a Psalm

Psalm 19:1–14

⌒

"Let the words of my mouth and the meditation of my heart
Be acceptable in Your sight,
O Lord, my strength and my Redeemer." (v. 14)

One of the most meaningful habits I have practiced in the last few years during my time of reading the Bible is to pray through a passage, thanking God for any truths revealed, confessing any sin highlighted in the passage that I might have committed, claiming any promises of God, asking for strength to obey any commands or godly examples, and many other things. Each passage serves as its own unique guide for prayer.

Let's try it with Psalm 19—in these 14 brief verses, God is unpacking a lot of wisdom for His people. In verses 1–6, David, who wrote this Psalm, talks about how all creation declares God's glory. Reflect on how an amazing sunset can take a person's breath away or how gentle waves can calm an anxious soul—these things are God's handiwork! He is the master artist, and the creation declares His power. Consider taking time just to sit outside, thanking and praising God for His creation.

In verses 7–11, David praises the incredible qualities and impact of the Word of God. God's Word is "perfect, converting the soul," and is "sure, making wise the simple" (v. 7); it is "right," bringing joy to the heart, and is "pure, enlightening the eyes" (v. 8). God's judgments are true *and* righteous, helping God's servants be warned (v. 11). Praise God for giving us His Word, which even more so than His splendid creation, reveals His glory and truth. His Word is His love letter to His children to guide us on how to live. Ask the Lord to give you a hunger for His Word.

In verses 12 and 13, David gives us some specific prayers to pray. First, pray that you would be cleansed from "secret *faults*" (v. 12)—these are "hidden" sins you may not even be aware of, things you may be doing or thinking that you do not realize are wrong. Second, pray that you would be kept from "presumptuous *sins*" (v. 13)—these are things you know are sins yet you do them anyway. David asks the Lord to keep him from letting sin have dominion or rule over him (v. 13). That's a wise prayer for us all to pray so that we are not slaves to sin, especially since God, not sin, is our Master!

In the final verse of this psalm, David prays that his words and the meditation of his heart would be acceptable to God. Then David praises God, who is his strength and Redeemer. Do you ever struggle with "taming your tongue"? Follow David's example in asking the Lord, who redeemed you and gives you strength, to help you speak only "pleasing" words and dwell on pleasing things.

Candi Finch

Prayer: *Consider taking time to pray through each section of this Psalm.*

Personal Reflection: ....

....

....

....

....

....

....

Why Should I Fear in the Days of Evil?

Psalm 49:1–20

"Why should I fear in the days of evil,
When *the iniquity at my heels surrounds me?" (v. 5)*

Our society prides itself on having the latest and greatest product on the market. Mistakenly, we have come to the conclusion that material possessions and wealth can answer all of our problems and fill a void in our lives that only Jesus can fill.

This wisdom psalm addresses and reflects on the inadequacy of wealth and the certainty of death. The question in verse 5 is the key to understanding the whole Psalm. The psalmist was concerned about being in a situation made dangerous by the sinful people who spent their time seeking wealth and prosperity instead of seeking after the Lord. The psalmist's tone in the question is one of confidence and assurance. He knew that he could trust in the Lord's protection when everyone around him was pursuing evil.

This psalm does not condemn those who have abundance of resources or wealth; it simply argues that those who pursue wealth, as though it will give their life meaning or contentment, are severely mistaken. Wealth cannot secure a lasting and fulfilled life. Only the blood of Christ can purchase eternal life. Money cannot prevent death. When the wealthy die, their wealth simply passes into the hands of others (v. 10). Only the wise person recognizes the limitations of money. Jesus taught His followers that "One's life does not consist in the abundance of the things he possesses" (Luke 12:15). The fate of those who trust in wealth compared to those who trust in God is contrasted in Psalm 49:13–15. The confidence that comes from being redeemed from the grave by the eternal God is far more valuable than money and possessions.

Do not fear the one who has an abundance of earthly wealth. Understand that true riches are found in knowing and living for God. As believers, it is important that we live and walk by the Spirit. If we do not, we certainly will become consumed with the materialism of other people and lose sight of God's sovereign plan for our lives. Although we may struggle, in the power of God, we can have the same resolve as the psalmist.

Jessica Pigg

Prayer: *When you pray, ask God to give you eyes to see as He sees. Ask Him to help you keep your eyes fixed upon Him and less on the things of this world. Tell God that you trust in Him alone and you desire to seek only after the riches that can be stored up in the kingdom of heaven. Finally, read Matthew 6:19–21, meditate on this truth, and pray to God for His provision.*

Personal Reflection: ....

....

....

....

....

....

....

Can God Forgive Me?

Psalm 51:1–19

༄

"Against You, You only, have I sinned,
And done this evil in Your sight." (v. 4a)

David wrote this psalm sometime after God sent the prophet Nathan to confront him in a straightforward but loving way (see 2 Sam. 11—12). As Israel's king, David served as the "pastor-in-chief" as well as commander-in-chief under the Lord's authority. When he chose to commit adultery and murder, trying to keep it secret, he sinned "big-time." When the Lord used Nathan to bring David face-to-face with what he had done, David acknowledged simply, "I have sinned against the LORD" (2 Sam. 12:13a).

A woman asking, "Can God forgive me?" often has long believed a lie that Satan uses to keep people from accepting God's forgiveness. The enemy tries to convince you that your sin is the worst and that its consequences are insurmountable. These are lies. The truth is that what blocks access to God's forgiveness is not how terrible the sin is but your own unwillingness to "come clean." Actually, when asked with sincerity—instead of making excuses for the sin or trying to explain it away—this question indicates that the heart is not hardened against the convicting work of the Holy Spirit, who wants to use the guilt to help you recognize your need for Him (John 16:8; 1 Cor. 11:32).

Look for the question, "Can God forgive me?" in Psalm 51. You won't find it. David knew already that God could forgive him because David knew God. Today, the same God offers forgiveness exclusively through Christ (John 3:16–17; Rom. 6:23). God forgives because the separation that sin causes between you and God (Is. 59:2) has already been overcome in the death and resurrection of His Son, Jesus Christ (see Acts 10:43; Rom. 3:22–25; 8:1–39). His blood covers any and all sin (Heb. 10:19). The forgiveness and cleansing He offers are free because of the great cost He paid (Rom. 5:8; 2 Cor. 5:21; Heb. 2:17–18).

In Psalm 51, David does not name his specific sins, perhaps because the Lord wanted every reader to be able to apply the pattern of prayer to her sin, whatever that sin is. If you or someone you know needs to seek God's forgiveness, let this prayer of confession and repentance serve as a much-needed model (cp. 1 John 1:7–9). David . . .

- went straight to God and requested "mercy" on the basis of God's character (v. 1);
- confessed, recognizing that God had seen everything and agreeing with God's just condemnation (vv. 3–4);
- acknowledged that fundamentally, his sin had sabotaged the one all-important relationship in life—his relationship with God (v. 4);
- prayed for God to cleanse, heal, forgive, and restore (vv. 7–14); and
- praised God for His righteousness.

Tamra Hernandez

Prayer: *Confess your sins. Thank the Lord for paying the price Himself to forgive any and every sin. Today, accept His grace and walk in obedience.*

Personal Reflection: ....

....

....

....

....

....

A Unique Collection

Psalm 56:1–13

"You number my wanderings;
Put my tears into Your bottle;
Are they not in Your book?" (v. 8)

In 1 Samuel 20, David questioned the thoughts and intents of King Saul, whom he had served so well. Jonathan, King Saul's son, confirmed David's suspicions that the King intended to kill him. David took flight from Jerusalem only to end up in the territory of an old enemy, the Philistines.

First, David found refuge in Nob, the city of the Priest, where he received provisions, including the sword of Goliath the Philistine (1 Sam. 22:10). Goliath, David's initial opponent, was noticed by King Saul. David's visit to Nob proved deadly for the priest who blessed him because he was observed by King Saul's chief servant, who informed the king of David's progress. David took flight from Nob to Gath, where he encountered Achish, the lord of Gath, in Philistine territory. There David pretended to have an insane moment to protect himself from destruction.

Although overwhelmed by enemies on every hand, David sensed God's presence. He was taken captive by God's preservation of his tears, the release of his bottled-up emotions. A book keeps a record of the drops of pain that were caused by the pursuit of his enemies. Trust and fear tugged against one another. Tears on top of tears were stored for safe keeping in the bottle of the Lord.

The fight to keep our emotions in check can end up brutal. To surrender to tears can appear as a sign of weakness. Instead, the collection of our tears by the Lord will prove as a sign of the past when we enter the land of no more: "And God will wipe away every tear from their eyes" (Rev. 7:17). In 2 Samuel 22, David sang a song to the Lord for deliverance from all His enemies and King Saul (vv. 1–51). After a time of tremendous suffering, the Lord brought victory and rest to King David.

I have lost sight of God on several occasions when battling both seen and unseen enemies. A season of unforeseen danger overwhelmed me. When my opponents were revealed, I trembled in disbelief. How could I allow someone to come so close who desired my destruction? Hidden agendas are very common to mankind. The motives are rarely understood, even when an explanation is given. The pain and agony experienced while searching for answers kept me in a state of suspicion. I wanted the freedom to trust my surroundings again, but new challenges kept me at bay.

Tear-stained eyes and weary days have made time stand still for me. When I surrendered to the act of forgiveness and recalled all the times the Lord rescued me in the past, I received strength to walk freely again. I joined the psalmist David who said, "This I know, because God *is* for me" (Ps. 56:9).

Elizabeth W. Luter

Prayer: *Ask for relief from the onslaught of your enemies. Spend time in the Word of God to increase your faith. Release your tears and fears into the Master's hands.*

Personal Reflection: ....

....

....

....

....

....

In God Alone

Psalm 62:1–12

෴

> *"My soul, wait silently for God alone,*
> *For my expectation is from Him.*
> *He only is my rock and my salvation;*
> *He is my defense;*
> *I shall not be moved." (vv. 5–6)*

Have you ever faced a problem so immense that, even after careful consideration and numerous sincere attempts, you could not see how it would possibly be resolved in a redemptive way? David was apparently in such a quandary as he wrote this psalm. He is known to be a resourceful man, well able to fend for himself in battle, whether against lions or men. Yet, here, he is admitting that he cannot face his adversary on his own. Interestingly, he does not spend any time coming up with a back-up plan in case his Plan A—depending on God—doesn't work. No, he is putting all his trust in God. There is no Plan B.

Several years ago, Brook was struggling with substance abuse. When confronted on numerous occasions, she repeatedly said she was going to stop. She rejected offers of recovery programs and addiction counseling. Brook thought she could handle the issue on her own. But, in the meantime, she betrayed family relationships and compromised her reputation with friends and employers.

One night, Brook chose to get high "one more time," but this time she was caught and the confrontation resulted in an ultimatum: Get help or go to jail. Help came in the form of a year-long, faith-based recovery program where she learned that only God could help her overcome her drug problem. While she is no longer in the residential part of the recovery program, Brook continues to surround herself with spiritual accountability to keep her studying the Word and depending on God. She understands that, when she depends on her own strength, she is susceptible once again to the desire to use—and abuse—drugs and alcohol. In order to stay clean and continue progressing in her recovery, she can't rely on a Plan B. Her life was restored by the God who is her "rock" and her "salvation." He was her only defense then, and He is her only defense now.

While substance abuse may not be our vice, we all need to stop relying on our own efforts to fix our problems, whether they are caused by our own poor choices or the hurtful choices of others toward us. We must reach out to the only One who **can** save and defend us and believe that He will. Then we can look with expectation for Him to do what only He can do. This takes Plan B off the table and has us putting all our attention onto the God of our salvation.

Judi Jackson

Prayer: *What have you tried to overcome in your own strength or willpower? Acknowledge that the Lord is able and wants to help you . . . that He alone is your salvation. Ask Him to be your rock, to defend you in this challenge so that you will draw near to Him and stay there!*

Personal Reflection: ....

....

....

....

....

....

....

No One Is Invisible to God

Psalm 68:1–6

"A father of the fatherless, a defender of widows,
Is God in His holy habitation
God sets the solitary in families;
He brings out those who are bound." (vv. 5–6a)

The daily news is flooded with tragic stories of hurting people in our broken world. Yet, everyday there are even more stories that go unheard—the stories of children dying from malnourishment and treatable diseases; stories of women in all corners of the globe struggling to survive after being abused or abandoned; and stories of institutional injustice and people subjugated for the financial gain of their oppressors. Many of these people must feel invisible and weighed down by their reality, which the world never notices. Who will provide safety for the abused, love for the fatherless, or provision for the widow?

Our God cares for the poor and the helpless. In the day of the psalmist, society did not care for the orphans, widows, or homeless. They were left destitute, with no one to take up their causes. The psalmist recognized God's compassion for the broken and lonely, and wrote that He is "a father to the fatherless" and "a defender of widows" (v. 5). The psalmist also described beautifully how God brings together those discarded by society, placing them in families (v. 6). Those who have no safe place and no providers find in Him the solace and comfort they desperately need.

The same God who defended widows and cared for orphans in the day of the psalmist continues to care for the downtrodden today. No one was invisible to God then, and no one is invisible to God now. Christ's body on earth, the church, is called to take up the cause that moves His heart. There are widows in your community who likely feel invisible—how could you let them know God cares? There are men and women in literal and figurative bondage—how could you be a part of setting them free? There are children who desperately need to live within families—how could you become a safe place for them?

When we participate in compassionate ministry for those whom society has rejected, we carry God's love to the individual, but we also display God's bountiful care to the world. The power of the gospel is that it compels us and enables us to meet the needs of those who need God's care. When we are faithful, God multiplies our efforts and turns skeptics into believers. Only when God's love and care for the individual is on display can a woman without Him recognize what she lacks.

Rhonda Harrington Kelley

Prayer: *Ask the Lord to open your eyes to the people around you who are neglected or abused. Reach out to share his love and salvation with those with physical and spiritual needs. See them like God sees them—people created in His image and for His purpose.*

Personal Reflection: ....

....

....

....

....

....

....

When I Am Old and Gray

Psalm 71:1–24

~

"Now also when I am old and grayheaded
O God, do not forsake me,
Until I declare Your strength to this generation,
Your power to everyone who is to come." (v. 18)

Older people who have known the Lord from their youth are quick to share their trust of Him as their rock, fortress, refuge, and hope (vv. 1–3). God is worthy of their continual praise because He has sustained them from the womb (v. 6). However, the challenge of an older person is often that nagging feeling that he is no longer useful to God. He longs for the Lord's continued presence with him (v. 9).

Those who are in their senior years must praise God because He has already responded to their prayers or because they know that God's answer is certain to come. As is the psalmist, those who are now closer to the end of life than to the beginning do well to remind the Lord of their continued need for His presence in their lives so that they can proclaim the Lord's power to future generations. How wonderful to come to the end of life with a positive outlook and with joy in the Lord. Whatever the troubles and afflictions, faith will triumph over all for those who put their trust in the Lord. No matter what your age may be, you always have a future when you are secure in your relationship with the Lord.

Because I am a grandparent, I love to read this psalm as a reminder to me of the stewardship of legacy I have the opportunity to impart to the next generation and even to my children's children. I want to share my faith with those coming after me, remembering the benchmarks in my faith journey. To tell my granddaughters how God has spoken to me and guided me in this journey creates for them spiritual roots stretching even to the generation before their parents and, in the process, teaching them some family history. Reading Scripture together, singing great hymns, talking about specific blessings God has bestowed on our family—all these record memories to be awakened in the future for our offspring and even the generations after them. I also treasure the years I can pray for those in these subsequent generations who may be called to take up my mantle and continue service to the Lord in some of the same ways I have served Him.

Dorothy Kelley Patterson

Prayer: *Review the Lord's faithfulness to you in the past and give Him thanks. Commit to Him that you will continue to trust Him whatever the future may bring. Ask Him to use you to declare His strength to the next generation.*

Personal Reflection: ....

....

....

....

....

....

....

....

Learning from Mistakes of the Past

Psalm 78:1–11

"That the generation to come might know them,
The children who *would be born,*
That *they may arise and declare* them *to their children,*
That they may set their hope in God,
And not forget the works of God,
But keep His commandments." (vv. 6–7)

Legacy is a many-faceted opportunity. Psalm 78 is a *maschil* (Hb., suggesting "teaching or giving insight into practical living"). In other words, it has a teaching purpose. As a parent and grandparent, I can leave to succeeding generations possessions, accessories, items with historical or sentimental value, passing on to those whom I love a reminder of me. However, the poet who penned Psalm 78 is writing about something intangible and far more valuable for the generations to come. He uses Israel's history to teach his lessons, describing the mistakes of Israel's forefathers, detailing the ways God's people had disobeyed Him despite the Lord's overwhelming blessings upon them. He begins with their deliverance from slavery in Egypt and continues with their conquest of the land of promise.

The mystery of ingratitude remains until this day. Despite the Lord's abundant mercy and outpouring of blessings, His people still rebel against Him as they did in the day of the psalmist. Yet we have a wonderful tool for passing along valuable insights in the lessons learned from past failures and from God's Word transferred from generation to generation so that each generation has the advantage of learning from the mistakes of those who have gone before.

Few families spend time together reading the Bible and praying. My husband and I were both blessed to be reared in homes with regular family worship. We incorporated this discipline in the daily routines of our home. On weekdays, we were more relaxed and flexible in our time at the dinner table. On Saturdays, we had a late and very leisurely breakfast, took time to answer questions about the biblical passage read, and shared requests for prayer. On Sundays we had some very insightful discussions of Sunday school lessons and/or the sermon as we traveled to and from church.

Family time around God's Word can be done in different settings and with whatever time is available. Yet for a toddler or child or teenager to hear his father read God's Word and perhaps make some comments on its importance and to remember his mother's voice praying for specific needs in his life become treasured memories—genuine "stones of help" for the future!

Dorothy Kelley Patterson

Prayer: *Consider asking the Lord's help for you in carving out some time for the family to gather around God's word in your home. If you are single, perhaps you can identify a young person in your extended family or one God has especially placed in your heart; then be creative in determining a time for you to share this spiritual legacy.*

Personal Reflection: ....

....

....

....

....

....

....

Brevity of Life

Psalm 90:1–17

~

"We finish our years like a sigh." (v. 9b)

The first person to die in Scripture was Abel, son of Adam and Eve, brother of Cain (Gen. 4:8). When Adam and Eve consumed the forbidden fruit, they died spiritually while continuing to live physically. When Cain killed his brother, Abel never moved from the place where he fell. Adam, Eve, and Cain truly realized the difference between spiritual death and physical death. The name "Abel" means "vapor" or "mist" or "breath." One moment he was here, the next moment he was gone. Even if we lived the 969 years of the lifespan of Methuselah, life is brief.

For a modern twist, one might look at Moses in this way: He was a journal keeper (Num. 33). He instituted the first 4-H Club for Keeping the Commands of God: Heart, House, Hand, and Head (Deut. 6). He was a song writer (Ex. 15). Near the end of his life, God commissioned Moses to write the very first Rock song (Deut. 32).

The 120 years Moses spent on earth divide into three major life events: 40 years in Egypt in the house of Pharaoh, 40 years in the desert of Midian herding sheep, and 40 years in the wilderness leading the mumbling, grumbling children of Israel, longing for those solitary desert days. Somewhere between Mt. Sinai where he received the laws of God and Mt. Nebo where he died in the arms of God, Moses became a psalmist.

Psalm 90:1–8 declares God is eternal. Man is temporary. God existed before the mountains that He fashioned. Man lives in the shadow of them. From everlasting (before the beginning) to everlasting (after the end), God is God. Man was formed from the dust of the ground. One might say that only God is "older than dirt!" A thousand years on our timetable is a blip on the radar from God's perspective. God is forever. Man is a one-day wonder.

Man lives from moan to moan to moan, completing his years like a barely-audible, last-gasp whisper (v. 9). No one is guaranteed a 70-year lifespan (v. 10).

After age 70, my grandmother said she was living on borrowed time. Her goal was to live to be fourscore (80 years old) and foursquare. Moses had discovered what every senior adult learns: Getting old isn't easy! The ever increasing "labor and sorrow" presses down with each passing year as the physical struggles pile up.

In response to these truths, Psalm 90:11–17 notes several bullet prayer points. TEACH us to highly value each day. ACCEPT our wisdom hearts as a gift. GRANT us mercy and lovingkindness. TRADE all of our days of affliction for days of gladness. REVEAL to us a clear understanding of Your plan. PERMIT future generations to experience your majesty. BLESS us with favor. CONFIRM that we are working in fields of Your choosing.

Becky Brown

Prayer: *As you go to the Lord in prayer, ask yourself these questions: Breath or death? Strength or sorrow? Then remember: Final sigh could be nigh. Lift God high!*

Personal Reflection:

Let Us Break Bread Together

Psalm 104:1–35

"These all wait for You,
That You may give them *their food in due season." (v. 27)*

Psalm 104 is a splendid psalm of praise for the Lord's provision for His creatures. This passage follows the account of creation in Genesis 1 then transitions
to the creation of the world and His gracious provision to all its inhabitants.
Indeed, every creature on earth looks to the Lord for His provision.

Our culture loves food. We are bombarded with visuals of food through
virtually every mode of communication. Television shows, magazines, books,
websites and social media keep food before us 24/7. Moreover, we are told, "We
are what we eat." We try to make good choices of what we put into our bodies.
However, we can be so concentrated on **what** we eat that maybe we forget the
purpose of why God has designed our bodies with the need for food. God has
designed us to be dependent on His provision, a constant, natural reminder that
we need Him, physically and spiritually.

A woman can easily focus on the meal and not on the **mealtime**. There is a
key difference. Wives and mothers usually have the responsibility for preparing
the food for their families. Mealtimes are so much more than what is presented
on our table. Mealtimes should be a time when the family comes together to
thank the Lord for His provision in our lives. It should be a time of love, encouragement, and joy as the family shares food and conversation to the glory of God,
focusing on the biblical truth in verse 27.

The family mealtime must be prioritized and protected. Commitment
is required from every person in the family. Parents may need to curtail
social outings and eliminate some extracurricular activities for the children.
Although it is a personal sacrifice, think of mealtimes as an opportunity to
honor God together.

Scripture provides several accounts of Christ enjoying meals in social
settings. In almost every account, the **food** isn't mentioned. The focus is on

the **fellowship**. Christ is reaching out to the outcasts of society (Luke 5:29–32; 14:12–14), encouraging his weary disciples (John 21:2), and teaching and admonishing those whom He loved dearly (John 12:1–2).

God has made our bodies to need continual nourishment through food, but we also need continual love, encouragement, and admonishment from one another. The table is the perfect place. We are reminded of our need for food and need for God through His continued provision in our lives.

Karen B. Allen

Prayer: *Thank the Lord for His provision in your life and pray He will send others into your life to share the joy and goodness He provides to His children.*

Personal Reflection: ....

....

....

....

....

....

....

....

Scripture Memory

Psalm 119:1–16

"Your word I have hidden in my heart,
That I might not sin against You." (v. 11)

Have you ever helped your children learn their memory verses only to find that they recalled them perfectly the next day but you could not remember the first word? You are not alone! Does that mean that Scripture memory is only for kids seeking to earn badges on Wednesday nights? Hardly.

The psalmist gives scores of reasons in this in-depth, lengthy psalm to demonstrate how passionately he loves the Word. Just a few verses into the chapter, we are given one of his chief motivations for memorizing the Word. He believes God's truth will serve as an aid to keep him from sinning. If he has the Word stored up in his heart, it will be brought readily to mind when situations arise requiring discernment. The psalmist obviously did not have the complete canon of Scripture that we have now. The inspired words of Paul reveal that the Word is also "profitable for doctrine, for reproof, for correction, for instruction in righteousness" (2 Tim. 3:16).

Why then are we often remiss about the process of hiding that precious Word in our hearts? Maybe we do think it is just for kids. Are we so busy that we are pleased with ourselves for reading a portion of the Bible on a regular basis but we lack diligence to actually memorize passages?

I have been convicted of my own lack of attention to this vital spiritual discipline in recent years. After doing a bit of research into some of the many memorization methods that exist, I was highly motivated to take the Charlotte Mason method and adapt it for my personal use. Instead of using a file box, I use a presentation book so I can photocopy pages from my Study Bible to place there. This approach works great for a visual learner. The method is simple and organized even as it facilitates review of previously learned verses. Other methods work too! Find one that you like and stop making excuses.

Pray about what passages of Scripture you should learn. If you are a new believer, it's wonderful to memorize passages rich in doctrine. If you are going through a difficult time, choose a passage that encourages and provides assurance. We should all be familiar with verses that will assist us in sharing the gospel with clarity. Be sure that the Lord will use this spiritual discipline to magnify your walk with Him in ways that you might not even imagine. And yes, it will certainly serve just as the psalmist said to discourage us from sinning against our Lord.

Mary K. Mohler

Prayer: *Ask the Lord to forgive you if you have not taken Scripture memory seriously. Ask Him to point you to the method, passages, and, if necessary, a mentor, to get started now. Get ready to be amazed as the Holy Spirit assists you in hiding the Word in your heart for life.*

Personal Reflection: ....

....

....

....

....

....

....

To the Very End

Psalm 119:105–112

"Your testimonies I have taken as a heritage forever,
For they are the rejoicing of my heart.
I have inclined my heart to perform Your statutes
Forever, to the very end." (vv. 111–112)

In this stanza of Psalm 119, the psalmist is on a dangerous and difficult road (vv. 107, 110). We have no trouble imagining ourselves on this perilous path—stumbling over obstacles and trying to avoid potholes. The righteous light provided by God's Word is a welcome help (v. 105). The Bible does not change our circumstances or make the difficulties go away, it simply reveals the danger, the way through it or around it, and shows us the way.

Even the weariest traveler is revived when helped along by the light of God's Word (v. 107). Our family once took a long hike in the mountains. Unaccustomed to the altitude and weighed down by our backpacks, we all grew very tired. We had come too far to turn back, but were beginning to despair of our youngest child making it to the campsite when we remembered the asthma inhaler in his backpack. He took a puff and soon skipped ahead of us all. We were glad to see him revived but were also frustrated that we had not remembered his medication sooner. We might all have enjoyed the hike a whole lot more if he had been strengthened.

The psalmist proclaims that he will not forget the law that he has at his disposal (v. 109). He vows to keep the Word, asks the Lord to teach it to him, and declares that he will not stray from it. If you want to avoid falling into sin or tripping over difficulties in your walk, you can follow the example of the psalmist. Keep God's Word close by reading, studying, meditating, and memorizing it. If there is something you do not understand, you can ask the Holy Spirit to give you insight and understanding, and you can seek out faithful teachers in the body of Christ. You will never experience the full benefits of God's Word unless you commit to staying on the path it illuminates.

On that camping trip I mentioned, one group took a wrong turn and did some wandering around in the mountains. They eventually arrived at the campsite, but they were colder, wetter, and far grumpier than necessary. God does help us get back on the path when we walk away from His precepts, but we always lose something in the straying. There is a deliberate decision in obeying God's Word. We must incline our hearts to His path—the one that will take us to the very end.

Christi Gibson

Prayer: *Take a few moments to rejoice in God's Word, thanking Him for the way He has guided you with His precepts in the past. Ask the Lord to show you ways that you can incline your heart to His statutes today and strengthen you to follow through to the end.*

Personal Reflection: ....

....

....

....

....

....

....

Unless the Lord Builds the House

Psalm 127:1–5

"Unless the LORD builds the house,
They labor in vain who build it." (v. 1)

The Bible includes many stories of families, both good and bad. God gives us examples of the joys and challenges of family life. In the first home, Eve disobeyed God and led Adam to sin (Gen. 3). Rebekah started out as a young woman sensitive to the Lord, but wound up showing partiality to Jacob, her youngest son, and deceiving her husband (Gen. 24:12–21). Jezebel led her husband, King Ahab of Israel, away from God and into the worship of idols (1 Kin. 19). God led Ruth, a girl from Moab, to follow her mother-in-law in worshipping the one true God and in going to live in Bethlehem (Ruth 1). There she met and married Boaz. In their lineage was King David and ultimately Jesus Christ.

Marriage is under attack today possibly more than ever before. We start our marriages so much in love with our husbands that we think we can't stand it. Then come some days that we just can't stand it! A woman came in from work one day and began packing a bag. Her husband asked, "What are you doing?" She replied, "I'm leaving. I just can't stand it anymore!" He pulled out a suitcase and started packing. She said, "What are you doing?" He replied, "I can't stand it anymore either. I'm going with you."

Throughout Scripture, God gives us principles for a healthy, holy, and happy marriage. Husbands are to love their wives as Christ loved the church (Eph. 5:22). Wives must submit to their own husbands as unto the Lord (v. 33). The wife should respect her husband. Finding ways to show respect for your husband is more important to him than showing you love him. He knows you love him, but he needs your respect.

Children are a blessing from the Lord. They are also a great responsibility. In the home, children get the first glimpse of God. Deuteronomy 6:6–9 gives the plan for instructing children. They see you serve God and love Him. They experience affection first in the home. They come to understand authority as the husband is head of the home and submission as the mother gives the example. They should experience unconditional love and acceptance. They should learn patience as they are disciplined in a just way, in love and not anger.

As we depend on the Lord and follow His guidance, we will not labor in vain. Accept your husband as God's gift to you. God knew exactly what you needed when He chose your man. Accept your husband's love as he can give it, knowing that men and women express love in different ways. Accept your children and choose joy in rearing them.

Barbara O'Chester

Prayer: *Ask the Lord to help you to depend on Him today in the challenges of family living. He will enable you to show your love in your home.*

Personal Reflection: ....

....

....

....

....

....

....

Monogamy—God's Perfect Plan for Marriage

Psalm 128:1–6

"Your wife shall be *like a fruitful vine*
In the very heart of your house." *(v. 3a)*

One man—one woman for life was God's ideal. The word "monogamy" comes from two Greek words: *monos*, meaning "one," and *gameō*, meaning "marry" or "take a wife." Literally, monogamy is marriage to one person. Genesis 2:24 says: "Therefore a man shall leave his father and mother and be joined [cleave] to his wife, and they shall become one flesh." This verse presents God's plan for a heterosexual, monogamous relationship in marriage.

Psalm 128 implies monogamy as it speaks of those who have an awesome reverence for the Lord. They will eat from the labor of their own hands. The wife will be fruitful and bear children. They will sit around their table in the heart of their home. It's a joyful blessed scene. Psychologists tell us that if a family sits down at the table for dinner four to five times a week, teenagers are far less likely to get involved in alcohol or drugs. Even if you bring in fast food, sit down and talk.

God allowed polygamy, but it was not His first plan. Lamech in Genesis 4:19 was the first man recorded as having two wives in the Bible. God had promised Abram a son but even Abraham, father of the faithful, friend of God, got tired of waiting and took his wife's suggestion to sleep with her maid Hagar. Trouble began as soon as Hagar got pregnant. She became arrogant and Sarai became jealous and mistreated her so badly that she ran away. God sent her back and told her to submit to Sarai (Gen. 16:1–13). Ultimately, Hagar and Ishmael had to leave permanently (Gen. 21). Thousands of years have passed and the enmity between the descendants of Isaac and Ishmael has grown more volatile.

In Matthew 19:4–6, Jesus quoted God's words in Genesis 2:24 reiterating God's plan of monogamy. Paul's teaching on marriage in Ephesians 5 presents the idea of one man and one woman for life. In 1 Peter 3:1–7, the author refers to monogamy when teaching wives to be submissive to their own husbands.

Although polygamy was prevalent among the Romans, monogamy was one factor that distinguished Christians in the New Testament era.

God's arithmetic says one plus one equals one. It's a **biological miracle** that two become one since it is a physical impossibility for one plus one to equal one. It is a **social miracle** for two families to be joined together. It is a **spiritual miracle** for marriage to be compared to the relationship between Jesus and His bride the church.

Some people in this country practice polygamy with devastating consequences for the women involved. Some of these same problems are experienced when Christian families divorce. Children are left feeling confused, hurt, and rejected. Too often they are forced to deal with step-parents and step-siblings and must divide up holidays and summer vacations. God's plan for marriage was perfect then and is perfect now!

Barbara O'Chester

Prayer: *Ask the Lord to help your home be a witness of His mercy and grace.*

Personal Reflection: ....

....

....

....

....

....

Every Life Is Special

Psalm 139:13–16

~

"For You formed my inward parts;
You covered me in my mother's womb.
I will praise You, for I am fearfully and wonderfully made;
Marvelous are Your works,
And that my soul knows very well." (vv. 13–14)

My children and I love playing around on Google Earth. It is so much fun to watch the satellite zoom across the globe and hone in on our home. (We can even spot the yellow slide from our swing set in our backyard.) For many of us, we may know *in our minds* we serve such an all-powerful, all-present and all-knowing God, but this passage reveals a God that hones in on us individually and personally—far surpassing Google Earth. God's love for us is seen in how He has created each one of us in His own image. The degree to which He has personalized His love and concern is deeply personal and is almost unfathomable. What a love and comfort this brings **to our hearts**!

Psalm 139 is a beautiful worship psalm that is deeply personal. God's attributes are revealed: omniscience (God knowing all things), omnipresence (God being everywhere at all times), and omnipotence (God's supreme power). David is meditating on the omnipotence of God and relishing in the fact that God has known him from his mother's womb. God knows us the way a painter knows his picture or a sculptor knows his statue. He knows us from concept to reality, from creation to completion.

How sad and unfortunate that one cannot read this passage in our culture without considering abortion! It is absolutely heartbreaking that this unthinkable tragedy remains legal in our country and is a societal "norm." We see through this text the sanctity of life as our divine maker established it (see also Jer. 1:5). We must faithfully remind those in our society "when" life begins, as stated so movingly in this passage.

Not only does God know us in the womb, but He also knows us our entire lives. We serve a sovereign God, actively molding and shaping our lives. What an encouraging thought that nothing in our lives catches God by surprise! John Calvin wrote: "We need not then wonder if God, who formed man so perfectly in the womb, should have an exact knowledge of him after he is ushered into the world."* As with the psalmist, when we meditate on the wonderful works of the Lord, a unique awareness of God's grace in our lives is revealed. The only fitting response as part of God's creation is a song of thanksgiving as we see modeled by David in this passage.

Karen B. Allen

Prayer: *Thank the Lord for purposefully and deliberately creating you and for His intimate care of every detail in your life. Ask the Lord for wisdom to know His perfect plan for your life.*

Personal Reflection: ....

....

....

....

....

....

* John Calvin, *Commentary on the Book of Psalms*, vol. 5, trans. James Anderson (Grand Rapids: Christian Classics Ethereal Library), notes on Psalm 139:15.

What Is the Passion of Your Heart?

Psalm 146:1–11

"Happy is he who has the God of Jacob for his help,
Whose hope is in the LORD his God." (v. 5)

Very early in my Christian walk, my spiritual mentor Verna Birkey shared with me a motto that consistently stimulates my passion to pursue becoming a woman after God's heart: "I am a personal representative of the living God, on assignment to make God visible to others around me" (Matt. 22:37). Psalm 146 provides some helpful guidelines to practically apply this motto to my daily life. Perhaps they will assist you in your journey to being known as a woman after God's heart.

The psalmist . . .

- **calls for a commitment to praise** (Ps. 146:1–2). Do I choose to praise God as an act of my will even when I do not like the circumstances? Remember that the Psalms are written to the will, not the emotions, and that contentment is an acquired character quality (Phil. 4:11–13).
- **challenges trust in God rather than people** (Ps. 146:3–4). Is my reflex reaction to trust my heavenly Father who can meet my every need or is my first response to rely upon people (Phil. 4:19)?
- **focuses on God's faithfulness to previous generations** (Ps. 146:5). Do I study the lives of people of the Old and New Testaments believing that God will faithfully care for me as He did for them (Heb. 11)?
- **offers assurance that God executes justice when I am wronged, provides for my physical needs, and always loves and protects me** (Ps. 146:7–9). Do I believe that there is no good thing that my heavenly Father will withhold from me if I am walking uprightly (Ps. 84:11)?
- **promises that God's truths are eternal** (146:10). Do I trust in the eternal Word of God rather than cultural or religious fads (Is. 40:6–8)?

When my Lord calls me home or comes for me, and when others sort through my belongings, I want my reading and viewing materials, files, correspondence, and all of the other items associated with my life to reflect my faith. My heart's desire is that what remains will validate that throughout my life as a believer I have loved the One who loved and redeemed me rather than affirming my teaching, management, or leadership skills. When I meet my heavenly Father, I yearn to hear Him say without hesitation, "Pat, you are truly a woman after my heart. Well done, my daughter. Welcome home!" I pray that is that passion of your heart as well.

Pat Ennis

Prayer: *Thank your heavenly Father for loving you, redeeming you, and making you a part of His eternal family. Ask Him to help you to learn to love Him with all your heart, soul, and mind.*

Personal Reflection:

A Woman Who Fears the Lord

Proverbs 1:1–7

ᗒ

"The fear of the LORD is the beginning of knowledge,
But *fools despise wisdom and instruction." (v. 7)*

Although "the fear of the LORD" is the climax of the Proverbs 31 description of the woman of strength, its path through the text of Scripture begins much earlier, and here in this passage we find a definitive phrase that is most helpful in unlocking its meaning. This phrase is the heart of the book of Proverbs, and this verse identifies "the fear of the LORD" as the beginning or starting point (or chief and principal part) in the sense of providing the foundation from which wisdom can grow. That wisdom includes an awareness of who God is and what He wants you to do.

Fearing the Lord is not just a "reverential trust" in Him. To fear the Lord is to know that He is not only watching what you do and listening to what you say but also reading your thoughts. You are continually aware that you are in His presence—the holy, just, all powerful God of the universe. You know that every thought, word, and action is open before Him and will be judged by Him. You fear that you will disappoint or hurt Him whom you love above all others. There is a controlling awe of His power and righteous retribution as well as a wholesome dread of displeasing Him.

As a child, I feared my father in much the same way. My motivation for obeying him was not fear of punitive retribution but rather a holy fear of love and trust that so possessed me that I dared not disobey because I did not want to disappoint him. He was so good to me that I wanted to make good grades; I wanted to obey him in my life choices. I did not want to bring shame or hurt to him or his name. In the same way, we are drawn in awe into God's presence. We are not frozen in terror, unable to make decisions or act, but we do not feel freedom to move solely according to our personal whims.

This "fear of the LORD" prepares the way for understanding wisdom and serves as an incentive for you to move forward in obedience. Your submission to the heavenly Father is through this process of reverent obedience. You will never become a woman of spiritual strength without being marked by "the fear of the LORD" in every area of your life. Not only is it the key to your personal success and praise from others, but also it is essential for your heavenly reward (Prov. 31:30).

Dorothy Kelley Patterson

Prayer: *Come to the Lord in humility and ask him to give you this spirit of humility and trust in His faithfulness. Open your mind, heart, and emotions—every part of your life—to Him, learning about Him and what He expects of you.*

Personal Reflection:

Marital Intimacy

Proverbs 5:1–23

~~~

"Drink water from your own cistern,
And running water from your own well." (v. 15)

When someone speaks of intimacy in marriage, sex is the automatic thought. However, true oneness in marriage is much more than physical intimacy. God wants us to enjoy marriage. The word "intimate" comes from the Latin *in timus*, which means "innermost." Everyone wants to experience an unconditional love and acceptance. Psychologists have described intimacy with words like openness, honesty, caring, and devotion.

This passage speaks of fidelity and an exclusive relationship. Intimacy was God's plan for lifelong marriage. The desire for sexual fulfillment is the rightful reward of marriage alone. God intends for the tender delights of love and the exciting spontaneity of passion to be woven into the marital union (Deut. 24:5; Eccl. 9:9). The best protection against infidelity is sexual intimacy in marriage.

In the book *The Mystery of Marriage*, the author states: "Marriage is not a joining of two worlds, but an abandoning of two worlds in order that one new one might be formed."* When we marry we leave life as we knew it. We leave our parent's home, their authority, and their credit cards. We leave some traditions behind to start our own traditions. We must also leave some difficult things. Sometimes women have had hard childhood experiences like rejection or abuse. We have to deal with these situations and let God bring healing.

Cleave means "adhere to" or "cling." A wife is to cling to her husband, not to cleave to the children. Jesus is our perfect example as He left His Father to come to earth and left His mother when He started His itinerant ministry. It was all for the purpose of becoming one with His bride, the church.

There are many aspects of intimacy in marriage. There is **spiritual intimacy**. Beginning in courtship, couples should share their personal spiritual journeys and continue growing together in the Lord. **Emotional intimacy** is sometimes difficult for a man because he may not want to appear weak. Ask God to help you understand his emotional needs. **Social intimacy** can be accomplished by having some couple friends with similar interests. **Intellectual intimacy** is important to the marriage relationship. Keep up with current events so you can have meaningful conversations and learn as much as you can about his business. **Recreational intimacy** is not always easy with the busyness of today's world, but try to find something you can do together for fun.

Marital intimacy requires work, but it is well worth the effort. God will bless your marriage with a special union as you both focus on God and each other.

Barbara O'Chester

Prayer: *Pray for your husband or future spouse. Ask God to help you be vulnerable with each other to create marital intimacy.*

Personal Reflection: ....

....

....

....

....

....

* Mike Mason, *The Mystery of Marriage: Meditations on the Miracle,* 20th Anniversary ed. (Colorado Springs, CO: Multnomah, 2005), 103.

The Craftiness of the Immoral Woman

Proverbs 7:1–27

"And there a woman met him,
With the attire of a harlot, and a crafty heart.
She was loud and rebellious,
Her feet would not stay at home.
At times she was outside, at times in the open square,
Lurking at every corner." (vv. 10–12)

"If you got it, flaunt it!" So goes today's advice to women around the world. Our culture would have us exploit every physical asset to our advantage in order to influence men. Think about the classic archetype of the femme fatale in movies who bats her eyelashes or uses some sexually suggestive tactic to manipulate a guy into doing what she wants. One of the original femme fatales is found right in Proverbs 7!

This married woman used her looks and words to ensnare and entice men into sin. She used the way she dressed with "crafty" intent (v. 10). She knew exactly what she was doing! She was seeking to trip up the young man who crossed her path by dressing in such a way that he would find her sexually attractive. She drew attention to herself and intentionally put herself in situations where she would be noticed (v. 12). The intent of her heart was not for the good of this young man.

The immoral woman of Proverbs 7 had a dangerous pattern in her life. She wore provocative clothing ("the attire of a harlot," v. 10); she put herself in compromising positions late at night (v. 9). Her demeanor was loud and rebellious (v. 11; cp. 9:13). When her husband was away on business, she is described as lurking at corners (v. 12). The picture of a black widow spider looking for its next victim comes to mind.

When the Proverbs 7 woman finally spotted a young man "devoid of understanding" (v. 7), she acted as the sexual aggressor. She grabbed him, kissed him, and pleaded with him shamelessly to come back to her house, talking in such a way to stimulate his sexual appetite (vv. 13, 15–18). She even tried to placate misgivings of the man by putting up a pseudo-spiritual façade, saying she had already been to the temple to make her offerings (v. 14). Her words, attire, and actions testified to the sad state of her heart; yet she still went through the motions religiously, putting on an act. However, her intentions are clear—she seduced the young man and led him like an animal to slaughter (vv. 21–23). This immoral woman of Proverbs 7 bears no resemblance to a woman who fears the Lord (Prov. 31:30).

Candi Finch

Prayer: *Have you ever had "crafty intent" like the Proverbs 7 woman in the way you dress, talk, or interact with people? Do you ever manipulate people to get your way? Confess any sinful practices to the Lord and commit yourself to thoughts, speech, and actions that are fitting for a woman who knows Christ (1 Tim. 2:9).*

Personal Reflection: ....

....

....

....

....

....

....

The Folly of the Foolish Woman

Proverbs 9:1–18

"A foolish woman is clamorous;
She is simple, and knows nothing." (v. 13)

The picture of the foolish woman is rather bleak and stands in stark contrast to wisdom (vv. 1–12). True wisdom begins with the fear of the Lord, not fear in the sense of being petrified by God, rather, a reverent obedience and honor of the Lord that is expressed in a submissive spirit (v. 10). A wise person chooses to keep herself under the control of God, so He can guide her in making wise choices and correct her when she strays from the path. A wise woman allows God to be in the driver's seat, navigating her life's journey.

On the other hand, the foolish woman takes a very different approach to life. The "fool" is not necessarily one who is intellectually defective. Instead, a foolish woman is one who is morally defective, choosing to reject wise counsel or not even seeking counsel at all. She lacks discernment, trusts in her own devises, and determines to follow her own desires. The word for "foolish" in Proverbs 9:13 signifies a person who is so stubborn in clinging to her own ways that she is unable to be moved by reasonable counsel.

This woman is characterized by a clamorous demeanor (v. 13), indicating a person who is so animated by her own passions that she is turbulent like a stormy and tempestuous wind that leaves disorder and havoc in its path. In addition, she is called simple, which may bring to mind a person who is not intellectually developed (v. 13). However, "simple" actually means a person who is morally underdeveloped; this woman has no preservative against evil in her life or any kind of moral fiber to resist temptation. Without Christ, we are all in this state! Without the power of the Holy Spirit or the Word of God to help us resist temptation, we have no power to lead a godly life.

Finally, this foolish woman is said to know nothing because she lacks any knowledge of what is right (v. 13). She is not satisfied to be in this state alone but tries to drag others into her way of life (vv. 14–18). Like the immoral woman of Proverbs 7, the foolish woman of Proverbs 9 leads others into sin, dragging people down to her level of depravity and immaturity (v. 18).

Candi Finch

Prayer: *As you read about the wise woman and the foolish woman, which description is more apt of your life right now? If you are allowing God to guide and direct your steps, pray for the continued strength to be obedient to His way of life and thank Him for the Bible, which gives you instructions on how to live. If you find there are areas of your life characterized by foolishness, would you confess that to the Lord and ask Him to help you to walk in the way of wisdom?*

Personal Reflection:

A Gracious Woman

Proverbs 11:1–31

ᦂᦂ

"A gracious woman retains honor,
But ruthless men retain riches." (v. 16)

Whenever we read an instruction or description directed specifically to women in God's precious Word, we should certainly take notice and evaluate ourselves accordingly. We have an idea of what it means to be gracious and know that this is a desired quality. We seek by God's grace to live a life characterized by being cordial, good-natured, hospitable, congenial, accommodating, friendly, and approachable. Graciousness. Yes, we seek to be gracious even as we hope to be the recipient of graciousness from others. The flip side is not a pretty picture at all. Who wants to be known as surly, aloof, rude, incompatible, irritable, hateful or even cruel? If we are honest, we will admit there are times when we sinfully exhibit those negative characteristics to our shame.

Proverbs 11:16 reminds us that a gracious woman in particular retains honor that is much more favorable in the sight of the Lord than ruthless men who retain riches. Would that we are mindful of the weight of our demeanor as it serves to bring either honor or shame to our Lord who has given His life for us. To be gracious toward those who have been gracious to us is much easier. What a challenge to be gracious to those difficult people whom the Lord has placed in our lives! Yet no exception is given for dealing with them. Proverbs 31:30 provides a critical reminder that our graciousness and charm can be deceitful when they are not offered with the right motives. If we do not fear the Lord with a reverence and overwhelming desire to please Him as seekers of His heart, then we are not worthy of praise or affirmation.

Peter makes the amazing statement that women should seek "the incorruptible *beauty* of a gentle and quiet spirit, which is very precious in the sight of God" (1 Pet. 3:4b). Don't we long to be very precious in the sight of God? How thankful we should be for these clear directives in the infallible Word of God.

Graciousness, coupled with a quiet and gentle spirit, should be at the forefront as we order our days.

Mary K. Mohler

Prayer: *When you read the adjectives describing what it means to be gracious and what it means to lack graciousness, are you convicted? Do you mentally put an asterisk by certain people in your life who challenge you in every way? Ask the Lord to forgive you for being gracious only when it is easy and not when it is hard. Ask Him to remind you continually of the unspeakable gift of your salvation in Christ alone that changes everything. Ask Him to equip you to be known as a gracious woman with a quiet and gentle spirit for His glory alone.*

Personal Reflection: ....

....

....

....

....

....

....

....

Motherhood and the Tool of Discipline

Proverbs 13:1–25

∽

"He who spares his rod hates his son,
But he who loves him disciplines him promptly." (v. 24)

I am the mother of four and the grandmother of nine. My children didn't have a chance at having a compliant will because their father and I are both extremely strong-willed, and we come from a long line of stubborn people. I lived by James Dobson's book, *The Strong-Willed Child,* when we were in the midst of parenthood. There were times that I was so exhausted, I felt like throwing in the towel on consistency in discipline.

At lunch one day after Bible study with a couple of friends, one of the moms was a little further down the road than I was with raising her children. My youngest had just thrown the food off her tray for the third or fourth time, and we were taking yet another trip to the bathroom. When I returned and plopped into my seat, I said, "She is wearing me out!" To which my friend promptly replied, "But you must win!" I said, "Just keep reminding me of that, because I am beyond fatigued!"

What my friend realized was that real love instills a respect for authority when our children are toddlers. If you want to have a well-disciplined teenager, you must put forth the effort when they are young. If you love your children more than you love yourself, you will be consistent, even when tired. When we fail to discipline, we are being lazy and taking the easy way out. The problem with that is, we will pay the consequences and so will our children.

The Bible is very clear that parents are responsible for training and disciplining their children (Prov. 22:15; 23:13; 29:15). Discipline is not pleasant at the moment, but "afterward it yields the peaceable fruit of righteousness to those who have been trained by it" (Heb. 12:11). Thus, we must be faithful to follow through with discipline.

Our children are all grown and married now, and by God's grace they are all walking with the Lord. Now my responsibility is to pray for them as they discipline their children and to encourage them when I notice that all-too-familiar sign of fatigue and desire to quit. God is faithful to His Word. We must train our children to obey the Lord and to obey us. This healthy respect for authority is all too rare in our day. But it will serve them well as they walk with the Lord and their fellow man.

Donna Gaines

Prayer: *If you are a parent, how are you doing with discipline? Have you and your husband discussed consequences for misbehavior, and are you in agreement? If not, ask the Lord to help you work together on this very important aspect of your responsibility as a parent.*

Personal Reflection: ....

....

....

....

....

....

....

A Strong Tower

Proverbs 18:1–14

"The name of the LORD is a strong tower;
The righteous run to it and are safe." (v. 10)

This wonderful proverb is meant to be paired with verse 11, which describes a rich man who trusts in his wealth and possessions for ultimate security. That seemed his only defense in trouble—"his strong city" and a "high wall" (v. 11). In contrast, the righteous person finds safety and security in the Lord, Who is our strong tower!

Strong towers were placed strategically in the corners of the ancient city. From the towers, the watchmen scanned the area for any threats by approaching enemies. They were tall and fortified heavily to both defend those within against attack and protect them against harm. They also served to steady the walls, anchoring and strengthening them to withstand whatever would come. What a beautiful picture of the place of security for the woman who truly believes in God!

This verse reminds us that when attacked and shaken, we can run to the Lord, whose very name displays His perfect character. In Him, we will find secure shelter and will not be defeated.

How beautiful are these names of God. He is:

- *Elohim:* "Powerful, Ruler, Majesty" (Gen. 1:1; Is. 54:5)
- *El-Shaddai:* "the Almighty God" (Gen. 17:1)
- *Adonai:* "Lord," "Master" (Josh. 5:14)
- *Jehovah:* "I AM," Self-Existent One (Ex. 3:14)
- *Jehovah yireh*: "The-LORD-Will-Provide" (Gen. 22:14)
- *Jehovah rapha':* "the LORD who heals" (Ex. 15:26)
- *Jehovah nissi:* "The-LORD-Is-My-Banner" (Ex. 17: 15)
- *Jehovah shalom:* "The-LORD-Is-Peace" (Judg. 6:24)
- *Jehovah ro'i:* "The LORD *is* my shepherd" (Ps. 23:1)
- *Jehovah tsidkēnu:* "THE LORD OUR RIGHTEOUSNESS" (Jer. 23:6)

- *Jehovah shammah:* "THE LORD *IS* THERE" (Ezek. 48:35)
- *Jehovah tseva'ot:* "the Lord of hosts" (1 Sam. 17:45)

Over 10 years ago, the doctors found a congenital defect in my heart valve that required repair. I thought I was absolutely prepared for the day of surgery, which was performed by the best heart surgeon in the country. I had prayed and enlisted others to do the same. But the moment came when I alone was being wheeled to the surgical suite. Looking around, I suddenly felt terrified. Though groggy and unable to concentrate well, His name came so sweetly to my mind and then my lips. I whispered aloud: "Jesus! Jesus!" Fear fled in the presence of *Jehovah shalom* and He hid me securely in the tower of His name. Call today on His name, and you will be saved! (Joel 2:32; Rom. 10:13).

Janet Wicker

Prayer: *Pray today with the psalmist:*

> Hear my cry, O God;
> Attend to my prayer.
> From the end of the earth I will cry to You,
> When my heart is overwhelmed;
> Lead me to the rock that is higher than I.
>
> For You have been a shelter for me,
> A strong tower from the enemy.
> I will abide in Your tabernacle forever;
> I will trust in the shelter of Your wings.   *Selah* (Ps. 61:1–4)

Personal Reflection: ....

....

....

A Good Wife

Proverbs 18:15–24

~

"He who finds a wife finds a good thing,
And obtains favor from the Lord." (v. 22)

As God surveyed all that He had created, He pronounced it "good" until He viewed the aloneness of Adam. "And the Lord God said, '*It is* **not good** that a man should be alone; I will make him a helper comparable to him'" (Gen. 2:18, emphasis mine). When God created Eve and gave her to Adam as his wife in a marital covenant relationship, he knew he had found "a good *thing*" and "favor from the Lord."

Sadly our society does not embrace this conventional wisdom, for marriage is now treated as an antiquated and useless institution. In the face of steadily declining marriage rates, "A record number of adults in America have never been married." A recent report from the Pew Research Center reveals that 50 percent of adults believe that: "Society is just as well off if people have priorities other than marriage" (www.pewresearch.org; September 24, 2014).

Why does God find it good that a man find a wife? Consider this:

- Together they would fulfill God's command to "be fruitful and multiply" and to "fill the earth" as godly children come from their union (Gen. 1:28).
- Each would find in the other a companion who would make up for what is lacking in the other (Gen. 2:18, 24).
- In beautiful oneness, they would reflect the wondrous glory of God as their marriage pictures Christ's relationship with the Church (Eph. 5:31–32).

Also notice this: The man is told that he is the one who "finds" a wife. Human initiative and personal work by the man are involved. The wife is also seen as "favor" granted from the Lord, which speaks of God's sovereign work in bringing two together for marriage.

I met my husband while we were both students at Southwestern Baptist Theological Seminary. It didn't take long for me to notice that quite a few of the young single ministers-to-be were searching for a wife. I had determined that I would never marry a preacher! One day, I ran into this student inside the rotunda as we were both racing to chapel service a little late. We quickly sat down together. Afterward, this handsome young man asked me to have dinner with him after classes. It seemed like a casual invitation, so I accepted. I found myself drawn to this devoted man of God, and amazingly he was drawn to me. We were engaged a few months later and married by the end of the year! Now, almost 40 years later, I pray that he says that he found a "good thing" and "favor from the Lord" when he found me! I know I certainly did!

Janet Wicker

Prayer: *Ask God to renew within our nation esteem for biblical marriage. Pray that you will be a Proverbs 31 wife who "does him good and not evil all the days of her life" (Prov. 31:12).*

Personal Reflection: ....

....

....

....

....

A Contentious Wife

Proverbs 19:1–29

⌒

"A foolish son is the ruin of his father,
And the contentions of a wife are a continual dripping." (v. 13)

The writer of Proverbs tells us that life in a family can be irritating and painful as well as pleasant and joyful. A foolish son—one who is unteachable, arrogant, disobedient, or immoral—is a disaster to his father. On the other hand, a wife who is contentious—argumentative and touchy—is irritating and ruinous like a continual dripping.

I shall never forget our first home, a tiny apartment in married housing at the seminary. One night, as I lay in bed trying to sleep, I kept being disturbed by the monotonous sounds of a constant dripping of water in the bathtub. I thought I could just ignore it, but it seemed to get louder and louder. Finally, I got up and did everything I could do to silence it. I tightened the spigot to try to stop the flow of water; I laid a cloth under the drip to muffle the sounds; and finally, I closed every door trying to shut it out. It seemed that nothing would work. After a restless night and little sleep, I called the plumber who came and fixed the awful nuisance the very next day!

Proverbs reminds me that I can be just like that to my husband when all I do is argue and oppose everything he says and does. For most husbands, the louder you get, the more determined he is to shut out what you are saying. If you think that all you have to do is make a long, eloquent appeal to win him over with your many words, you will soon learn that you are getting on his last nerve! Your contentious quarreling will not get you what you want!

I learned another lesson about constant dripping as I walked through my beautiful dining room one morning. Pieces of the ceiling were strewn on the top of the dining table and a drip of water was hitting it as well. After hurriedly climbing into the attic (and moving the table), we learned that an overhead pipe had been pierced by a small nail and a very slow drip of water had been hitting that spot for a period of time. It did its damage by weakening the wallboard on the ceiling until it had begun to collapse onto the table below. Quickly, the plumber was called and came to the rescue! He sealed the hole, and a carpenter restored the damage in the ceiling. What an expensive disaster, but I got it! While this constant "dripping" of unkind argument and disrespectful strife toward my husband irritated him, it could ruin our marriage if I did not stop!

Janet Wicker

Prayer: *Repent today of any words that are disrespectful and contentious toward your husband. Ask God to control your tongue and the words you say to bring blessing instead of irritation and destruction to your marriage.*

Personal Reflection: ....

....

....

....

....

....

....

....

The Challenge of Godly Discipline

Proverbs 22:1–15

"Train up a child in the way he should go,
And when he is old he will not depart from it." (v. 6)

This well-known verse has usually been considered a promise to parents who reared their children with consistent spiritual nurturing. However, some parents have experienced disillusionment and hurt as their children moved away from what they were carefully taught in the home and church. Two factors must be considered: God has given every individual free will to make her own choices, and some will make poor choices despite the good teaching and guidance of their parents. Also, Satan targets godly families in order to derail their faith and keep them from faithful service to Christ.

Nevertheless, parents have the responsibility to teach their children biblical truths, to model what they are teaching in their own lives, and to inspire the child's willing embrace of what is being taught by careful and constant supervision of and interaction with the child. Parenting is hands-on in more than one way!

There is another interesting caveat in understanding this verse. Some suggest "the way he should go" is a reference to "God's way;" others suggest it as the child's "natural bent." Although the first interpretation has merit, this verse may have a double message—not just a promise that impacting your child with every means for firmly planting faith in his heart will produce fruit unto righteousness, but it may also be a warning about the wiles of the devil.

The most literal rendering of the Hebrew text from my translation of the verse is "Train up a child according to his own way, and he will never depart from going his own way." In this case, the verse warns parents that they must break the willfulness of the child early and throughout their time of parenting in the home. Allowing a child to have his own way can come into play without warning. Perhaps her choices in early years are good ones, and her desires are holy and right. A parent can then be lulled into trusting the child, allowing her to slip into a self-willed lifestyle. A determination to have her own way keeps a child from becoming obedient to going God's way.

Parents must claim the promise and give themselves to careful spiritual nurturing of each child in the home. But they must realize that doing all the right things will not harness the willfulness of the child. Rather they must use diligence in helping the child to obey in whatever choices she must make, correcting her lovingly and firmly but without growing weary in the task!

Dorothy Kelley Patterson

Prayer: *If you are a parent or if you work with children or young people in any setting, ask the Lord to give you a discerning spirit to identify even the smallest spark of rebellion in the child's life. Pray for wisdom to know how to train the child and for strength to see the task to the finish line.*

Personal Reflection: ....

....

....

....

....

....

....

A Paradigm for Biblical Womanhood

Proverbs 31:1–9

"The words of King Lemuel, the utterance which his mother taught him." (v. 1)

King Lemuel ("unto God" or "one dedicated to God") may be a reference to Solomon, a symbolic name for an ideal king, or an allusion to a king whose origin is not clearly identified. Whoever is referenced in this verse bears a name given by his mother as a testimony to her faith. Even though a king, this man is not ashamed to acknowledge the influence of his mother on his life and even to give her credit for her wisdom. In a sense, he is immortalizing her life and influence in the presentation of the divinely designed paradigm of womanhood (31:10–31).

This wise mother uses endearing epithets to describe her beloved son: "son of my womb" and "son of my vows" (v. 2). Mother and son obviously had a close and loving relationship. Of interest is the fact that this book of wisdom begins with wise words from a father (1:8) and now closes with words of wisdom from a mother (31:1). For you as a woman, it is even more significant that Lemuel's mother is the inspired messenger for these words formulating the extraordinary portrait of a "virtuous wife" or, as according to my own translation, "a woman of strength."

In this prelude, the mother begins with warnings for her son (vv. 3–7). She notes the danger of distractions to his divinely assigned responsibility of governing his people. Then she moves into a poem of praise for a woman of strength, whose household would be far beyond the ordinary woman in any generation. Yet the description moves from the inner character of the woman (Prov. 31:10–12, 17, 25, 30–31) to how this works itself out in commitments to her family (vv. 11, 23, 28) and to the management of her household (vv. 13–15, 21, 27) as well as to service in her community (vv. 20, 26). She does not overlook personal attractiveness (v. 22) and giftedness (vv. 16, 18–19, 24). Her standard of excellence sets her apart to be admired and emulated.

The "virtuous wife" is a helpful partner who makes her husband's work in the community more effective, bringing honor to him and to their family by her own deeds (v. 23). The vivid and varied details penned in this account make this woman one to whom other women can reach out and touch in some way. She lifts the standard high, inspiring godly women to excellence throughout the generations.

Dorothy Kelley Patterson

Prayer: *Set your heart apart in devotion to the Lord, coming before Him sincerely and often, asking Him to develop in you an inner beauty that will then work itself out in practical ways in all of your life relationships and assignments. Ask the Lord to make you "heart healthy" and worthy of His commendation.*

Personal Reflection: ....

....

....

....

....

....

....

Inner Beauty

Proverbs 31:10–31

⌒

"Charm is deceitful and beauty is passing,
But a woman who fears the Lord, she shall be praised." (v. 31)

The book of Proverbs ends just as it began—with an admonition to fear the Lord. In Proverbs 31 we are introduced to the Virtuous Woman, the woman who is revered for her fear of God. She is not a perfect woman, as some have thought; she is godly. She is not striving; she is living out of the center of a life that fears or reveres God, and her values and choices prove it. This woman has found security in her relationship with the Lord. Her value system is not that of the world. She has not allowed the world to conform her to its ways, but has rather been "transformed by the renewing of . . . [her] mind" and is able to discern the will of God (Rom. 12:2).

Our culture is constantly bombarding us with messages about how we are to look and dress and what size we should wear in order to be valuable. The world says that youth, wealth, and celebrity are important. But a woman who knows the living God does not live for such superficiality. She realizes that true beauty is within and is reflected in how we imitate Christ and how we treat others. What purse she carries or what car she drives is not even on her radar screen. Instead, she is living to love her Lord and to serve Him more readily. She lives from an eternal vantage point, devoted to advancing God's Kingdom agenda. Thus, He entrusts her with "true *riches*" (Luke 16:11). The Lord is able to work through her and accomplish more than she could "ask or think, according to the power that works in" her (Eph. 3:20).

A wise woman lives and makes decisions based on God's Word. She is free to love and respect her husband and care for her household without demanding they meet unmet needs in her life. She also cares for the poor, and "on her tongue *is* the law of kindness" (Prov. 31:20, 26). She builds others up instead of tearing them down.

God alone is our source for wisdom, strength, grace, love, and joy. These virtues flow forth from a woman who recognizes her heart is more important than her outward appearance. The "virtuous wife" is simply a picture of a woman whose life reflects her relationship and commitment to God (vv. 10–31). I encourage you to allow her—this woman whom God praises—to be a role model for you.

Donna Gaines

Prayer: *Ask the Lord to show you if you are more concerned about your outward appearance than your heart. Do you truly fear the Lord and desire to honor Him above yourself or anyone else?*

Personal Reflection: ....

....

....

....

....

....

....

....

Anticipating the End

Ecclesiastes 7:1–13

"The end of a thing is better than its beginning;
The patient in spirit is better than the proud in spirit." (v. 8)

Have you ever been misjudged or mistreated? If you are a living, breathing human being then the answer is likely "yes" to both questions. When we or someone we love is wronged, often our automatic human response is to launch into defense mode. Our strong need for validation can drive us at times to react hastily in the moment, only to later realize that in so doing we forsook the long-term view of the situation and perhaps even the outcome that God desired to bring about. The focal verse serves as a biblical "stop sign" to keep us from doing just that.

Traditionally, authorship of Ecclesiastes is attributed to Israel's third king, Solomon, the son of David. The theme of the book is hinted at early on, as in Ecclesiastes 1:2 he says, "Vanity of vanities . . . all *is* vanity." The Hebrew word used there for vanity, *hevel*, is different than the Hebrew word that is used in the Third Commandment to say, "You shall not take the name of the Lord your God in **vain**" (see Ex. 20:7a). Another word for "vain" (Hb. *shaw*'), meaning "hollow, empty," is used. But in Ecclesiastes, the word *hevel*, or vanity, actually means "vapor." Solomon then is not saying that all of life is **hollow**, but rather it is a **vapor**.

Vapors are real; they have substance; but as their description suggests, they do not last. Solomon seems to be begging the question then, "How should I live in this vapor of life?" He answers that question in the other great wisdom text attributed to his pen, the book of Proverbs, which gives advice on how to live a righteous life. Yet in Ecclesiastes 7:8, Solomon also sheds light on the best way to live "in the midst of the vapor." The reader is encouraged to "take the long view" and to be patient enough to see matters worked out, rather than take them pridefully into their own hands.

Are you in a situation now where you run the risk of being tempted to make hasty responses? If not, it probably won't be long until you face a decision. Those situations are very real; they have substance; but remember, they won't last forever. Commit this verse to memory and allow the Holy Spirit to use it in your life to help you take deep breaths rather than give short replies. Ultimately you must trust in HIS plan and HIS sovereign defense of your life.

Courtney Veasey

Prayer: *Consider God's ability to see both your present circumstances and all that is yet to come and offer praise for the guidance He gives for every season. Ask Him to cultivate in you a spirit of patience and a willingness to place matters both great and small into His capable hands.*

Personal Reflection: ....

....

....

....

....

....

....

A True Woman

Ecclesiastes 7:23–29

"And I find more bitter than death
The woman whose heart is snares and nets,
Whose hands are fetters.
He who pleases God shall escape from her,
But the sinner shall be trapped by her." (v. 26)

When I was a little girl, my granddaddy and I would fish with rods and reels, but my favorite way to catch fish was through a trot line. We would lay out the line, consisting of a series of wound-up springs with bait at the end. When the fish took the bait, the spring would snap and trap the fish with a sharp hook. Late in the evenings, my granddaddy and I would go back and gather the trapped fish from that day. A trot line was quick and effective in trapping fish, much easier than sitting for hours with a fishing pole.

Sadly, in the same vein, some women trap men just as effectively. Instead of springs and worms, they use a false pretense of love, seductive words, and flattery. According to Solomon, her "heart *is* snares and nets, Whose hands *are* fetters" (Eccl. 7:26). Solomon, who wrote both Ecclesiastes and Proverbs, warns men about the woman with the "attire of a harlot, and a crafty heart" (Prov. 7:10). He goes on to describe the dire situation, "With her enticing speech she caused him to yield, With her flattering lips she seduced him" (v. 21). As she seduces this young, foolish man, he is described as going "after her, as an ox goes to the slaughter" (v. 22).

Most women would not classify themselves as a crafty harlot (Prov. 7:6–10); but, because of our sin nature, we all are vulnerable. How do we avoid becoming a trap for the men around us? We do as Solomon did. "I applied my heart to know, To search and seek out wisdom and the reason *of things*" (Eccl. 7:25). In contrast to the woman who traps men with her sin, a true woman does her husband "good and not evil / All the days of her life" (Prov. 31:12). Instead of "enticing speech" and "flattering lips," a true woman living out her

God-given purpose "opens her mouth with wisdom" and speaks words of kindness (Prov. 31:26).

Do you pursue a deeper knowledge of God or do you follow the fleshly desires of your heart? Every day you choose to be a crafty woman or to be the true woman God created you to be. Wise women are hard to find, but, when found, they are worth far more than rubies (v. 10). Be a wise woman for the men in your life. Instead of leading them astray, encourage them to pursue Christ even more.

Melanie Lenow

Prayer: *Ask God to show you areas in your life where you need to die to your fleshly desires and pursue Him more. Ask for forgiveness for the times when you have been more crafty than wise in your relationships with men.*

Personal Reflection: ....

The Blessing of Marriage

Ecclesiastes 9:1–18

"Live joyfully with the wife whom you love all the days of your vain life which He has given you under the sun, all your days of vanity; for that is your portion in life, and in the labor which you perform under the sun." (v. 9)

Every time my husband performs a wedding, he shares a quote that is dear to my heart with the bride and groom: "Your spouse may not be perfect but that spouse is perfect for you." A couple doesn't take long to realize that love is much more than physical attraction or infatuation. If the purpose of marriage is happiness, then most couples would feel a need for a new marriage every two to three years.

Scripture cites the many reasons God has ordained marriage: relationship and fulfillment (Heb. 13:4); procreation (Gen. 1:28); protection (Eph. 5:25); completion (Gen. 2:23); and as a means to display God's glory to the world through the relationship between Christ and His church (Eph. 5:31–33). Modeling God's love for His church is key to Christian marriage—the grand display of spiritual reconciliation. It is striving in our relationships to make God happy rather than ourselves, which is completely against our sin nature. Being married forces one to confront some character issues she would never otherwise confront. Godly marriages help prune and sanctify us. In this sense, a marriage can be a platform for the gospel. It can point a lost world to a truth beyond what is natural in our flesh and away from this world and into the next.

Biblical love stands in contrast to the love our culture knows from romance novels and sensual movies. Secular love always looks so exhilarating, but Christians know the difference. Believers understand the sinful struggles our spouses face, knowing that we all have hearts stained by sin. Dying to self is a daily struggle, but dying to yourself is the key ingredient to a joyful and lasting marriage. In other words, a good marriage is not something you find, it is something toward which you work.

What Christian wife wouldn't want to live joyfully with her husband? The catalyst for this verse is seeking holiness and happiness within the marriage union, two individuals becoming one together in pursuit of a shared vision for God's glory in their marriage. Then, and only then, the couple will know a joy that the world cannot grasp.

Karen B. Allen

Prayer: *Thank the Lord for your spouse if you are married. Let your relationship with your husband point you to what you really need most of all—God's love and presence in your life. Ask the Lord to deepen your love for Him and your spouse. Ask the Lord to reveal hidden sins in your own heart that would prevent a closer relationship. Petition the Lord to show you ways to love your spouse as you show him appreciation.*

Personal Reflection: ....

....

....

....

....

....

Enjoy Life and Remember

Ecclesiastes 11:7–10

~~~

Rejoice, O young man, in your youth,
And let your heart cheer you in the days of your youth;
Walk in the ways of your heart,
And in the sight of your eyes;
But know that for all these
God will bring you into judgment.
Therefore remove sorrow from your heart,
And put away evil from your flesh,
For childhood and youth are vanity." (vv. 9–10)

Today's women are bombarded with messages that happiness and joy come from possessions, positions, and pleasures. In October 2009, *Time Magazine* published a special report entitled, "The State of the American Woman," subtitled "A new poll shows why they are more powerful—but less happy." The report states that while women have more power, more possessions, more money, more position, and more pleasure, they are less fulfilled than at any other time in history.

The writer of Ecclesiastes knew about position, power, pleasure, influence, and possessions. King Solomon became king at the age of 24, and he never lacked for material things. His conclusion was that all was vanity. He writes to instruct and warn. Though he was writing to young men, he challenges women of today to live out their lives in the "light." Women should enjoy their lives. Life is short, and there is a very thin line between light and darkness, or more specifically, between life and death.

King Solomon challenged his young men to remember the "light is sweet" but days are dark (vv. 7–10). Solomon encouraged young men to live their lives to the fullest, to enjoy life. Have fun but know that God brings everything into judgment. In other words, life should not be without enjoyment and fun, but this earthly life is not the sum of your life. You cannot live lives of pure indulgence, obtaining what you desire or you want for your family, and expect fulfillment or happiness. As another wise woman said to her children: "At the end of the day, you are the only one looking back at you in the mirror."

Live your life in a state of joy for all that earth has for you and for all God has provided. As women, we must evaluate our lives in light of the Word of God and the will of our Savior. Are you living this life or are you enduring life? There should be joy. Look around and choose to enjoy life.

Diane Nix

Prayer: *Pray, remembering who is the giver of life and joy. Ask the Lord to reveal to you areas of want and indulgence. Ask Him to help you to know how to choose joy in daily activities and to look only to Him as the supplier of all things. Pray, thanking Him for the joy of this life and eternal life to come.*

Personal Reflection: ....

....

....

....

....

....

....

Remember Your Creator

Ecclesiastes 12:1–7

"Remember now your Creator in the days of your youth,
Before the difficult days come,
And the years draw near when you say,
'I have no pleasure in them.'" (v. 1)

"Youth is wasted on the young," said playwright George Bernard Shaw. I asked my teenage daughter her thoughts on the meaning of this quote. "We waste our youth trying to grow up so fast, and we do 'brainless' things, trying to feel older, trying to avoid being a kid, when in reality older people would do anything to enjoy youth again—taking it slowly and staying young." How many times have you wished you could know what you know today and be young again? Solomon moves from confusion and depression, brought about by pondering the meaning of life, to focusing heavenward: "Remember your Creator in your days of youth" (v. 1).

The call to remember is more than just casually bringing God to our minds. It is the choosing to "fear God" or respect Him (12:13). To remember is to choose not only the fear of God but also to embrace obedience in daily life. While you are young, look to God. Keep your eyes toward heaven in the midst of your youthful days. Remember who made you. As I have repeated to my girls through the years until today, "Remember whose you are and who you are!" Remember and do not lose focus.

God our Creator can keep us from mistakes that will harm us and plague us in the years to come. In my ministry, I have met with countless women who carry guilt, shame, the lack of forgiveness, and other emotional pains from decisions they made in the days of their youth. Many of these women had knowledge of our Lord even in the midst of times when their faith was faltering.

What about you? Do you allow self-doubt or shame to discourage you? Don't allow these immature emotions to control you. Instead, remember your

Creator. He loves you and is at work in you. When your faith falters, put away foolish thoughts that are centering on you and trust Him to reveal His purposes for your life.

Diane Nix

Prayer: *Ask the Lord to reveal areas of want and indulgence in your life. Ask Him to help you to know how to choose joy in everyday activities and to look only to Him, the supplier of all things. Pray you will continue growing older and wiser in the Lord and that He will direct your steps.*

Personal Reflection: ....

....

....

....

....

....

....

....

Don't Awaken Love before It's Time

Song of Solomon 2:1–17

"Do not stir up nor awaken love
Until it pleases." (v. 7b)

Singleness meant one thing: virginity. If you were single, you had not been in bed with any man. If you were to be permanently single, you were never going to be in bed with any man.

That was a hundred years ago, of course. But even a hundred years ago anybody who quite seriously believed that and acted on it would be seen as an oddity by many people. Perhaps we were in the minority. I can't be sure about that. Certainly the majority *professed* to believe that sexual activity was best limited to husbands and wives, whether or not their private lives demonstrated this conviction. Now, however, times have changed, they tell us. For thousands of years, society depended on some semblance of order in the matter of sex. A woman knew that she possessed a priceless treasure, her virginity. She guarded it jealously for the man who would pay the price for it—commitment to marriage with her and with her alone.

Somehow we've gotten the idea that we can forget all the regulations and get away with it. Times have changed, we say. We're "liberated" at last from our inhibitions. We have Sex and the Single Girl now. We have freedom. We can, in fact, "have it all and not get hooked." Women can be predators if they want to, as well as men. Men aren't men unless they've proved it by seducing as many women as possible—or as many men, for we may now choose according to "sexual preference." We can go to bed with those of the opposite sex or those of our own. It doesn't matter. A mere question of taste, and we all have a "right" to our tastes.

The reason my roommates and I believed that singleness was synonymous with virginity was not that we lived a hundred years ago when everybody believed that. It was not that we didn't know any better. It was not that we were not yet liberated or even that we were just plain stupid. The reason is that we were Christians. We prized the sanctity of sex.

In forfeiting the sanctity of sex by casual, nondiscriminatory "making out" and "sleeping around," we forfeit something we cannot do without. There is a dullness, monotony, sheer boredom in all of life when virginity and purity are no longer protected and prized. By trying to grab fulfillment everywhere, we find it nowhere.

Elisabeth Elliot

Prayer: *Ask the Lord to help you model His approach to sexual purity in your interactions with other people. Are there any ways in which you may be "awakening love" before its time?*

Personal Reflection: ....

....

....

....

....

....

An excerpt from Elisabeth Elliot's *Passion and Purity*, written in 1984, where she discusses her days in college and ideas she and her roommates held about sexual purity and not "awakening love" before the proper time (pages 21–23).

Sexual Purity

Song of Solomon 4:1–15

"A garden enclosed
Is my sister, my spouse,
A spring shut up,
A fountain sealed." (v. 12)

When I was a girl, my mother talked to me about sexual purity. She said, "Once your virginity is lost it can never be regained." Sexual immorality leaves scars on the soul that are difficult to overcome. One girl testified that a one-time slip left a stain she could not get rid of even though she knew that God had forgiven her.

In Song of Solomon 4:12, Solomon speaks of the purity of his bride—an enclosed garden, a spring shut up, and a fountain sealed. The greatest gift a bride can give her groom is her purity. She can enter marriage without guilt or regret. The call for sexual purity is no longer directed just to teenagers.

Never before, in my many years of life, has there been so much sexually provocative material available literally at our finger tips. If surveys are true, as many as 30 percent of women are involved in pornography. This is astounding! At a recent seminar, three of six women in positions of Christian leadership confessed to years of addiction to pornography. Statisticians report that it is an addiction harder to overcome than cocaine. Many people have left their mates after participating in "chat" rooms.

A movie came out in February of 2015, which from all reports is filled with perverted sexual material. A television reporter seemed to take joy that it was being well received in the "Bible Belt." God's purpose for Christians is to live in the world but not to be of the world. He puts us here to be a light in a crooked and perverse generation, to show the way to Him.

First Peter 1:13–15 says, ". . . Gird up the loins of your mind . . . not conforming yourselves to the former lusts, *as* in your ignorance; . . . to be holy in all *your* conduct." The mind is the gateway to your soul. Philippians 4:8 instructs that "Whatever things are true, . . . noble, . . . just, . . . pure, . . . lovely, . . . of good report, . . . meditate on these things."

God has given us liberty with our husbands in sexual matters. However, He draws the line on adultery and sexual perversions such as homosexuality, bestiality, and incest. In 2 Corinthians 10:4–5, God suggests weapons mighty in power to overcome temptations: the name of Jesus, the Word of God, the blood of Christ, and the Word of our testimony. The same power that raised Jesus from the dead comes to live in you when you receive Jesus as your Savior. It is possible to walk in victory. You must learn to use God's power within you to remain sexually pure in your mind and your actions.

Barbara O'Chester

Prayer: *During your prayer times, ask the Father to help you to think on things that are pleasing to Him as you avoid sexual immorality.*

Personal Reflection:

Marital Conflicts and Transforming Love

Song of Solomon 5:2–16

"His mouth is most sweet,
Yes, he is altogether lovely.
This is my beloved,
And this is my friend,
O daughters of Jerusalem!" (v. 16)

Many couples today will face a conflict over sexual intimacy during their marriage. Solomon and the Shulamite woman were no exception, despite their passionate love for one another. This passage describes the couple's first conflict. Solomon came to his wife's door late at night; she was already in bed. Despite her love for her husband, she hesitated and explained that her feet were already clean! She sent the message to her husband that she did not desire his love, and he left before she could change her mind and open the door to him. Sounds like some things have not changed since the first century!

As soon as the Shulamite woman realized that she had offended her husband, she set in search for him. She enlisted the help of the "daughters of Jerusalem," likely friends of the bride or the women who made up her royal court. The Shulamite woman told them that she was "lovesick," and they responded by asking her what made her man so much better than all the rest. This question stirred in the bride the realization that Solomon's love for her was an unselfish one. She knew that he truly cared for her, desired the best for her, and was committed to her growth, as should every husband!

The description that follows the daughters' question reveals not merely the physical attraction that the bride felt for her husband but a deeper appreciation of his character. She said his head was like "the finest gold," referring to his wisdom and authority as king (v. 11). She described his face with words that captured his tenderness and kindness for her, as well as her interest in what he had to say (vv. 12–13). She described his body in a way that suggested his leadership, strength, and trustworthiness (vv. 14–15). She even noted that his mouth was "sweet," suggesting that his speech reflected his good character (v. 16). Last, she described him as "altogether lovely," someone who has not just a lover, but a friend (v. 16). Her husband was her "beloved" and "friend"!

Married couples will inevitably experience conflicts as they learn to live together—differences of opinion, awkward communication, and opposite perspectives. Abraham and Sarah quarreled over her childlessness (Gen. 16:50), and Job disagreed with his wife about his illness (Job 2:9–10). The Scripture also provides guidance to husbands and wives when they face conflict. Selfish needs and desires can be replaced by unselfish love and sacrifice. As the apostle Paul taught, "Love bears all things, believes all things, hopes all things, endures all things" (1 Cor. 13:7). Marital conflict can be transformed into love with the help of the loving heavenly Father.

Rhonda Harrington Kelley

Prayer: *Do you love your husband like the Lord loves him? Seek to overcome marital conflict with transforming love.*

Personal Reflection: ....

....

....

....

....

....

Sexual Intimacy in Marriage

Song of Solomon 7:9–13

"I am my beloved's,
And his desire is toward me." (v. 10)

Sex was God's idea. In the beginning, God created man and woman, designed our bodies to fit together and instilled a desire in us for each other. Then He gave us marriage to make it legal and moral. God set marriage as the boundary for sexual activity.

Today's passage gives a beautiful picture of conjugal love between the Shulamite woman and her husband. Notice that she is the one who initiated this episode. She expresses her deep love in speech as well as action. She receives him joyfully.

The most important thing in a woman's enjoyment of sex is her attitude. Lovemaking cannot be enjoyed if sex is considered wrong. Some women bring inhibitions into marriage. Throughout Scripture, God speaks approvingly of the physical relationship. Proverbs 5:19 says to a husband regarding his wife: "Let her breasts satisfy you at all times; And always be enraptured with her love."

Four concepts regarding the act of marriage are introduced in 1 Corinthians 7:2–5:

1. The husband and wife have sexual needs and desires that are to be satisfied in marriage.
2. When one marries, control of one's body is forfeited. The wife belongs to her husband and vice versa.
3. The husband and wife are forbidden to refuse to meet their mate's physical needs.
4. The act of marriage is approved by God.

A person's attitude about her body affects sexual intimacy. I have never met a woman who was completely satisfied with her body. We must realize that God made us and must accept ourselves. We are "fearfully *and* wonderfully made" (Ps. 139:14). If we don't love ourselves, we won't believe anyone else can love us.

If your attitude about your husband is not right, you cannot enjoy making love to him. If you come into the experience with unresolved anger or resentment, sex will turn into a duty instead of a joy. Make a list of your husband's good points, and thank God every day for 30 days for these good traits. You will find that God will change your heart toward your husband.

God made man and woman different in every way. A man is aroused by sight, sound, and fragrance. A woman's arousal comes through touch. We must understand these differences and act accordingly.

Sexual fulfillment doesn't happen overnight. It takes work. Practice makes perfect. We have three daughters. When Shannon was about four, she made an embarrassing comment while playing in Sunday school. She was putting her dolly to bed when in her little high-pitched voice, she said, "We have a happy room at our house." All the teachers listened with curiosity. The preacher has a happy room?

"Where is your happy room, Shannon?"

"It's mama's and daddy's bedroom. They go in there and just giggle, giggle, giggle."

Do you have a happy room?

Barbara O'Chester

Prayer: *Ask the Lord to help you love each other freely and joyfully.*

Personal Reflection: ....

....

....

....

God's Love for Rebellious Children

Isaiah 1:1–20

"Hear, O heavens, and give ear, O earth!
For the Lord has spoken:
'I have nourished and brought up children,
And they have rebelled against Me.'" (v. 2)

The parable of the prodigal son told by Jesus is a well-known story of a young man who asks for his inheritance prematurely (His father was still alive!), then quickly and wastefully spends it. When all is lost, he returns home to his father to beg for mercy; the father receives him joyfully (Luke 15:11–32).

Jesus used parables to teach a spiritual truth. In this story, the father represents our heavenly Father. He has an inheritance for us, to be given at an appointed time, when Christ returns. To be a prodigal is to waste the earthly blessings of God in this life as a replacement for the heavenly blessings God has for us, to live this life as if there is no eternity with God.

The prophets of the Old Testament often described the nation of Israel as a child who rejected the Lord, though He "nourished and brought up" His people. Chapter 5 of Isaiah depicts God as Judah, one who loved a vineyard, cared for it, and expected good grapes but only found wild grapes. In Isaiah 1, Judah is described in the following ways: rebellious, sinful, evildoers, corrupt, turned backwards as well as with wounds, bruises, and sores not treated. Even the land was desolate, burned with fire, and overthrown by strangers.

All of us have rebelled against God's goodness. We can do no other, because we are all sinful. Isaiah describes us as sheep who have all gone astray (Is. 53:6a). Some mothers know the heartbreak of raising a child who has rejected God and is wasting gifts, talents, resources, and opportunities, living life as if there is no eternity with God. Because of the love the mother has for her child, she grieves over the rebellion.

The hope for all of us is the fact that God is greater than our sin. Though we rejected His love, He did what we could not; He paid for the sin Himself in the person of Jesus Christ. "And the Lord has laid on Him the iniquity of us all" (Is. 53:6b). Jesus is our hope for freedom from rebellion and the hope for our prodigal children, as well.

Although no one can make another person accept God's love, we can have faith in the ability of God to save our prodigals. We can be faithful to pray that they would repent and turn to God. We can humble ourselves and ask them for forgiveness for where we have been lacking as a parent. We can continue to love the prodigal and trust that God is working.

Karen Yarnell

Prayer: *Thank the Lord that He loves you and your prodigal. Ask Him to give you faith and wisdom in this difficult situation. Diligently pray for your prodigal.*

Personal Reflection: ....

....

....

....

....

....

Living in an Upside-Down World

Isaiah 3:1—4:1

"And in that day seven women shall take hold of one man, saying,
'We will eat our own food and wear our own apparel;
Only let us be called by your name,
To take away our reproach.'" (4:1)

The women of Isaiah's day, "the daughters of Zion," bore some of the responsibility for the desperate social situation denounced by the Lord (3:16–17). He pronounced judgment on these woman in several ways:

- They were wicked and unrepentant (3:17—4:1).
- They were proud and arrogant, which was apparent even in the way they moved about. They thought more highly of their own needs than those of others (3:16).
- They were immodest, attracting attention to themselves in a flirtatious and haughty way (3:16).
- They were materialistic, not only with many possessions but focusing on material things as the means for enhancing their status and comfort without regard for the needs of others (3:16, 18–23).

As a result, the Lord would take away everything in which they had placed their trust: physical beauty, material possessions, and confident self-assurance (3:17, 24).

The prophet then moves to address the women of Zion in light of the coming siege of Jerusalem, which would leave few men in the city. He prophesies that there will be "seven women [to] take hold of one man," pleading with him to take them into his household. They would be ready to give up their expected material provision just to have a marriage contract. Their determination to reverse roles and assume domination in the household would be stripped away.

They will long for the legal and social protection provided by marital union (4:1).

The lesson for women in this generation is to note the complete social and economic breakdown occurring with the final destruction of Jerusalem and the desperate conditions that followed. When we embrace a lifestyle that inherently rejects the priorities of the Lord and assignments found in the creation order (Gen. 1—2) and ignore His design for the home and the respective roles of husband and wife within marriage, we remove ourselves from the umbrella of His protection. We pursue living according to our own whims and receive the judgment that brings. When the moral breakdown of a nation reaches its women, the most devastating impact is on the home. Nothing is more tragic than the aftershock such destruction brings in the absence of the formative influence needed for the younger generation.

Dorothy Kelley Patterson

Prayer: *Seek God's face to examine your own priorities. Learn from the women of Jerusalem the dangers of upending divine assignments. Ask the Lord to help you see clearly His direction for you, especially as you invest in the next generation.*

Personal Reflection: ....

....

....

....

....

Accepting the Call

Isaiah 6:1–13

"Also I heard the voice of the Lord, saying:
  'Whom shall I send,
  And who will go for Us?'
Then I said, 'Here am I! Send me.'" (v. 8)

Were you ever given the task of delivering bad news to someone, knowing that there would be unfortunate consequences? I remember an unpleasant incident in my first career as a high school French teacher, when I observed one of my best students cheating on a major exam. Quietly, after the exam, I told her what I had seen, informing her that her grade average would consequently suffer. I was as upset as the student!

In today's text, the prophet Isaiah found himself in the unenviable position of being the bearer of bad news to his own people; yet he was willing to go nonetheless! Israel had "cheated" on the Lord; they spurned "the Holy One of Israel," drawing divine judgment upon themselves (5:24). Isaiah 5 speaks of judgment through impending war and captivity, while Isaiah 6 speaks of a slightly different judgment: God will refuse Israel spiritual comfort because they had grown deaf to God's voice and blind to His works, desensitizing their hearts to God's leading (vv. 9–10). Isaiah's bad news was that this situation would continue until they had been thoroughly judged for sin (vv. 11–12).

What could have motivated Isaiah? As he was worshipping in the temple, the Lord God revealed Himself in all His glory and splendor, surrounded by flying seraphim (Hb., "burning or fiery ones"). These beings covered their feet and faces with wings because of God's blinding holiness and called to one another: "Holy, holy, holy *is* the LORD of hosts" (vv. 1–3). The whole temple shook and "filled with smoke" (v. 4).

Awestruck, Isaiah watched this scene unfold, fearing for his life. He cried out: "Woe *is* me, for I am . . . a man of unclean lips, And . . . my eyes have seen the King, The LORD of hosts" (v. 5). A seraph touched his lips with "a live coal

. . . from the altar," purifying him for the Lord's presence and preparing him to be the Lord's messenger (vv. 6–7). God asked the poignant question: "Who will go for Us?" Isaiah responded willingly: "Here *am* I! Send me." Isaiah was willing to go and felt prepared as well.

The Lord called my husband and me as church planters among refugees from communist Romania who had settled in Australia, and the International Mission Board was ready to send us. The Lord had prepared us over many years. My husband Titus readily accepted, but I hesitated. "Here am I," but not, "Send me." The Holy Spirit worked in my heart to convict me that this open door for the gospel meant that God wanted us there. And so, by faith, I finally said, "Send me!"

Stefana Dan Laing

Prayer: *You can decide to follow Jesus because the Lord atoned for your sin, and He is able to sanctify you by the Holy Spirit. Ask Him to send you wherever He needs you; then go willingly!*

Personal Reflection: ....

....

....

....

....

....

Birth of Christ Foretold

Isaiah 7:1–17

〰️

"Behold, the virgin shall conceive and bear a Son,
and shall call His name Immanuel." (v. 14b)

Isaiah 7:14 is among the most well-known messianic prophecies. It is quoted in almost every Christmas pageant because it so clearly teaches the truths of the virgin birth and incarnation. Born of the virgin Mary (Matt. 1:18), Jesus was God incarnate, who came to bring God's gracious salvation to humanity by paying the penalty for our sins on the cross. This verse adds beauty to an already beautiful, celebrative season.

Yet few of us are acquainted with its darker, historical context of political turmoil and military unrest nor how the prophecy given by Isaiah was initially fulfilled in his own day (perhaps in the birth of Isaiah's own son; 8:3–4, 8, 10). God sent Isaiah to King Ahaz to offer a message of hope. As a descendant in the royal line of David, Ahaz ruled the southern kingdom of Judah. Ahaz's rule was threatened by two neighboring states (Israel and Syria), and he feared being deposed and replaced by a puppet regime. Isaiah came to tell him that those two kings would instead be defeated by Assyria, thus securing his throne. The birth of the child was to be a sign to Ahaz that God would do this because of His faithfulness to His covenant with David (2 Sam. 7:14). Even though the Assyrian Empire would dominate the entire region (8:7–8), the Lord would still be with Judah; He would not allow the Jews to be completely destroyed at that time (vv. 8, 10).

The message of hope to Ahaz was twofold. First, it proclaimed God's continuing faithfulness to His covenant promises, no matter how dire the circumstances may seem. Ahaz was surrounded by enemies, and the Assyrian empire was an ever-present threat. The Assyrian king had the military might to conquer Jerusalem at any time (humanly speaking), but God's sovereign covenant promises to David concerning his heirs remained, and so Ahaz was safe. We can have confidence in the promises of God given in His Word.

Second, the message included a promise of God's abiding presence with His people. The name "Immanuel" means "God with us," and its ultimate fulfillment appeared in Jesus' taking on flesh and living "among us" (Matt. 1:23; John 1:14). In Isaiah, it also referred to God's presence with His people as long as they were faithful. As believers, we have assurance that God is with us: We are not alone, even when it seems the whole world is against us. As in the past, so even now, "Immanuel" is a beacon of hope in any dark situation!

Stefana Dan Laing

Prayer: *Thank God for His faithful promises to His people, for signs of His presence amid dark circumstances. Praise Jesus, God incarnate, who humbled Himself to be born as a baby, to live among us as a weak and vulnerable human being. Glorify the Spirit, who overshadowed the obedient and humble virgin Mary of Nazareth, the instrument of Immanuel's coming.*

Personal Reflection: ....

....

....

....

....

....

....

The Danger of Complacency

Isaiah 32:9–15

~⌒~

"Rise up, you women who are at ease,
Hear my voice;
You complacent daughters,
Give ear to my speech.
In a year and some days
You will be troubled, you complacent women;
For the vintage will fail,
The gathering will not come.
Tremble, you women who are at ease;
Be troubled, you complacent ones." (vv. 9–11a)

In this passage, the prophet Isaiah addresses the over-confident women of Israel with warnings of pending judgment. His prophecy came to pass when the Assyrian armies invaded in 701 B.C. and destroyed the countryside, leaving only Jerusalem standing in the midst of a barren land stripped of any promise for harvest. The proper response for the women in the face of such a warning should have been belief in the words of God, which should have led them to mourning and repentance. Instead, these women are characterized by complacency, demonstrating a lack of spiritual sensitivity and rejection of obedience to the dire situation their nation faced.

Could it be said that Christians today are like those complacent daughters of Jerusalem? Do we take a casual attitude to life, preferring to be at ease, burying our heads in the sand instead of seeing the dire situation facing people today? A complacent person is self-satisfied with negligence and carelessness towards life, having an overconfident attitude in the face of adversity because she prefers simply not to face facts. Instead of being alert and having an understanding of her situation, she remains smug and self-satisfied with her laissez-faire approach to life. In the movie *Gone with the Wind*, Scarlett O'Hara demonstrated a complacent spirit when she refused to face the realities of her life after the war. In one memorable scene, she sighs heavily and says, "I will just think about that tomorrow." When tomorrow comes, she continues to refuse to confront her situation.

Contrary to such a complacent approach to life, believers should have a sense of urgency. We are commanded to be alert, sober-minded, and clear-headed (1 Pet. 1:13). Every person who does not know Christ is under a death sentence far worse than what the daughters of Jerusalem faced in Isaiah's day, and Christians are always to be ready to share the good news of the gospel (1 Pet. 3:15). Unfortunately, too many believers approach their relationship to Christ with the same spiritual insensitivity and disobedience as the daughters of Jerusalem, knowing what the Word of God says but refusing to heed it. I pray that you would not be complacent or careless Christians but women of God who are obedient to Him and passionate about accomplishing the His plan and purpose on earth.

Candi Finch

Prayer: *Are there any areas of your life where you are complacent? Ask the Lord to search your heart. Also, are there any people in your life who need to hear the gospel? Ask the Lord to give you boldness and opportunity to talk to them about Christ.*

Personal Reflection: ....

....

....

....

....

The Word of God Stands Forever

Isaiah 40:1–11

*"The grass withers, the flower fades,
But the word of our God stands forever." (v. 8)*

As a result of their sin and disobedience, God's people were in exile in Babylon. Yet through Isaiah, God is merciful to send a reminder that He sees their suffering and hears their cries. God must bring consequences for our sins, yet He always shows tenderness and compassion in the midst of the consequences. God reminds His people that He is in control of everything (vv. 3–4). He has power over our most powerful enemies and will be our one and only deliverer.

Isaiah uses an analogy that relates to each of us. We all witness grass and flowers dying without the necessary water or sunshine. This process happens so quickly and many times is out of our control. In my home, I even witness flowers and plants dying when I am watering, fertilizing, and grooming them daily. Admittedly, I am not a gifted gardener, but I can certainly appreciate what Isaiah is proclaiming. People come and go in our lives in similar fashion (v. 7). Leaders arise and are taken down, sometimes for reasons we can see and other times for reasons we cannot fathom. Power, wealth, influence, and prestige do not last forever.

However, Isaiah proclaims that in contrast to what is temporary, "the word of our God stands forever." Israel could be comforted knowing that all the promises God made to them will remain. Even though they must suffer consequences for their sins, they are not left without hope. God is alive and well and will see that His Word stands forever. We can be certain that even in the uncertainties of life and the people, God is constant. He is faithful and His mercies are new every morning (Lam. 3:22–23). God's Word cannot be changed. It is the same yesterday, today, and forever.

My passion in life as a wife and mother has been to saturate my heart and mind with God's Word and to speak it as often as possible in my home. I have more scriptures displayed in my home than I can count. I have been singing

Scripture songs to my girls since their birth. I made a commitment to the Lord when my girls were toddlers to correct them as necessary with Scripture. I desire to saturate their hearts and minds with God's command not my own. I will fade away at some point, but God's Word will remain long after I am gone. Also, as circumstances and situations change, our rules have to change, but God's Word and truth is constant. I firmly believe one of the greatest impacts we can make in the lives of those around us is sharing God's Word in every situation. He is able to provide everything we need for every moment.

Carmen Howell

Prayer: *Trust the Lord to help you love His Word and His truth more than anything. Seek His help to memorize it so that you might know it, live it, and share it.*

Personal Reflection: ....

....

....

....

....

....

....

The Lord Never Faints or Grows Weary

Isaiah 40:21–31

"Have you not known?
Have you not heard?
The everlasting God, the LORD,
The Creator of the ends of the earth,
Neither faints nor is weary.
His understanding is unsearchable." (v. 28)

Isaiah reminded Israel, God's people, who God was in this rich passage. His people were suffering in bondage and beginning to believe that God had abandoned them. In their difficulties, they had forgotten the power and love of their God. Isaiah began by stating that God is the Creator of all. There is no beginning or end in Him. He has always been and will always be. He "neither faints nor is weary" (v. 28). He cannot be exhausted by anyone or anything. He will not give up or give in! "His understanding is unsearchable" (v. 28).

When no one understands our thoughts, pain, confusion, doubts, tears, or joy, God understands. He knows all, sees all, understands all. At our weakest point, when we have nothing left to give physically, emotionally, or spiritually, He will give us the "power" to be sustained and strengthened. This power is not from without but from within. He gives power from nothing. Incredible!

Isaiah also admonishes them that everyone needs God. Age, education, station in life does not matter. Everything will fail us. Yet, do not be discouraged because He will not fail and He is able (Eph. 3:20).

In closing this passage, Isaiah gives us the promise that He is all-sufficient and will see us through every single challenge. However, you will notice it begins with waiting (Is. 40:31). God's help does not always come when we think we need it; His help comes when He knows we are ready for it! Yet, if we are willing to wait, He will "renew" our strength. He will exchange our weakness for His strength.

God's children will soar on the mountaintops like eagles, run through the valleys and not be tired, and walk through the daily struggles and chores of life and not faint. He cares about the big things and the little things. He has not forgotten His people Israel, and He has not forgotten about us either. He is the one who will make the darkness light around us and in us. Therefore, we must wait and trust His heart and His timing.

God knows exactly where you are and the struggles that you face today. He is not weary, anxious, or surprised by your struggles. He is ready to help you conquer them—trust Him and rise above your problems at the perfect time. Trust Him for today and forever.

Carmen Howell

Prayer: *Thank the Lord for reminding you of His power, love, and understanding of your circumstances. Trust Him more today than yesterday and learn His Word while you wait on Him to renew your strength.*

Personal Reflection: ....

....

....

....

....

....

Fear Not

Isaiah 41:1–10

~

"Fear not, for I am with you;
Be not dismayed, for I am your God.
I will strengthen you,
Yes, I will help you,
I will uphold you with My righteous right hand." (v. 10)

Because of their disobedience, God's people were walking through difficult days. The consequences of turning away from God were causing them to become weary and to question both His promises and His love for them. He reminds them in this passage that He has redeemed them. He has set them apart. Although He must punish sin in light of His holiness, His covenant with them has not changed. He has not cast them away (v. 9). They must look past their circumstances to Him.

God says there is no reason for fear, discouragement, or desperation. He is right here with you. He is the same powerful God who has provided for and protected you until now. He continues to encourage and promise His strength and help.

God does not say that He will remove our difficulties, but He does assure us that He will provide everything we need. He says "I will uphold you with My righteous right hand." He will not allow anything that is not just because He is not capable of unrighteousness. He will make all things right in my perfect time and plan.

In the midst of difficulty and pain, God will protect, sustain, and provide according to what is and what will always be right. Do not dwell on the circumstances and people around you. Look to God, Your Redeemer. He alone will bring justice to all!

This Scripture is a command—not an option. If you truly know Jesus, you will trust His heart. Even though His discipline sometimes seems heavy and you cannot see His purpose, you must walk in confidence and peace knowing that He is your God. He will strengthen and help us even when you are suffering for your own mistakes. God is incredibly kind; He does not leave you to make amends for your own mistakes. He is always with you to help and strengthen you. He will lead you to righteousness as you trust in Him. You need not fear any man, circumstance, or even death, because He will prevail in you and through you. When your days, your life, and your struggles are surrounding you in darkness, God can and will bring light, joy, and hope.

Carmen Howell

Prayer: *Ask the Lord to help control your fear of the people or circumstances in your life. He will bring light to your darkness! Trust Him because He loves you with an everlasting love. He will strengthen and help you.*

Personal Reflection: ....

....

....

....

....

....

....

God Will Be with You

Isaiah 43:1–7

"But now, thus says the Lord, who created you, O Jacob,
And He who formed you, O Israel:
'Fear not, for I have redeemed you;
I have called you by your name;
You are Mine.
When you pass through the waters, I will be with you;
And through the rivers, they shall not overflow you.
When you walk through the fire, you shall not be burned,
Nor shall the flame scorch you.'" (vv. 1–2)

As God's daughters, when we sin we still face the consequences of our actions. We may be tempted to believe that God has abandoned us. However, this passage gives hope to those walking through the Lord's "chastening" (Heb. 12:11). Israel was experiencing the Lord's punishment but received this encouragement (see Is. 42:18–25). He had not redeemed them to then abandon them. When they were unjustly enslaved by Pharaoh, God had delivered His people with His "mighty hand" (Deut. 7:8). Even in the most challenging of circumstances God promised to be with them (Is. 43:2).

If you are a child of God, redeemed from the bondage of sin through faith in Jesus, you can be certain God will not abandon you (1 Pet. 1:18–19; Gal. 3:27). He promised that He would never leave or forsake you (Heb. 13:5). John wrote, "See what great love the Father has lavished on us, that we should be called children of God" (1 John 3:1). And nothing can separate you from that love (Rom. 8:38–39). But can you really trust God to be there with you in the waters and fires?

Moses led the Israelites out of Egyptian captivity. No sooner had they departed than the Egyptians started pursuing them in chariots all the way to the sea. Had God led them out of Egypt just to let them die? God had Moses extend his hand over the sea so that the children of Israel crossed on dry ground while the Egyptians were covered with water (Ex. 14). God was with them in the waters.

During the Babylonian exile Daniel's three friends might have doubted God's presence. They had chosen to obey God by refusing to bow to the king's golden image, knowing that the penalty was to be thrown into "the midst of a burning fiery furnace" (Dan. 3:6). Upon hearing their staunch refusal to bow, the king heated the furnace seven-times hotter than usual. Expecting their instant death, the king looked and saw four men walking loose inside—the form of the fourth man "like the Son of God" (v. 25). The men exited unscathed. God was with them in the fire. The same God who was with the Israelites as they crossed the sea on dry land and was with Daniel's friends in the fiery furnace is with you.

Erika N. Mercer

Prayer: *Confess any known sin to God and ask Him for forgiveness. Thank God for His presence even when you have not obeyed Him.*

Personal Reflection: ....

....

....

....

....

....

The Potter and the Clay

Isaiah 45:1–13

*"Shall the clay say to him who forms it, 'What are you making?'
Or shall your handiwork say, 'He has no hands'?" (45:9b)*

The process of making pottery fascinates me! The heavy, wet lump of clay is placed in the center of a flat platform. The platform moves by turning slowly, gradually increasing with intensity. Potters work by shaping clay. Their hands leave that ugly glob of spinning clay only for very quick moments, sliding to another spot to continue shaping. The vessel is cured and painted, then fired at extremely high temperatures. The curing process includes specified periods of shelf time for it to set. The end product is a completely unique and usable vessel.

In Jeremiah 18, God called Jeremiah to come to the potter's house to receive a special message. That message became much clearer when I personally served as an apprentice to a master woodcarver. The first day I watched him turn wood into a beautiful bird, I got it. The piece of wood was in one hand and his knife was in the other. The clump of wood, like the lump of clay, becomes beautiful and usable in the hand of the Master.

Isaiah 45:9–10 provides a picture of the proper response to our Maker. We are not to question Him, only rest in His hands, allowing Him to shape us as He desires. We are not clay or wood. We are living, breathing human beings blessed with freedom of choice. The safest place is in the hollow of the hand of God.

Isaiah 64:8 complements Jeremiah 18:1, completing the thought from Isaiah 45. In the lyrics of a song of prayerful worship, I have described the potter and clay relationship this way: "Now, O Lord, You are our Father. We are the clay. You are the Potter. Take our lives. Shape our days. Hold and mold our hearts in the image of The Savior. By Your hand we would be broken, cleansed by the words that You have spoken. Search our souls. Make us whole, willing worthy vessels in the service of the Master."

Dr. Sam Gore, professor of art at Mississippi College since 1951, is beloved for his live demonstrations of clay sculpture. In approximately 20 minutes, he creates the head of Christ from a 13-pound lump of clay. With tears of conviction, joy and amazement, I recently watched Dr. Gore sculpt his 800th head of Christ. The sculpture was of the Potter.

I was the sound technician that evening. As he made final preparations, I asked when he would like for me to begin playing the background music. "Well, young lady, I would like you to start the music the moment I touch the clay." Wow! Adam was the first human note in the symphony of creation. The music of salvation began when God touched the clay and formed the first man.

Becky Brown

Prayer: *Ask God to mold and shape you into His vessel—willing, worthy, ready-to-be-used for His glory.*

Personal Reflection: ....

....

....

....

....

....

....

My Ways Are Not Your Ways

Isaiah 55:1–13

"'For My thoughts are not your thoughts,
Nor are your ways My ways,' says the LORD.
'For as the heavens are higher than the earth,
So are My ways higher than your ways,
And My thoughts than your thoughts.'" (vv. 8–9)

Although created in the image and likeness of God, men and women will never be equal to God. He is in an entirely different realm and is above all. This focal passage is a reminder of the necessity to understand that the Lord's purposes and will for our lives is not what our finite minds often think (vv. 8–9).

The prophet Isaiah urged the people to seek the Lord and turn from their wicked ways. We must turn from any way in our life that is not pleasing to the Lord. He reminded the people to "Seek the LORD while He may be found, Call upon Him while He is near" (v. 6). There is great danger if we continue to live in a lifestyle that is not pleasing to the Lord. Dear sister, remember we are not promised tomorrow. If we desire to know God's will and His best for our everyday lives, we will make sure that there is nothing hindering our fellowship with Christ.

"If I regard iniquity in my heart, The LORD will not hear" (Ps. 66:18). Sin separates us from God. Isaiah 55:8–9 reminds us of the great contrast between God and mankind. We must turn to God so we will be able to discover more fully who He is and how we are impure. Only Christ can wash away our sins and make us pure. This passage is a call for purity of heart and focus. In order to hear from a Holy God, we must have clean hearts that are receptive to His voice.

In a fallen and broken world, the temptation is to follow a path other than God's path. It should bring great comfort that we have a Creator who knows the direction we should follow and has designed a way for us to live that is best for us. As you surrender to the holy God and see a true picture of your unholy self, you must confess your sins before Him. Only then will you be able to know His purposes and His ways. He is your Shepherd and knows the best path for you to follow. He wants you to seek His face and daily surrender to be the woman He desires you to be. There is no greater path!

Monica Rose Brennan

Prayer: *Thank the Lord for His ways that are so much higher than ours. Confess your sins before the Lord, asking for strength to surrender daily to His will for your life. Praise Him for His purposes for your life, and submit to live a life that is pleasing to Him.*

Personal Reflection: ....

....

....

....

....

....

....

....

Formed in the Womb

Jeremiah 1:4–19

⤶

"Before I formed you in the womb I knew you;
Before you were born I sanctified you;
I ordained you a prophet to the nations." (v. 5)

The heavenly Father does a marvelous work in a woman's body when she is carrying a child. Within just a few weeks of conception, a baby's little heart is beating and limbs start to develop. A few weeks later, a baby's central nervous system is pieced together and his eyes and nose are developing. In the last few weeks before birth, the baby's lungs prepare him to take his first breath of air. No other time whispers so clearly of God's design; His value of life is woven into the creation of life!

Jeremiah focuses attention not only on the intricacy of the formation of our bodies but also on God's plan to draw us to Himself. God created you for a relationship with Him. How amazing to think that He knew you—in fact, he knew your whole life—before you were ever born! It's hard to imagine being capable of relationship before you entered the world, but think about how a mother loves her baby before he enters the world.

In the months before your birth, your mother carried you with her everywhere. She may have spoken to you about her day, called you by name, or run her hands along her growing belly as you kicked her. If you are a mother, you can recall this prenatal experience with your own child. In the days and weeks leading up to labor, you may have wondered about the shape of your baby's lips or the sound of her cry. Before a woman gives birth, she already has a bond with the baby in her womb. A mother loves that baby more than words can say.

That immense affection a mother feels for her child is a small reflection of the way God loves you. Even before He created your tiny, developing body, He loved you enough to send His Son to die for you. As He weaved together your body, He bestowed on you the dignity of being His most beloved creation.

God's love for you goes hand-in-hand with His intimate knowledge of your heart and your life. His foreknowledge of you included every choice you would ever make in your life. He already knew every sin you would commit, and yet He still desired to call you His beloved child. Sister, never question your Father's deep love for you. Be reassured that He has been present in every moment of your life, even when you were still in your mother's womb.

Laura Landry

Prayer: *Thank the Lord for His unending affection for you and His plan to draw you to Him. Ask Him to open your eyes to His sovereign ways in your life.*

Personal Reflection: ....

....

....

....

....

....

....

A Bride Never Forgets

Jeremiah 2:30–37

"Can a virgin forget her ornaments,
Or a bride her attire?
Yet My people have forgotten Me days without number." (v. 32)

Most women have special plans for their wedding day before ever being engaged. Plans take months, even years. Many women already know how they want their hair arranged, which wedding dress, and what accessories long before the big question is asked and the wedding is arranged.

Do you remember your wedding dress and jewelry? I am sure you do! When that day came for me, it was so simple because I had already thought through every detail including the wedding theme: "In His Time." Many brides also spend a lot of money to have their wedding dresses placed carefully in a special box after the wedding day. I needed no reminder to wear my dress on the day I had been anticipating since I was a little girl! I was ready to meet my groom!

The prophet Jeremiah confronts the sin of forgetfulness in the lives of the people of Israel (v. 32). He uses the example of a bride not forgetting her wedding dress or ornaments though Israel had forgotten God. How often we forget the things that matter most in life and begin to take them for granted!

The children of Israel had taken their eyes off God and had forgotten the reason for their existence. We are the bride of Christ, and He gave His life for us. Just as Jeremiah was urging the people to turn back to God in this passage, so we must evaluate our lives to determine our focus in life. Have we turned our eyes away from our Groom—God Himself? Have we allowed other things to creep into our lives? Have we been deceived concerning why we were created—to glorify God?

Many things in life demand your devotion and attention—your husband, children, ministry, hobbies, friendships, etc. While there is nothing wrong with giving devotion and attention to these important demands, nothing should ever take the place of God. The moment your focus drifts away from Christ, you begin to enter into idolatry. "No one can serve two masters; for either he will hate the one and love the other, or else he will be loyal to the one and despise the other. You cannot serve God and mammon" (Matt. 6:24). As the bride of Christ, your Groom is to come first in everything. May you never forget who He is and the calling He has given you to be His Bride!

Monica Rose Brennan

Prayer: *Ask the Lord to help you keep your eyes on Him so you will be a bride who never forgets her Bridegroom. Ask Him to forgive you for the times you have forgotten and have allowed other things to take His place. As His bride, you ought to seek His face daily to gain strength in Him.*

Personal Reflection: ....

....

....

....

....

....

....

....

Lying Words

Jeremiah 7:1–15

~~~

"Do not trust in these lying words, saying, 'The temple of the LORD,
the temple of the LORD, the temple of the LORD are these.'" (v. 4)

In Hebrew, to repeat something three times is like underlining, italicizing, and using a bold font—all three—for emphasis. By repeating the phrase "the temple of the Lord" three times, the Jews living in Judah, the southern kingdom of Israel, or their religious leaders were emphasizing their reliance on **the temple** for their security and identity.

Around 100 years before (722 B.C.), the Lord had judged the northern kingdom of Israel by allowing the Assyrian Empire to conquer and capture them. The northern kingdom had been ruled by a series of wicked kings who set up their own worship centers (plural) and Samaria as their capital. Surely the southern kingdom had been spared because **they** had restored worship of the Lord in His temple (singular) under King Josiah (ca 622 B.C.; see 2 Kin. 22:1—24:25). Those who entered the temple's gates "to worship the LORD" (Jer. 7:2) had to be in good standing with Him, right? After all, in Judah, the people worshipped the right God in the right place. The Lord would never let anything happen to Judah because His temple was there.

Through the prophet Jeremiah, the Lord confronted the notion head-on. In verse 4, He commands: "Do not trust in these lying words"; in verse 8, He accuses: "Behold, you trust in lying words that cannot profit." The question is, why would the Lord call their profession of trust in His temple "lying words?"

The way the Lord refers to the temple offers a big clue. Throughout this sermon, He calls it "the LORD's house" (v. 2) and "this house, which is called by My name" (three times, vv. 10–11, 14; cp. v. 30). He also prompts remembrance of "My place which was in Shiloh, where I set My name at the first" (see Josh. 19:51; 1 Sam. 1—4). What was important about His house was not the building but the worship conducted there. He called His people's devotion to the temple an outright lie because their conduct apart from the temple told another story.

Shamelessly guilty of oppression, theft, murder, adultery, lying, and idol worship (Jer. 7:6, 9–10), the people yet had the audacity to enter the Lord's house without repentance.

Not unlike many Sunday-only "Christians," were they? The Lord wanted their "ways" and their "doings" to match their professed worship of His name. Are you trusting in any "lying words"—claiming to belong to Jesus but living like you don't know Him? Or do your "ways" and "doings" confirm that you are, indeed, His daughter?

Tamra Hernandez

Prayer: *If you claim to trust in Jesus Christ as your Savior, then ask Him to keep "cleaning house" and allow Him to work on a specific area of hypocrisy in your life starting today.*

Personal Reflection:

Women's Intense Grief Because of Wars

Jeremiah 15:1–9

"She languishes who has borne seven;
She has breathed her last;
Her sun has gone down
While it was yet day." (v. 9a)

Nothing in this world is more unnatural than for a mother to bury her child. As we learn from the life cycle, age should always precede death; it's the natural order of things. But when a mother loses a child, it goes against that pattern, and the pain and grief felt are inexplicable. Perhaps Jeremiah 15 is so deeply sobering because it strikes at the heart of a woman at her lowest point.

Jeremiah, a prophet sent by God to talk some sense into the lives of the children of Israel, explains to the people their punishment for being so easily swayed and led by the evil king, Manasseh (v. 4). War is coming and it will devastate their country, their cities, and their homes.

Using the vivid picture of a mother with seven sons, that quintessential picture of perfection for a Hebrew household, and how quickly she is brought from glory to ruin having "breathed her last," Jeremiah shows how truly horrible this judgment will be for them. A mother who was once fully content in what she had been given by Yahweh will now groan with the grief of what sin does to her family. Her dreams are gone; her life has ended; the sun has set (vv. 7–9). And she has been left with nothing but grief. They left God (v. 6), and war has now come (v. 8). Sin called the shots, and they are the ones left bleeding. What was once her pride and joy is now her shame and misery.

This is a grave yet accurate picture of what sin does to a person's life! God desires to fill our lives with abundance (John 10:10; Eph. 3:20), but sin leaves us lifeless. The whole point of Christ's death is to eradicate our sin problem so that we could live life with Him! His salvation is not just for heaven **one day**; it is for **today**. He did not die to save us from eternal hell **someday** just to make us live an earthly one right now. Peace, protection, security, contentment, love, acceptance, value, guidance, a voice, and all those other things women seek after can all be found today in Christ. But sin comes in like a thief, like a lion, and kills your spirit. It strips you bare of the protection and goodness of God without which you cannot survive.

Sarah Bubar

Prayer: *Which sin is controlling your life? We all have them! Confess yours to the Lord. Come to Him in humility, seeking forgiveness for areas of your life where you, like the children of Israel, listened to the enemies of God and thereby brought war into your life. Do not wait until it is too late, until the consequences of sin have devastated your home beyond recognition.*

Personal Reflection:

Deceitfulness of the Heart

Jeremiah 17:9–10

⤺

"The heart is deceitful above all things,
And desperately wicked;
Who can know it?" (v. 9)

"Just follow your heart!" These words have been spoken by many well-meaning individuals seeking to offer advice or counsel. As women, we put a great deal of emphasis on feelings. We are emotive creatures, given the capacity to feel deeply. Emotion was one of God's great gifts to women to be used for His purposes and glory as we live in the world He created.

In the garden of Eden, a woman's feelings led her to commit the first sin. Eve saw "that the tree *was* good for food, and that it *was* pleasant to the eyes, and a tree desirable to make *one* wise" (Gen. 3:6). In that instant, sin entered her heart and her relationship with the Lord was broken. Eve's heart was deceived by the master liar. From the very beginning, Satan's intention was to dethrone God from the hearts of His people. His method of choice was deception; if he could cause Eve to believe that God was not good and that His Word was not true, he could stake his hold over her heart.

The mind is described as "the seat of thought and reason" while the heart is the "seat of emotions." The mind and the heart are inextricably bound together, each affecting the other. How you think influences how you feel, and vice versa!

Unfortunately, my heart doesn't always tell me the truth. Satan whispers lies to bind the people of God today just as he did with Eve; he tries to convince you and me that God is not good and that His Word is not true. When a door of opportunity closes, I begin to feel as though God's plan for me really isn't good. When His Word tells me what I don't want to hear, I begin to believe that the Scriptures may not be applicable to me after all.

Deception keeps a person from truly experiencing the Christ-life as God intended. Jesus said to His disciples, "If you abide in My word, you are My disciples indeed. And you shall know the truth, and the truth shall make you free"

(John 8:31–32). The key to seeing Christ enthroned in our hearts and ruling our emotions is: knowing and walking in TRUTH! Allowing the Word of God to take up residence in the heart ensures that Christ will be the master of your feelings and that your feelings will not control you.

Kristin Yeldell

Prayer: *Take comfort in knowing that Christ knows you completely and that He loves you. Are you tempted to believe that God's plans for you are not good? That His Word is not true? Confess that to Him and recommit your heart to walking in His ways and His Word. May Christ be enthroned in the home of your heart today and every day!*

Personal Reflection: ....

....

....

....

....

....

....

Satisfaction and Trust in God the Father

Jeremiah 31:1–14

"For I will turn their mourning to joy,
Will comfort them,
And make them rejoice rather than sorrow.
I will satiate the soul of the priests with abundance
And My people shall be satisfied with My goodness, says the LORD." (vv. 13b–14)

What brings you satisfaction? A well-cooked meal (preferably with bacon!), a well-crafted book, a relaxing nap, or perhaps that first sip of coffee or tea in the morning. As a non-morning person, I find that the first sip of strong black tea in the early hours of the day is so satisfying, like a calming balm coursing through me. The feeling of peace and tranquility on a quiet morning as I sip my hot tea is wonderful. In a simple way, a cup of hot beverage brings me pleasure and happiness. Satisfaction is defined as a finding pleasure when my needs have been met.

The prophet Jeremiah told the remnant of Israel that they would find true satisfaction in the future. The interesting thing, though, is that God's people would be satisfied with God's goodness (v. 14). What they needed for fulfillment, happiness, and pleasure is the very character of God Himself, the fact that He is good and trustworthy. Wealth, power, and fame are fleeting and would never bring real, lasting satisfaction to the children of God.

Consider how God displayed His character as a caring Father to His people in this passage. He claimed them as His people, despite their rebellion against Him (v. 1). He reminded them of His everlasting love and kindness toward them (v. 3). He cared enough to bring restoration to them, healing any broken places (vv. 4–5). He promised to gather them together and lead them so they would not stumble (vv. 8–9). When the people were powerless to redeem themselves or pay their own ransom, God the Father stepped in and took care of them (v. 11). He satiated the soul, making it "like a well-watered garden" (vv. 12, 14). God turns sorrow to joy and comforts His people in their distress (v. 13).

Better than any human father, God knows what is truly best for His children. He knows what will bring satisfaction, happiness, and pleasure because He is our Creator! As much as I love crispy bacon and a good cup of black tea, those things cannot bring me lasting satisfaction. The ultimate pleasure and happiness of human beings is found in a relationship with God. And, He never disappoints! His character has been proven over and over again, and His goodness never ends.

Candi Finch

Prayer: *Has there been a time in your life where you put your trust in God for your salvation? If not, would you consider trusting Him today? Remember, God made you, and you will only find lasting satisfaction in a relationship with Him. If God is your Father, thank Him for your salvation and for His goodness toward you.*

Personal Reflection:

Failure to Consider the Consequences of Sin

Lamentations 1:1–22

⤳

"Her uncleanness is in her skirts;
She did not consider her destiny;
Therefore her collapse was awesome;
She had no comforter.
'O LORD, behold my affliction,
For the enemy is exalted!" (v. 9)

Tears streamed down her cheeks as she sat across from me in my office. She told me how she never wanted to hurt her family and how she never intended to let it go on for so long. Before she took the stage as a worship leader, others looked to her marriage as the one of their dreams. She never imagined that **she** would become the woman who sat on the back pew in church, hoping that she wouldn't hear the whispers or notice the sideway glances. Her sin had robbed her of her reputation, her ministry, her friends, her husband, and even her children. My heart was absolutely broken to hear of her loss.

"When I was with him, I knew it was wrong, but I never stopped to consider the consequences. I was so caught up in the moment—and now that moment will impact the rest of my life," she said. "I know that God still loves me, and that He has forgiven me," she continued, "but will He restore my future?" She knew that her sin did not change God's character. He was still merciful and still good. Yet sin had taken her further from God than she ever wanted to go and cost her more than she had ever wished to pay. The consequence of her wrong choice was the utter collapse of the beautiful life she had built. Now, it was hard for her to imagine a future so different from her past.

In this passage in Lamentations, "she" refers to the people of Israel. The nation of Israel was spiritually and militarily weak. As a result, they were subject to God's wrath, and He punished them. Over and over in the Old Testament, the Israelites wandered away from God in sin. However, the beauty of the story is that God disciplines them, and then brings them back to Himself. He forgives the people who wander away from Him still today.

If you find yourself today utterly broken by sin, be reassured that God's love for you and pursuit of you never ceases. He can make beautiful things from the ashes of your life. If you are living in sin, learn from the example given in the book of Lamentations. Stop and consider the pain that comes when you disobey the Father. His plan is for your good. His law is to protect you. Repent, sister, and turn back to the Lord!

Laura Landry

Prayer: *Ask the Lord to guide you as you examine your heart today. Ask Him to reveal to you the hidden sins with consequences you have never considered. Plead with Him to break your heart for what breaks His, and ask Him to make you holy in His sight.*

Personal Reflection:

What Does It Take to Get Your Attention?

Lamentations 2:1–22

"See, O Lord, and consider!
To whom have You done this?
Should the women eat their offspring,
The children they have cuddled?
Should the priest and prophet be slain
In the sanctuary of the Lord?" (v. 20)

Have you ever come across a passage in Scripture and wondered what in the world is going on? Why is the author talking about women eating their own offspring (v. 20)? Whenever you come across such a verse or passage that you have trouble understanding, consider what is stated before and after the focal passage. This book of Lamentations is chiefly a song of grief over the siege, fall, and destruction of Jerusalem.

The mourner was acting as a representative of the nation as he expressed deep grief not only over the tragic events that had transpired but also over the situation precipitating those events. Rather than citing the national upheavals as the major reasons for Judah's demise, the author cites spiritual reasons instead. Judah's worst enemies were the people themselves, who with willful sin violated their covenant with Him many times over. God had sent prophets to plead with the people to turn back to Him and repent, but they had refused to listen.

In chapter two of Lamentations, the mourner describes the utter destruction of the city (vv. 1–9) and the weeping of the people over their shattered lives (vv. 10–22). The Jews were utterly devastated because of the horrors of the Babylonian siege. Children were starving and were victims of cannibalism by the desperate population. God tried to protect and warn them, knowing that if the people did not heed His counsel, then dark days would follow.

As the city lay in ruins and the people acted in atrocious ways, such as verse 20 mentions, grief finally gripped the people's hearts. The spiritual devastation and gravity of their sin became apparent when they could see the physical destruction and the low depths to which the people had sunk in order to survive. Can you imagine how different their lives would have been if they had simply listened to God's warnings in the first place?

Unfortunately, Christians can be just like the people of Jerusalem. We try to ignore the Holy Spirit's warnings when we start down the path of sin. We may turn a blind eye to the consequences, but the situation gets so serious that we are only left with destruction and devastation around us. The people of Jerusalem would warn us. Don't make the same mistake! Listen to what God tells you to do!

Candi Finch

Prayer: *Is God trying to get your attention about unconfessed sin in your life? Would you ask the Lord to search your heart to see if there is anything you need confess? Then, would you ask the Lord to give you the strength to be obedient to Him as you go throughout your day?*

Personal Reflection: ....

....

....

....

....

We Are NOT without Hope

Lamentations 3:1–33

*"'The Lord is my portion,' says my soul,
'Therefore I hope in Him!'" (v. 24)*

As I have led women's leadership conferences, I have noticed something that has surprised me. Many women who are seeking to be equipped to lead other women are themselves in crisis. I am not surprised that women deal with difficulties. In over 40 years of walking with the Lord and serving in ministry, I too have faced numerous trials that almost destroyed me. But what does surprise me is how women in leadership are not walking in the hope that is theirs through Christ.

Jeremiah is depressed and in despair, weeping over the destruction of Jerusalem (vv. 17–20). But in the next few verses, he refocuses on God and God's love. As he does, Jeremiah has hope despite the painful situation. He recalls God's mercies, goodness, and faithfulness and commits once more to put his hope in Him.

Have you recently considered how good God has been to you? How He offers new mercies every single morning? Anyone who says she follows Christ cannot be without hope. He is the living testament of God's love!

Paul expresses that "we do not give up" because we have the gospel, the good news of Jesus and what He has done for us. Paul faced multiple disasters (beatings, imprisonments, shipwrecks) but was able to say: "We are hardpressed on every side, yet not crushed; we are perplexed, but not in despair; persecuted, but not forsaken; struck down, but not destroyed" (2 Cor. 4:8–9).

To me personally, this promise means that no matter what happens or what attacks the devil may make on me or my loved ones, I will not give up but stand firm in my hope that never fails. I recently experienced a situation that should have made me fall apart, but instead I claimed God's promises and relied on his faithfulness. I prayed for peace in that storm, and He showered me with His presence, which led to that peace.

The longer we walk with God, the more we witness His love and goodness in our lives, the quicker we are to turn to Him and trust that He will handle each difficulty. He is "good to those who wait for Him," to the person who seeks Him," and it is good to "wait quietly" for deliverance (Lam. 3:25–26). The problem with us is that often we are not patient in our waiting. Instead of struggling through the next crisis, seek Him and His deliverance. He promises to be faithful!

Chris Adams

Prayer: *What difficulty are you facing right now? Pray and ask Him to show you how to wait patiently for Him to work it out. Ask Him to give you prayer partners to pray you through the "patient wait." Pray that He will show you how to "hope in Him" (v. 24).*

Personal Reflection:

Are You Hard-Hearted?

Ezekiel 3:4–9

"But the house of Israel will not listen to you, because they will not listen to Me;
for all the house of Israel are impudent and hard-hearted." (v. 7)

A callous is simply an area of thickened dead skin, which, for the most part, has no feeling. If you talk with a serious guitarist, she will tell you that the sooner calluses are developed on your fingers, the easier it will be to play the guitar. Believe it or not, there are actually steps you can take to form guitar calluses. For the guitarist, it's a good thing.

In today's verse, God tells Ezekiel that the people of Israel are hard-hearted (calloused). He also describes them as rebellious (Ezek. 2:6; 3:26; 5:6). How did their hearts become calloused? What were the steps they took to have "heart calluses"? They "despised My judgments and did not walk in My statutes, but profaned My Sabbaths; for their heart went after their idols" (20:16). Over time, the people of Israel had combined following God with following the gods of the nations around them. Unlike guitar calluses, these calloused hearts were anything but good.

An important fact is that hardened hearts do not develop overnight but gradually. There were times when the people of Israel humbled themselves and were obedient to God. In fact, less than three decades earlier, the people, under King Josiah, had recommitted themselves to God (2 Kin. 23:1–3). But it wasn't long before they "transgressed more and more, *according* to all the abominations of the nations" (2 Chr. 36:14). Their hearts became calloused toward God as they incorporated the culture of the people they lived among. God's people had forgotten they were called to be a holy, set-apart people.

While God described these people as hard-hearted, calloused, and rebellious, He did not plan to leave them that way. His promise to Ezekiel, and ultimately to His people, was to return them from exile (Ezek. 11:17), give them unified hearts (11:19), and a heart of flesh—one ready to obey God (vv. 19–20). This promise was for restoration of the people to their Creator God.

That promise of restoration is ours today through the sacrificial death of Jesus Christ. Upon placing faith in His death, burial, and resurrection, you receive a new heart that is ready to follow hard after God (2 Cor. 5:17). Your calloused heart is replaced with a heart of flesh, soft and moldable toward the things of God.

Denise O'Donoghue

Prayer: *If you have never accepted Jesus Christ as your Lord, ask Him to give you a heart of flesh and show you how to follow Him. If there are areas in your life where you might be yielding to the culture around you, ask God to reveal them to you. Ask Him to forgive you for any ways that you may have become hard-hearted towards Him.*

Personal Reflection: ....

....

....

....

....

....

....

Whom Do You Worship?

Ezekiel 8:1–18

⌒

"So He brought me to the door of the north gate of the Lord's house; and to my dismay, women were sitting there weeping for Tammuz. Then He said to me, 'Have you seen this, O son of man? Turn again, you will see greater abominations than these.'" (vv. 14–15)

Every so often I go to a nail salon to have a pedicure. One of the first things I see, as I walk into the salon, is a small idol with fruit and other offerings around it. I smell the incense as it burns by the idol. You've probably seen this too. I am saddened that these people are worshipping an idol, yet at the same time I think, how could they do that? Worse, I pridefully think, "I would never worship an idol."

Tammuz was a fertility god, an idol of the ancient Akkadians. It was thought that he died every year with the harvest and would then live again with the spring rains. Perhaps the weeping women were waiting, afraid he would not come again to bless the spring planting. What is really ironic about this scenario is that they were sitting at the actual gate of the temple of the Lord, the very Creator of all living things, yet they chose to worship another god (v. 16).

Before becoming incredulous at the thought of these women worshipping an idol, consider a definition of idol. Tim Keller, in his book *Counterfeit Gods*, defines an idol as "anything more important to you than God, anything that absorbs your heart and imagination more than God, anything you seek to give you what only God can give."* Well, now, that steps on my toes! How about yours?

Are we like the women weeping over Tammuz in the shadow of the temple, claiming to be followers of God yet worshipping idols? Could it be that we are absorbed with our homes and the stuff that fills them? Our bodies and the stuff we put on them? Our time and how we want to spend it? Could it be that you allow these or similar things to "absorb your heart and imagination more than God?" The Lord told Ezekiel that what these women were doing was an abomination. May these words of God be a wakeup call for you to check your own heart and evaluate whom you truly worship.

Denise O'Donoghue

Prayer: *Pray Psalm 139:23–24:*

> *"Search me, O God, and know my heart;*
> *Try me, and know my anxieties;*
> *And see if there is any wicked way in me,*
> *And lead me in the way everlasting."*

Ask the Lord to reveal to you anything that is more important to you than Him. Prayerfully wait for the Holy Spirit to answer. Ask the Lord to forgive you for allowing anything to take His rightful place as most important; then ask Him to help you properly worship Him alone.

Personal Reflection: ....

....

....

....

....

....

....

* Timothy Keller, *Counterfeit Gods* (New York, NY: Penguin Group, 2009), xvii.

Putting Trust in the Wrong Things

Ezekiel 16:1–30

૮ꝋ

"But you trusted in your own beauty, played the harlot because of your fame, and poured out your harlotry on everyone passing by who would have it." (v. 15)

The prophet Ezekiel had a very straight word with the people of Jerusalem in this passage. The beginning of the chapter talks about God's tender care and love for the people (vv. 1–14); yet instead of trusting in Him, they trusted in themselves, other nations, and other gods. God had nurtured them when they struggled (v. 6), made them beautiful and attractive (v. 7), and enabled them to thrive (v. 7). He loved them and entered into a covenant with them so that in a very real sense the people were in a committed relationship with Him (v. 8). Like a loving husband, he provided for their needs and gave them many beautiful things (vv. 9–13), and because of His care for them, their fame went out among the nations (v. 14).

Instead of telling the other nations about their great God, the people turned from Him and trusted in their own fame and beauty (v. 15). Though they had entered into a covenant with God, they cheated on Him ("played the harlot") with other nations and gods. Everything they had was because of God, yet they allowed themselves to be puffed up with pride. The intoxicating allure of other people's praise made them forget their God. They trusted in temporary and fleeting things instead of God, who is a solid Rock and an unshakable fortress.

Who or what do you put your trust in for salvation? Is it the Lord or do you think your good works will get to go to heaven someday? The Bible says that the only way to heaven is through a relationship with Jesus Christ (John 14:6); we can't do anything to earn our salvation (Eph. 2:8–9). And, once in a relationship with Christ, God wants us to trust in Him alone each day and not be unfaithful to Him with other gods or idols or religions.

If you are already a believer, in what do you put your trust each day? Do you think your looks are what will make people like you or give you success in life?

The Bible warns that beauty is passing (Prov. 31:30). Many think a pretty face, a stunning outfit, or a certain size figure is where a woman's worth is found. The culture certainly stresses such things! Or, is fame or being well-known and liked by many people where you find value? There is nothing ultimately wrong with wanting to be beautiful or well-liked, but that is not where your worth should be found. Your worth and value are found in a relationship with God!

Candi Finch

Prayer: *Spend a few moments thanking God for the sacrifice He paid for us so we can have a relationship with Him.*

Personal Reflection: ....

....

....

....

....

....

....

Knowing the Difference between the Holy and Unholy

Ezekiel 44:10–31

⌒

"And they shall teach My people the difference *between the holy and the unholy, and cause them to discern between the unclean and the clean." (v. 23)*

Do you know how new treasury agents in the Department of the Treasury are trained to recognize counterfeit money? In their first days on the job, they don't study the history of forgery or pour over endless variations of fake bills. No, they sit in a room and study real money. They feel and touch the uniqueness of the paper, study each nuance of different bills, and smell the fragrance of real money. In this type of training, new treasury agents will become so familiar with the real thing that it will be easy for them to spot a fake.

In the same way, God desires that each of His children become so immersed in His Word that it would be immediately apparent when a counterfeit belief or idea crosses her path. In Ezekiel 44, God gave instructions to the priests. One of their most important duties was to teach the people to recognize the difference between holy and unholy things. The priests were to equip the people with discernment that enabled them to distinguish those things honoring the Lord and those ways of living and thinking that did not honor Him.

Certainly, today, pastors are entrusted with the same task of training believers to be discerning. However, there are many other ways that you and I can train our senses to know the difference between the godly and ungodly. Listening to the teaching and preaching of trusted, godly leaders is a good start. Spending time studying God's Word each day is another. Just like those new treasury agents, it is so important for children of God to pour over the "real thing." As we learn what God says about how to live and think, how to react in difficult circumstances, and how to treat people, the more we can line our lives up under God's way.

Being around people who model God's way of life is also a great way to learn how to discern between the holy and the unholy. Let's be honest. We don't have to work hard to be exposed to unholy people, things, and ways of living!

Those ideas scream at us from TV shows, billboards, magazines, social media, and in many other forms. That is why it is so important for you as a Christian to make sure you are spending time around God's people and putting yourself in places and circumstances where you are exposed to God's way of thinking.

Candi Finch

Prayer: *Are you able to spend time with God studying His Word on a regular basis? Thank God for His Word, and ask Him to help you to recognize the difference between holy and unholy ideas and ways of life.*

Personal Reflection: ....

....

....

....

....

....

....

Purpose in Your Heart Not to Defile Yourself

Daniel 1:1–8

*"But Daniel purposed in his heart that he
would not defile himself...." (v. 8a)*

Daniel and his friends were probably around 15 years of age when they were taken captive and transported to Babylon. They were ripped from their homeland and separated from their families and then immersed in a culture completely foreign to everything they had ever known, forced to learn a new language, new cultural customs, and even given new names that referred to foreign gods. Everything familiar to them was stripped away! All of the events described in Daniel 1:1–7 were completely out of Daniel's hands. However, much can be learned from this young teenager about how to stand strong in adverse situations and honor God in the midst of a pagan culture.

Verse 8 marks a clear transition from a description of circumstances beyond Daniel's control to an account of his own decisions. Daniel made up his mind that he would not compromise or defile himself with practices, customs, and behaviors that would be displeasing to God. Daniel and his friends could have used their exile, distance from Jerusalem, and indeed, the destruction of their worship sanctuary to excuse the application of the rules of their faith. Yet, in the years of their youth, as much as in adulthood and old age, Daniel and his companions demonstrated uncompromising faith, even at the risk of their lives (1:8; 3:18; 6:10). God had called Israel to be a nation set apart as a witness to unbelievers, and this group of exiles determined to remain holy even as their nation was disciplined by the Babylonian conquest.

What does it look like today to "purpose in our hearts not to defile our-selves"? To defile means to corrupt something and make it impure. It is possible for us to compromise our lives by letting ungodly things have an influence on us. Are there any customs, practices, and behaviors that you or I may have adopted that really go against God's standards? If so, we must clean out our closets, so to speak, and get rid of anything that would cause us to sin or compromise our beliefs. That may include cutting out forms of media that cause you to dwell on ungodly things, changing clothing styles that skirt the line of modesty, or possibly even eliminating "corrupt talk" (Eph. 4:29). Remember, the end result of not conforming to the culture is often the opportunity to be a witness for God just like Daniel and his friends.

Candi Finch

Prayer: *Praise the Lord for the example of Daniel and his friends in how to live life in an ungodly culture and how to react to circumstances beyond your control. Then, examine your life, asking the Lord to convict you of any ways you may be defiling yourself with thoughts, habits, or behaviors that are more like the culture than like Christ.*

Personal Reflection:

Standing Strong in the Fiery Furnace

Daniel 3:1–18

～

"Shadrach, Meshach, and Abed-Nego answered and said to the king,
'O Nebuchadnezzar, we have no need to answer you in this matter.
If that is the case, our God whom we serve is able to deliver us from
the burning fiery furnace, and He will deliver us from your hand, O king.
But if not, let it be known to you, O king, that we do not serve your gods,
nor will we worship the gold image which you have set up.'" (vv. 16–18)

Every book of the Bible was included in the canon of Scripture for a specific reason. The book of Daniel, for instance, preserves the history of how God's people survived and maintained their identity through both the destruction of Jerusalem in the sixth century B.C. by the Babylonian king, Nebuchadnezzar, and their 70-year captivity in Babylon, which followed. The Jewish people should not have survived that attack and further punishment, but they did survive; and the account of Shadrach, Meshach, and Abed-Nego gives a good indication as to why (Dan. 3).

Bonfires may be a good idea, until some crazy guy decides to douse the fire with gasoline, and then your eyebrows may go missing. We've all been there. These three friends faced danger when they refused to bow down to a golden image that had been set up by King Nebuchadnezzar. He became so enraged by Shadrach, Meshach, and Abed-Nego's unwillingness to worship the idol that he not only arranged for them to be thrown into a furnace, but he also commanded that the heat of the fire be turned up seven times the usual temperature! Yet these three Jewish boys held their ground. They declared that whether or not God decided to deliver them physically, He was still the only One worthy of their allegiance.

Shadrach, Meshach, and Abed-Nego's ability to make such a courageous stand of faith did not simply come to them in that moment of trial. Rather they had spent a lifetime facing smaller "fires," and every stand they made along the way added up to this great moment of testing. Every single day of your life counts. It matters what you watch, what you hear, what you wear, what you say, what you do with your time and resources. Have you discovered God to be most worthy of your worship in these things? Are the choices you are making today preparing you to be one who can and will take a stand for the faith when your day of "facing the furnace" comes? He requires nothing less than your best at all times. Then God will give you everything more in return.

Courtney Veasey

Prayer: *Praise God for the joy you have in knowing Him. Proclaim His worthiness, and ask that He make you stand firm in days of trial. Display your wonder and worship before Him alone today.*

Personal Reflection:

Can People Tell You Know the Lord?

Daniel 4:1–18

◡◠

". . . But you are able, for the Spirit of the Holy God is in you." (v. 18b)

Have you ever wondered what people think of Christianity when they observe your life? In the mundane, routine moments of the day, would someone glancing at you or me from across the room see a difference in us, maybe in the way we react to a rude person or how we treat a waitress or maybe even how we talk to members of our family? Does the way we live out our faith in our lowest moments such as when tragedy strikes or when death darkens our doors point to the strength, hope, and joy people can experience only by knowing Christ?

Throughout Daniel's life journey from a young teenager to an old man, he lived without compromise as an exile in a foreign land. His life of faithful devotion gained him favor with God, and the people around him took notice. In fact, his life of integrity distinguished him from his administrative peers and garnered the respect of the ruling authorities.

Nebuchadnezzar, the first king of Babylon where Daniel served, recognized that the "Spirit of the Holy God" was in him (v. 18). Then, when Nebuchadnezzar's son Belshazzar experienced a truly puzzling event, the queen counseled Belshazzar to consult Daniel because he was a man "in whom *is* the Spirit of the Holy God" (5:11). When Darius became king, "Daniel distinguished himself above the governors and satraps, because an excellent spirit *was* in him" (6:3). Over and over again, people sought out Daniel because they recognized that he was wise and the God he served was holy and powerful.

Remember, Daniel was surrounded by a people and culture that tried to get him to change his beliefs and customs. Nevertheless, instead of being conformed to the Babylonian culture, he had an impact on those around him. It is the difference between a potato and a coffee bean. If you put them side by side, the potato seems like it would be stronger than the small little bean. However, when a potato is put in a pot of boiling water, the once stalwart vegetable turns mushy. The heat of the water slowly causes the potato to weaken as it soaks up the boiling water. When you put a coffee bean in boiling water, the exact opposite happens. Those tiny, insignificant beans flavor the water and cause the clear liquid to take on the taste and smell of coffee.

This is ultimately how a Christian should impact her world! No matter how "hot" the circumstances, God wants us to impact the culture around us so that we have the opportunity to point people to Him (Rom. 12:2).

Candi Finch

Prayer: *Can people around you tell that you know Christ? Pray that as you go about your day today that you talk and act in a way that points people to the hope found only in Christ.*

Personal Reflection: ....

....

....

....

....

....

....

....

The Danger of Pride

Daniel 5:1–30

"But when his heart was lifted up, and his spirit was hardened in pride, he was deposed from his kingly throne, and they took his glory from him." (v. 20)

Is pride always a bad thing? Perhaps not. You can be proud of your husband when he receives a well-deserved promotion. Similarly, you can be proud of your child when she makes a good grade after studying hard. So, when is pride dangerous?

Nebuchadnezzar, king of Babylon, is the subject of today's reading. King Nebuchadnezzar's pride resulted in his losing the kingly throne and its glory. So, how is the pride of Nebuchadnezzar different from the pride mentioned above, i.e., pride in the accomplishments of others?

Daniel 2 gives insight to this important question. It records a conversation between Daniel, a Jewish exile, and the king. Daniel had been summoned to interpret the king's dream. Daniel explains: "You, O king, *are* a king of kings. For the God of heaven has given you a kingdom, power, strength, and glory; and wherever the children of men dwell, or the beasts of the field and the birds of the heaven, He has given *them* into your hand, and has made you ruler over them all" (vv. 37–38). Eventually Nebuchadnezzar ran into trouble. He forgot the interpretation of the dream and took credit for his own power and glory.

Later King Nebuchadnezzar, while surveying his country, exclaims: "Is not this great Babylon, that **I have built** for a royal dwelling by **my mighty power** and for the honor of **my majesty**?" (Dan. 4:30). King Nebuchadnezzar failed to acknowledge that all he had was given to him by God—his kingdom, his power, his strength, and his glory. As a result of his pride and arrogance, King Nebuchadnezzar was driven into the wilderness to live like an animal (vv. 31–33).

You and I likely do not walk on the roof of our homes exclaiming that everything in our sight is due to our greatness and our vast power. However, like King Nebuchadnezzar, perhaps we take credit for things that God has given to us by His hand. Have we, over time, forgotten that He is the source of all that we have?

"When pride comes, then comes shame; But with the humble *is* wisdom" (Prov. 11:2). Our culture will lure and entice us to exalt ourselves. It will feed our pride. Let us seek a humble heart and a teachable spirit, all the while giving God the glory.

Denise O'Donoghue

Prayer: *Ask the Lord to reveal areas in your life where dangerous pride might be an issue. Ask Him to forgive you for instances in your life where you have failed to acknowledge Him as the giver and have instead taken credit for yourself. Ask for a humble spirit. Thank Him for all that you have received from His hand and ask for godly wisdom to govern it well.*

Personal Reflection: ....

....

....

....

....

....

....

The Patterns That Steer a Life

Daniel 6:1–17

"Now when Daniel . . . went home. . . . in his upper room, with his windows open toward Jerusalem, he knelt down on his knees three times that day, and prayed and gave thanks before his God, as was his custom since early days." (v. 10)

Daniel's integrity and wisdom as a high-ranking administrator in the government of Darius were legendary. Even his enemies recognized Daniel's exemplary leadership and found his character to be unassailable (v. 5). Daniel's knowledge of Darius's decree (v. 7) failed to discourage his disciplined pursuit of the Lord. Three times daily, he sought the Lord, opening his window and looking toward Jerusalem with no effort to conceal his activities or to deceive his detractors by appearing to comply with the ungodly edict. He made no effort to change his place of worship despite his knowledge that they were watching his every move. He did not disrupt his pattern for praying in humility and obedience.

This crisis did not deter Daniel but instead created a desire in his heart to go to the Lord with the crisis. Because of his exemplary life, even the king was agonizing, trapped in his own legal system (v. 14). Yet the strict law of the land meant that Darius must send Daniel to the den of lions.

Daniel was taken captive as a young man. How did he develop this devotion to the Lord? Being immersed in a pagan culture at a young age must have made it difficult for him to keep his faith—much less faithfully exercise his commitments to the living God. Yet he continued doing what he had done before, placing his petitions before the Lord and trusting Him for the outcome. Although the text does not say how Daniel learned to seek the Lord, he did so "as was his custom since early days." We can assume that his parents, and perhaps especially his mother, had a part in establishing these godly patterns of seeking the Lord regularly and in all matters in his life.

Mothers play a pivotal role in preparing their babies, children, and teens for the world in which they must live with many evil influences. Mothers are uniquely gifted with nurturing sensitivities to exert amazing influence over their offspring. Such influence does not come with quality time here and there but with the investment of a life in quantities of time, energy, and creativity—and prayer. "The woman who rocks the cradle that rules the world" is not the only successful woman, but "the woman who spends much time on her knees in behalf of her children" will also see overwhelming victories!

Dorothy Kelley Patterson

Prayer: *Lift your children and the young people who cross your path before the Lord. Pray specifically for their spiritual nurture. Teach them by word and by life example what it means to seek the face of the Lord.*

Personal Reflection: ....

....

....

....

....

....

....

....

Gomer—Hope Lost Can Be Restored

Hosea 1:1–3

∽

When the LORD began to speak by Hosea, the LORD said to Hosea:
   "'Go, take yourself a wife of harlotry
   And children of harlotry,
   For the land has committed great harlotry
   By departing from the LORD.'
So he [Hosea] went and took Gomer, the daughter of Diblaim. . . .".
   (vv. 2–3a)

Hosea's marriage is interwoven with his prophetic work. God planned to teach about Israel's unfaithfulness to the Lord through the betrayal of Hosea's wife. The prophet lived during Old Testament times and was a devout servant of God. Hosea obeyed God and married Gomer, an immoral woman. What a painful way to learn a lesson!

Hosea and Gomer marry, and she gives birth to three children—Jezreel, Lo-Ruhamah, and Lo-Ammi (vv. 4, 6, 9). The children of Hosea and Gomer followed in her sinful footsteps and are described in the Bible as "children of harlotry" (v. 2). The prophet Hosea must have felt hopeless as Gomer lived an adulterous lifestyle and their children rebelled against God. Dreams of a fruitful ministry for the young preacher seemed destroyed.

Gomer shamelessly committed adultery with numerous men and was enslaved by them (Hos. 2:2, 5; 3:1–2). Her husband rescued her, forgave her, and remained faithful to her despite his public humiliation. Gomer experienced some consequences for her sin, a period of discipline and time of renewal before resuming marital privileges. Hosea's faithfulness and compassionate love is a picture of God's unfailing love when His children are unfaithful. Gomer's life also illustrates the depth of God's forgiveness and restoration.

Iris Blue may be considered a modern-day Gomer. Raised in church, she rebelled from her faith and became promiscuous. As a teenager, she ran away from home, became addicted to drugs, and was arrested for armed robbery.

After her incarceration, someone witnessed to her, and she was genuinely saved. Jesus changed her life dramatically. In her testimony, Iris proclaims: "I knelt down a tramp and stood up a lady!" God forgave her of her sin and restored her life. Though she served time in prison, she now serves the Lord. Recently she commented: "After serving an eight-year sentence in Texas, I am now serving Jesus forever – forgiven, clean, and new (2 Cor. 5:17). Thanks to Jesus, the older I get, the 'newer' I get!" God offers that same redemption to all.

The lesson from Gomer's life is clear: **Hope lost can be hope restored**. Because Hosea had faith in God, he did not give up on his marriage. God instructed Hosea to marry Gomer, bring her home, and redeem her as his own. Hosea obeyed God and his marriage was restored. His faithfulness to God and to marriage strengthened his life and ministry. While Gomer is a negative example, her restoration to God and to her husband gives hope and confidence even to those who sin against God.

Rhonda Harrington Kelley

Prayer: *Thank the Lord for His faithfulness and forgiveness! Ask Him to bring hope and restoration to you and others who fail to follow Him.*

Personal Reflection: ....

....

....

....

....

Do You Pursue Other Lovers?

Hosea 2:1–13

"She will chase her lovers,
But not overtake them;
Yes, she will seek them, but not find them.
Then she will say,
'I will go and return to my first husband,
For then it was better for me than now.'" (v. 7)

The book of Hosea is a true story about how God's prophet Hosea rescues his wife Gomer from an adulterous life. God uses the storyline of Hosea and Gomer to teach about His love for Israel even though they have committed adultery against Him. Israel's adultery was committed because they turned away from the Lord to worship idols, figuratively pursuing other "lovers" (v. 2). "Children of harlotry" refers to the children being born as a product of the adulterous unions of the wayward wife and her lovers (v. 4). These particular children figuratively represent the idolatrous Israelites who had no right to identify themselves as God's sons and daughters. The adulterous wife is described as one who has been deceptively convinced that her lovers, rather than her husband, have provided for her (v. 5).

Due to the adulterous wife seeking other lovers, the Lord chose to make her idolatrous pursuits unpleasant and unrewarding. The imagery implies that the Lord would entrap or frustrate the efforts of His people (vv. 6–7). The Lord does not force those who belong to Him to remain faithful to Him. However, He does actively work against their rebellious pursuits in order to show them that living in obedience to the Lord is far more rewarding than the short lived pleasures of their idolatry. Verse 7 does not specifically promise redemption, but it does anticipate it. No assurance that Israel's relationship with the Lord will be restored is given until verses 14–23, it is only expected. The fact that Israel will seek her "husband" anticipates the promise: *"That* you will call Me 'My Husband,' And no longer call Me 'My Master'" (v. 16). A wife seeking elsewhere for the provision that only her faithful husband could provide her constituted betrayal. Israel had done this, they had chased after other idols seeking the things that only the Lord could provide for them (v. 8).

What do you pursue? Do you pursue other lovers, or do you chase after what is pleasing to the Lord? Our Lord is jealous; He desires your complete attention and worship. Only in the will of God do you find what is needed.

Jessica Pigg

Prayer: *When you pray, ask the Lord to forgive you for all your sinful pursuits. Then commit to memory Matthew 6:33 so that when you pursue something other than God you will remember: "Seek first the kingdom of God."*

Personal Reflection: ....

....

....

....

....

....

....

....

The Promise of Restoration

Hosea 2:14–23

"Then I will sow her for Myself in the earth,
And I will have mercy on her who had not obtained mercy;
Then I will say to those who were not My people,
'You are My people!'
And they shall say, 'You are my God!'" (v. 23)

Hosea the prophet (Hb. "help, deliverance, salvation") ministers mainly in the northern kingdom of Israel (Ephraim). On the surface, this nation looks to be enjoying a time of prosperity and substantial growth. However, with a closer look, moral corruption and spiritual adultery permeate the people of Israel.

Although remembered as a place where the people grumbled against the Lord, the wilderness also signifies the place where the people of Israel had to rely on God to provide for them (v. 14). Time after time God spoke comfort to His people and promised to restore to them what He had previously stripped away, even declaring that He would make the "Valley of Achor as a door of hope" (v. 15). The name "Valley of Achor" (Hb. "trouble") was given to the place where the sin of a man named Achan had brought great turmoil upon the Israelites following the battle of Jericho. It was at this place of restoration that God's people would respond (Hb. 'anah, "call or cry out") to the Lord, just as they had done before when the Lord first brought them out of Egypt and forged the covenant at Mount Sinai.

In verses 19-20, five of the Lord's attributes are given to characterize His commitment to the people of Israel. Righteousness and justice denote God's perfect fairness in His treatment of Israel (v. 19). It is the righteousness and justice of God, not Israel, that restores them. Love and compassion describe God's steadfast commitment to Israel (v. 19). In verse 20, it is God's faithfulness that is contrasted to Baal's fickleness and Israel's unfaithfulness.

These five attributes were considered to be comparable to the bride price for His marriage to the people of Israel (v. 19). During this time, the bride price was an amount of money or property paid by the groom or his family and given to the parents of the woman he was to marry. This bride price would not only reveal to the woman's parents his commitment to marriage, it would also prove to her parents that he was able to provide for her.

Does your relationship with the Lord need to be restored? Just like the bride price, the Lord has sent His One and Only Son to die on the cross for your sins. The blood of Jesus was shed in order to purchase you and have a covenantal relationship with you.

Jessica Pigg

Prayer: *Ask the Lord to restore your relationship with Him. Confess your sins to the Lord. Remember that Jesus provides forgiveness of sins to those who ask. Now seek to live in the righteousness of God. Pray asking God to give you the strength to live victoriously in the righteousness that only He can provide.*

Personal Reflection: ....

....

....

....

....

....

....

Weighing Sorrow and Joy

Joel 1:1–12

"All the trees of the field are withered;
Surely joy has withered away from the sons of men." (v. 12b)

Have you ever had an "Alexander" day? You know, the "terrible, horrible, no good, very bad" kind?* This kind of day occurs where everything that could go wrong does, and as quickly as your emotions unravel, your joy plummets into the depths of despair. Okay, maybe things are not that catastrophic, but we do get cranky! The prophet Joel describes this kind of sorrow in terms of locusts plaguing the land in which God's people are living (v. 4).

The nation of Israel had once again wandered from their God; He no longer had their undivided admiration. They continued with their religious customs, but it was all empty. The outward worship did not make its way into their hearts. So when the plague descended, the land was stripped bare, and joy withered away with the vegetation (vv. 11–12).

Joy can be like a litmus test to see where our true contentment lies. If joy vanishes as obstacles sprout up choking our productivity, our joy may be misplaced. Life is not easy! We all have those days when it is hard to smile about what is happening in our lives. Surely this is how Israel felt. Their fields were dried up, not because they had not worked their land, but because an outside force had wreaked havoc on their crops leaving death and destruction in its wake. All they could see was barrenness as they looked at their hopeless land.

Before you give the people of Israel too hard a time, first look inwardly at your own life. How many of you are simply going through the motions of church attendance and religious practices, completely devoid of a thriving and deepening walk with the Savior? You put on a good face for Sunday mornings, but by Monday afternoon you are tired of the task. You are dried up and withering away, and your human joy fades along with you.

Often you forget on those Alexander days that you still have much for which to rejoice. There is still the forgiveness of your sins, a Savior who loves you unbelievably, and an eternity with Him. But when your focus and your contentment is wrapped up in your current situations, joy can be as flexible as a child's Slinky®, descending with each step. Hard times will come into your life. While you cannot control those outside forces and what they will bring, you can choose joy over sorrow.

Sarah Bubar

Prayer: *If you have lost your joy because of circumstances, examine the basis of your joy. When the stuff of life makes you feel dried up, ask God to remind you that He is the refreshing Living Water that can satisfy your soul's thirst and barrenness. Evaluate areas in your life where you might be going through the motions of faith.*

Personal Reflection: ....

....

....

....

....

....

....

* Allusion to Judith Vorst, *Alexander and the Terrible, Horrible, No Good, Very Bad Day* (New York, NY: Simon & Schuster, 1972).

Sons and Daughters Shall Prophesy

Joel 2:28–32

⁓

"And it shall come to pass afterward
That I will pour out My Spirit on all flesh;
Your sons and your daughters shall prophesy. . . ." (v. 28a)

The day of the Lord seems so far into the future that it really holds no bearing on our present lives. To be fair, it can be so confusing to the average Christian, given varying views on the specifics of the end of our present earth as we know it, that many authors, pastors, and speakers shy away from the topic to avoid confusion or controversy. However, most Christians agree: It is going to be a bad day for anyone who is found outside Christ and a glorious, yet sobering one for those inside Christ.

Joel wrote this verse as prophecy, Peter quoted it thousands of years later on the Day of Pentecost in Acts 2, and we can still apply truths from it! The Word of God is active and reveals the heart of God. That is exactly what we see in Joel 2:28—God's heart for women.

First, notice that on that day the Spirit of God will be "poured out" (Hb. *shaphak*, "spill, shed"). Pouring implies a liberal drenching. Like a cup of invigorating water being dumped over your head on a hot summer day, you are doused in its overflowing refreshment. The prophet paints a picture of God's Spirit being poured over his people. Second, the prophet is no longer speaking on God's behalf. "All flesh"—"sons and . . . daughters," "old men" and "young men," "menservants and . . . maidservants" alike—are all conduits of the Spirit of God delivering a message to His people (vv. 28–29).

The Spirit of God is available to women as to men. We are included in those promises of God mentioned in Ephesians 1:13: "sealed with the Holy Spirit of promise." The Spirit is poured out on us in the same way that it is poured out on men. The question is not whether or not a woman can prophesy (see Acts 21:9) but if she can prophesy in her own way even if it is contradictory to the Lord's guidance to women as recorded in Scripture (Eph. 5:32; 1 Tim. 2:12).

God has given women a voice that speaks directly into the lives of other women like nothing else. How exciting to know the heart of God is proactive for us as women!

Sarah Bubar

Prayer: *Are you actively being used by God according to His will, or are you limiting your usefulness by your insecurities, fears, or pride? Lay those at His feet, and allow Him to use you to the fullest. Confess areas where you have been resistant to God's plan for you as a woman. Ask Him to reveal His heart to you today!*

Personal Reflection: ....

....

....

....

....

....

....

The Deafening Roar

Amos 3:1–8

"Can two walk together, unless they are agreed?" (v. 3)

Life was good for the nation of Israel! Economic prosperity and international peace characterized their days. If *Time Magazine* had been around, Israel would have been included in a list of "Top Places to Live in the Ancient Middle East." But from God's perspective, Israel was headed for destruction. Justice could not be found in the land. The righteous and the needy were oppressed in order to further the prosperity of the powerful. Though faithful in "religious works," the people were characterized by injustice and moral failure. God had spoken to the people through His law and commandments. Now, He roared through His prophet Amos (Amos 1:2).

God is good and never executes judgment without warning (3:7). This nation, chosen by God among all nations (v. 2), had been given His Word through the law: They had been provided with the knowledge needed to live holy lives. God was now speaking His Word through the prophet, Amos, a sheep breeder from the southern nation of Judah (7:14). Amos declared God's judgment on the neighboring nations, first, then focused on Judah, and last, Israel. The people responded by commanding the prophet **not** to prophesy.

This disagreement was not between strangers. God knew Israel intimately. The nation and God had entered into a covenant, a binding agreement. God had been faithful to the covenant and had acted mightily on their behalf. But, an agreement is only an agreement if both parties agree. Though faithful to commit religious acts, the people lived sinful lives as if they did not know God. They did not agree with God when He addressed their sin; they no longer walked with Him. Like a child who covers his ears so that he will not hear the instructions of a parent, so Israel was refusing to listen to the prophet.

Sin deafens the ears and blinds the eyes of the sinner. It also hardens the heart toward God and His Word and toward others. A commitment to sin, whether open or hidden, will separate us from sweet intimacy with our God who loves us. He is holy and cannot tolerate sin. Even being faithful to attend and serve in church cannot keep one in fellowship with God if they are living in rebellion to His Word.

Can you hear God roar? He is calling to His people, the ones for whom He has acted mightily, the ones He knows as His own. Even in the punishment God is good because it is for the sake of redemption (Ps. 107). Will you agree with the Lord and walk in fellowship with Him?

Karen Yarnell

Prayer: *Ask God to show you areas where you do not agree with Him and His Word. Do you harbor a secret sin? Is there a sin that you nurture? Ask the Lord to overcome this sin in your life and bring you into sweet fellowship with Him.*

Personal Reflection: ....

....

....

....

....

....

....

You Have Not Returned to Me

Amos 4:1–13

*"Hear this word, you cows of Bashan, who are on the mountain of
    Samaria,*
Who oppress the poor,
Who crush the needy,
Who say to your husbands, 'Bring wine, let us drink!'" (v. 1)

Amos directly addressed the lavish lifestyle of the women of Israel in his proclamation of God's judgment, comparing them to cows from the area of Bashan, known for its lush pastures and abundance of well-fed cattle. Their home, the mountain of Samaria, was where the capital city was located, the court of nobility. These were the elite women of the day, their abundant lifestyles envied. But, in truth, these women were oppressing the poor and crushing the needy so that they could indulge themselves, inviting their husbands to share in their debauchery.

Israel knew the sting of correction—famine, drought, pestilence, plague, and burning. "'Yet you have not returned to Me,' Says the LORD" (vv. 6, 8–11). God had caused difficult situations for His own people so that they would call to Him. They refused to listen to His words through the law. Also, they refused to call on God when He sent correction. And, they refused to listen to His prophet Amos. Therefore, they were to come face to face with God.

God's people would not encounter the god the "cows of Bashan" worshipped. Israel's God is not the god of man-made idols. He is not a god that indulges their excessive pleasures. He is not a god that turns a blind eye to the injustices suffered by the poor and needy. He is the God who formed the mountains; the God who creates the wind; the God who has revealed Himself to man; the God who makes the day turn dark; and the God who strides across the mountains. He is "the LORD God of hosts" (v. 13).

When the children of God choose a life of self-indulgence, we form God into the image that pleases us. We do not really change the nature of God, we just convince ourselves that God is like us and ignore the correction He gives.

We do not acknowledge the great power of God. Because of this tendency to form God in our image, corporate worship is important. In the house of God, declaring His name, works, and character reminds us of the true God we worship. Here we see the end of the wicked. "My steps had nearly slipped. . . . When I saw the prosperity of the wicked. . . . Until I went into the sanctuary of God; *Then* I understood their end. . . . *But* God *is* the strength of my heart and my portion forever" (Ps. 73:2b–3, 17, 26).

Karen Yarnell

Prayer: *Do you find yourself desiring to emulate the lifestyles of women who do not worship God? Ask the Lord to help you understand the end of a life in rebellion to Him. Pray the words of Psalm 73.*

Personal Reflection: ....

....

....

....

....

....

....

In Evil Times, Seek the Lord

Amos 5:4–27

"Seek good and not evil,
That you may live;
So the LORD God of hosts will be with you." (v. 14a)

Many years before the time of Amos, Moses stood at the base of Mount Sinai and proclaimed to the nation of Israel the words of the Lord. From the God who loved them and was giving them the Promised Land came commandments and instructions. God knew that the people would rebel and, from the start, made provision for repentance. He told them that if they did not worship Him that they would be sent into captivity; but from the place of bondage, if they sought Him with all their hearts, they would find Him. "But from there you will seek the LORD your God, and you will find *Him* if you seek Him with all your heart and with all your soul" (Deut. 4:29).

God's specific message through Amos to the descendants of Israel was the same. They had rebelled against the commandments of God. His chief grievance against them was their idolatry (Amos 5:25–27). They were His people, yet worshipped the pagan gods. Their lack of love for God meant a lack of love for others. Instead of basing the society on the ordinances of God, they oppressed the poor and needy, taking bribes and corrupting their courts. How a society crumbles when there is no just law!

The people had transgressed, rebelliously crossed the boundaries God had set (vv. 10–13), and they had sinned, missed the standard of righteousness (vv. 21–24). Because of their transgression, the religious acts of service were unacceptable to the Lord. God loathed their obedience to religious ritual, which was accompanied by duplicitous hearts. The material wealth and military power characterizing Israel could not provide security from the sure judgment of God.

Was there hope? Yes, seek God, who is good, Amos instructed. Hate the evil that God hates. Establish justice; live according to God's covenant law. "For what great nation *is there* that has God *so* near to it, as the Lᴏʀᴅ our God *is* to us, for whatever *reason* we may call upon Him?" (Deut. 4:7).

When a woman urgently seeks something she has lost, she looks everywhere for it. She looks under and in everything then moves things around, trying to remember where she placed it. She seeks and searches until the situation is resolved. This sense of urgency is what the Lord desires of His children, a complete commitment to finding Him, all else put aside in order to discover His presence and please Him. Loving God includes a hatred for the sin that grieves Him. Regardless of the evil around us, we can seek Him with a pure heart.

Karen Yarnell

Prayer: *Ask the Lord to examine your heart and reveal to you where you love something or someone more than you love Him. He can change your heart as you seek Him.*

✎ **Personal Reflection:** ....

....

....

....

....

....

....

In God's Garden

Amos 9:11–15

"'I will plant them in their land,
And no longer shall they be pulled up
From the land I have given them,'
Says the LORD your God." (v. 15)

Life began in a garden, planted and cultivated by God. His plan, His desire was the fellowship of humanity with Himself. Adam and Eve lived in the abundant garden of Eden, in the presence of God. But when they chose to disobey God's instruction, they no longer wanted fellowship with God; they wanted to hide (Gen. 3:8). Disobedience led to broken relationship.

History repeats itself!

Again, God prepared an abundant land for His people, the Promised Land. By His great power, He brought Israel into the land "flowing with milk and honey." He protected and provided for them in the land. His very presence was in the tabernacle of David, and later the temple of Solomon. God drew near to this people whom He called His own. Again, the people disobeyed His instruction and broke fellowship with God, bringing about the sure judgment that Amos prophesied.

God is greater than history!

Even in the pronouncement of judgment on Israel, Amos proclaims hope to the people. A remnant will be saved. This remnant will not be great because of its own wealth or military power. It will be great because God "will plant them in their land, And no longer shall they be pulled up" (Amos 9:15). Never again will they be like a weed that is ripped out of the soil, roots and all, to be cast away. In this garden, the harvest will be so abundant that gathering will continue until the next planting season (v. 13).

This fertile land will be good because God will be present. He will rebuild the tabernacle of David (v. 11). As Isaiah also prophesied, "In mercy the throne will be established; And One will sit on it in truth, in the tabernacle of David,

Judging and seeking justice and hastening righteousness" (Is. 16:5). From the descendants of King David, Jesus the Messiah would be born. His people would not only include the nation of Israel, but also the Gentiles (Amos 9:12; Acts 15:16–18).

God will accomplish His purpose!

The fellowship of God and humanity will become an eternal reality. "Behold, the tabernacle of God *is* with men, and He will dwell with them, and they shall be His people. God Himself will be with them *and be* their God" (Rev. 21:3b). In love, God created every person for fellowship with Him, though we separate ourselves from God by our sin. In love, He sent Jesus, who sacrificed His life so that we could be forgiven. In love, God is preparing a new garden for fellowship with His children.

Karen Yarnell

Prayer: *God is faithful in His love for His creation. Thank Him for His great love. Have you separated yourself from God by sin? In prayer, ask God's forgiveness and turn from your own ways.*

Personal Reflection: ....

....

....

....

....

....

A Proud Heart Sets Itself against the Lord

Obadiah 1–16

~

"For the day of the Lord upon all the nations is near;
As you have done, it shall be done to you;
Your reprisal shall return upon your own head." (v. 15)

An unharmonious sound in music is called dissonance. Interestingly, the most dissonant are the tones that are closest together. For example, a white key and the very next black key on the piano played at the same time sounds unresolved. The unresolved tension between siblings is similarly dissonant, and more so when their descendants continue the conflict. The setting of Obadiah is the conflict between the descendants of the twin sons of Rebekah, Jacob and Esau.

Jacob, the second twin, was chosen by God to be the one through whom the Messiah would be born. Therefore, to fight against Judah (Jacob's descendants) was to be in direct opposition to the Lord and His plan. Edom, Esau's descendants, had a hatred for their brother nation and watched as Judah was being conquered. They aligned with Judah's enemies, preventing anyone from escaping. They were fighting against the Lord (Ezek. 35). In Judah's day of captivity, day of calamity, and day of distress, she found no help in Edom but instead an enemy.

Because their home was a seemingly impenetrable fortress in a high, rocky mountain, Edom thought they had the perfect defense. They soared like eagles and dwelt among the stars (Obad. v. 4). Edom's pride proved to be its destruction (v. 3).

Pride is a false hope. Pride puffs up, like an overinflated balloon full of air but with no substance. The Edomites wrongly assumed that they could not be defeated. God said that He would bring them down (v. 4). "Pride *goes* before destruction, And a haughty spirit before a fall" (Prov. 16:18).

Pride is deceptive. Pride causes one to believe things that are untrue. Those in the confederacy with Edom, the ones who peacefully shared their meals, would be the ones to betray Edom. Edom's security was a false security.

As Esau had betrayed his brother, so his friends would betray him. "When pride comes, then comes shame" (Prov. 11:2a).

Pride causes one to hurt others. With coldness, Edom watched as Judah was defeated and taken captive, refusing to help. Brother Esau acted the same as the enemies of Judah, rejoicing in their destruction and aiding in the process. "By pride comes nothing but strife" (Prov. 13:10a).

Edom's pride set the nation in opposition to the Lord, but God is near the humble.

> For thus says the High and Lofty One
> Who inhabits eternity, whose name *is* Holy:
> "I dwell in the high and holy *place*,
> With him *who* has a contrite and humble spirit,
> To revive the spirit of the humble,
> And to revive the heart of the contrite ones." (Is. 57:15)

Karen Yarnell

Prayer: *In pride, is your heart set against the Lord? Ask the Lord to reveal your pride. Pray that He would bring brokenness then restoration (Ps. 34:18).*

Personal Reflection: ....

....

....

....

....

God Loved Nineveh When No One Else Did

Jonah 1:1–17

"Now the word of the LORD came to Jonah . . . , 'Arise, go to Nineveh, that great city, and cry out against it; for their wickedness has come up before Me.'" (vv. 1–2)

Why did Jonah respond to God's command by running the other way? The book of Jonah opens with the Lord's clearly telling the prophet Jonah to go to Nineveh and call the people to repent from their wickedness (vv. 1–2). Instead of traveling to Nineveh, the reluctant prophet fled to Tarshish, away from the presence of God. Jonah disobeyed and went the other way, as far from God's direction as he could go.

Jonah was a servant of God, the son of Amittai from Gath Hepher near Nazareth (2 Kin. 14:25). He was a Hebrew prophet during the reign of Jeroboam II, king of northern Israel. He preached repentance to the people but didn't want to go to Nineveh. Jonah was afraid to go to the Assyrian city. In his heart, he wanted them to experience the justice of God due them.

Nineveh was located in Assyria, a pagan nation known for its barbaric warfare. In the tenth and ninth centuries B.C., the Assyrian army committed atrocities as a warning to their enemies not to resist being conquered. Their cruelty is depicted in stone carvings now displayed in the British Museum in London, such as soldiers playing catch with the heads of their victims. Fear of the Assyrians was widespread, obviously influencing the prophet Jonah's refusal to take God's message of salvation to them. No one loved Nineveh, not even the prophet Jonah. No one, that is, except God!

God demonstrated His love for the people of Nineveh. He warned them through the prophet Jonah to repent in 40 days or be destroyed (Jon. 3:4). Though Jonah expected destruction like Sodom and Gomorrah (Gen. 19:12–29), God offered them forgiveness. Jonah was disheartened that his prediction of their doom did not come to pass. The sinful Ninevites believed God's message spoken through Jonah (3:5–10). God loved them and saved them from the penalty of their sin. However, Jonah did not respond in love—"It displeased

Jonah exceedingly, and he became angry" (4:1). Can you imagine? A preacher was disappointed when everyone who heard his message repented from his sins.

God loved Nineveh when no one else did! What a beautiful picture of God's unconditional love! God loves everyone, even the most sinful. He offers forgiveness, for even the gravest sin. He loves all people and seeks to save them. No sin is great enough to separate the repentant sinner from the seeking Savior!

Rhonda Harrington Kelley

Prayer: *Praise God for His unfailing love. Thank Him for loving you in spite of your sin. Return to God if you have strayed and be willing to share His message of love—even to those who are not easily loved.*

Personal Reflection:

It's Never Too Late to Pray

Jonah 2:1–10

"Then Jonah prayed to the Lord his God from the fish's belly. And he said:
'I cried out to the Lord because of my affliction,
And He answered me.'" (vv. 1–2a)

You know the story! God spoke; Jonah ran. A storm brewed; a fish was fed. Jonah cried; God answered. The prophet Jonah ran from the Lord when he was told to take the message of repentance to Nineveh. God caused a storm at sea, and Jonah was thrown overboard. He was swallowed by a great fish, and finally called out to God. The patient heavenly Father heard his cry and answered because **it's never too late to pray!**

Jonah began his prayer from the belly of the fish with confession and praise. His prayer is structured as a psalm of thanksgiving with a heartfelt expression of gratitude to God for His previous work in Jonah's life. In these first two verses, the prophet cried out to God, acknowledging his sin, and accepting the consequences: "You cast me into the deep . . . The waters surrounded me . . . The earth with its bars *closed* behind me forever" (vv. 3–6). God heard Jonah in his despair and forgave him: "Yet You have brought up my life from the pit, O Lord, my God" (v. 6b). Even in his judgment, Jonah remembered the Lord and rejected the pagan idols (vv. 7–8). He proclaimed, "Salvation *is* of the Lord" (v. 9b). Then "the Lord spoke to the fish, and it vomited Jonah onto dry *land*" (v. 10). God answered Jonah because **it's never too late to pray!**

What about you? Have you run from God like Jonah, heading in the direction opposite to where He sends you? Have you followed your own desires and disobeyed the Lord's directives? Have you possibly experienced the painful consequences of your rebellion? It may be time for you to pray. Don't wait. Cry out to Him now because **it's never too late to pray!**

Let Jonah's prayer provide a pattern for you as you pray. Verses two through nine suggest these heartfelt responses as you pray:

- Cry out to God;
- Confess your sin;
- Consider your condition;
- Claim His forgiveness;
- Call on His name.

Like Jonah, believe the promises of God to hear, forgive, and save. He will answer you because **it's never too late to pray!**

Two thieves hung on crosses and were crucified on either side of Jesus Christ. One sought mercy from the Messiah as he was dying: "Lord, remember me when You come into Your kingdom" (Luke 23:42). And the Lord Jesus heard him and answered, "Assuredly, I say to you, today you will be with Me in Paradise" (vv. 43). As the thief was dying, he was saved by the Savior because **it's never too late to pray!**

Rhonda Harrington Kelley

Prayer: *Be grateful that it's never too late to pray. Take a few minutes to confess your sin and call upon His name.*

Personal Reflection: ....

....

....

....

....

It's Never Too Late to Obey

Jonah 3:1–10

"Now the word of the Lord came to Jonah the second time . . . So Jonah arose
and went to Nineveh, according to the word of the Lord." (vv. 1–3a)

Jonah is not known for his obedience. In fact, he is remembered for his disobedience. The prophet deliberately chose not to follow the directives of God.
He turned away from Nineveh and suffered the consequences. While trying to
escape God, a storm brewed at sea. Jonah was cast into the sea and swallowed
by a large fish. He called out to God, who saved him. Jonah's first rejection of
God's plan did not disqualify him from kingdom service.

God is a God of second chances! Jonah was given another opportunity
to obey God. After his rescue at sea, God spoke again to Jonah: "Arise, go to
Nineveh, that great city, and preach to it the message that I tell you" (v. 2). The
second time, Jonah obeyed—he immediately went to Nineveh as commanded
by the Lord, and he delivered the divine revelation (vv. 3–4). Passionately he
cried out to the Ninevites he once feared: "Yet forty days, and Nineveh shall be
overthrown!" (v. 4b). Jonah learned that God had given him and his enemies a
second chance. Scripture says: "So the people of Nineveh believed God" (v. 5a).
Wow!

The disobedient prophet was given another opportunity to proclaim
God's truth to a disobedient nation; and when he did, everyone listened and
turned to God for mercy. Jonah was blessed as were the people of Nineveh.
He was given another prophetic ministry, and the Ninevites were spared the
wrath of God. When they repented, "God saw their works . . . and God relented
from the disaster that He had said He would bring upon them, and He did not
do it" (v. 10). Jonah and the Ninevites all learned that it is never too late to
obey God.

Hearing God speak is not enough. It's what we do with what we hear that
sets the course of our lives. Listening to God is the beginning of obedience, but
what we learn is that it is pointless to hear God if we do not do what He says.

James wrote it this way in the New Testament: "But be doers of the word, and not hearers only" (James 1:22). Jonah was a hearer and finally became a doer when he obeyed God.

If God nudges you to speak to a friend about Jesus, you are not obedient until you do it. If He challenges you to know His word, you are not obedient until you systematically study the Bible. If He calls you to serve Him, you are not obedient until you minister to others. It's never too late to obey—hear the word of God, then do it!

Rhonda Harrington Kelley

Prayer: *Thank God for speaking to you. Then don't stop at hearing. Make a commitment to obey God when He speaks.*

Personal Reflection: ....

....

....

....

....

....

If God Can Use a Worm, He Can Use You

Jonah 4:1–11

". . . God prepared a worm, and it so damaged the plant that it withered." (v. 7)

Late one night on the campus of Baylor University, I was studying with my boyfriend in the library. While I was studying a textbook, he was reading his Bible. With great enthusiasm he said that he found a Scripture verse that would change my life. He read Jonah 4:7 (NASB): "God appointed a worm when dawn came the next day and it attacked the plant and it withered." Huh? A verse about a worm will change my life? I don't even like fish bait. Well, that wise boyfriend became my husband, and he's been preaching his "worm sermon" for years.

What life-changing lessons can we learn from a worm? Chapter 4 begins with Jonah pouting, angry at God for not punishing the Ninevites as the prophet had prophesied (v. 1). Jonah whined to God, even as he acknowledged the deity of God. He begged God to let him die to free him from his humiliation (vv. 2–3). Instead of fulfilling Jonah's prophecy to destroy the Ninevites if they failed to repent, God spared them when they turned to Him.

When God refused to let the prophet die, Jonah fled again, this time finding refuge under a tree outside of Nineveh (vv. 4–6). It was in the shade of the large tree that God taught the prophet a big lesson through a little creature. God sent a small worm to eat the large plant and eliminate the shade protecting the prophet (v. 7). Then God prepared a powerful wind along with the hot sun to torture Jonah (v. 8). When he whined again, God asked him a pointed question: "*Is it* right for you to be angry about the plant?" (v. 9). Jonah was more worried about the death of the plant than the suffering of the people of Nineveh (vv. 10–11). God taught Jonah to love all His creation.

What can you learn from the worm in Jonah 4:7? He was a God-appointed worm with a God-appointed task at a God-appointed time with God-appointed results.

- **God-appointed worm.** He was created by God and chosen for His work.
- **God-appointed task.** He had a specific job assigned by God.
- **God-appointed time.** At a precise time in history, God asked him to accomplish a timely task.
- **God-appointed results.** When the worm faithfully followed God's commands, God guaranteed His perfect results.

Learn a lesson from a worm! Know that God has chosen you. He has a purpose for you and will work through you in His time. He guarantees the results. If God can use a worm, He can use you!

Rhonda Harrington Kelley

Prayer: *Find a quiet place for reflection. Thank the Lord for loving you and working through you like He did for the little worm!*

Personal Reflection: ....

....

....

....

....

....

....

God Is Watching

Micah 2:1–5

~

> "Woe to those who devise iniquity,
> And work out evil on their beds!
> At morning light they practice it,
> Because it is in the power of their hand." (v. 1).

Have you noticed that some people think they can step on and use others to get what they want without personal consequence? Perhaps a supervisor took the credit for a project you did, so he could get a promotion. Maybe at a loved one's death a family member took more of the inheritance than she was allotted. Can they really get away with it? Micah records the accusation the LORD made against His people who thought they could. They were devising "iniquity" and planning "evil." The rich oppressed the poor because they could. By force they took the land that God had specifically allotted to the respective tribes as their divine inheritance (v. 2). The strong robbed and manipulated the weak rejecting God's commands and authority in their lives.

God responded clearly. His patience had run its course with their arrogant deeds. They had planned ruin for others, but God was planning disaster against them. When God carried out His judgment, the people would be humbled (v. 3). Furthermore, the individuals who had performed these deeds of wickedness would no longer be allowed to join the assembly in covenantal activities (v. 5). In God's sovereign timing they received the consequences for their sin.

God does not turn a blind eye when His commands are ignored. He hates a "heart that devises wicked plans" and "feet that are swift in running to evil" (Prov. 6:18). We should never think that God will overlook sin—the sin of others or our own. People may think that they can do wrong and get away with it. Perhaps they think, "After all, it worked last time." However, such an attitude is prideful. It resembles the actions of Eve in the garden. She knew God said that if she ate from the fruit of the tree in the midst of the garden she would die. Yet, Eve ate the fruit anyway, believing that she would not receive the consequence

God had promised (Gen. 3:1–6). While rebellion against God seems to go unpunished at times, His timing is beyond our understanding. It is natural to desire quick severe judgment for others and slow merciful judgment for ourselves. God is "longsuffering" and wants everyone to repent, but He will surely avenge the oppressed according to the measure of His justice (2 Pet. 3:9; 2 Thess. 1:6–10). The rich Israelites thought they could steal from the poor without penalty. However, they soon realized that God had been paying attention after all.

Erika N. Mercer

Prayer: *Ask the Lord to help you trust His justice and timing in your life. Ask the Lord to reveal if there are any areas where you are walking in pride and disobedience.*

Personal Reflection: ....

....

....

....

....

....

....

A Warning to Leaders

Micah 3:2–15

"Her heads judge for a bribe,
Her priests teach for pay,
And her prophets divine for money.
Yet they lean on the LORD, and say,
"Is not the LORD among us?
No harm can come upon us."
Therefore because of you
Zion shall be plowed like a field,
Jerusalem shall become heaps of ruins,
And the mountain of the temple
Like the bare hills of the forest." (vv. 11–12)

Do you think having good leadership is important? The prophet Micah records the influence of Israel's leadership on the well-being of the nation (vv. 9–12). Apparently, the wealthy Israelites were not the only ones disregarding the Lord. The leaders of the people were also living in flagrant disobedience. The judges, the priests, and the prophets were all doing whatever served them best.

The religious leaders' "ministry" was about personal profit instead of serving the Lord sincerely and training the people. Instead of speaking what the Lord desired, the prophets spoke whatever paid them the best.

The judges were concerned with their income instead of their integrity. The leaders claimed that the Lord was with them, but they had strayed far from Him (v. 11). Their choice to serve themselves instead of God would result in the total destruction of "Zion," a synonym for Jerusalem. Even the temple, the "house of God," would not survive (v. 12).

Leaders act as influencers in the lives of those who follow them. If a leader's heart is turned toward the Lord, she can help turn around a nation, a women's ministry, or an organization. Conversely, a bad leader can do great damage. The life of Queen Esther offers an example of positive leadership, and the life of Queen Jezebel presents an example of negative leadership. Both women had great influence during their lifetime, but their legacies are dramatically different.

Scripture instructs us to make "prayers, intercessions, *and* giving of thanks . . . for kings and all who are in authority, that we may lead a quiet and peaceable life in all godliness and reverence" (1 Tim. 2:1–2). We must take seriously the influence of those in leadership positions both in the local church and in the secular sphere and pray diligently for them. Leadership positions in the church are crucial but come with the warning that teachers "shall receive a stricter judgment" (James 3:1). This should not scare women away from stepping up to lead in biblically supported roles. Rather, it should challenge us to be humble and pray fervently that we would stay close to the Lord and influence people for their good—whether we have public positions of authority or lead through our influence as mother, friend, or co-worker.

Erika N. Mercer

Prayer: *Pray for those in leadership in your church and nation. Seek the Lord to reveal any areas where you are influencing people negatively, and ask for help as you lead those in your sphere of influence toward His heart.*

Personal Reflection: ....

....

....

....

....

What Does the Lord Require of You?

Micah 6:1–8

~

"He has shown you, O man, what is good;
And what does the LORD require of you
But to do justly,
To love mercy,
And to walk humbly with your God?" (v. 8)

The Lord had presented a compelling case against His people. Their offenses were many. It was time for them to answer His accusations, but what could they say? He had done only good to them, and they were without excuse. With such a collection of offenses, what sacrifice would be sufficient to bring to the Lord to obtain forgiveness (vv. 6–7)? God used this opportunity to remind them that he had already revealed to them what is good in His sight. Three specific directives were given for their continuous action.

The first directive is **to do justly**. This means that God's people should do what is right—hating what is evil and loving what is good (Amos 5:15). The desire "to do justly" should come from recognition that God, the "God of justice," only does what is right (Is. 30:18). He is not even tempted by evil (James 1:13).

The second directive is to **love mercy**. Loving mercy means having a devotion to "unfailing love." God is characterized by His mercy and unfailing love. None equals God in unfailing love (1 Kin. 8:23; John 3:16). It should not surprise you that the greatest command is to "love the Lord your God with all your heart, with all your soul, and with all your mind," and the second greatest is to "love your neighbor as yourself" (Matt. 22:37–39). God puts a high priority on loving mercy.

The final directive is **to walk humbly with your God**. Walking humbly before God necessitates the recognition that you occupy a lowly position in relation to God. He is the Creator and the Almighty God (Gen. 1:1; 17:1). The psalmist David wrote, "The fool has said in his heart, '*There is* no God.' . . . There is none who does good" (Ps. 14:1). Recognizing God for who He is becomes the first step toward pleasing Him.

What does the Lord require of you? First you must recognize your position before Him. Praying a prayer will not save you if you are still reigning as "god" in your life. To please the Lord you must humble yourself before Him and hold nothing back. Eternal life is for those who surrender all they possess, desire, and enjoy to the Lord for Jesus' sake and the sake of the gospel (Mark 10:30). Humble yourself before the Lord and commit yourself to living His way. Love the Lord with all your heart. Do what is right out of a humble heart and love for God. This is what the Lord requires of you.

Erika N. Mercer

Prayer: *Praise the Lord for who He is. Express your love for Him. Ask God if there is anything that you are holding back from Him.*

Personal Reflection: ....

....

....

....

....

....

....

Who Is a God like You?

Micah 7:8–20

"Who is a God like You,
Pardoning iniquity
And passing over the transgression of the remnant of His heritage?

He does not retain His anger forever,
Because He delights in mercy.
He will again have compassion on us,
And will subdue our iniquities.

You will cast all our sins
Into the depths of the sea." (vv. 18–19)

What does your name mean? Solomon says that "a good name is to be chosen rather than great riches" (Prov. 22:1). In biblical times, a name was interconnected with a person's character and reputation. Micah means "Who is like the Lord?"—a fitting name for a prophet of God. Ironically, Micah asks God, "Who *is* a God like You?" (Mic. 7:18). Micah focuses the conclusion of His prophecy on God's compassion. Although God is sometimes portrayed as a "God of wrath" in the Old Testament and then as a "God of love" in the New Testament, this passage clearly discredits that notion. God's character is constant through His entire revelation in the Scriptures. He is a God of justice, and He is a God of mercy ("faithful love").

The book of Micah is filled with many judgments since Israel had sinned grievously against the Lord. Nevertheless, the people of Israel are left with a word of hope—a word related to the compassionate character of God.

God established His covenant with Abraham promising to make him into a great nation. God said He would bless him, make his name great, and bless "all the families of the earth" through him (Gen. 12:1–3). Generations later God continued to fulfill His part of that covenant with faithful love (Mic. 7:20).

Although "the remnant of His heritage" had to be purified through exile, God would not forget His covenant (v. 18).

Jesus is the ultimate fulfillment of what is described. He came first to the Jewish remnant so that those who placed their faith in Him might have their sins cast into "the depths of the sea" (v. 19). Even on the excruciating cross Jesus continued to express compassion for His murderers, saying, "Father, forgive them" (Luke 23:34). However, He also was the source of blessing to all the families of the earth who placed their faith in His atonement on the cross. His death provides a means for our sins to be forgiven today. John reminds us that "if we confess our sins, He is faithful and just to forgive us *our* sins and to cleanse us from all unrighteousness" (1 John 1:9). His compassion is incomparable and begs the question, "Who *is* a God like You?"

Erika N. Mercer

Prayer: *Thank God for His consistent character through the generations and for His gift of Jesus and the forgiveness of sin. Ask God to help you walk in that forgiveness and to help you express this truth with others.*

Personal Reflection: ....

....

....

....

....

....

The Justice of God

Nahum 1:1–6

"God is jealous, and the LORD avenges;
The LORD avenges and is furious.
The LORD will take vengeance on His adversaries,
And He reserves wrath for His enemies.
The LORD is slow to anger and great in power,
And will not at all acquit the wicked." (vv. 2–3a)

When you think of the people who have caused the deepest hurts in your life, does anger flare? Do you seethe with hatred toward them? Do you sense a strong desire to get even? Perhaps you have acted on these emotions. The desire to take revenge when you or someone you love has been treated unfairly or cruelly comes naturally for sinners (a category from which none is exempt). Whether the "payback" impulse is warranted or not—i.e., whether the guilty party inflicted pain on purpose or accidentally—followers of Christ, however, must reflect the Master's character by leaving vengeance to Him. He has stated plainly, "Vengeance is Mine" (Deut. 32:35; Rom. 12:19; Heb. 10:30). The right to avenge "my rights" or to "set the record straight" lies exclusively in God's domain.

When you are mistreated, persecuted, or oppressed, to know that God is in charge and that He does take vengeance is comforting. God sent the prophet Nahum, whose name means "comfort," to preach such a message. God had already judged the northern kingdom of Israel by allowing them to be conquered by Assyria (in 722 B.C.), a notoriously cruel empire. Now He was allowing the Assyrians to oppress the southern kingdom of Judah because of their sin. Consequently, God's people questioned how He could tolerate such evil. Through Nahum, God reveals several truths that discourage His people from doubting His faithfulness, from despairing of hope, and from destroying themselves with bitterness.

First, because of His absolute holiness, the Lord is **jealous** (Hb. *qana'*, "burn with zeal"). He is a passionate advocate for the well-being of His people, yet He refuses to ignore wrongdoing. He demands and exacts justice. If you belong to Christ, rest assured that your heavenly Father is not only concerned but that He is actively opposes abusers.

Second, the Lord **will take vengeance**. The Lord avenged the suffering of His people under Assyrian cruelties. As Nahum prophesied, Nineveh, the Assyrian capital, was completely destroyed (612 B.C.). Likewise, "payday is coming" for those who hurt, abuse, mistreat, persecute, and oppress others, particularly those who belong to Christ. Human anger at such perpetrators does not compare to the righteous fury and power of Almighty God. Notice, however, that this wrath is directed specifically at "His enemies."

Third, the Lord is **slow to anger**. He is not quick-tempered, impulsive, or rash. When He punishes and renders judgment, He upholds His own perfect standard of justice.

Tamra Hernandez

Prayer: *Praise the Lord for His great power both to deal justly with those who are cruel, refusing His rule, and to give grace to those who repent.*

Personal Reflection: ....

....

....

....

....

A Stronghold in Distress

Nahum 1:7–11

"The LORD is good,
A stronghold in the day of trouble;
And He knows those who trust in Him." (v. 7)

Everyone has experienced or will experience some form of pain, suffering, or turmoil that is extremely severe—something held so closely and dearly could have been taken away quickly; division in the church amongst friends and family that has left you grieved in your spirit; or perhaps you have prayed about something for so long you have become weary and faint, no longer having the words to communicate to a God whom you know is there but feels so far away. Confusion comes when bad things happen to good people. There are things we hold so dearly that when jeopardized can cause us to despair even of life itself!

Nahum writes of the distress the people of Judah were experiencing. Judah was experiencing much pain, conflict, and suffering from the Assyrians. This encouraging verse is a reminder of the goodness of God in the midst of anguish of spirit (v. 7). Regardless of our situation, God is in control, and He is sovereign.

God is a "stronghold." He is the Protector, Sustainer, and Deliverer of His people. When the world is falling apart, God offers security and strength to endure, when trust is placed in Him. We can trust that He cares and is there to comfort us though His plans are unclear. Even when we have cried so hard that we cannot cry anymore, God is present! God cares! This truth is our stronghold!

Dear sister, you are so special to God. There is absolutely nothing unknown or impossible to Him! One of the key principles in this comforting Scripture is that the refuge found in Him during periods of distress and anguish. In other words, run to Him! Run to Jesus! He is there waiting to give you comfort and direction regardless of the situation!

Let God be your hiding place as you pour out your heart to Him. He will hear your prayer as you look to Him, and He will strengthen your heart, mind, and spirit. He is the great Comforter! In times of distress, find comfort in the truth that Christ is making you more into the woman He desires you to be, and He will never leave you nor forsake you, regardless of what you are experiencing (Heb. 13:5).

Monica Rose Brennan

Prayer: *Ask the Lord to be your stronghold. Submit to His will even when you don't understand how He is answering your prayer. Ask Him to give you the strength you need to endure suffering and pain. Ask Him to make you more into the woman He desires you to be as you go through difficult times in life. Thank Him for using suffering in your life to draw you closer to Him.*

Personal Reflection: ....

Beautiful Feet

Nahum 1:12–15

ᨑ

"Behold, on the mountains
The feet of him who brings good tidings
Who proclaims peace!
O Judah, keep your appointed feasts,
Perform your vows.
For the wicked one shall no more pass through you;
He is utterly cut off." (v. 15)

Isn't it a wonderful thing to receive good news? Do you remember the first person who declared to you the good news of Jesus? They have beautiful feet! Have you taught someone else the good news of Jesus? Then you have beautiful feet! According to Isaiah:

How beautiful upon the mountains
Are the feet of him who brings good news,
Who proclaims peace,
Who brings glad tidings of good *things,*
Who proclaims salvation,
Who says to Zion,
"Your God reigns!" (Is. 52:7)

We have the opportunity not only to look to the One "bringing good tidings, who proclaims peace" but to be messengers of that same peace that we have received. In the book of Nahum, the Lord is reminding His people of His justice and their peace. Although the people of Judah were experiencing oppression from the Assyrians due to their sin, eventually Judah would experience the peace experienced after repentance and return to God.

Just as Nahum brought comfort to Judah by encouraging them to look to the One bringing peace, so Christ has given a message to proclaim! The grace of

God is so profoundly seen in this verse. God will protect His beloved people! He is faithful! God has called His children to be peacemakers as well! Sometimes people do not want to listen to the message that can save their souls. The gospel is good news. However, some are not open to accept the Truth! Just as we are reminded in the book of Nahum of God's faithfulness, we must also be faithful in proclaiming truth and peace regardless of the opposition or responses of others!

Another theme in this passage is that wicked people will be destroyed. Remember that vengeance belongs to the Lord and He alone will judge. Pray to trust in the Lord when evil occurs and act justly and live righteous lives for His glory! In our world today there are so many who need to hear the powerful message of peace found only in a personal relationship with Christ. Dear sister, may you be used as His instrument of peace to remind others of God's everlasting faithfulness for His people and the justice that He will bring.

Monica Rose Brennan

Prayer: *Ask the Lord to make you His instrument of peace. Thank Him for His faithfulness in your life and the lives of others. Ask Him to help you be a messenger of His gospel and help others experience the peace that only He can give. Thank Him for being a God of justice. Ask Him for opportunities to show peace to others who are in need.*

Personal Reflection: ....

....

....

....

....

Stumbling Blocks to Holiness

Habakkuk 1:12–17

"Are you not from everlasting,
O LORD my God, my Holy One?
We shall not die.
O LORD, You have appointed them for judgment;
O Rock, You have marked them for correction.
You are of purer eyes than to behold evil,
And cannot look on wickedness." (vv. 12–13a)

Why is holiness so uncool? Not only among lost people, but it is also unpopular among Christians. Some Christians have simply abandoned holiness as a meaningful concept, trying to be more like the world instead of God. The word "holy" conveys the meaning of something that is set apart or purified or consecrated in order to be devoted to God; and biblically, holiness is a positive concept! The Bible is very clear that our God is holy; in Habakkuk 1:12, He is named the Holy One. And, because He is holy, God calls His people to be holy (Lev. 11:44). So, why do some believers shun holiness? Below are just two reasons it appears that Christians may stumble over the concept of holiness.

Pharisee Syndrome: You know those people who act "holier than thou." Sometimes we struggle with holiness and obedience because we think of holiness as a negative thing and identify it with the Pharisees or hypocrites rather than God. The problem is that Christ held up the Pharisees as the exact opposite of holiness—their "holier than thou" attitude fired Him up (Matt. 23:27–39). You see, Christians aren't just supposed to "act" holy and then lord it over other people. Christians are to be holy inside and out. When Jesus said that the Pharisees were hypocrites and full of all uncleanness, He was saying that they were not even in the ballpark of holiness. Some of us run from holiness because Pharisaical Christians have given it a bad name, and we don't want to be perceived like them. However, people were never meant to be our standard of holiness—God, the Holy One, is the standard.

Holiness Is Too Hard: Another stumbling block to holiness is our attempt to make ourselves holy instead of letting the Holy Spirit help us. Do you get discouraged when you struggle with sin or do you forget to ask God for help in the midst of temptation (1 Cor. 10:13)? Or, do you live out a "Lone Ranger" Christianity, acting like you don't need fellow believers when God has given us each other to help us in our weaknesses (Eccl. 4:9–12) and to encourage us to good deeds (Heb. 10:24)? Our desire should be to be more like Christ in word, thought, and deed today than we were yesterday. We need the help of the Holy Spirit and fellow believers for that to happen. We can't become holy in our own strength.

Candi Finch

Prayer: *Are you stumbling over the concept of holiness? Seek the Lord's help in making you holy like He is holy, repenting of any sinful thoughts, words, or actions.*

Personal Reflection: ....

....

....

....

....

....

....

The Just Shall Live by Faith

Habakkuk 1:12—2:4

"But the just shall live by his faith." (2:4b)

If you have ever had a nightmare about being in (or watching) a desperate situation but feeling paralyzed to act, then you come close to understanding what Habakkuk must have experienced when the Lord revealed to him the imminent judgment of Judah, the southern kingdom of Israel. Although the Jews living in Judah had witnessed Assyria's devastation of the northern kingdom (722 B.C.), they were rapidly heading toward a similar fate and for some of the same reasons.

In Judah, Habakkuk saw "violence" without God's intervention (1:2–3), "iniquity," "trouble," "plundering," "strife, and contention" (v. 3). He had cried out to the Lord so long about what he saw, with no apparent result, that he wondered when God would ever do something about it (v. 1). God's law and His justice seemed "powerless" to stop "the wicked" from surrounding "the righteous" and twisting His truth to their own advantage (v. 4).

In reply, the Lord showed Habakkuk how He was going to use Babylon to punish Judah. If we had video footage documenting the destruction of Jerusalem in 586 B.C. by the Chaldeans (Babylonians), perhaps understanding the "burden which the prophet Habakkuk saw" would be easier (1:1, 5–11). Bewildered, he asked the Lord, who cannot "look on wickedness" (2:13), why He would allow brutal pagans to overrun Judah, even for their "correction" (vv. 12–17).

The Lord insisted that judgment was certain (vv. 2–3), but He gave the prophet hope for those who did remain faithful to Him in a violent world rapidly heading toward certain judgment. The "appointed time" of God's judgment on the godless Babylonians also would "surely come" (v. 3). God would punish His people for their "unfaithfulness" (1 Chr. 9:1; Dan. 9:7), **and** He would judge the Babylonians for their sinfulness, idolatry, and cruelty (Hab. 2:5–20; Is. 13:1—14:23).

The Lord also pointed out the clear contrast between "the proud" and "the just" (Hab. 2:4). The proud, whether unfaithful Jew or ruthless Babylonian, trust in themselves—in their own strength, religious practices, ethnicity, and accomplishments—instead of in "the Lord [who] is in His holy temple" (v. 20). The just don't live that way. The Hebrew word for "just" here is *tsaddiq*, someone who **is** "upright" or "righteous," who loves and obeys the Lord. A just person is faithful to the Lord and wholeheartedly trusts in Him.

In this violent world, rapidly heading toward certain judgment, today is a good day to reevaluate where you stand with the one God who "will justify" both Jews and Gentiles the same way—through "faith in Jesus" (see Rom. 1:16–17; 3:1–31). Are you "proud," relying on yourself instead of relinquishing everything to the Lord? Or are you "just," living by faith in Jesus?

Tamra Hernandez

Prayer: *Thank the Lord that He is righteous. Surrender any resistance to His Spirit's correction, allowing Him to make your life more Christ-like today than it was yesterday.*

Personal Reflection: ....

....

....

....

....

....

The Lord Is My Strength

Habakkuk 3:1–19

⁓

"Yet I will rejoice in the LORD,
I will joy in the God of my salvation." (v.18)

I **will** rejoice! Choosing joy is just that—a choice. There will be plenty of opportunities to allow the circumstances of your day or another person to steal your joy. But they can only take it if you allow them to do so. We must each come to the point in our lives that our joy is grounded in our relationship with Christ. When He becomes our joy, no one and nothing can take it away.

Habakkuk's book in the Old Testament portrays a passionate dialogue between Habakkuk and the Lord. Habakkuk lived in a time when a Babylonian invasion of Judah and Jerusalem's captivity appeared to be imminent. He began by complaining and trying to inform God how He should move on Judah's behalf. He ends in chapter three with a prayer. By the end of the prayer he has moved from complaining to trusting God, and with his trust came great joy!

You, too, will move from complaining to expressing and experiencing joy if you will place your trust in the Lord. Your joy does not come from your circumstances but from the Lord Himself. He is the One who loves us with an everlasting and unconditional love. Once we surrender to this indescribable love, all fear will be cast out (1 John 4:18) and our desires will be changed. When we begin to love the Lord and long for Him, not just His blessings, we will experience an even deeper level of intimacy, which will overflow into joy.

I delight in my children and grandchildren. They bring me such great joy, that I sometimes find it difficult to express my deep emotions or to put into words my feelings of utter pleasure just to be in their presence. They do not have to do anything to elicit this bliss—just their "being" is enough. Earthy relationships are but a glimmer of the truth of heavenly relationships.

The Bible speaks of God's delight in us (Ps. 16:3). He willingly paid the price with the death of His only Son to set us free from sin. We cannot respond in any way but with awe, wonder, and delight, as well as a desire to please and obey! This, my friend, is when joy—inexpressible and full of glory—will flow forth from your inner person (1 Pet. 1:8).

Donna Gaines

Prayer: *How would you rate your level of joy? Are you allowing circumstances to rob you of the joy God desires for you to exude as you revel in His great love and faithfulness? Confess anything preventing you from placing your trust in the Lord and rejoicing in the God of your salvation.*

Personal Reflection: ....

Tender Care and Love of the Lord

Zephaniah 3:1–13

~∽~

*"The L*ORD *is righteous in her midst,*
He will do no unrighteousness.
Every morning He brings His justice to light;
He never fails,
But the unjust knows no shame." (v. 5)

Zephaniah prophesied in Judah's history during a time when the people had turned from the Lord and her priests were telling the people what they wanted to hear. God's rebuke to the people went unheeded, as their hearts grew cold. Zephaniah called the people to seek the Lord (Zeph. 2:3) but they refused to listen.

In chapter 3, the prophet indicted all their leaders. They were all dishonest, and the priests and prophets in particular were arrogant and profaned the sanctuary and God's law. The Lord's presence was in their midst, and they had His law by which to live; yet they denied Him with their lives.

Interestingly, history repeats itself. Except for a relatively small righteous remnant in America, our own nation has turned away from our Judeo-Christian roots and has launched down the broad path that leads to destruction. A few modern-day prophets and preachers cry out in the name of the Lord, yet, in America, "the unjust knows no shame." In fact, the wicked not only continue in their sin, but also heartily encourage others to join them (Rom. 1:32).

The Lord is still righteous and He continues to command, "Be holy; for I *am* holy" (Lev. 11:44–45; 1 Pet. 1:16). God has given each Christian His Holy Spirit in order that believers might become partakers of His divine, holy nature (2 Pet. 1:4). We have the power of the Spirit living within us to enable us to love and obey God. But in order to obey God, we must know the truth to allow us to discern the lies of the world, our flesh, and of the evil one (James 3:15).

When we repent of our sin and return to the Lord in humility, He is faithful to graciously forgive and restore us to Himself. He is ever so patient and long-suffering. That is why Zephaniah exhorted the people to "seek the Lord" (Zeph. 2:3).

I don't know where you are in your walk with Christ, but heed the words of this faithful prophet to put your faith and trust in the Lord. God alone is righteous and just, and He never fails. Right now He is awaiting your return, and He longs for you to repent and obey Him so that you might experience His blessings, the greatest of which is His presence. May He be "righteous in your midst" today!

Donna Gaines

Prayer: *What is your current plan for reading through the Bible? Do you have a specific time and place where you meet with the Lord daily? Ask Him to help you be faithful to read His Word and live it out. Truly, our Lord longs to extend His tender care and love to those who will seek Him with all their hearts.*

Personal Reflection:

God's Promise of Redemption

Zephaniah 3:14–20

"At that time I will bring you back,
Even at the time I gather you;
For I will give you fame and praise
Among all the peoples of the earth,
When I return your captives before your eyes,'
says the Lord." (v. 20)

My father is a very patient man, but even patient men have a threshold of tolerance that can be crossed when their children display a certain degree of disobedient behavior. When I crossed that threshold as a child, there was no question as to what would come next. First my father would issue a spanking, which usually took place before bedtime. After taking my licks, I would put on my pajamas and sniffle my way into bed; and like clockwork, Dad would then come back in the room. He would lie beside me in the bed, and I would refuse to look at him partly because I was mad and partly because I was embarrassed by my behavior. Then, without fail, he would speak these words of love to me: "I am the only man on earth who will always love you. Even though I love you, and because I love you, sometimes I have to spank your rear end." I had that speech memorized by the third grade!

The children of Israel who lived in the southern kingdom of Judah in the mid-seventh century (around 630 B.C.) had consistently disobeyed God, and had become complacent in their evil ways. Like my father, but much more so, God is also very patient. The psalmist declared, "The Lord *is* merciful and gracious, Slow to anger, and abounding in mercy" (see Ps. 103:8; cp. Pss. 86:15; 145:8). Yet, even God has a threshold of tolerance, which once crossed, requires disciplinary actions to be necessary. The wicked behavior of the people of Judah, indulging in foreign religious practices and worshipping false gods while mocking their own God, had crossed that line.

God raised up the prophet Zephaniah to tell the people of Judah of the coming judgment and discipline God was going to bring their way. But also like my father, God's purpose in disciplining them was not meant to be mean or to flex his "God muscles," but rather it was because He loved them. Zephaniah 3 is a reminder that God would restore His people after their correction was complete, and it demonstrates that they would be all the better because of it. Are you in a season of being disciplined by the Lord? If so, receive the correction of your perfect Father in heaven and know that His ultimate plans are always for your good, never otherwise.

Courtney Veasey

Prayer: *Praise God for His perfect parenting skills. He uses them to shape your life. Ask Him to help you submit to His will and His authority in all your days.*

Personal Reflection:

Consider Your Ways!

Haggai 1:1–11

"Now therefore, thus says the LORD of hosts: 'Consider your ways!'" (v. 5)

The brief book of Haggai, with only 38 verses, is a powerful reminder to believers to make sure we keep the "main thing" the main thing. King Cyrus of Persia allowed any Jewish person in his kingdom to return to Jerusalem to help rebuild the temple. In 537 B.C., the first group of exiles, numbering close to 50,000, arrived in Jerusalem. As the Israelites began to rebuild, they faced opposition from their enemies in the surrounding lands. The Jewish remnant became discouraged and left the work of rebuilding the temple God called them to do. They concentrated on building their own houses instead. Over 16 years later in 520 B.C., God sent His prophet Haggai to call His people back to their main task. Over a four-month period Haggai admonished the people to consider their ways, be convicted of their sins, be encouraged by God's faithfulness, and be assured of God's promises.

The remnant's indifference toward God's house lying in ruins revealed that their hearts were far from Him. They were being disobedient to the primary task God had given them to do. Enemies and everyday life had distracted God's people. As Haggai outlined the adversities the people had faced as a result of their disobedience, he continued to urge the people to "consider" their ways (1:5, 7; 2:15, 18). This word was one of Haggai's favorites to encourage the Israelites to pause and reflect carefully on their lives and their decisions.

Have you ever heard the saying, "Good is the enemy of the best?" There is a lot of wisdom in that brief sentiment! Good things can sometimes distract us from spiritual priorities such as prayer and devotional time. Just as the Israelites were busy about their lives while God's temple lay in ruins, we can miss God's vision for our lives if we are busy about the wrong things.

Haggai told the Israelites to refocus their eyes on the Lord. Taking our eyes off the Lord even for a second can mean choosing a good but, in the end, vain path. When you stay attentive to the Lord, He gives you clear vision and wisdom for the best and most meaningful work He has for you. Sometimes the godliest thing we can do is say "no" to some really good opportunities or activities in order to say "yes" to the one thing God has specially equipped us to do. Don't miss out on God's best by settling for just good enough!

Candi Finch

Prayer: *Take a few moments and consider your ways. Is there anything on which you have neglected to follow through but that you know God has asked you to do? Or, is there anything on your "to do" list that wouldn't be on God's "to do" list for you? Pray that you would have wisdom and discernment in how you spend your time today.*

Personal Reflection: ....

....

....

....

....

....

....

....

Encouragement and Promise

Haggai 2:1–9

"'... Be strong, all you people of the land,' says the Lord,
'and work; for I am with you,' says the Lord of hosts." (v. 4)

Have you ever gone through something so devastating that you questioned if you would ever be the same person again? Truth be told, you aren't the same; trouble fundamentally changes you, leaving you scarred and wounded. You may have healed from the pain and, through forgiveness, buried the bitterness your heart could have embraced, yet you know that deep down inside, you're different. You wonder if you will ever get back to the old you.

Haggai finds Judah at this low point in life. Having just repaired the ruined temple at the heart of their worship, they were about to dedicate it to God, but they were discouraged. In the past, the temple was a grand spectacle of elaborate design only Solomon could accomplish, but now, it looked nothing like it once did. Although complete, it was primitive and basic, functional but hardly glorious. Now, it was scarred.

God ached for the people as they saw what the effects of sin had done to their temple. He asked them to remember what it once was (v. 3). "In comparison with it, *is this* not in your eyes as nothing?" He questioned (v. 3). God, then, encourages His people to be strong. Repeating this charge three times for the purpose of emphasis, similar to our exclamation points or all caps when we write a letter, God was telling his people to BE STRONG!

God gave the ultimate pep talk. He wanted His children to be encouraged, but He also wanted them to work, to keep plodding along, not to give up the fight, not to count themselves out because they were wounded. God had given them a temple again; and although it was simple, they could enter into it and worship Him rightly. Furthermore, He didn't leave His people in a hopeless state. He reminded them that a day would come when His temple would be filled with glory greater than it had before (vv. 7–8).

Life has mountains and valleys. Sometimes after walking through a valley, depression can develop because we remember the mountaintop and hate the valley. We remember the view from above and how wonderful life looked from there, but the view from the valley is dark and shrouded by the forest of doubt. Maybe a recent valley in your life has left you hurt and confused, BE STRONG! Maybe your relationship with God looks nothing like it once did, BE STRONG! Maybe you've lost your way through the valley, BE STRONG! And work! The Lord is with you (v. 4).

Sarah Bubar

Prayer: *If you've recently walked through a valley and cannot seem to return to the person you once were, remember God is with you. Keep moving forward in your relationship with Him. Ask Him for ways that you can be restored.*

Personal Reflection:

Don't Despise the Day of Small Things

Zechariah 4:1–14

"For who has despised the day of small things?
For these seven rejoice to see
The plumb line in the hand of Zerubbabel.
They are the eyes of the LORD,
Which scan to and fro throughout the whole earth." (v. 10)

There is a universal idea: Life should be exciting. It should hold some grand love story, some thrilling adventure, or some heart-pounding pursuit. When we were children, no one said, "I want to do nothing when I grow up." No! Instead, we had dreams of traveling the world and being the best at something exciting. Living a boring life filled with mundane tasks was not a viable dream.

The small things in life are often despised: laundry, dirty dishes, cleaning our house, making meals, grocery shopping. Those tasks seem to go unnoticed and unappreciated. "It's only noticed when it doesn't get done," I've heard women say: If we're not careful, we can see the small things in life and loathe them to the point of discontentment. The Lord was discouraging His people from loathing the mundane. The small things accomplished the work of rebuilding His temple, as seen in Zechariah 4.

The book of Zechariah is filled with visions from the Lord for His people as they were rebuilding the temple where He lived. There were eight visions total, and chapter 4 explains the fifth one, the gold lamp stand and olive trees (vv. 1–14). Zechariah's prophecy affirmed that Zerubbabel was going to complete the temple. Using the illustration of a plumb line, Zechariah acknowledged that the Lord was watching over the construction of this temple. A plumb line is an instrument used by builders to ensure that the building is level. Utilizing the force of gravity, the construction is built according to the direction of the plumb line, not the direction that looks straight. In reminding His people that "small things" were involved in the project, God reminds His people that the construction would not happen overnight. It was going to take time.

Have you ever wished you could fast forward, to move on to more exciting times, a more exciting life? We often want to speed through dating so we can become married, speed through the first years of marriage so we can become parents, speed through child-rearing so we can have the house to ourselves again. Spiritually, we want to speed through a dry quiet time to get to a vibrant contagious walk with Christ. In life, we want to experience grand love, a thrilling adventure, and hot pursuit. Perhaps what is missed in the mundane is this fact: God is our grand love, His will is our thrilling adventure, and He has been in hot pursuit of us before we were ever born!

Sarah Bubar

Prayer: *Through which part of your life are you wanting to fast forward? Take time to stop and reflect on what God might be teaching you in the mundane details of life.*

Personal Reflection: ....

....

....

....

....

....

....

Hearts like Flint

Zechariah 7:4–14

～

"But they refused to heed, shrugged their shoulders,
and stopped their ears so that they could not hear. Yes, they made
their hearts like flint, refusing to hear...." (vv. 11–12a)

"I want my airplane pajamas!!!!" Griffin screamed at me through the tears streaming down his red four-year-old face. Clearly, I was not delivering on the expectation my ward had placed on me when I became his babysitter earlier that day. His vacation was immediately spoiled by the unrelenting babysitter hired by his parents' swanky hotel to care for him: ME! I stood there, my mind reeling with what to do, where to find, make, GLUE airplanes onto his train pajamas. "Griffin," I tried to console, "I'm so sorry, buddy, but your parents didn't pack your airplane pajamas. They must still be at home." His hands immediately clasped his ears, his shoulders rose as he inhaled air, only to exhale it in the loudest scream imaginable, "But I want my airplane pajamas!" Although I could not see his heart, I was sure of this: I just watched it turn to flint!

Zechariah found hardened hearts when he confronted the people with their disobedience. They made their hearts like flint. Flint is a hard dark rock. It has an almost glassy texture at its core, but a rough porous texture to its surface. Used to make the whittled points of spears or arrows, it is sharp enough to slice through a target. What a sobering picture of sin! Sin causes the heart to be hard and impenetrable when lives are used as weapons of war toward others. In this state, we cut to the quick our intended target. The saddest part is that the Israelites did this to themselves. When confronted with truth (vv. 5–6), when encouraged to change their ways, when told to show love to those around them (v. 9), their proverbial hands rose to their ears and shrugging their shoulders, they shouted, "We will not yield!" Although hardness to God was their choice, it was also going to bring more hardship into their lives (vv. 13–14).

I will probably never meet Griffin again. However, I will never be able to forget him. He showed me outwardly what my heart feels inwardly toward God when I am slow to submit to Him and His leading, when I justify my sins, or when I outright demand my own way. I become like Griffin, red-faced, tears flowing, and angry that I am not getting what I think I deserve or need. If left unchecked, if left unconfessed to fester in my mind, my heart will inevitably turn to flint as well. Sin will always take me farther than I ever meant to go, affecting me in ways I never imagined.

Sarah Bubar

Prayer: *Pray Psalm 139:23–24 and Ezekiel 36:22–32 over your life. Come honestly before your God, confessing your sins, knowing that He can create a new heart of flesh in you.*

Personal Reflection:

The Lord Restores His People

Zechariah 10:1–12

~

"I will bring them back,
Because I have mercy on them.
They shall be as though I had not cast them aside;
For I am the LORD their God,
And I will hear them." (v. 6b)

My family and I embarked on a huge project in 2002. We renovated an 1840 hotel and restaurant in our hometown in upstate New York. It was a beautiful building in its prime, but time had taken its toll, and it was in a dilapidated state. Within the kitchen of this poor, broken building there was a table. I immediately saw potential in its structure and devoted all my time and energy on this one piece of furniture. Certain family members thought I was crazy. "It's just the butcher's table; it's ugly and worn," they argued with me. But I knew that if I could strip away all that was ugly about its frame, I could turn it into something beautiful.

As I spent my days working on my solitary project, I thought of the restoration process through which the Lord often guides each of us. Sin comes into our lives like a thief robbing us blind. We give it more and more of ourselves, hoping the thief will be satisfied and leave our lives, but it does not; instead, sin lies to us (v. 2). It just continues to take and never give, until we are left resembling a worn old butcher's table in a forgotten kitchen. Then one day, light breaks through. We are bought with a high price by the One who makes all things new (2 Cor. 5:17; Rev. 21:5). Although there is pain in the process, the stripping process is for our good because God uses it to build up and restore.

Zechariah highlights the restoration process in this passage. God is looking forward to the day when He can fully and completely restore His people. Again and again, the prophet reminds the reader why God restores: His presence is always with them (Zech. 10:3–5), He has compassion on them; He is Yahweh, their personal God; and He has redeemed them (v. 6–8). All of His reasons are based on who HE is in relation to His people and not the other way around. What an encouragement to know God still relates to me in the same way. When He looks at me, redeemed by the precious blood of Christ, He doesn't see my sin because I have been crucified with Christ (Rom. 8:1; Gal. 2:20; Col. 3:3). An exchange took place: my guilt for His freedom, my sin for His righteousness, my life for His life (2 Cor. 5:21). In this process, the restoration makes me new. I am not forgotten. I am not ugly. I am not worthless. I am restored to more beauty than I could ever accomplish on my own.

Sarah Bubar

Prayer: *Praise the Lord for His restoration process in your life. Think about what it means to be hidden in Christ, and rejoice that you have been redeemed.*

Personal Reflection: ....

....

....

....

....

....

....

God Hates Divorce

Malachi 2:10–17

"'For the LORD the God of Israel says
That He hates divorce,
For it covers one's garment with violence,'
Says the LORD of hosts.
'Therefore take heed to your spirit,
That you do not deal treacherously.'" (v. 16)

Malachi 2:16 **does not say** that God hates people who have had a divorce; instead He hates divorce. Why is this an important distinction? Because if statistics are accurate, you or someone you know has been touched by divorce. More than fifty percent of all marriages end in divorce today, grieving the heart of God. His plan for marriage is to reflect a larger truth about the way He relates to and loves His people (see Day 4 devotion on Gen. 2:24–25 and Day 298 devotion on Eph. 5:22–33).

Malachi's day was not much different than today; divorce was a serious problem back then as well. Israelites were divorcing their wives and marrying pagan women (Mal. 2:11–12). Throughout the ancient Near East, all marriages were considered bound by law, but Yahweh was especially clear with His people about the lifelong commitment demanded by this spiritual covenant of marriage. Though the law of Moses permitted divorce (see Day 34 on Deut. 24:2–4), God, as clearly presented in Malachi, rejected the breaking of the marriage vows.

In fact, God is not only a witness in marriage; He considers marriage a life-long covenant (Mal. 2:14). What is a covenant exactly? It is a serious, binding commitment for life. It is not a simple contract between two parties; marriage is a three-way covenant between a man, a woman, and God. Jesus said about marriage: "What God has joined together, let not man separate" (Matt. 19:6). One does not enter into a covenant lightly nor should one dissolve it easily. In Malachi's day, God expresses the serious nature of a man who had dealt "treacherously with the wife of his youth" by divorcing her—He **hated** it (Mal. 2:14–15).

Why do you think God uses such strong terms like dealing treacherously, hate, and covering one's garment with violence (an expression referring to defiling one's character)? The reason is that a husband in a marriage covenant was to represent the way God loves and cares for His people, but when a human husband deals treacherously with his wife, he corrupts the picture. "Dealing treacherously" refers to a conscious or willful betrayal of trust, and God as a husband would never betray the trust of His people. Malachi commands the Israelites to "take heed" and watch themselves carefully (v. 16). Just like the New Testament passages that warn believers to be alert, clear-headed, and on guard (see 1 Pet. 1:13 and 5:8), believers today must take the threat against marriage seriously.

Candi Finch

Prayer: *Pray that Christians will recapture God's high view of marriage and be alert to any threats that may seek to distort God's design for marriage.*

Personal Reflection: ....

....

....

....

....

....

God Does Not Change

Malachi 3:1–7

"For I am the Lord, I do not change." (v. 6a)

As a music major in college, I endured four semesters of ear training. Some students were naturally gifted with this ability, which for most is an acquired skill. After hearing the tonic chord, the anchor note of a musical key, we would sight-read melodies, identify chord structures, and even write out the music we heard. The first notes were usually easy, but somewhere along the way, I would miss a note and, in a matter of seconds, be completely lost. Progress felt slow and often out of reach. Frustrated, I asked a professor's advice—the secret to having a brilliantly skilled ear. His answer stuck with me: "Always remember where the anchor is. Never forget the sound of a key's foundation. When you read a note, look at it according to its relationship to the tonic chord. You may still stumble and get lost, but you will know where you are and what adjustments you need to make."

God's unchanging character is the foundation for our spiritual ears. He is the anchor note by which we can determine where we are and what adjustments we need to make. He will be exactly who He has revealed Himself to be, at all times, in all situations. Even more, He will continue to be Himself on the basis of who He is, not who we are or what we have done (2 Tim. 2:13). We can stake our lives on God's promises in the confidence that He will be and do everything He has promised.

God does not want you to wonder where you stand with Him. In Christ, all of the promises of God are a constant, faithful "Yes" (2 Cor. 1:20). He Himself is the guarantee for our salvation and our future. To allow your feelings to control how you relate to God and how you live is easy. When you fail, you wonder if God will forgive you. He has already promised to forgive you when you honestly and humbly confess (1 John 1:9). When you face setbacks, sickness, and struggles, you wonder if He is still present, but He has already promised to work all of it together for your good (Rom. 8:28). When you see your own shortcomings, you wonder how God could use you, when He has already promised to fulfill His purpose for your life (Ps. 138:8)

All of the promises of God have been given to you in full, and they are as reliable as the unchanging faithfulness of God Himself. Even when you get off track, you can reset your life on the basis of His constant character. Because He is faithful and without even the slightest shadow of change, you can anchor your life on the foundation of His Word (James 1:17).

Katie McCoy

Prayer: *What promises of God do you find difficult to believe? How does His unchanging nature give you confidence and security? Thank God that He never changes.*

Personal Reflection:

Will You Rob God?

Malachi 3:8–12

"Will a man rob God?" (v. 8a)

A tithe of our money reveals our hearts! When I first married, I had no teaching or knowledge about the tithe and its purpose. I did not know what Scripture taught about tithing. Our small salary and the cost of living in a big city led us to believe we could not afford to give away a tenth of our income. Father God had much to teach me. He stretched me time and time again to trust Him with my finances.

After six months of marriage with money tight, we realized that writing our tithe check the following morning would deplete our entire checking account. We would not have any grocery money for the next week. I went into the kitchen to look in the pantry and start making a plan. By faith and in obedience, we wrote the check, got on our knees to pray, and then went to bed trusting God with our finances.

The next morning, we walked down the crowded hall of the church when the mother of one of our youth reached out and pulled me to the side. She explained that she had been carrying around our wedding gift and our Christmas gift for the past six months. Christmas had passed, and we were in the New Year. She handed me an envelope and a brown paper gift bag, neither of which looked like a Christmas gift. I carried it with me to worship. During worship, I placed the offering envelope with our tithe in the plate as it was passed, breathing the prayer of provision.

When we returned home that evening and opened the card, it was a sweet Christmas greeting. I read the message on the cover then as I opened the card, a check fell from inside and landed in my lap. My husband read it and then handed it over to me, saying, "God is good, and He provides."

That personal experience taught me that God always meets our needs very specifically. Six months earlier, the day of our wedding, this caring woman wrote a check for the very amount that we had tithed that Sunday. Speechless, we both slid off the couch to our knees. We were aware that in the early days of our marriage God was speaking to us specifically and purposely for the days ahead. Do you trust God with your money? Do you faithfully return to Him a tithe of all He gives you?

Diane Nix

Prayer: *Ask God to reveal any sin in your management of money. Repent and return to the Lord. Ask Him for help in regard to your giving. Pray specifically for God to order your steps in your finances. Thank the Lord for the ability to make money and for the ability to give so that others may know your God.*

Personal Reflection: ....

....

....

....

....

....

....

Jesus' Family Tree—and Yours

Matthew 1:2–6

*"Salmon begot Boaz by Rahab, Boaz begot
Obed by Ruth, Obed begot Jesse." (v. 5)*

What faces do you see in your family tree? Do some names fill you with delight and others with embarrassment? Matthew's Gospel begins with the genealogy—family tree—of Jesus Christ. Unlike most genealogies of his day, Matthew named five women among the men, including Rahab and Ruth (v. 6). God chose these two Gentiles, a former prostitute and a Moabite woman, to be foremothers of the promised Messiah, Jesus.

Rahab the harlot protected the two spies Joshua, the Israelite leader, sent to survey the land before his army attacked. She committed herself to the God of Israel. Joshua spared her life when his soldiers marched against the city of Jericho. Rahab identified with God's people by marrying Salmon of the tribe of Judah.

Although God banned marriage to Moabites, an Israelite who immigrated to Moab during famine married Ruth. After his death, Ruth moved to his homeland with her widowed mother-in-law Naomi, choosing to trust the God of Israel. Her care for Naomi caused others to respect her. Ruth married Rahab's son, Boaz. Ruth's son, Obed, was the grandfather of King David. God's grace allowed both Rahab and Ruth—unlikely choices for the Messiah's family tree—to play an important role in His plan of redemption.

The Lord has blessed my family tree. When I think of Grandma, two words come to mind: sacrificial service. This homemaker took care of one family member after another: her invalid brother, five daughters, and numerous grandchildren. Whenever anyone had problems, her spare bedroom became home for one night—or for months. She exemplified love-in-action.

Grandma's humble service continues in her youngest daughter, my mother. At age 87, she still organizes and delivers "funeral meals" for her church. She leads the prayer shawl knitting ministry. Weekly she calls homebound members of her Bible study class. She serves as a prayer warrior for the whole family. My grandmother's and mother's lives encourage me to follow in their steps of love for and service to the Lord. Will I leave that kind of legacy?

What about you? You may not find inspiration in your family tree. Through faith in Jesus Christ, however, God will adopt you into His family, giving you godly examples to follow in a church community and in His Word, and using you as part of His plan of redemption. You can choose to grow a new branch to your family tree, one that future generations will view with joy and respect. What faces *will you see* in your family tree?

Sharon Gritz

Prayer: *Thank God for your family tree—both the inspiring and the upsetting faces. Like Rahab and Ruth, commit yourself to the one true God. Ask Him to shape you into a woman who reflects the character of His Son, Jesus Christ, a woman whose future generations will rejoice to have in their genealogy.*

Personal Reflection: ....

....

....

....

....

....

Sexual Purity: The Example of Jewish Betrothal
Matthew 1:18–25

"Then Joseph her husband, being a just man, and not wanting to make her a public example, was minded to put her away secretly." (v. 19)

Jewish betrothal was not like modern-day engagement. Today, an engagement can be broken until the couple says, "I do." In Jewish culture, a betrothal was a binding contract between a man and a woman. The families of the bride and groom were usually involved in the arrangement and, following a formal betrothal, the groom prepared a home for his new bride. Even though there was no physical intimacy, the couple was considered married. They belonged to each other. In fact, the only way to break a betrothal was a divorce. Unfaithfulness was not premarital promiscuity but adultery.

When Mary was found to be pregnant, Joseph, knowing the baby was not his, had reason to believe Mary was unfaithful. He had the right to take Mary before the religious leaders, accuse her of adultery, and publicly divorce her. Not only would her marriage prospects have been damaged, if not completely dashed, but she would also have been humiliated. Instead, Joseph chose to sever his betrothal quietly and discretely, sparing her the shame. When God revealed His plan to Joseph through an angel in a dream, He assured him that Mary had not been unfaithful but was carrying the Messiah, conceived by the Holy Spirit.

While this story is primarily about Christ's virgin birth, it also illustrates the importance of sexual purity before marriage. Many people today claim that the importance of virginity is something created by society, that it should not be emphasized. Some have mistakenly held up virginity as the defining measure of a woman's character, even equating physical abstinence with purity (Matt. 5:27–28). As a result, many make the opposite mistake of separating one's sexual behavior from overall personal character. However, while sexual purity is not the only expression of character, it certainly cannot be separated from it.

Scripture presents sexual purity as beginning in the heart, with physical behavior being an expression of the heart (1 Thess. 4:3–8). The truth is that none of us is perfectly pure. Whether in body or in the heart, we have all fallen short of God's perfect standard and need the blood of Jesus to cleanse us and make us pure. But, no matter what your history, you can walk in restored purity through God's forgiveness and the power of the Holy Spirit (Gal. 5:16).

Ultimately, the choice to practice sexual purity before and after marriage is an act of worship. We live in such an "anything goes" world that following God's plan for sexuality is one of the most countercultural sacrifices of worship to be made (Rom. 12:1–2).

Katie McCoy

Prayer: *Are you walking in sexual purity, both physically and spiritually? Take a moment to renew your commitment to following God's design for your sexuality.*

Personal Reflection: ....

....

....

....

....

....

....

How Can You Enjoy Blessedness?

Matthew 5:1–9

⟜⟜

"Blessed are those who hunger and thirst for righteousness,
For they shall be filled." (v. 6)

The Sermon on the Mount, especially the **Beatitudes**, is a well-known biblical passage, familiar to believers and unbelievers. The passage is about achieving righteousness not by works but by living a life consistent with genuine repentance and faithful obedience. In doing so, you will bear fruit to honor Christ and influence the world. Such a journey requires a complete change of heart, manifesting itself beyond mere deeds in order to produce fruits worthy of presenting to the Lord (Matt. 5:20).

Values of the modern, as well as in the Greco-Roman world—wealth and fame—were actually devalued in Christ's kingdom. He turned things upside-down to reflect what really matters to Him.

Blessed (Gk. *makarios*), also translated "happy," may reflect the idea of "good fortune." However, more accurate is the idea of expressing congratulations based on the favor of God upon an individual. Only God bestows blessedness—not on your demand or for exemplary behavior—but as a characteristic of God Himself exclusively available to believers. Outward circumstances do not affect or restrain blessedness. Rather this spiritual discipline is formed within as a result of Christ's working in your life.

Scripture does not describe poverty as the path to spiritual blessing. Here the emphasis is upon emptying yourself to make room for God—you recognize that you cannot satisfy your own needs and must look to God. To be **poor in spirit** puts your focus on God's power instead of your own resourcefulness. Most people do not consider sorrow a blessing, and indeed spiritual payments are not due as a response to grief. However, as a believer **mourns** over her sin, the Holy Spirit does His work to give comfort and enable her to persevere even in the midst of suffering and sorrow. The **gentle** are not weak and cowardly, but they are willing to harness their lives with God-control and be content with whatever challenges appear.

Those who hunger and thirst for righteousness recognize the insatiable hunger God has placed in the heart for Himself—often described as a God-shaped vacuum. So a believer does not seek to be full of righteousness in order to be blessed, but the one blessed will yearn for righteousness, which will always be part of the faith journey.

These first four Beatitudes describe the character of one who is filled with the Spirit of God and who is determined to mold a life worthy of that commitment. Each beatitude builds upon the previous one and prepares for those that follow.

Dorothy Kelley Patterson

Prayer: *Ask the Lord to start this building project in your heart. Strip away the outer veneer, affirming your own inadequacy. Mourn over your sinfulness. Invite the Lord to control your life, and acknowledge your hunger for the necessary filling to sustain you on your spiritual journey.*

Personal Reflection: ....

....

....

....

....

....

Persecution in the Midst of Blessings

Matthew 5:10–12, 43–48

꙳

"Blessed are those who are persecuted for righteousness' sake,
For theirs is the kingdom of heaven." (v. 10)

The Beatitudes are etched on the hearts of believers who take the faith journey seriously. The emphasis moves from the character of the one who has been filled with the Spirit of God (Matt. 5:3–6) to how that Christ-like character is to exhibit itself in the believer's relationship to others. For example, once you have been stripped of pride, you become tenderhearted toward one another. Then you find self-restraint and a submissive spirit, so that ultimately you are motivated to hear and to do the will of God.

This Spirit-filled life prepares you to relate not only to other believers but also to unbelievers. You are moved to pity and compassion as you grieve over the suffering of others. **The merciful** embrace God's way with an act of the will, not merely in their doing deeds to awaken praise from others but in their displaying faith that is working itself out in meeting the needs of others (v. 7).

The pure in heart have disciplined their lives so that they are committed to set-apartness unto the Lord (v. 8). This holiness is marked by a difference in your thoughts and motivation. This holiness draws you to be obsessed and controlled by God.

The peacemakers have a spirit of forbearance instead of retaliation. They seek to forgive wrongs and to restore fellowship. The desire is not just to end conflict but to bring healing. Such peace with others only comes when you have peace with God (v. 9).

Those who are persecuted for righteousness' sake have come the full circle and will receive the same reward as those described in the first beatitude (v. 10). Persecution was considered a blessing in Christ's kingdom because a person could thereby empathize with the sufferings of Christ. The steadfast loyalty that marked such a commitment could not be broken. A reward in heaven awaited the person who persevered. Those who are insulted and persecuted because of Christ do not find joy in the persecution itself, but they are reminded that as they drink the cup of His sufferings, their patience springs from within their hearts and thus provides for them strength to endure suffering. They find a new intimacy with Christ and have the potential to be blessed because of bearing testimony for Him (vv. 11–12).

Dorothy Kelley Patterson

Prayer: *Only Christ can prepare your heart for a godly response to those who delight in causing you pain and suffering. Place your burdens before Him and seek the joy of perseverance—a blessing Christ wants to give to those who suffer in His name. Ask the Lord to prepare you to bear your testimony faithfully regardless of circumstances that unfold to make that journey difficult.*

Personal Reflection: ....

....

....

....

....

....

....

The Ministry of the Blessed Woman

Matthew 5:13–16, 38–42

"You are the salt of the earth; but if the salt loses its flavor, how shall it be seasoned? It is then good for nothing but to be thrown out and trampled underfoot by men." (v. 13)

Jesus encouraged those who followed Him to display characteristics that would set them apart from the prevailing culture of the world. This countercultural mandate does not mean separating yourself from the people immersed in that ungodly culture; rather believers are called out to change the culture. Salt and light are powerful elements that bring change wherever they are used. Nothing enhances flavor and keeps food from decaying as effectively as salt—but only if it is pure and unadulterated. Its base, sodium chloride, will not lose its saltiness and effectiveness unless it is diluted or mixed with impure substances. So believers can serve a wonderful purpose in the world by bringing the flavor of the Lord and His character into full effectiveness, but to do so demands that they maintain intimacy and fellowship with the Lord so that the Spirit fills and enables them to function in an effective way (v. 13). Yet salt must touch what is to be purified and preserved. Believers must reach out and touch those whose lives they want to influence.

A beacon of light also transforms a room or area into which its beam shines. D. L. Moody said, "A holy life produces the deepest impression. Lighthouses blow no horns; they only shine." The darkness prohibits movement and any effective work, but the light dismisses darkness and provides an atmosphere in which effective work may be done. Believers also have this purpose in the world—to light up the darkness and make possible kingdom work (v. 14). Light may also be used to symbolize purity so that it becomes an excellent metaphor for God's revelation of Himself. Jesus is identified as the true light (John 1:9; 8:12, 14). People who do not know Christ as Savior are lost in darkness, and believers have the beacon of light to point them to Christ.

Influence is a gift from God. I believe this is especially true for women. The maternal, nurturing nature that God has implanted in women is a natural conduit for enhancing influence. We cannot be content only to prevent decay as salt certainly does, but we must be proactive to add flavor through Christian virtues to the world in which we live. We must commit ourselves to preserving biblical values. For the sake of our children and grandchildren, we must also flood our venues of influence with a beacon of light—light that comes from the gospel within our hearts. We need to unveil biblical truth and to show how that truth changes lives and accomplishes the purposes of God

Dorothy Kelley Patterson

Prayer: *Ask the Lord to make you salt and light so that you can change your home, your neighborhood, your city, your state, your nation, and even the world!*

Personal Reflection: ....

....

....

....

....

....

....

Jesus—The Ultimate Lawgiver

Matthew 5:17–20, 27–30

*"For assuredly, I say to you, till heaven and earth pass away, one jot
or one tittle will by no means pass from the law till all is fulfilled." (v. 18)*

"The Law and the Prophets" is a reference to the Old Testament Scripture—all of it. Jesus without question affirms the Old Testament as God's Word. And Jesus Christ is the fulfillment of the prophecies. He is the ultimate subject of the Old Testament, which points to Him, as well as the New Testament, which records His life and ministry. Jesus also affirms the thoroughness of His acceptance of the inspiration of the Old Testament, arguing that not a "jot" (the smallest letter in the Hebrew alphabet) or "tittle" (a small extension of a Hebrew letter used to differentiate it from another letter) will be lost. He honored the Law, including every syllable of all its words and even the small strokes of each letter in the words.

Jesus proved that He is the true interpreter of the Law. His interpretation opposed that of the Pharisees, who charged Him with destroying the Law. He denied their charge (vv. 17–20). In fact, Jesus fulfilled the Law by:

- fully obeying it;
- submitting to its condemnation as He took the place of all who transgressed the Law (v. 28);
- stressing His own messianic authority as equal to the authority of the Law;
- proving that the inferences from the religious leaders were false;
- living up to the righteousness demanded by the Law;
- fulfilling predictions regarding the promised Messiah;
- stressing the ethical and moral rather than the ritual demands of the Law; and

- viewing His messianic mission as the means whereby the righteousness of the kingdom might be fulfilled through His work as the Mediator (Heb. 9:15).

The coming of Christ brought some of the Law to completion, but other requirements await His return (v. 18).

Matthew 5:31–48 includes six illustrations of the kind of righteousness Jesus required of His followers. Jesus, just as the Law, condemned murder, adultery, divorce, oath-taking, and retaliation. However, He also went beyond the letter of the Law in denouncing hatred, lust, and pride, as well as the attitudes that stood behind these sins. His summary statement contains the ultimate challenge for a believer: "You shall be perfect, just as your Father in heaven is perfect" (v. 48). The biblical meaning of "perfect" offers a different understanding that reaches beyond the absence of mistakes. The word has the sense of "complete" or "mature." Accordingly, Jesus' challenge to the believer is a journey, not a sinless life. You are admonished to use great effort and endurance to complete the journey before you in a God-glorifying way.

Dorothy Kelley Patterson

Prayer: *Seek the Lord's help in your journey. Affirm to Him your love of His Word and determination to be obedient to the mandates of Scripture. Ask His help in guiding you through your journey, climbing the mountains as well as walking through the valleys.*

Personal Reflection: ....

....

....

....

The Danger of Lust

Matthew 5:27–30

"I say to you that whoever looks at a woman to lust for her has already committed adultery with her in his heart." (v. 28)

Have you heard the expression, "Be careful little eyes what you see"? Jesus takes it a step further in the Sermon on the Mount when He warns against looking on a woman in lust. He is essentially saying, "Be careful little mind what you think." In this one simple statement, Jesus is affirming sex as only appropriate between a husband and wife, encouraging men not to view women as physical objects, and calling Christians to a very high standard of sexual purity in both actions and thoughts.

Sisters, we live in a "porn-positive culture" that has perverted and twisted sex. Instead of being a gift designed by God to be enjoyed by a man and woman in a committed, marriage relationship, sex is used by our sin natures and Satan as a tool to ensnare us. Second Peter 2:19 warns that we are slaves to whatever has mastered us. Unfortunately, many people—men and women—are slaves to some form of sexual immorality and lust.

Consider pornography. Contemporary secular culture considers viewing or reading some form of pornography as "victimless" recreation; just a harmless diversion that is "safe" because it doesn't "hurt" anyone else. Frankly, that's just naïve. The first victim pornography takes down is the person viewing it by creating an appetite in the mind for things that cause lust, which brings forth sin (James 1:14–15). Jesus knew the danger of feeding lusts in the mind; thus He warns about adultery in the heart.

Think about the progression: When a woman spends time fantasizing or lusting in her heart about sexually explicit material, the allure can lead her to want to see it and then move her to acting out what she has seen. James 1:14–15 warns: "But each one is tempted when he is drawn away by his own desires and enticed. Then, when desire has conceived, it gives birth to sin: and sin, when it is full-grown, brings forth death." Start viewing lust as a destructive tool used by the enemy to ensnare—the Bible warns: "Can a man take fire to his bosom, And his clothes not be burned?" (Prov. 6:27).

Since lust and pornography are often regarded as a "man-only struggle," many women have an added sense of shame and guilt when they find themselves struggling with these sins. Sin entangles men and women, and the problem will not go away by itself. If you struggle with lust, you must seek the Lord's transformation: "Create in me a clean heart, O God, And renew a steadfast spirit within me" (Ps. 51:10).

Candi Finch

Prayer: *Do you struggle with dwelling on lustful thoughts? Ask the Lord to reveal any influences that may be causing you to stumble and ask Him to help you turn from that sin and set your mind on godly things.*

Personal Reflection:

Don't Lay Up for Yourselves Treasures on Earth

Matthew 6:19–34

⌣

"Do not lay up for yourselves treasures on earth, where moth and rust destroy and where thieves break in and steal." (v. 19)

Financial gurus warn that cars and computers may be the top two depreciating consumer products in America. As far as cars are concerned, the depreciation rate varies by the model but, overall, simply driving a new car off the sales lot lowers its resale value. Computers are not all that different. Few things seem to be outdated as fast as electronics. Some companies roll out new versions of their product every year or so, leaving many people holding the retired "has-beens" in their hands while others run after the "latest and greatest."

In the first part of Matthew 6, the words of Jesus focus the reader's attention on things of lasting value: doing charitable deeds on behalf of the Father, not oneself; praying to an audience of One (the heavenly Father) and not for the attention of others; and fasting for God's reward and not man's approval. Jesus models a prayer that acknowledges the holiness of God and the dependence of the pray-er on His sovereign presence and purpose. Then, in a summary statement, Jesus warns that earthly treasures are susceptible to earthly problems like moths, rust, and thieves.

Jesus could have added natural disasters to this list. In August 2005, the wind and rain of Hurricane Katrina left much devastation in its wake. As several levees breached throughout the New Orleans area, hundreds upon hundreds of homes were flooded, some to the roofs and others just inches deep. But no matter the depth of the water, loss was felt. Soggy carpets, waterlogged couches, deluged cars, moldy clothes, and rotten food were the norm as the water subsided and reality dawned. An estimated 22 million tons of waste was hauled away during the recovery process. A *New York Times* writer reported that this amount of trash could fill the Empire State Building 40 times.* And this was just one city affected by one natural disaster.

In the journey of life, sometimes your possessions, people in your life, even your own dreams can steer your heart and get in the way of God-given opportunities to reach out to a lost and hurting world. You may have more, but you are not better.

Jesus wasn't saying that the basics of food, shelter, and clothing aren't important. Instead, He wanted His followers then—and now—to stop focusing on the outside trappings and focus on the matters of the heart because "where your treasure is, there will your heart be also" (Matt. 6:21).

Judi Jackson

Prayer: *If the Holy Spirit convicts you about the importance you place on earthly possessions, repent and ask Him to show your excess. Follow His leading to share what you do not need with someone who will be blessed by your act of sacrifice.*

Personal Reflection: ....

....

....

....

....

....

* Jennifer Medina, *New York Times,* October 16, 2005. See http://www.nytimes.com/2005/10/16/national/nationalspecial/16garbage.html?pagewanted=all&_r=1&.

Herodias—A Power-Hungry Woman

Matthew 14:1–12

"So she [Salome], having been prompted by her mother [Herodias], said 'Give me John the Baptist's head here on a platter.'" (v. 8)

Herodias was a crafty, greedy woman of the first century. She was a member of the Herodian dynasty, perhaps one of the most despised leaders history has ever known. Her name is a feminine form of the name Herod. She rose to her position in a dishonorable way, demonstrating that she was a power–hungry woman from the beginning.

Herodias, born in Tiberias on the Sea of Galilee, the daughter of Aristobulus, son of Herod the Great, married her uncle Philip. She and Philip had a daughter Salome, who later conspired with her mother to destroy John the Baptist. Herodias soon tired of Philip and was wooed by a third son of Herod the Great, Herod Antipas. Attracted to the beautiful Herodias, he divorced his Arabian wife and caused the divorce of his brother in order to marry his sister-in-law. Oh what a tangled web sin weaves!

Elevated to a position of political power through an incestuous relationship, Herodias brought out the worst in her new husband Herod. At the same time, John the Baptist was preaching in Israel. He seemed a threat to the dynasty because of his popularity with the people and his courage to confront their sin. Herod had John the Baptist imprisoned and was angry to be confronted for his own sin (vv. 1–5).

The plot thickened at Herod's birthday party when his seductive step-daughter asked for the head of John the Baptist on a platter. Manipulated by her mother, the wicked daughter followed her despicable plan and brought his head on a platter to Herodias (vv. 6–12). Evil ran throughout the members of the Herodian dynasty.

No one is uglier than a wicked woman! When I think of truly evil women, I envision the Wicked Witch of the West in *The Wizard of Oz*. She is sinister and creepy in contrast to Dorothy, who is sweet and kind. The witch causes chaos wherever she goes and tries to lure Dorothy to her evil ways. Like Herodias, the witch sought the power of others, trying to steal Dorothy's magical ruby-red slippers. In the movie, everyone (except the witch) lives happily ever after. However, in reality and in this biblical account, the ending is very grim. Because John the Baptist was killed in such a gruesome way, Herodias and her daughter Salome are remembered for their evil nature and are counterparts to Jezebel of the Old Testament.

The moral of this tragic tale is: Don't let your desire for power go to your head. And, don't influence others to sinfulness. Herodias used her husband King Herod Antipas and her daughter Salome as instruments to orchestrate her tragic crime. Be warned that power-hungry people get their just desserts!

Rhonda Harrington Kelley

Prayer: *Have you ever known a power-hungry woman like Herodias? Beware of her snares. Ask the Lord to protect you from the deceit of others.*

Personal Reflection: ....

....

....

....

....

....

The Syro-Phoenician Woman—A Desperate Mother

Matthew 15:21–28

"Then Jesus answered and said to her 'O woman,
great is your faith! Let it be to you as you desire.'" (v. 28)

The relationship between this mother and daughter is a stark contrast from Herodias and Salome introduced in the previous chapter of Matthew. This Canaanite woman lived in the Gentile region of Tyre and Sidon. She trusted in Jesus as God, the One with divine powers. She begged Jesus: "Have mercy on me, O Lord, Son of David! My daughter is severely demon-possessed" (v. 22). In desperation, the worried mother sought help from the only One who can heal.

A friend's young child recently had a near-drowning experience. As her little one lay lifeless in intensive care, this desperate mother called out to God for help. The family and friends prayed fervently for healing. God intervened in this crisis situation and saved the small child's life. His healing has been a powerful testimony of faith to believers and unbelievers alike.

The Syro-Phoenician woman believed Jesus could save and perform mighty works. She worshipped Him and called out to Him saying, "Lord, help me!" (v. 25). Her faithful life was recognized by Jesus who claimed He had only come for "the lost sheep of the house of Israel" (v. 24). She knew Jesus had come to save the Gentiles as well as the Jews. Her confidence in Christ resulted in her greatest blessing; Her daughter was healed of her disease. It was not the mother's love for her child but her faith in the Savior that brought healing. "Then Jesus answered and said to her, 'O woman, great *is* your faith! Let it be to you as you desire'" (v. 28).

Christ began His ministry to the Gentiles when He encountered this desperate mother. He ministered to other desperate women in the course of His time on earth. Jesus always responded with compassion and concern. He stopped what He was doing and gave personal attention, affirmed the individual's faith, and taught a powerful lesson. Whether or not a miracle was performed, meeting with Jesus always impacted the life of a woman desperately seeking Him.

Are you desperately seeking the Lord? Do you desire Him more than anyone or anything? Be a desperate disciple of Christ. Sing to God with Michael W. Smith in his moving song "Breathe:"

This is the air I breathe;
This is the air I breathe;
Your holy presence living in me.

This is my daily bread;
This is my daily bread;
Your very word spoken to me.

And I I'm desperate for you,
And I I'm lost without you.*

Let it be to you as He desires!

Rhonda Harrington Kelley

Prayer: *What is your greatest need today? Take your burdens and concerns to the Lord who cares for you. He is desperately seeking you, and He longs for you to desperately pursue Him.*

Personal Reflection: ....

....

....

....

* Artist: Michael W. Smith; Album: *Worship*; copyright 1995 by Mercy/Vineyard Publishing. See http://m.musicnotes.com/sheetmusic/mtdFPE.asp?ppn=MN0051473.

Jesus' Teaching on Divorce

Matthew 19:1–11

◡◠◡

"So then, they are no longer two but one flesh. Therefore, what God has joined together, let not man separate." (v. 6)

Have you seen those old cartoons where a villain with a slick mustache hatches an evil scheme and then strokes his mustache with his fingers while cackling ominously? Every time I read this passage in Matthew 19 about the Pharisees questioning Jesus about divorce, I picture those old cartoon villains. You see, the Pharisees asked Jesus a loaded question to "test" Him; that word for test means they did so with malicious intent (v. 3).

Divorce was a hotly debated topic between two different rabbinic schools of Shammai and Hillel. The Pharisaic schools disagreed about the significance of Moses allowing a man to divorce his wife if he found some "uncleanness" in her (Deut. 24:1; see Day 34 devotion). The Shammai school took the strict view that divorce was allowed only in cases of sexual immorality, while the Hillel school held that the statute could be applied to practically any action that displeased a husband. In the modern era, such a position would have provided grounds for seeking a divorce if a wife burned her husband's breakfast! Both of these groups had taken the permission granted by Moses and made it a command or mandate. In the process, they had allowed human choices and circumstances to circumvent God's plan and purpose.

The Pharisees were probably hoping Jesus would offend at least one of the groups with His answer about any lawful reason for divorce. However, rather than citing the teaching of one of the popular rabbis, Jesus responded by pointing His listeners back to God's ideal plan for marriage found in Genesis 2:24 and reminding them that marriage is a covenant between a man, a woman, and God ("what God has joined together"). Jesus models how we should handle hotly debated topics—always go back to what the Word of God says on an issue.

Because marriage was a metaphor used by the Lord to illustrate His own relationship to believers and to the church (Eph. 5:22–33), Jesus had an uncompromising word for any who broke the vows of marriage. Ultimately, God's answer to this problematic issue was not found in laws, legal codes, traditions, or even human choices. God returned to His creative design for the man and woman, their holy committed union, and His plan to use that sacred union as a tool for revealing Himself and His faithfulness. God does not concede His principles to popular opinion nor does He lower His standards because He knows His standards are for our good. Conversely, it is also important to remember that God redeems and restores all who seek Him and His forgiveness.

Candi Finch

Prayer: *As topics like divorce get debated both inside and outside the church, pray that believers would model the approach of Jesus in handling these tough questions by letting God's Word be the final authority.*

Personal Reflection:

Zebedee's Wife—An Ambitious Mother

Matthew 20:17–28

"Then the mother of Zebedee's sons came to Him with her sons, kneeling down and asking something from Him. . . . 'Grant that these two sons of mine may sit, one on Your right hand and the other on the left, in Your kingdom.'" (vv. 20–21)

Most Christian mothers pray that their children will follow the Lord and accomplish great things. They hope that their children will serve the Lord and be recognized for their kingdom ministry. However, there is a great difference in beseeching God for His work in the lives of your children and taking matters into your own hands. The ambitious mother in this passage did not wait for God to speak truth directly to her children, she approached Jesus with her own plan for their lives.

Meet the characters in this story. Zebedee was a fisherman on the Sea of Galilee, in Capernaum on the northern shore. The Bible does not describe his personal faith, but his sons were among the inner circle of Jesus Christ. He married Mary, who followed Jesus and ministered to Him (Mark 15:40–41). They had sons James and John, two of the first disciples of Jesus. The sons worked with their father in the fishing business until they heard the call from Jesus: "When He [Jesus] had gone a little farther from there, He saw James the *son* of Zebedee and John his brother, who also *were* . . . in the boat with the hired servants, and went after Him" (Mark 1:19–20).

Can you imagine this mother's joy when her sons were called to serve with the Messiah? My sweet mother-in-love prayed for her five children faithfully. She sincerely desired that they follow the Lord and serve Him. When her only son was called to the ministry rather than to continue the family business, she rejoiced. She believed her son accepted a higher calling, to preach the gospel. Unlike Zebedee's wife, Mom Kelley was not selfishly ambitious for her children. She trusted God with their lives and prayed for them to heed His call. What a significant lesson for mothers today!

As Christ's impending time of suffering drew near, His servanthood was emphasized. He repeatedly told His disciples He would suffer, be killed, and on the third day be raised to life (Matt. 20:18–19). The disciples were still expecting a political Savior, so they continued to desire rank and rewards in His kingdom. This mother wanted her sons to fill higher positions than the other disciples. As always, Jesus responded with a profound biblical teaching: "Whoever desires to become great among you shall be your servant. And whoever of you desires to be first shall be slave of all. For even the Son of Man did not come to be served, but to serve, and to give His life a ransom for many" (Mark 10:43–44).

Rhonda Harrington Kelley

Prayer: *Spend some time reflecting on the servanthood of Jesus. Pray for God's will not your ambition for yourself and those you love.*

Personal Reflection:

The Wise and Foolish Virgins

Matthew 25:1–13

*"Then the kingdom of heaven shall be likened to ten virgins who took
their lamps and went out to meet the bridegroom." (v. 1)*

Jesus often told parables, stories to teach a life lesson. His parables often turned the ears of the people to eyes as they visualized His truth. He shared the parable in this passage after foretelling the end times (Matt. 24) and just days before His crucifixion (Matt. 27). Only recorded by Matthew, the parable of the wise and foolish virgins, as well as the parable of the talents in the following passage, teach the importance of personal preparation for the return of Jesus (25:14–30).

The context for this teaching by Jesus was a wedding, a time of celebration as well as traditional customs. Ten virgins who were bridesmaids waited with the bride to meet her bridegroom. Five wise virgins took a supply of oil with their lamps while five foolish virgins took only their lamps. They slept as they waited for the bridegroom. When the bridegroom arrived at midnight, the naïve ladies realized they were unprepared, not enough oil for their lamps. They were denied entry to the wedding feast. The bridegroom told them: "Assuredly I say to you, I do not know you" (v. 12; cp. Matt. 7:21–23). Their lack of preparation disqualified them from entry into the presence of the bridegroom.

In the same way that a bride attends to every detail of her wedding day, a Christian should attend to every detail, preparing for the appearance of her Bridegroom, Jesus Christ. Spiritual preparation must be made ahead of Christ's return; it cannot wait until the last minute. From the time of salvation until the Lord's return, the Christian should be getting her affairs in order. The message of this parable is clear: The day and time of the return of Jesus is imminent though unknown. He may come today, or He may delay; believers must be prepared. "Watch therefore, for you know neither the day nor the hour in which the Son of Man is coming" (Matt. 25:13).

I have lived all my life along the Gulf Coast of the United States, which is hurricane territory. As a child, I learned to prepare the hurricane basket in

June to last through the season which ends in November. The basket is filled every year with flashlights, batteries, and candles in case the power goes off. Water bottles and nonperishable foods are purchased in case a storm traps you in your home. Then the waiting and praying begins, but the preparations have been made.

While virgins and hurricanes can only be likened to the kingdom of heaven (v. 1), the lesson is clear—be prepared! If it is important to be prepared for the special events of life, it is even more important to be prepared for the return of Jesus, our Savior and Lord.

Rhonda Harrington Kelley

Prayer: *Take a spiritual inventory of your life. Are you prepared for the Lord's return? Be wise not foolish as you wait.*

Personal Reflection: ....

....

....

....

....

....

....

The Two-Talent Christian

Matthew 25:14–30

"Well done, good and faithful servant; you have been faithful over a few things, I will make you ruler over many things. Enter into the joy of your lord." (v. 23)

Have you been faithful to use the gifts God has given you? This well-known parable speaks to the crucial issue of how a believer manages—or stewards—her gifts. In this story, talents can be understood in three ways: your natural ability, your spiritual giftedness, and your opportunities. The number of talents given in this story are often thought to imply the value of the servant, but that is not so. The text clearly states that both the five-talent and two-talent servants were given the same praise and the same reward by the master (vv. 21, 23). There is no reason to believe that the one-talent servant would not have received the same.

How do we understand the differences in these three servants as it applies to us today? I suggest that the five-talent women are those who are unusually gifted. They can do many things and manage them all very well! Not wealth nor fame but their abilities and gifts help them take full advantage of many opportunities. Two- and one-talent women are those with some natural abilities and spiritual gifts, yet perhaps with fewer opportunities to use them.

The world runs on two-talent people! Most of us do not have extraordinary giftedness or exceptional opportunities. Thousands of pastors, staff members, and lay people serve God faithfully in small churches, small towns, or rural communities across our nation. These are "two-talent" people in the sense that their opportunities have been limited to some degree. Most of them will never pastor a mega-church, publish a book, or have a national platform. Yet they faithfully and joyfully serve in the field where God has placed them, investing their time and energy in His kingdom (see 2 Cor. 10:13).

The master praised the five- and two-talent servants, calling them "good and faithful." What a contrast when we notice that he described the one-talent servant as "wicked and lazy." That seems harsh, at first reading. But if we understand "wicked" to mean working against God's purposes, then it becomes clear. If we are poor stewards of the gifts and opportunities He has invested in us, then we have no part in His kingdom work.

The point of this parable is not how many talents you have been given, but your willingness to use them faithfully and develop them for the glory of your Master. Be a faithful two-talent Christian!

Susie Hawkins

Prayer: *Ask the Lord to help you see the gifts He has given to you, as well as opportunities that may be right in front of you! Pray that you will serve faithfully, working with God's purposes in your life, as well as Kingdom purposes.*

Personal Reflection:

Pilate's Wife—An Intuitive Woman

Matthew 27:11–26

*"While he [Pilate] was sitting on the judgment seat, his wife sent to him,
saying, 'Have nothing to do with that just Man, for I have suffered
many things today in a dream because of Him.'" (v. 19)*

The name Pontius Pilate is known by Christians worldwide because of the role
he played in the crucifixion of Jesus. He was the Roman governor of Judea who
hated the Hebrews. He assumed power about A.D. 26 and brought into Jerusalem
the influence of Caesar, in defiance of the Jewish law. Luke documented his
reputation: "There were present at that season some who told Him about the
Galileans whose blood Pilate had mingled with their sacrifices" (Luke 13:1).

In this passage, Jesus appeared before Pilate as His trial began. Pilate
asked Jesus a direct question: "Are You the King of the Jews?" (Matt. 27:11a).
Jesus simply answered: "*It is* as you say" (v. 11b). Thus, the inscription over His
head on the cross: "THIS IS JESUS THE KING OF THE JEWS" (27:37). Jesus
truly is the King of the Jews, the Lord of lords, and the Prince of Peace!

Pilate obviously thought Jesus was innocent. According to Roman custom,
he could release a prisoner. He gave the crowd the choice of Jesus or "a notori-
ous prisoner called Barabbas" (v. 16). While Pilate was sitting on the judgment
seat, his wife reported a disturbing dream. She sent a warning to him saying:
"Have nothing to do with that just Man" (v. 19). Like the wife in Shakespeare's
Macbeth, she strongly encouraged her husband to wash his hands of the whole
matter. While the details of the dream are not recorded, Pilate's wife clearly
believed Jesus was innocent, and she worried that her husband's position would
be harmed if he convicted Jesus.

Unfortunately, Pilate did not heed the warning of his intuitive wife. He
released Barabbas as the people requested, and "delivered *Him* to be crucified"
(vv. 25–26). The blood of Christ was on the hands of Pilate and his children. The
circumstances of Pilate's death are unknown, though some say he was exiled

and committed suicide. One thing is certain, Pilate should have listened to his intuitive wife.

Intuition is a sense of understanding without conscious reasoning. God gives women that special ability of perception and discernment. Abigail in the Old Testament showed discerning intuition in her evaluation of the danger to her household from David and his men. She wisely intervened to protect her husband Nabal and his property (1 Sam. 25:2–35). Her godly intuition was a blessing to her family.

What about you? Do you have feminine intuition? Do you sometimes have a sense or feeling about a situation or person? Seek the Lord's direction to clarify your thoughts, then share them appropriately. Always verify your intuitions with the truth of God's Word.

Rhonda Harrington Kelley

Prayer: *Thank the Lord for giving you His thoughts and commit to being a discerning Christian woman.*

Personal Reflection: ....

....

....

....

....

....

Women and the Great Commission

Matthew 28:16–20

*"Go therefore and make disciples of all the nations, baptizing them
in the name of the Father and of the Son and of the Holy Spirit." (v. 19)*

If you could give a statement or tweet with parting words, what would you write? Jesus' final words are found in these verses on which we base our call. He left His followers with this most important message found in Matthew 28:16–20. The Great Commission is the mission of the local church as well as a call for every believer.

For some church members, evangelism is seen as the pastor's responsibility. We want to be part of a church that is going into all the world and taking the gospel or good news that Jesus Christ died for our sins. We trust that the pastor will teach and disciple people. However, we may miss the fact that Jesus gave these words for the pastor, the church, and for us as believers.

Summing up your life as a tweet, would the most important thing be going and telling people about Christ? If your heart desires to take Christ to the nations, how would you go about accomplishing this huge task?

One of the best ways you can start is by committing your life to Christ. When you believe that God sent Jesus to die on the cross for you and ask forgiveness for your sins, then God is faithful to forgive you (1 John 1:9) and to help you know how to live for Him. Because of His Holy Spirit, God will always be with you and will let you know how to be witnesses (Matt. 28:20). As a follower of Jesus, God says that you are to show others how they, too, can become disciples or learners of what makes up a life committed to Christ.

The Great Commission says that we are to go, make disciples, baptize, and teach all that we have learned. We learn the Scriptures by studying and praying. Then as we go, we teach others what we have learned. It is an awesome task; yet God helps us to accomplish His will one day at a time. As we are obedient to the Lord, He will be with us and help us know what to say and do. He never meant for us to do it alone.

Are you a woman with a Great Commission heart? Do you heed the parting words of Jesus to go and make disciples of all nations? Let your life be a Great Commission statement as you take His gospel with you everywhere you go.

Jaye Martin

Prayer: *Recommit your life to the Lord. Ask Him to teach you something from His Word so that you may share with others while at the grocery store and running errands. Be sensitive to the needs of others and look for ways to share the hope of Jesus to this lost world.*

Personal Reflection: ....

....

....

....

....

....

....

Simon's Mother-in-Law—A Willing Servant

Mark 1:29–31

～

"But Simon's wife's mother lay sick with a fever . . .
so He came and took her by the hand and lifted her up,
and immediately the fever left her. And she served them." (vv. 30–31)

The account of Jesus healing Simon's mother-in-law touches the hearts of women. Do you know women just like this precious saint? As soon as she was healed, she immediately began serving others. There is never a convenient time for a woman to be ill. It is difficult if not impossible to stop life to recover from an illness. We always have so many things to do and so many people in our care. The fact that three of the four Gospels include this miracle of Jesus should encourage you (Matt. 8:14–17; Mark 1:29–31; Luke 4:38–39). While not many details are known, this faithful servant made a significant impact on the Savior.

Jesus performed many miracles during his ministry on earth. The healing of this willing servant was the first recorded in Scripture. Why did Jesus perform miracles? Why did He heal some and not others? Jesus performed miraculous signs and wonders to reveal His divine nature and to work supernaturally in the lives of His children (Matt. 10:34; John 4:48). The God who had the power to create has the power to heal. People who are healed by God have the responsibility to respond to Him in love and service.

While little background is provided for this nameless mother-in-law of Simon Peter, she was obviously a woman of faith. She must have developed a servant spirit before her illness because when she was healed by Jesus, she immediately began serving others. She must have been know by all of the disciples because, "they told Him [Jesus] about her at once" (Mark 1:30). Her illness must have been serious as the disciples reacted with urgency. Jesus healed her, and she expressed her gratitude through service. The proper response to the work of Jesus in your life is service to others.

My mother is a faithful servant of the Lord. She shares life and ministry with me, offering hospitality in our home. She volunteers monthly at the

Friendship House and Global Maritime Ministry in New Orleans. And, she supports friends who have personal needs. Mother serves the Lord willingly because she loves Him dearly.

What about you? Are you a willing servant of the Lord? Even when you are tired or sick, do you desire to serve others? God needs you to be His hands and His feet in the world. He works through you to accomplish His mighty ministry. Respond like this sweet servant. When Jesus takes your hand and lifts you up—serve. Serve the Lord willingly, giving Him the glory for all that He accomplishes through you.

Rhonda Harrington Kelley

Prayer: *Take a deep breath and feel the hand of the Lord on your life. But don't sit still. After He speaks to you, get up and serve!*

Personal Reflection: ....

....

....

....

....

....

....

Jairus's Daughter—A Young Woman Healed

Mark 5:21–23, 35–43

⌇∽

"Then He took the child by the hand and said to her, 'Talitha cumi,'
which is translated, 'Little girl, I say to you, arise.'" (v. 41)

Much of the earthly ministry of Jesus was spent around the Sea of Galilee. This passage records the healing of Jairus' daughter by the sea. Have you ever been to Israel? A trip to the Holy Land helps the Scripture come to life in a believer. It is awe-inspiring to walk where Jesus walked. The Sea of Galilee is one of the most meaningful places in Israel, in a very beautiful setting.

Located in the region of Galilee in northern Israel, this sea is really a freshwater lake surrounded by hills. This major commercial center in the time of Jesus was a crossroads for travel in the ancient world. Fishing was an important industry. Many prosperous towns developed along the shore, including Capernaum, Tiberias, and Bathsaida.

Jesus had been in the Galilee area for a while when He crossed over the sea from where He had cast a legion of demons out of a man (Mark 5:1–20). He then encountered Jairus, a ruler of the synagogue. How interesting that a Jewish leader would seek a miracle from Jesus! This desperate father pleaded earnestly with Jesus to heal his child: "My little girl lies at the point of death. Come and lay your hands on her that she may be healed, and she will live" (vv. 22–23).

Have you ever begged God to work a miracle in your life or in the life of one you love? When facing extreme illness or a devastating situation, to cry out to God for His supernatural intervention is natural. When you know God can heal, you want Him to perform His mighty works on your behalf. Like this heartbroken father, you plead with God for help and hope. God always hears and answers, but He does not always heal. You should pray in accordance to His will and accept His perfect plan, knowing that He will be with you whatever the result.

As Jesus followed Jairus to his house, a multitude of people followed. In the crowd, a woman with "a flow of blood for twelve years," touched Jesus and was healed (v. 25). What a compassionate Savior! On the way to perform a miracle, He healed a young woman.

Jairus received word that his daughter had died. Jesus assured him, "Do not be afraid; only believe" (v. 36). Then Jesus performed an even greater miracle than healing, He raised the young girl from the dead. With tenderness and love, Jesus spoke, "Little girl, I say to you, arise" (v. 41). And immediately, the twelve-year-old girl arose and walked. Everyone was amazed!

Rhonda Harrington Kelley

Prayer: *Jesus invites everyone to "come boldly to the throne of grace, that we may obtain mercy and find grace to help us in time of need" (Heb. 4:16). Take your problems to the Lord and leave them there.*

Personal Reflection: ....

....

....

....

....

....

....

Woman with an Issue of Blood—A Woman of Faith

Mark 5:24–34

*"Immediately the fountain of her blood was dried up,
and she felt in her body that she was healed of the affliction." (v. 29)*

Many nameless women are mentioned in Scripture. Though their names are not remembered, their stories were recorded. The details of their lives often teach a profound lesson applicable today. Mark describes a nameless woman who reached out to Jesus in the midst of a large crowd. Surrounded by many people, Jesus knew He had been touched by someone in need. In this passage, the strong faith of this weak woman is evident (vv. 24–34).

No wonder the woman was desperate! She had suffered with chronic hemorrhaging for twelve years. She had tried everything, including many doctors. Nothing or no one had helped. In fact, she was in more pain and had less money because her treatments had been expensive and costly. In a last resort, the sick woman reached out to Jesus, touching the hem of His garment.

While the three synoptic Gospels include this encounter, the passage in Mark cites more details (Matt. 9:18–26; Mark 5:25–34; Luke 8:43–48). Each reference states that the woman came from behind Jesus, could barely reach Him in the crowd, and only touched the edge of His robe. She spoke no words and made no eye contact with Jesus. However, the omniscient Lord knew what had happened. The puzzled disciples could not understand how Jesus knew that someone had touched Him (Mark 5:31). God in the flesh knew without a doubt that His divine power had been poured out to heal someone of faith.

The response of this woman to Jesus proclaims the great message. She trembled with fear, fell at His feet, and told the whole truth (v. 33). This woman of faith knew that she was in the presence of God. Jesus affirmed her: "Daughter, your faith has made you well. Go in peace, and be healed of your affliction" (v. 34).

There was a period of several years that I struggled with a chronic health problem. I went to several doctors and endured many tests to determine why my heart raced rapidly without warning and how to treat my condition. At times, I was discouraged and frightened. But, my faith sustained me through the struggle. Oh, how I rejoiced when finally some answers were found! I know only in part the joy of this woman who experienced the healing touch of Jesus.

The woman's faith was so strong that just touching the garment of Jesus would prove life-changing. What about your faith? Do you believe that any encounter with Jesus can bring you healing and wholeness? Reach out to Him in faith today. Trust Him to change your life. Then, like the woman with an issue of blood, go in peace!

Rhonda Harrington Kelley

Prayer: *Reach out and touch Jesus as did this woman of faith. Esteem Him as God, fall at His feet, and share your heart with Him.*

Personal Reflection:

The Widow with Two Mites—A Faithful Follower

Mark 12:41–44

"Then one poor widow came and threw in two mites ... she
out of her poverty put in all that she had, her whole livelihood." (vv. 42, 44)

In Mark 12, Jesus teaches the people about hypocrisy. Some people sought recognition and power while stealing from the poor and pretending to be religious
(12:38–40). The Savior did not notice those flaunting their positions or possessions. He pointed out the one who gave her all.

Widows faced even greater challenges in ancient times than today. They
had less capacity for earning money than slaves. Without the help of family
and friends, widows often became destitute and homeless. According to Jewish
law, widows without means of support became the responsibility of the people,
just as the orphans and strangers (Deut. 14:29). In the New Testament, specific
advice is given by Paul for Christians to care for the widows (1 Tim. 5:3–16). The
family of faith, the church, is called to provide for the material and spiritual
needs of widows (Acts 6:1).

This woman of meager means did not let her lack of funds lead to a lack
of faith. She gave all that she had, trusting that God would care for her. Jesus
used this humble widow to summarize all the lessons of His ministry in this
last public teaching. Her small amount of money did not make a big difference
to the church budget. Unlike the arrogant givers, she knew that everything
belonged to God. Her tiny offering brought joy to Jesus: "Assuredly, I say to you
that this poor widow has put in more than all of those who have given to the
treasury" (Mark 12:43).

The attitude of the heart matters most to God. Large sums of money from
the stingy giver are less important to God than a small offering from a sacrificial giver. Those who give out of their abundance are not praised by God, but
one who gives all she has is acknowledged for her faith (v. 44).

Our sweet Mom Kelley was a widow on a fixed income. She carefully
watched her budget and was always concerned that she might outlive her

money. At times when she thought her money was tight, she would not buy chicken at the grocery. One time, she ordered a vegetarian plate at a fancy New Orleans restaurant because it was the cheapest item on the menu. Even when she was worried about her finances, Mom Kelley never failed to tithe. She always gave money to missions, to her family, to others—not for show, but out of the sincerity of her heart. I always think of Mom Kelley when I hear the story of this widow with the two mites. Sacrificial giving is praised by God!

Rhonda Harrington Kelley

Prayer: *Do you trust God with what you have? Are you willing to give all that you have to Him? Seek to live like this faithful widow, who was totally dependent upon God.*

Personal Reflection:

She Did What She Could

Mark 14:1–9

‿◡◠⁀

"She has done what she could. She has come beforehand
to anoint My body for burial." (v. 8)

Have you ever been hurt because your sacrificial gift of time or effort went unnoticed by your husband or child, by your parent or sibling, by your friend or foe? Instead of dwelling on what is not said or on gratitude not given, offer your kind deed done for someone else as your gift to Christ. He will receive it as a gift to Himself, and your testimony will be etched in the stones of eternity as bringing honor to Him. They will then honor you as He did Mary of Bethany.

The Passover, commemorating the Israelites' last night in Egypt, was an important national celebration for the Jews. On that night, the angel of death had passed over all who had displayed on their doorposts the blood from sacrifices offered (Ex. 12:5–14):

When Mary anointed Jesus, she lovingly gave her attention to His personal needs.

- She poured out her ministry to Him with a sacrificial gift—"an alabaster flask of very costly oil of spikenard" (Mark 14:3).
- She performed a selfless task—"poured it on His head" (v. 3).
- She offered her service to Christ even at the risk of public criticism and scolding as some were expressing indignation to one another (v. 4).

Jesus then expressed gratitude to her and recorded her testimony for generations to come (v. 9).

The legacy of Mary has so touched me that I have written in the notes to my family concerning my own death and burial that I want these words on my tombstone: "She did what she could." As I have moved into my senior years, I am so often disappointed and discouraged because I cannot seem to accomplish all in my heart to do for my family and for my Savior. But I do keep trying. I would love for Jesus to have a commendation like He gave to Mary for me.

When a woman offers to Christ her committed devotion in service to Him personally—as did Mary—or to someone else in His name, she will always be rewarded. Perhaps the one she serves or to whom she gives sacrificially will express loving gratitude, but far more important to her is the commendation of the Savior. He does indeed note every deed of lovingkindness done in His name (Heb. 6:10). Do what you can with what you have while you can where you are, and perhaps you, too, will hear these encouraging words said about you!

Dorothy Kelley Patterson

Prayer: *Search your own heart for ways to honor the Savior and express your devotion to Him. Give yourself to doing the tasks—however simple and unimpressive—that honor Him. Wait for His commendation of your faithful service.*

Personal Reflection: ....

....

....

....

....

....

....

Elizabeth, Mother of John the Baptist— A Spiritual Mentor

Luke 1:5–45, 57–66

࿊

"Then she spoke out with a loud voice and said, 'Blessed are you among women, and blessed is the fruit of your womb!'" (v. 42)

Do you have a mentor—someone who shares her life with you, a wise woman with spiritual maturity who invests her knowledge and experience into your life? Mentoring is a God-ordained, perfect plan for human relationships. The Bible instructs women to teach the next generation about God, His redemptive works, and His call to holy living (Ps. 145:4). The apostle Paul mentored many young men in the faith (like Timothy and Barnabas), and he instructed believers to imitate him (1 Cor. 4:14–21; 1 Thess. 2:7–8). Spiritual mentoring is a mutually beneficial relationship, teaching the younger woman and encouraging the older woman.

Mary the mother of Jesus had a wonderful spiritual mentor, her cousin Elizabeth (Luke 1:39–45). Elizabeth was the daughter of a priest and married a priest named Zacharias. She was a woman of integrity and obedience: "Righteous before God, walking in all the commandments and ordinances of the Lord blameless" (v. 6). Luke gave her a great character reference in his Gospel!

Elizabeth was unable to conceive a child. An angel appeared to Zacharias with a promise from God that Elizabeth would bear a son—not just any son, but one who "will be great in the sight of the Lord . . . will turn many of the children of Israel to the Lord their God. He will also go before Him [Jesus] in the spirit and power of Elijah" (vv. 14–17a ; see vv. 8–22). Wow! What a precious promise from God to this older couple! Elizabeth would conceive in a miraculous way, and their son would be a great servant of God.

The Scripture confirms fulfillment of the prophecy. Elizabeth conceived a son who would be called John (vv. 23–25). At the same time in the city of Nazareth, an angel appeared to the virgin Mary with news that she had been chosen by God to conceive the Son of God through the work of the Holy Spirit (vv. 26–38). Mary humbly accepted her role in the messianic prophecy. The angel sent the pregnant Mary to her expectant relative Elizabeth for nurture and care. God's divine plan brought these two godly women together to await the births of their respectively anointed sons.

Elizabeth and the babe in her womb knew they were in the presence of the Holy One when the pregnant Mary entered their home. Filled with the Holy Spirit, Elizabeth proclaimed: "Blessed are you among women, and blessed is the fruit of your womb!" (v. 42). Mary responded to her cousin's proclamation with a song of praise, Mary's Song or The Magnificat (vv. 46–55). She stayed in the home of Elizabeth and Zacharias for three months (vv. 56). What a joyful time the two expectant mothers must have shared as the righteous Elizabeth extended hospitality and wise advice to young Mary. Elizabeth gave birth to John the Baptist who was a powerful preacher and forerunner of Jesus (vv. 57–66). The special mentoring relationship is illustrated beautifully in the lives of Elizabeth and Mary.

Rhonda Harrington Kelley

Prayer: *Thank God for spiritual mentors in your life. And make a commitment to mentor younger women.*

Personal Reflection: ....

....

....

....

....

Mary of Nazareth—Being a Christ-Bearer

Luke 1:26–56

〰

*"Then the angel said to her, 'Do not be afraid, Mary, for you have
found favor with God. And behold, you will conceive in your womb
and bring forth a Son, and shall call His name Jesus.' (vv. 30–31)*

And Mary said:
  'My soul magnifies the Lord,
  and my spirit has rejoiced in God my Savior.
  For He has regarded the lowly state of His maidservant;
  For behold, henceforth all generations will call me blessed.'" (vv. 46–48)

Before Jesus was born, a young virgin named Mary responded to a heavenly
summons and allowed God's Spirit to become flesh. She gave her body to be
the chalice into which the life of God was poured. A chalice is a cup. What Mary
did is what you and I are meant to do, every one of us, every day, no matter
where we are or what the circumstances—to carry Christ into this world. We
are like chalices, empty vessels willing and ready to be filled with the life of God.
Cleaned out in the process, we are poured out for others. Our lives illustrate
what God is like much more by what we **are** and **do** than by what we say. We
incarnate Christ by taking up our crosses and following Him, doing exactly as
Jesus did when He was obedient to the Father.

When the angel went to Mary, he said, "'Greetings, you who are highly
favored! The Lord is with you.' Mary was greatly troubled at his words" (vv. 28–29
NIV). The angelic message was alarmingly clear and Mary's response was awe—
and bewilderment. When something interrupts what we are doing (the angel
interrupted Mary's housework, I suppose), most of us fret. God's message to Mary
would have seemed to most engaged girls an enormous inconvenience, even a
disaster. For her, it caused a moment of puzzlement (how could this be?). Then,
as far as we know, she raised no objections about what would happen to her or

her fiancé. Her answer came very simply, "Be it unto me according to Thy word" (v. 38).

Whether or not an angel ever comes to us, we might be troubled at some of God's words to us as well. We might wish we'd never heard them. But our response should be modeled on Mary's and that of her Son Jesus—immediate obedience. Like someone holding out a cup to be filled when a drink is offered, we need to put our hearts forward right when God offers to pour Himself into us for an assignment, large or small. It's the attitude of a Christ-bearer.

Elisabeth Elliot

Prayer: *Thank God for the example of obedience in the life of Mary. Ask the Lord to help you to follow her example of immediate obedience in your life today as you go about your daily tasks.*

Personal Reflection: ....

....

....

....

....

....

....

An excerpt from Elisabeth Elliot's *Be Still My Soul* (pages 7–9).

Anna—A Faithful Prophetess

Luke 2:36–38

~~

"[Anna] served God with fastings and prayers night and day." (v. 37b)

Anna was an elderly prophetess who recognized the Messiah when He was brought to the temple for dedication (vv. 36–38). Daughter of Phanuel of the tribe of Asher, she was an 84-year-old widow who served the Lord faithfully along with Simeon the prophet. She instantly recognized baby Jesus as the promised Messiah and proclaimed His deity to others. Anna was confident in the message of redemption offered by Jesus. What a blessing for her to witness the arrival of the Messiah she had been expecting.

Why did this humble widow recognize the Savior when no one else did? She was a woman of deep faith and total commitment. This brief account in Scripture teaches a powerful lesson about faithfulness. Luke 2:37–38 provides specific instructions for living a faithful life: Anna "served God with fastings and prayers night and day." She gave thanks to the Lord, and spoke of Him to all those who looked for redemption in Jerusalem.

In her life, this faithful prophetess practiced spiritual disciplines, which provide an example for us today. Throughout history, other faithful Christians have served God faithfully. Lottie Moon was a missionary to China in the late 19th and early 20th centuries. She spent nearly 40 years ministering to the Chinese people and building a missions focus among Baptist women. At approximately the same time in history, Annie Armstrong was building a missionary base in North America and became a founder of the Woman's Missionary Union. These women were faithful in serving the Lord and speaking of Him to others. Today there are faithful believers who give their all to the Lord as did Anna.

Are you a faithful follower like Anna? If not, you can begin practicing these spiritual disciplines today. If so, you should continue in them, growing in your personal relationship with Jesus Christ. Serve Him with your whole heart, devoting your life to ministry in His name. Pray fervently, seeking to know God and His will for your life. As God directs, fast or refrain from eating food in order to focus on him. Practice these disciplines diligently day and night. Rejoice in God's goodness and thank Him for your blessings. Speak to others about God's work in your life, and share the gospel.

Anna was a woman who worshipped and witnessed. She faithfully praised God and worshipped Him, serving full-time in the temple. She did not keep God's blessings to herself. She was a witness of His saving grace. Her life is a testimony to us of what our lives should be to others. All believers should worship and witness.

Rhonda Harrington Kelley

Prayer: *Thank God for revealing Himself through Jesus Christ. Renew your commitment to worship Him and witness of Him faithfully.*

Personal Reflection: ....

....

....

....

....

....

....

The Widow of Nain—A Grieving Mother

Luke 7:11–17

*"When the Lord saw her, He had compassion on
her and said to her, 'Do not weep.'" (v. 13)*

There is no greater sorrow than for a mother to lose her precious child. In this passage, Jesus encounters a funeral processional as He traveled with His disciples to the town of Nain, south of Nazareth. He had healed the centurion's servant in Capernaum (Luke 7:1–10) and now had compassion on this grieving mother. Her loss was compounded by the fact that she was a widow with only one son. She was left alone to care for herself, no husband or child still living.

Picture the scene of this funeral procession as Jesus witnessed it. The dead man's body was carried in a casket, surrounded by his family and friends. The mourners, including his mother, were distraught. What a surprise when they met Jesus and His party of travelers along the road. While they recognized Jesus as a prophet, none of them ever imagined that He could give life to a dead man.

Jesus stopped to comfort the grieving mother. He tenderly spoke to her: "Do not weep" (v. 13). Then He touched the coffin and commanded the dead man: "Young man, I say to you, arise" (v. 14). Miraculously, the widow's son sat up and spoke. In fear and awe, the crowd glorified God saying, "A great prophet has risen among us and God has visited His people" (v. 16). The report of the miracle spread around Judea.

New Orleans is known for its jazz music (and for its delicious food). A jazz funeral often takes place to honor prominent individuals, especially musicians. A typical jazz funeral processional includes a brass band as well as family and friends who walk from the church or the funeral home through the streets of the city to the cemetery. The music while parading to the cemetery is somber, reflecting deep sorrow and sadness felt by the loved ones. However, after the burial, the tone of the music changes to upbeat music with a second line of the mourners, twirling parasols and waving white handkerchiefs. Tunes like "Just a Closer Walk with Thee" are replaced by "When the Saints Go Marching In."

Sorrow from the loss of a loved one is replaced by the joyous hope of heaven. For Christians, sorrow from loss is lessened by the hope that a believer who has died is now in the presence of the Lord for all eternity.

There was a great "jazz funeral" in Nain the day Jesus miraculously brought the dead man to life! The mourners left the city parading in sadness but returned after the miracle in a "second line," praising God for giving life to the widow's son. Her grief turned into pure joy!

Rhonda Harrington Kelley

Prayer: *Reflect upon loss in your own life, then rejoice over the work of God in your life. Joy comes in the morning!*

Personal Reflection: ....

The Sinful Woman—A Forgiven Sinner

Luke 7:36–50

"She has washed my feet with her tears and wiped them *with the hair of her head . . . has not ceased to kiss My feet . . . has anointed My feet with fragrant oil . . . her sins,* which are *many, are forgiven, for she loved much." (vv. 44–48)*

Jesus had another divine encounter in the town of Nain. He met an unnamed woman who is called in Scripture "a sinner" (vv. 37, 39). Perhaps she was a prostitute, causing the Pharisees to be shocked at her intrusion and behavior. Not only did she enter Simon's home uninvited, but she was a woman and a sinner. Then she did the unexpected, she poured expensive perfume over the feet of Jesus, washing His feet with her tears, wiping them with her hair, and kissing His feet (vv. 37–38). While the Pharisees were horrified, Jesus was honored. He rebuked the foolish men and responded with love and grace to the sinful woman.

While the Pharisees questioned the deity of Jesus, the woman demonstrated true faith. Jesus taught a lesson when He spoke to Simon, telling a parable about two debtors (vv. 40–42). Did Simon understand what Jesus was saying and that He found Simon rather than the sinner guilty? One debtor owed much money, while the other owed less. Both debtors were forgiven by the creditor. Then Jesus asked Simon the probing question: "Tell Me, therefore, which of them will love him [the creditor] more?" (v. 42). Simon the Pharisee knew the correct answer in his head, but he responded hesitantly from his heart (v. 42). Jesus taught a lesson on forgiveness when He saved the sinful woman and sent her away in peace. Undoubtedly, the Pharisees learned that Jesus was not just a prophet; He is God Incarnate, the Messiah, Savior of the world.

What can we learn from this sinful woman who was forgiven by Jesus? She saw her need for the Savior, received His love and forgiveness, and gave her all to Him. How do you respond to Jesus? Jesus calls you to see your own sin, accept His forgiveness, and sacrifice everything to Him.

Simon welcomed Jesus to his home but failed to extend true hospitality. He did not follow typical customs for greeting a guest. He did not offer to wash Jesus' feet, welcome Him with a kiss, or anoint His head with oil. While the host neglected his common courtesies, the sinful woman sacrificially extended hers. She took an alabaster jar filled with a costly perfume, stood weeping behind Jesus, washed His feet with her tears, kissed His feet, and anointed them with the fragrant oil (vv. 37–38). This tender demonstration of faith teaches an eternal truth. The sinful woman fully understood the forgiveness of Christ and was unashamed for others to know her love for Him.

Rhonda Harrington Kelley

Prayer: *No matter how you come to Jesus, you can leave in peace. He saves and forgives even the greatest sinner. Claim that promise.*

Personal Reflection: ....

....

....

....

....

....

....

Women Who Followed Jesus

Luke 8:1–3

*"And certain women who had been healed of evil spirits and infirmities—
Mary called Magdalene, out of who had come seven demons, and Joanna,
the wife of Chuza, Herod's steward, and Susanna, and many others
who provided for Him from their substance." (vv. 2–3)*

As you read through the Gospels, watch Jesus as He interacted with all sorts of people—the outcasts and the rulers, the poor and the wealthy, men and women. Believers today have the advantage of witnessing in the Bible how Jesus responded to the needs of women, opening doors for women to serve in biblically appropriate ways. Although women may occasionally feel misunderstood by some men, Jesus never misunderstands them because He created and designed women uniquely. He knows us better than we know ourselves!

Luke, among the four Gospels, gives the most attention to the women involved in Jesus' life and to those who received ministry from Him. Unique to Luke is the account of the women who supported Christ's work (vv. 1–3). These women had been healed of various diseases by Jesus. Seven demons were cast out of Mary called Magdalene. Luke does not specify how Joanna, the wife of Chuza, Herod's steward, and Susanna were healed; but they were among the many supporting Jesus from their own possessions.

Women would not typically be a part of the party traveling with itinerant preachers in the first century. What is also surprising is that Jesus recognized women as full-fledged disciples, something completely unheard of in His day. These women not only gave sacrificially of their resources, but they also exhibited extraordinary devotion and selfless service to Jesus, giving of their time and energy to be a part of His traveling ministry. In a day when women were often mistreated, Jesus treated women with dignity and respect and valued their service to Him.

Jesus still affirmed that women and men had some distinct roles in the home and in ministry settings (i.e., Jesus did not ever put a woman in a teaching or authoritative role over men, cp. 1 Tim. 2:11–15). Nevertheless, He also encouraged women to learn about the faith (Luke 10:38–42), befriended women (Luke 8:1–3), and showed concern and care for women (Luke 7:11–17). Jesus modeled for us how men and women are to live and serve together.

In the example of Mary Magdalene, Joanna, and Susanna, we see women who had an active faith. Too many Christians today are content to fill a pew on Sunday, and then live for themselves the rest of the week. However, we should serve Christ just as much on Monday in our homes or at our jobs or as we do on Sundays when we gather for worship.

Candi Finch

Prayer: *Thank God for His loving care and concern for women and for the example of Mary Magdalene, Joanna, and Susanna as they served the Lord. Consider also how you can serve the Lord with your time today.*

Personal Reflection: ....

....

....

....

....

....

....

The Disabled Woman—Bound No More

Luke 13:10–17

*"And He laid His hands on her, and immediately she was
made straight, and glorified God." (v. 13)*

Life with a disability is difficult. Whether permanent or temporary, physical or mental, a personal condition impacts the individual and her family. The woman in this passage had suffered physically for a long time. She had "a spirit of infirmity for eighteen years and was bent over and could in no way raise *herself* up" (v. 11). She was noticed by Jesus as He and the disciples traveled through her city in Perea on their way from Galilee to Judea. Seated in the synagogue as Jesus began to teach, the disabled woman was blessed by a passing glance, which led to a miracle moment.

The synagogue was filled on the Sabbath with many religious people. In the large crowd, Jesus noticed the woman who was bent over. He initiated the encounter, recognizing her faith. "He laid *His* hands on her, and immediately she was made straight, and glorified God" (v. 13). It was the touch of the Master's hands that healed the woman!

As they often did, the religious leaders challenged the healing work of Jesus on the Sabbath—the day of rest. Jesus called this one a hypocrite and then cited the many ways they worked on the Sabbath (vv. 15–16). The adversaries of Jesus were shamed, the large crowd rejoiced, and the disabled woman was healed. Legalism did not blind Jesus to the needs around Him.

Do you know someone with a persistent, serious disability? Those handicapped individuals with a strong personal faith can have a powerful impact on healthy and unhealthy people alike. The testimony of Joni Eareckson Tada has been used by the Lord through the years to spread the gospel and encourage the disabled. Paralyzed in a diving accident when she was 17, Joni has lived as a quadriplegic in a wheelchair without use of her arms or legs, hands or feet. She has adapted to her disability in amazing ways, painting with a brush between her teeth. She has written books, spoken worldwide, and founded an organization to minister to the disabled. The mission of Joni and Friends International is "to accelerate Christian ministry in the disability community." Unlike the woman in Luke 13, Joni has not been healed physically by Jesus. Instead, she was healed spiritually and has ministered faithfully to others who are disabled.

What can you learn from the disabled woman and Joni Eareckson Tada? Whether healed or not, handicapped or not, everyone should praise the Lord for His mighty works. Are you filled with praise today? Find ways to glorify God whether or not you are suffering.

Rhonda Harrington Kelley

Prayer: *Examine your heart to see if you are grateful to the Lord for His mighty works. Rejoice in who God is and what He has done in your life to bring about healing and hope. Pray for God to strengthen those you know with disabilities.*

Personal Reflection: ....

....

....

....

....

....

....

The Woman with the Lost Coin—A Persistent Sleuth

Luke 15:8–10

"And when she has found it [the lost coin], she calls her friends, and neighbors together, saying, 'Rejoice with me, for I have found the piece which I lost!'" (v. 9)

Do you have a habit of losing things? Does there seem to be a black hole in your house consuming your lost items? Whether your keys, your sunglasses, a sock, or an earring, misplacing an important item is so frustrating. Occasionally, I seem to hide things from myself. I put them in a logical place but fail to remember that good idea later. Often times the lost object is right where it was supposed to be, and I just didn't see it. Other times someone else can find it. Unfortunately, some lost objects are never found.

Jesus told three parables in Luke 15—about a lost sheep, a lost coin, and a lost son—to illustrate God's love and concern for every lost sinner (vv. 3–7, 11–32). In each case, the Father/Shepherd lovingly seeks what has been lost. While one coin today seems of little value, a coin in that day was very valuable. One silver coin was worth a full day's wage (Matt. 20:2). The value was not only financial for the woman; it was emotional. The coin was probably a part of her headdress, her actual savings account for her dowry, or it may have been a wedding gift.

Jesus lovingly told the parable emphasizing the woman's determination in her search and joy in her discovery. She lights a lamp, sweeps the house, and searches carefully—turning everything around her upside down. She does not stop her search until she finds her coin (Luke 15:9). Then she erupts into joyous celebration when her beloved coin is found, calling her friends and neighbors to rejoice with her (v. 10). Can't you picture that party?

I recall a wonderful celebration when a lost item was found. Mom Kelley lost her checkbook. She always prayed about everything she lost. She asked me and all her friends to pray about her lost item. After several days, I went to her apartment. My mother joined us, and the three of us with flashlights in hand looked everywhere for her checkbook. I turned her recliner chair over, and there was the checkbook! The three of us jumped up and down, squealing with joy. We ended our celebration with prayer, thanking God for helping us find the checkbook. We thanked Him for persistently searching for us, His lost children.

Jesus concluded His parable with the biblical lesson: "There is joy in the presence of the angels of God over one sinner who repents" (v. 10). God and His angels rejoice when a sinner returns in repentance to Him. This woman's joy is a beautiful picture for us to recall and replicate.

Rhonda Harrington Kelley

Prayer: *Rejoice that God has searched for you and others who are lost. Persist in seeking the lost as you share the gospel message.*

Personal Reflection:

The Persistent Widow and Her Importunate Prayer

Luke 18:1–8

"Now there was a widow in that city; and she came to him [the judge] . . .
he said, '. . . because this widow troubles me I will avenge her, lest by
her continual coming she weary me.'" (vv. 3–5)

Although Jesus preached sermons and shared parables between the woman with the lost coin (13:8–10) and the widow in this passage, the theme of His message was often the same—persist in your faith. Jesus encouraged His disciples to pray persistently as the coming of God's Kingdom on earth would be sudden and without warning (17:20–37). To make His point, Jesus included a widow as an illustration.

The introduction to Jesus' parable was short and sweet: "Men always ought to pray and not lose heart" (18:1). In the body of His message, Jesus contrasted a dishonest judge and a helpless widow. The judge did not believe in God or respect others (v. 2), while the widow trusted God and respected the system (vv. 3–5). She had no power of her own, so she went to the judge who had authority, petitioning him for justice against her adversary.

Though the exact nature of the conflict with her enemy is unknown, surely a grave matter irritated the widow. Rather than taking matters into her own hands, she worked through the system, returning again and again to file her complaint with the judge. The reluctant judge finally ruled in her favor, not because he believed in God or the widow. He was worn out from her persistent pleas. Our Holy God has all power and listens to His persistent children in their needs, offering mercy and love.

Christians are to pray persistently like this widow. E. M. Bounds, a great theologian of the twentieth century, has written about prayer and importunity. In his book *The Necessity of Prayer,* he says "Importunate prayer is the earnest, inward movement of the heart toward God; the throwing of the entire force of the spiritual man into the exercise of prayer."* This widow earnestly threw herself at the judge, pleading for his favor. That is how all Christians should approach God the Father in prayer. Persevere in prayer! Do not give up or become discouraged, God is not an uncaring judge but a righteous, loving Father.

Christians do not always persist in their faith or in prayer. My dad, Bob Harrington, was an evangelist known as The Chaplain of Bourbon Street. He left the Lord and our family after years of effective ministry. A prodigal for 18 years, Dad returned to the Lord with a new message—"Loving the Left Back Right." He believed many Christians on church pews have spiritually left the Lord. They are no longer persistent in their faith, prime targets for temptation from the devil. We must persist in our faith and encourage other believers to persevere. The heavenly Father is waiting for you to earnestly seek Him.

Rhonda Harrington Kelley

Prayer: *Thank God for persistently seeking you. Then spend time in importunate prayer.*

Personal Reflection: ....

....

....

....

....

....

* E. M. Bounds, *The Necessity of Prayer* (1929), reprinted in *The Complete Works of E. M. Bounds on Prayer* (Grand Rapids, MI: Baker, 1990), 30.

A Woman's Worth and Mission

John 4:27–42

"And many of the Samaritans of that city believed in Him because of the word of the woman who testified, 'He told me all that I ever did.'" (v. 39)

When Jesus sat down with the woman at the well, He broke societal barriers in more than one way. First, she was a Samaritan. The roots of hatred ran deep between the Israelites and the Samaritans for many reasons. The Jews excluded the Samaritans from worship in Jerusalem because they considered them unclean due to their mixed blood. Jesus chose to speak with a woman who was an outcast to other Jews because of her ethnicity. Also, Jesus spoke with a woman—something not sanctioned in Jewish culture. Do you think Jesus considered the message He would be sending by His actions?

Of course He did! Our God is a deliberate God. In fact, Jesus clarifies that He was doing His Father's will by speaking with this woman (v. 34). Jesus confronts culture with His higher plan, demonstrating His value of women. His knowledge of this woman's life shows that He cared about her personally. His offer of salvation shows that He loved her and had a plan for her eternity. God reveals in this passage that He knows you personally, sees you as valuable, and intends salvation for **you** as well.

Christ's encounter with the woman at the well led to her repentance, and His forgiveness changed her life. She was so transformed by Jesus that she immediately returned to her village and claimed that she had met the Messiah. What makes this story so beautiful is that Christ not only offered the living water to women, He also included them in His plan to expand the Kingdom. When the disciples discovered Jesus speaking with this woman, they expressed their confusion. The fact that Jesus responded by explaining that the fields were ready for harvest clearly reveals that this woman was a part of His plan to share the gospel. You have a role in growing the Kingdom as well!

Scripture tells us that "many of the Samaritans of that city believed in Him" because the woman at the well testified about Jesus (v. 39). If you are a follower of Jesus, then you have a personal story of when you first met Him just like this woman. This is your testimony, and sharing it has the power to bring others to Jesus. Tell people how assured you are of His personal love for you and His offer of living water. Ladies, the fields are still ready for reaping. What role will you play in the harvest? How could God use your testimony to reach others?

Laura Landry

Prayer: *Thank the Lord for valuing you personally and including you in His plan to expand the Kingdom. Ask Him to give you opportunities to share your testimony today.*

Personal Reflection:

The Adulteress—A Forgiven Woman

John 8:1–11

"Then those who heard it, being convicted by their conscience, went out one by one, beginning with the oldest even to the last. And Jesus was left alone, and the woman standing in the midst. When Jesus had raised Himself up and saw no one but the woman, He said to her, 'Woman, where are those accusers of yours? Has no one condemned you?'" (vv. 9–10).

The story of the woman caught in adultery offers no better picture of how Jesus replaced legalism with grace. A woman who had been caught in the act of adultery was brought to Jesus. The custom of the time was for both offenders to be put to death by stoning. The religious leaders intended to trap Jesus when they asked Him, "But what do You say?" (v. 5). Jesus was in the business of forgiving sinners, but the Pharisees believed that even Jesus would be unable to overlook such a serious sin. They confronted Him with the law, evoking the name of their forefather Moses (v. 5). In this teaching, Jesus brought together a high moral standard and loving mercy—polar opposites that the religious leaders of the day had never been able to balance.

Rather than join them, Jesus stooped down and started writing on the ground with His finger. Certainly this behavior took everyone by surprise! His unorthodox method of addressing their question was powerful and effective. One by one, everyone who stood to accuse the woman walked away. Precisely what Jesus wrote that day is unknown, though many have speculated that perhaps He began listing the hidden sins of the woman's accusers. The mystery of what Jesus wrote in sand is not as important as the mystery of His unmerited favor toward us, broken sinners like the adulterous woman.

Two lessons are to be learned from this passage of Scripture. First, Jesus does not condemn you nor does He overlook your sin. The reality is that Jesus does not judge you by human standards. Rather, you are held to His perfect standard—one that you could never reach with your own efforts. Jesus offers forgiveness and covers you in His righteousness when you accept Him as your

Savior. His victory over sin on the cross is what enables you to leave your sin behind and begin to walk in truth.

Second, Jesus calls us to extend His grace to others. Jesus said, "He who is without sin among you, let him throw a stone at her first" (v. 7). Religiosity and judgment do not draw the lost to salvation or the wandering Christian to restoration. Christ's words convict us of our own sinfulness and teach us to balance the high moral standard of God with His loving mercy and forgiveness.

Rhonda Harrington Kelley

Prayer: *Thank Jesus that He does not condemn you but rather enables you to live a righteous life by His grace. Ask Him to help you replace condemnation with a heart for sinners like His.*

Personal Reflection: ....

....

....

....

....

....

....

Martha of Bethany—The Original Home Management Expert

John 11:5; 12:1–2

". . . And Martha served." (12:2)

I grew up in the era when clothes were actually ironed. I was always intrigued when Mom would take a wet, wrinkled garment and, with the combination of the iron's heat and her pressure, transform the garment from an unacceptable to a wearable condition. Wanting to follow her model, I would ask to "help." She first taught me how to iron her embroidered dishtowels. More important than the ironing skill Mom imparted, her servant's heart challenged me to be excited about exhibiting servanthood and assimilating her homemaking skills in my home. Though I am a Certified Family and Consumer Scientist by education and profession, I learned the "how-tos" of managing a home by assimilating what my mother modeled.

Martha of Bethany, a significant woman who impacts our Christian faith, offers a clear portrait of effective home management. When you think of the Luke 10:38–42 description of Martha, at first glance it appears that her active, extroverted personality casts her into the light of a natural servant. Servanthood is often defined as making someone else successful. Mark 10:44–45 reminds us that whoever of you desires to be great is to be a servant and that our Lord Jesus set the example for servanthood. Martha certainly fits that description. Thinking and acting quickly, she welcomed Jesus and His disciples into her home (Luke 10:38). She definitely got things done and made things happen, both qualities of a strong servant (v. 40).

The passage also communicates that Martha is a reactor. Instead of asking Mary to assist her, she voiced her frustration to her guest of honor (Luke 10:40). How often do we react rather than stepping back from the situation and thinking through what is the biblical response? Martha offers both a positive model in her work ethic and a poor model in her reaction to someone she loves.

Martha teaches one way of managing life. Her management style clearly got things done and made things happen. A probing question to ask, however, is "what were the eternal benefits of her activities?" Perhaps if she had been willing to sit with Mary, both then could have served together, thus sharpening one another.

I am always reminded of the poignant message of Charles Hummel's small but convicting book *Tyranny of the Urgent!* when I read about Martha. His concluding words remind us that "If we continue in the word of our Lord, we are truly His disciples. And He will free us from the tyranny of the urgent; free us to do the important, which is the will of God."* May we be quick to assimilate Martha's positive qualities so our activities reflect true servanthood.

Pat Ennis

Prayer: *Consider placing in your heavenly Father's hands all of your management skills (or lack of them). Earnestly seek His guidance on how to use them as a humble servant.*

Personal Reflection: ....

....

....

....

....

....

* Charles E. Hummel, *Tyranny of the Urgent!* (Downers Grove, IL: InterVarsity Press, 1967), 15.

Mary of Bethany—Sit, Listen, Ponder, Serve

John 12:3–8

"Then Mary took a pound of very costly oil of spikenard,
anointed the feet of Jesus, and wiped His feet with her hair." (v. 3)

What management strategies would you use to describe a woman who is an effective servant in our Lord's kingdom? Well organized, hard worker, and flexible might be appropriate choices. More than likely sit, listen, ponder, and then serve would not be ones you would choose. Why? Because they do not **appear** to produce an immediate outcome. Yet management experts tell us that if our time is limited to complete a project, we will make more progress if we plan first and then take action.

Mary of Bethany offers the ideal role model to the twenty-first-century woman who wants her life to have a far-reaching spiritual impact. Mary's friendship with Jesus and her choice to sit at His feet, listen to His teachings, and ponder His words, allowed her to develop a spiritual insight and understanding of things that others did not see. Mary was the only one who realized Jesus' time on earth was drawing to an end (Mark 14:6–9). Rather than being concerned about offering her Lord a gourmet meal with short-lived benefit, Mary chose to worship Him. Her example of knowing her Savior well enough to understand that He wanted her heart more than her skills at that point in His ministry is important to us as Christian women. Once we have sat at His feet, listened to His teachings, and pondered His words, we are more likely to love Him completely (Matt. 22:37). Only then will we be able offer service to His Kingdom with potential eternal results.

Pondering Mary's devotional life offers us guidelines for ours:

- Read and study God's Word (2 Tim. 2:15).
- Linger in sweet prayer (Phil. 4:6; 1 Thess. 5:17).

- Commit to memory His life-changing Word (Ps. 119:11).
- Meditate on things of the Lord (Phil. 4:8–9).

If we practice these simple guidelines, we can then view life's circumstances through the lens of true servanthood and will be ready for each day's special assignment.

Time regularly spent with God bears fruit that only grows in the shade of His presence. Consider these thought-provoking words of nineteenth-century Scottish lecturer Henry Drummond in his classic work, *The Greatest Thing in the World*: "Talent develops itself in solitude; the talent of prayer, of faith, of meditation, of seeing the unseen."* Will you choose to sit, listen, ponder, and *then* serve so that your efforts will have an eternal impact?

Pat Ennis

Prayer: *Seek your heavenly Father's wisdom for how best to sit, listen, and ponder at this season of your life. Ask Him to help you acquire Mary's character qualities so that He will say of you that you chose "that good part, which will not be taken away" from you (Luke 10:42).*

Personal Reflection: ....

....

....

....

....

* Henry Drummond, *The Greatest Thing in the World* (Old Tappan, NJ: Fleming H. Revell, 1981), 44.

Mary Magdalene—A Devoted Follower

John 20:1–18

∽

*"Mary Magdalene came and told the disciples that she had
seen the Lord, and that He had spoken these things to her." (v. 18)*

Devotion is simply love and loyalty for a person or cause. Women in general are devoted because we were created by God to be relational. When we love someone or something, we really love them. Women are devoted to their husbands, children, grandchildren, and extended family. We love our friends and even our neighbors or co-workers. We are loyal to our schools and organizations. Any person near to our hearts or sensitive to a cause we support will receive our unfailing love and loyalty.

Devotion to God demands even more commitment. Christians are to "love the Lord your God with all your heart, with all your strength, and with all your mind, and your neighbor as yourself" (Luke 10:27). Mary Magdalene was a devoted follower of Jesus Christ who loved Him wholeheartedly.

First introduced in Scripture by Matthew, Mary Magdalene is included with women who followed Jesus (Matt. 27:55–56). Her name is mentioned 14 times in the New Testament, in each of the four Gospels. Little is known about her life before Jesus. She was from the village of Magdala on the shore of the Sea of Galilee and has been popularly identified as a prostitute, though there is no textual evidence of this view. Luke records that she was "healed of evil spirits and infirmities . . . out of whom had come seven demons" (Luke 8:2). Mary Magdalene was devoted to Jesus because He saved her and healed her.

Mary's devotion was evident throughout the ministry of Jesus. She supported the Lord's work financially and cared for Him personally. She was faithful to the Savior through His death on the cross and resurrection from the grave. Scripture documents her love and devotion in the following ways. Mary Magdalene:

- witnessed the crucifixion and burial of Jesus (Matt. 27:55–61);
- reported the empty tomb to Peter (John 20:1–2);

- spoke to the two angels in the tomb (John 20:13);
- saw the risen Lord before any others (vv. 16–18); and
- delivered a message from Jesus to the disciples (Matt. 28:10).

The Lord richly rewarded Mary Magdalene for her faithfulness. She experienced first-hand the miraculous works of the prophesied Messiah, ministering to and with Him. She witnessed His resurrection to life as had been promised.

Mary Magdalene was a devoted disciple who ministered to Jesus, witnessed His crucifixion, and discovered the empty tomb. Are you devoted to Jesus? Do you love Him with all your heart? Do you follow His commands faithfully? Do you serve Him as He calls you? The Christian life demands daily devotion to Jesus. Renew your commitment to Him and grow daily in your discipleship.

Rhonda Harrington Kelley

Prayer: *Spend some time now in prayer. Tell the Lord of your love and devotion. Commit to living in a way that reflects your devotion to Him.*

Personal Reflection: ....

....

....

....

....

....

Sapphira—A Deceitful Woman

Acts 5:1–11

"Then Peter said to her, 'How is it that you have agreed together to test the Spirit of the Lord? Look, the feet of those who have buried your husband are at the door, and they will carry you out.'" (v. 9)

After God sent the Holy Spirit to Christians on the day of Pentecost, the church began to grow rapidly. New believers worshipped and prayed together, studying under the apostles' teaching. In the early church, those who came to faith often sold their possessions and shared the proceeds communally. Their personal sacrifice provided for the basic needs of all the believers and no one among them lacked (4:34). Scripture does not suggest that the apostles required members of the church to support each other, but rather the practice was done willingly.

The story of Ananias and his wife Sapphira is found in this context. The two were owners of a parcel of land, which they chose to sell for the benefit of the church. However, when they had the money in their hands, in crept the temptation to keep some for themselves. They devised a plan to give part of the proceeds to the apostles to provide for the needs of the believers and to keep the rest. When Ananias took the proceeds to the church, God revealed his deception to the Apostle Peter. Peter pointed out to Ananias his lie to the Holy Spirit, and then Ananias literally dropped dead.

Several hours later, not knowing what had happened to her husband, Sapphira came to the church. Peter questioned her to see if she had been a willing participant in her husband's scheme or if he had acted alone. She revealed her lack of integrity when she told Peter that the amount they donated was the whole of what they had received for their land. Sapphira was caught in a lie, and she too fell dead. What Ananias and Sapphira sowed in deceit, they reaped in God's judgment and their premature deaths.

In the early days of the church, the issue of integrity was of the utmost importance. If it had not been for the fervor and devotion of the early Christians, the gospel message would not have continued to spread around the world.

Believers who did not live transformed lives were a threat to the survival of the church as a whole. The deaths of Ananias and Sapphira demonstrated to the others how serious God was about keeping His church pure.

The testimonies of individual believers continue to affect the integrity of the church today. Pretending to be more generous than you truly are is only one of the types of hypocrisy found in the present-day church. Examine your own heart, and commit to protecting the integrity of the church through your personal witness.

Laura Landry

Prayer: *Thank the Lord for the gift of the Holy Spirit, who comforts and convicts. Ask Him to help you live in a manner worthy of the gospel of Christ.*

Personal Reflection: ....

....

....

....

....

....

....

Conversion and the Spread of the Gospel

Acts 8:26–40

*"Now as they went down the road, they came to some water.
And the eunuch said, 'See, here is water. What hinders me from being
baptized?' Then Philip said, 'If you believe with all your heart, you may.' And he
answered and said, 'I believe that Jesus Christ is the Son of God.'" (vv. 36–37)*

Just before He ascended to heaven, Jesus gave the command to His followers to carry the gospel message to Jerusalem, Judea, Samaria, and the ends of the earth (Acts 1:8). Philip, or "Philip the Evangelist" as he is often called, was a Christ-follower who took Jesus' commission seriously, and he became one of the first missionaries of the early church. He began by going to Samaria, the home of an unclean people who were considered heretics by the Jews. While Philip was ministering in a Samaritan city, the Holy Spirit prompted him to go down to the desert road that connected Jerusalem with Gaza.

When Philip arrived at the road, he found an Ethiopian eunuch, a high official of the Queen of Ethiopia and in charge of her entire treasury, riding in his chariot. The eunuch must have adhered to some form of Judaism, since he had come from worshipping in Jerusalem and was reading from the book of Isaiah. When Philip asked if he understood what he was reading, the eunuch expressed confusion about the passage in Isaiah 53. He asked Philip to whom the prophet was referring when he wrote about the sheep being led to slaughter.

The Holy Spirit had led Philip directly during this divine appointment. Philip was able to share with the eunuch the truth of Jesus the Messiah, about whom the prophet wrote in Isaiah 53. The gospel message was so clear and powerful that the eunuch immediately asked to receive baptism! After Philip baptized him, the Spirit performed a miracle and he disappeared. The eunuch returned home rejoicing. Tradition maintains that Candace, the Queen of the Ethiopians, was converted as well.

The only facts known about Candace are based on the conversion of her servant. His decision to follow Christ gave the eunuch greater status than even the queen. He became a child of the heavenly King and was involved in the early spread of the gospel.

The Holy Spirit who led Philip to meet the eunuch on the desert road and lead him to Christ is the same Holy Spirit who dwells within believers today. Is the Holy Spirit at work in you, speaking the gospel through you to those whom you meet? Let the conversion of the Ethiopian eunuch, a servant of Candace, be an example of a faithful witness to the gospel of Jesus Christ.

Laura Landry

Prayer: *Ask the Lord to help you become more sensitive to the prompting of the Holy Spirit. Commit to be faithful when the Lord gives you the opportunity to be a witness.*

Personal Reflection: ....

....

....

....

....

....

....

....

Dorcas—Adorned with God

Acts 9:36–43

*"This woman [Dorcas] was full of good works and
charitable deeds which she did." (v. 36)*

A phrase in this focal verse speaks straight to my heart—*"which she did"* (v. 36). Dorcas was a woman in the early church known for her good works because she actually did them. I often think of calling a sick friend, baking a cake for a grieving family, or visiting a lonely shut-in. However, my thoughts are not always implemented because of the busy demands of my life. According to this Scripture, I am only "full of good works and charitable deeds" if I actually do them!

Dorcas lived among the Greeks in the first century in Joppa, a city located about 40 miles west of Jerusalem along the Mediterranean coast. Her Greek name was Dorcas and her Aramaic name was Tabitha, both mentioned in this passage. She was a beloved woman, who was called by Luke a "disciple" or committed follower of Jesus Christ (v. 36).

This disciple had a heart for the Lord and concern for others. She worshipped the Lord and served Him faithfully. She saw the needs of widows and made them clothing. When Dorcas became ill and died, those who received her good gifts wept and mourned (v. 39). They sent for the apostle Peter who was ministering in a nearby city. He knelt down beside her and prayed for Dorcas. The power of the Holy Spirit worked through Peter to restore her to life, and she returned to her good works (vv. 40–41). As a result, many people believed in the Lord (v. 42).

The good works of Dorcas did not save her or bring her back to life. Her faith in Jesus Christ brought about her salvation. Her good works were a natural result of her salvation. Because Dorcas loved the Lord, she loved others. Because she served the Lord, she served others. Because her Lord was full of good works, she "was full of good works and charitable deeds which she did" (v. 36). This sweet servant was honored by the Lord and her friends for serving the poor and needy. She is a biblical example of generosity and goodness for Christian women today.

My mother Joyce Harrington is like Dorcas—she is full of good works. Mother has skilled fingers like Dorcas, too, sewing baby blankets and cross-stitching tea towels. She shares these gifts of love with family and friends who treasure them forever. She bakes pound cakes and volunteers at mission centers, serving others with her time and energy.

Paul instructed women in the church to "adorn themselves . . . with good works" not with "braided hair or gold or pearls or costly clothing" (1 Tim. 2:8–15). So ladies, let's be like Dorcas and adorn ourselves with good works!

Rhonda Harrington Kelley

Prayer: *Reflect on this lesson from the selfless servant Dorcas. Seek ways to do good works in the name of Jesus.*

Personal Reflection: ....

....

....

....

....

....

....

Mary, Mother of John Mark—Hostess to the Early Church

Acts 12:5–12

"So, when he had considered this, he came to the house of Mary, the mother of John whose surname was Mark, where many were gathered together praying." (v. 12)

John Mark was the author of the second gospel, as well as a companion to Peter, Paul, and Barnabas on their missionary journeys. John Mark was passionate about people coming to know Jesus as their Savior and wrote his gospel primarily to convince the Gentiles that Jesus was the Son of Man. Mary, the mother of John Mark, likely came to know Jesus through the witness of her son. A woman of means, her conversion gave her the desire to offer what she had for the use of the church. She had a home large enough for many believers to gather, and she kept her doors open even during what was an intense time of persecution. Her home probably served as a regular place of worship for the Jerusalem church because Peter went straight there after angels delivered him from prison.

Peter had been held in prison under constant guard as he awaited trial before King Herod Agrippa I. King Herod had just killed James, and Peter knew that execution would likely be his fate as well. The believers in Jerusalem gathered in Mary's home to pray for Peter's release. Despite the fact that Christians were being persecuted, arrested, and even murdered, Mary continued to invite them to gather in her home. God used a willing woman to provide safe-haven for many believers in Jerusalem.

Mary, the mother of John Mark, is just one of the many women whom God used in growing the early church. Jesus had broken the mold of Jewish religion, empowering women to have an active role in spreading the gospel and expanding the kingdom. One common role for Christian women at the time was to be the hostess of a house church. Others such as Priscilla (1 Cor. 16:19), Lydia (Acts 16:14), and Nympha (Col. 4:15) are also mentioned in Scripture as hostesses of house churches.

Jesus continues to call women today to use their resources to grow the church. Opening your home to friends and neighbors or even hosting church gatherings connects you to the legacy of these women who helped build the early church. Apart from hospitality, there are many other gifts that the Lord can use to advance the gospel through faithful women. Accept Christ's invitation to include women like you in building His church. Determine to use your gifts to bless others, no matter what the cost.

Laura Landry

Prayer: *Thank Jesus for breaking the mold and calling women to participate in ministry. Ask the Lord to show you what gifts He has given you that He could use to expand the church. Commit to be a part of the legacy of women who have offered their gifts to advance the kingdom.*

Personal Reflection: ....

....

....

....

....

....

....

Rhoda—A Joyful Maid

Acts 12:12–17

"And as Peter knocked at the door of the gate, a girl named Rhoda came to answer. When she recognized Peter's voice, because of her gladness she did not open the gate, but ran in and announced that Peter stood before the gate." (vv. 13–14)

Joy, a fruit of the Spirit in the lives of Christians, was definitely the mood of Rhoda, the maid of John Mark's mother. The apostle Peter was in prison, and members of the church were praying all night for his release (12:5–11). An angel of the Lord appeared in the jail, where Peter was bound with chains between two soldiers. The angel told the apostle to arise quickly; his chains fell off, and he put on his sandals. Peter escaped in a miraculous way and went directly to the house of Mary, the mother of John Mark.

Rhoda, a young servant and follower of Jesus, was not only working in the home of Mary but also worshipping with other believers. They had prayed all night for Peter. Can you imagine Rhoda's surprise when she answered the door in the wee hours of the night and heard the voice of Peter? She was so excited about their answered prayers that she ran inside without opening the gate (vv. 13–14). Her joy in the Lord should be an example for Christians today.

Joy is the happy state of mind that results from knowing and serving God. Recorded in Scripture more than 150 times, joy is obviously an important virtue of faith (Gal. 5:22–23) and should be evident regardless of the circumstances (James 1:2–3). For Christians, joy is not temporal but eternal, not based on circumstances but on Christ. Joy is a blessing to the believer and a witness to others.

Rhoda was joyous in her service. She worked not only out of obligation but with true happiness. While most servants were not happy in their work, Rhoda had a different attitude of heart. Are you joyful on the job? Are you happy as you work around the house? **Rhoda was also joyous in her response.** She was so excited to hear Peter's voice that she forgot to let him in the house. Do you respond with joy to God's work in your life? **Rhoda shared a joyous message.**

She spoke to the church members with such excitement that they thought she was crazy. Does your zeal for the Lord at times look to others as craziness? We can learn from this joyous servant how to have true joy in the Lord.

Little else is known about Rhoda, but the young girl's enthusiasm has made a profound impression on Christians through the centuries. The joyous maid who was joyful in her service shared her joy with others. Be a joyful worker like Rhoda, sharing God's grace through the witness of your life and your words. Let your joy be contagious to others!

Rhonda Harrington Kelley

Prayer: *Rejoice in the Lord as you spend time in prayer. Then, share your joy with others.*

Personal Reflection: ....

....

....

....

....

....

....

....

Lydia—A Life with Purpose

Acts 16:11–15

"Now a certain woman named Lydia heard us. She was a seller of purple from the city of Thyatira, who worshiped God. The Lord opened her heart to heed the things spoken by Paul." (v. 14)

Lydia came from Thyatira, though she was living in the city of Philippi when she met Paul and made a decision to follow Christ. As an influential business-woman, she sold articles dyed purple, a prized color of royalty and wealth. While she worked full-time as a merchant, Lydia also served the Lord faithfully. She witnessed of her faith to others and hosted the church in her home.

On a Sabbath day, Paul went outside the city gates to the river where women typically gathered for prayer (v. 13). It was there he met Lydia and shared the gospel message with her (v. 14). When Lydia was saved, she led family members and friends in her household to faith in Christ. They were all baptized in that same river and began to serve the Lord, ministering to Paul and Silas as well as other disciples (v. 15). Lydia visited Paul and Silas when they were imprisoned (vv. 16–24) and hosted them in her home upon their release (vv. 40).

In this passage, five verbs guide us in living with purpose as did Lydia: heard, worshipped, opened, baptized, persuaded.

- Lydia **heard** the word of the Lord (v. 14a). Purposeful living responds to hearing from God in prayer, through his Word and through the godly counsel of others.
- Lydia **worshipped** the Lord (v. 14b). Purposeful living results in the worship of God personally and in corporate settings, praising Him in song and learning from His Word.
- Lydia's heart was **opened** to the message of the gospel (v. 14c). Purposeful living relies on a personal relationship with Jesus Christ.

- Lydia was **baptized** with her entire household in an act of obedience and as a testimony of faith in Christ (v. 15a). Purposeful living reveals the transforming work of salvation in an individual's life.
- Lydia **persuaded** others; she passionately spoke of her conversion and convinced the disciples to stay in her home (v. 15b). Purposeful living rejoices in the work of God, testifying to others and serving Him faithfully.

My dad was dramatically converted on April 15, 1958. While he went to the Baptist church in his hometown for a revival service to find prospects for his insurance business, he found the Lord instead. On the seventh pew of the church, during the seventh stanza of "Just As I Am," Dad heard the gospel, worshipped the Savior, opened his heart in salvation, was baptized and began preaching, and has persuaded others with the gospel message since his conversion. Like Lydia and my dad, we must live lives of purpose as we trust and follow Christ.

Rhonda Harrington Kelley

Prayer: *Have you heard the Lord speak to you and opened your heart to Him? Spend time in worship and prayer. Now live a life with purpose.*

Personal Reflection: ....

....

....

....

....

A Fortune-Telling Slave Girl—Rescued and Valued

Acts 16:16–24

"But Paul, greatly annoyed, turned and said to the spirit, 'I command you in the name of Jesus Christ to come out of her.' And he came out that very hour." (v. 18b)

As Paul and Silas made their missionary journey through Macedonia, they came to a town called Philippi. Although the town is now uninhabited and in ruins, its name will always be remembered because of the church that started there. Paul later wrote the book of Philippians to encourage and admonish the believers in Philippi, and his words continue to instruct the church today. The impact of Paul's ministry in Philippi was great despite the opposition and difficulty that he faced there.

One sign of the truth of the gospel was Paul's casting a demon out of a slave girl. While Paul and Silas were preaching in Philippi, a girl with a spirit of prediction started following them around and antagonizing them. Despite the fact that her "gift" for telling the future was clearly demonic, her owners encouraged her practice of fortune-telling because it made a profit for them. The girl was reduced to the money that she could generate for those who enslaved her. Many women find themselves in slavery today; they are stripped of value and treated as a commodity.

The girl disrupted the preaching and ministry of Paul and Silas in the town, no doubt the enemy was trying to prevent the establishment of the church in Philippi. Frustrated by the disturbance, Paul turned and spoke to the girl with the authority that God had given him. It is interesting that Paul did not condemn the girl. Rather Paul spoke directly to the demonic spirit, which he knew was within her, casting it out in the name of Jesus Christ.

Not only did the demon flee, but the girl was also rescued from her spiritual slavery. Paul did not see a mere aggravation when he saw this poor girl. He saw someone who was in bondage and who deserved to be freed. God assigns value to every person, even a female slave who was worth nothing in the pagan culture of the first century.

As the story continued to unfold, Paul and Silas were thrown in prison because of their action on behalf of the slave girl. Yet, the plans of the enemy were foiled again, and God sent an earthquake to loose their chains. Ultimately, God's display of power and His plan to use Paul and Silas led to the establishment of one of the most fruitful branches of the early church. Recognize your personal value in the eyes of the Most High God and believe that He is at work even in the midst of strong opposition.

Laura Landry

Prayer: *Thank God that He is powerful to overcome the work of the enemy and that He values you. Believe He has a plan to use you.*

Personal Reflection:

Damaris—Counter-Cultural Commitment

Acts 17:22–34

"And when they heard of the resurrection of the dead, some mocked, while others said, 'We will hear you again on this matter.' So Paul departed from among them. However, some men joined him and believed, among them Dionysius the Areopagite, a woman named Damaris, and others with them." (vv. 32–34)

The sermon at Mars Hill is one of the most important moments in the ministry of Paul. The rocky hill in Athens sits high above the rest of the city, just adjacent to the Acropolis. From this point today, one can see the bustling modern city below and the ancient ruins of the world's most legendary architecture above. There is a sense of connection with some of the greatest minds who ever lived as you stand and take in such an incredible feat of mankind. The spot was equally well-known and celebrated in the time of Paul.

The Acropolis represented the pinnacle of Greek civilization. It was a vast civilization that continues to influence culture today, and here—at the highest point in their capital city—was a sparkling white beacon of human achievement. The temples to many different Greek gods still stand there, as striking and beautiful as they ever were. The Areopagus was the high court of Athens. The highest officers in Greek civic life and some of the most powerful judges in the world determined justice.

Presenting a message in that context would have unnerved me. Yet Paul, in true Pauline fashion, did not bat an eyelash in intimidation or fail to take advantage of an opportunity to share the gospel. Paul found a connection point with his audience (their altar to an "unknown god"), and then presented God as the true Lord over heaven and earth (vv. 23–24). His sermon demonstrated how Paul effectively adapted the gospel message to his audience. He did not change the truth of the gospel but rather the manner in which he presented it. While many dismissed Paul and others even ridiculed him, there were a few in the crowd who accepted Christ's resurrection as proof that the God of whom Paul spoke was the true God.

One of these believers was a woman, and she is mentioned by name in the passage. Little is known about Damaris, but she was presumably a prominent member of society and participant in Greek civic life. Despite the fact that everything Paul had said was in conflict with her cultural practice of philosophy and idol worship, she recognized the truth he presented and had a transforming experience through Jesus. Damaris had the courage to accept the call of Christ, even when it most likely caused her to be ridiculed and cast out of intellectual society.

Laura Landry

Prayer: *Express your gratitude to God for examples of people with courage and commitment to the truth in God's Word. Commit to follow Christ, even in the face of ridicule or judgment.*

Personal Reflection:

Priscilla's Ministry

Acts 18:24–28

*"So he [Apollos] began to speak boldly in the synagogue.
When Aquila and Priscilla heard him, they took him aside
and explained to him the way of God more accurately." (v. 26)*

Priscilla and her husband Aquila were quite the dynamic duo in the first century! Priscilla was a Jewess who left Italy with her husband Aquila to live in Corinth after Claudius expelled all the Jews from Rome. They were tentmakers by trade just like the Apostle Paul. When they moved to Corinth, they were introduced to Paul (Acts 18:1–3). After coming to faith in Christ and being trained by Paul, they hosted a church in their home in Corinth (1 Cor. 16:19). They also traveled with Paul to Ephesus and stayed there to minister to the believers while Paul continued on his missionary journey (Acts 18:18). Later, this couple returned to Rome, opening their home to believers there (Rom. 16:5). Paul commended them as his fellow workers, who risked their own lives for Paul (vv. 3–4).

While the testimony of this couple's life is a wonderful example for men and women today, some scholars want to cite the example of Priscilla's teaching Apollos (Acts 18:26) to support abolishing the teaching of 1 Timothy 2:12, which states that a woman should not "teach" or "have authority over a man" in the church. This misinterpretation of Scripture is tragic in a sense because in wanting to say more than the Bible says about Priscilla, these scholars distract from the very noteworthy ministry Priscilla did have alongside her husband. The text speaks for itself; it needs no embellishment.

Furthermore, the account of Apollos with Priscilla and Aquila cannot contradict 1 Timothy 2:12 for several important reasons:

- **Priscilla taught alongside her husband.** She was not teaching Apollos by herself but assisting her husband. The text does not indicate how this teaching was done, but clearly Priscilla and her husband taught Apollos.

- **The content of the teaching was evangelistic.** Aquila and Priscilla taught Apollos critical truths about the Christian faith. He did not have a full understanding of Christ because he only knew the baptism of John (Acts 18:25). They explained the way to God to him more accurately.

- **The teaching occurred in a private place and not in a public assembly or class.** Aquila and Priscilla invited Apollos into the privacy of their home so they could help him more accurately understand the very nature of the Christian faith.

For these reasons, this account of Priscilla, Aquila, and Apollos cannot be viewed as contradicting the clear teaching of other passages of Scripture.

Candi Finch

Prayer: *When approaching the Bible, pray that the Holy Spirit would give you discernment so you do not say more or less than the Scripture actually says. Also, thank the Lord for the example of Priscilla and her husband Aquila who served the kingdom of Christ by offering hospitality, learning about their faith, and sharing it with fellow believers.*

Personal Reflection: ....

....

....

....

Daughters of Philip—Second Generation Christians

Acts 21:7–11

"On the next day we who were Paul's companions departed and came to Caesarea, and entered the house of Philip the evangelist, who was one of the seven, and stayed with him. Now this man had four virgin daughters who prophesied." (vv. 8–9)

On the day of Pentecost, God fulfilled the promise of Jesus that He would send His Spirit to be with the believers on earth. Thousands of new Christians were added to the church on that day, and the Holy Spirit sparked a fire in their hearts to set about spreading the gospel and expanding the kingdom. One of the Christ-followers who dedicated himself to this work was Philip, whom Luke referred to as "Philip the evangelist" in the book of Acts (v. 8). Philip was the first missionary for the church and is remembered for sharing the gospel with the Ethiopian eunuch.

Philip evangelized all the towns along the Mediterranean coast until he came to Caesarea Maritima. At Caesarea by the sea, Philip settled down, raised a family, and likely planted a church. Paul and Luke came to visit him there while on their way to Jerusalem about 20 years later. As Luke documented this stop on his missionary journey with Paul, he decided to make mention of Philip's "four virgin daughters who prophesied" (v. 9). What was it about these four young women that made them important enough to be remembered in Scripture?

First of all, these daughters of Philip represented the fulfillment of a prophecy from the book of Joel, which Peter quoted on the day of Pentecost (Joel 2:28; Acts 2:17). The fact that these young women "prophesied" was evidence that the Holy Spirit dwelt within them and their eternity was secure. God truly had sent His Spirit to be with the believers, and the proof was in their spiritual gifts. The daughters represented the expansion of the church and the spread of the gospel. They were second-generation Christians.

The fact that they were "virgins" likely meant that they had devoted themselves wholeheartedly to ministry. Although we are given no details about the specific ministries of these women, other passages of Scripture describe the gift of prophecy in New Testament times as speaking "edification and exhortation and comfort" (1 Cor. 14:3). They likely ministered specifically to the women of the church, discipling them into mature faith as their godly father had discipled them (1 Tim. 2:12).

No matter what their specific role may have been, it is clear that Philip's daughters made an impact on the early church. You are a daughter of the King, on whom He has bestowed at least one spiritual gift. What will be the lasting impact of your service to Christ in the church?

Laura Landry

Prayer: *Ask the Lord to reveal to you how you can use your spiritual gifts to edify believers and exhort the church. Thank Him for the gift of the Holy Spirit, which He bestows on men and women equally.*

Personal Reflection: ....

....

....

....

....

....

....

Drusilla and Bernice—Rejection of the Truth

Acts 24:24—25:23; 26:28–32

*"And after some days, when Felix came with his wife Drusilla,
who was Jewish, he sent for Paul and heard him concerning the faith
in Christ. Now as he reasoned about righteousness, self-control,
and the judgment to come, Felix was afraid and answered,
'Go away for now; when I have a convenient time I will call for you.'" (vv. 24–25)*

As Paul traveled across the Roman Empire during his missionary journeys, he frequently ran into trouble with the local officials and wound up in jail because Christianity was seen as a threat to the pagan empire as well as the established Jewish religion. When his preaching caused a stir among the Jews, the Romans often tried to silence him.

Paul arrived in Jerusalem and was welcomed by the Christians there. However, when the Jews found out that Paul was back in town, chaos ensued. The Roman authorities stepped in, arrested Paul, and brought him to Felix, the governor in Caesarea, who failed to find a reason to prosecute Paul. However, Felix did not want to cause another riot among the Jews, so he held Paul in jail for two years until Festus took over as governor of the province.

Drusilla and Bernice were Jewish sisters who descended from Herod the Great. Drusilla was married to the Roman governor, Felix, who with Drusilla, heard Paul preach the gospel as a result of their curiosity about the commotion. In fact, Scripture says that Felix conversed with Paul often while he was in jail (24:24–25). However, nothing in the text suggests that either Felix or Drusilla ever accepted Jesus as Savior despite the conviction they felt.

In Acts 25, Bernice traveled with her brother, King Agrippa, to visit Festus after he had taken over for Felix. Because Agrippa was a Jewish leader, Festus suggested that he should hear Paul's case while he was in town. The next day, Agrippa and Bernice heard Paul's defense in which he made the gospel message quite clear. Bernice had a reputation for immorality and displayed her self-importance by entering the courtroom with "great pomp" (v. 23). She, like her sister, rejected Jesus as the Messiah and did not receive salvation, despite her belief that Paul was innocent.

Both Drusilla and Bernice heard the truth and had opportunities to respond, but they chose not to put their faith in Jesus (Acts 24:24–25; 25:28–31). You can hear the gospel with your ears but not respond with your heart. Many women attend church their whole lives and even claim to believe the Word of God but do not yield their hearts to the lordship of Jesus.

Laura Landry

Prayer: *If you have not yet accepted the truth of Jesus, do not delay in acknowledging Him as the true Messiah and your personal Savior. If you are a believer, thank God for His conviction that led you to repentance and salvation.*

Personal Reflection: ....

....

....

....

....

....

....

The Roman Road to Salvation

Romans 3:9–30; 6:15–23

*"For the wages of sin is death, but the gift of God
is eternal life in Christ Jesus our Lord." (6:23)*

Have you ever used a map app or another navigation tool to find your way from one place to another? These tools can be helpful, but one wrong direction and you are miles away from where you intended to go.

God wants you to know how you can get to heaven. Many verses in the Bible lead us, and we can be sure that all of them give us clear direction for becoming a believer in Christ and knowing the way to get to heaven.

The Roman Road is a list of Bible verses from this New Testament book, giving the reader direction for getting to heaven. We can trust God's inspired Word (2 Tim. 3:14–17). When we follow His plan, there is no way to take a wrong turn. "For I am not ashamed of the gospel of Christ, for it is the power of God to salvation for everyone who believes" (Rom. 1:16a). The Roman Road makes the message of salvation easy to know and to share with others.

Everyone has done wrong things or sinned (3:23). The payment for our sin is death or eternal separation from God, but the gift of God is eternal life with Christ (6:23). This means that God sent Jesus to provide for our salvation. He is a gift to those who believe. God has demonstrated His love for us; and though we were sinners, He sent Jesus to die for us and thus pay for our sins (5:8). If we believe in our hearts and confess with our voices, the Bible says that all who call on Him will be saved (10:9–10, 13). When we believe in Jesus, we will have peace with God (5:1); there is no longer condemnation for those in Christ (8:1), and we will never be separated from Him (8:38–39). We will have Him to help us to know how to live while on earth, and we can know that we will go to heaven to live with Him when we die.

God's directions to heaven are found in the Roman Road and can be trusted. If we follow these verses by believing in Christ and confessing with our mouths, they will show us the way to heaven. There are no wrong turns, and God will guide us every step of the way.

This pathway to God is only available through Jesus. No other route is correct. Use the Bible as your navigation tool to eternal life, as well as for direction for your life on earth. May you know His peace at every turn!

Jaye Martin

Prayer: *Seek salvation through Christ and plan to share it with others as you follow His clear plan of salvation.*

Personal Reflection: ....

....

....

....

....

....

....

Bodies as Living Sacrifices

Romans 12:1–8

*"I beseech you therefore, brethren, by the mercies of God,
that you present your bodies a living sacrifice, holy, acceptable to God,
which is your reasonable service. And do not be conformed to this world,
but be transformed by the renewing of your mind, that you may prove
what is that good and acceptable and perfect will of God." (vv. 1–2)*

Discipline, for a Christian, begins with the body. We have only one. It is this body that is the primary material given to us for sacrifice. If we didn't have this, we wouldn't have anything. We are meant to present it, offer it up, give it unconditionally to God for His purposes. This, we are told, is an "act of spiritual worship." The giving of this physical body, comprising blood, bone, and tissue, worth a few dollars in chemicals, becomes a spiritual act, "for such is the worship which you, as rational creatures, should offer."

The Jerusalem Bible translates is this way: "Think of God's mercy, my brothers, and worship Him, I beg you, in a way that is worthy of thinking beings, [that is, a note tells us, "'in a spiritual way,' as opposed to the ritual sacrifices of Jews or pagans"] by offering your living bodies as a holy sacrifice."

More spiritual failure is due, I believe, to this cause than to any other: the failure to recognize this living body as having anything to do with worship or holy sacrifice. This body is, quite simply, the starting place. Failure here is failure everywhere else.

"He who would see the face of the most powerful Wrestler, our boundless God," wrote Alonso de Orozco, "must first have wrestled with himself." Only one who has taken seriously the correlation between the physical and spiritual and begun the struggle can appreciate the aptness of that word "wrestle." Habits, for example, hold a half nelson on us. That hold must be broken if we are to be free for the Lord's service. We cannot give our hearts to God and keep our bodies for ourselves.

The Christian's body houses not only the Holy Spirit Himself, but the Christian's heart, will, mind, and emotions—all that plays a part in your knowing God and living for Him. In my case, the "house" is tall; it is Anglo-Saxon, middle-aged, and female. I was not asked about my preferences in any of these factors, but I was given a choice about the use I make of them. In other words, the body was a gift to me. Whether I will thank God for it and offer it as a holy sacrifice is for me to decide.

Elisabeth Elliot

Prayer: *Are there any sinful habits that are preventing you from honoring the Lord with your whole body, including your heart, will, mind, and/or emotions? If so, confess your sin, and ask the Lord to help you to be "transformed" by the power of His Word and Holy Spirit.*

Personal Reflection: ....

....

....

....

....

....

An excerpt from Elisabeth Elliot's *Discipline: The Glad Surrender* (page 43).

Please Be My Guest

Romans 12:9–21

". . . Given to hospitality." (v. 13)

If you were asked to define biblical hospitality, how would you choose to describe it? The topic and the definition should be dear to our hearts as believers; for as we practice hospitality, we share what we have with those whom God brings into our lives. Biblical hospitality is focused on having a heart for service, asking our heavenly Father to creatively stretch what we have to offer refreshment to others, as well as using our time and energy to add joy to our daily lives.

Hospitality is the art of creating a generous, friendly, pleasant, and nourishing environment. I believe most Christian women desire this type of environment for their homes and want to be known as hospitable women. However, for the Christian woman, becoming a hospitable woman requires more than just developing the needed skills in entertaining, food preparation, or home management (although, developing these skills will free you up to focus on people as your priority). For hospitality to be extended with love and graciousness, a wise woman understands God's definition of hospitality.

The Greek word *philoxenia* used in the New Testament for hospitality literally means "love of strangers." The word has two parts—*philos* meaning "loving" and *xenos* meaning "a stranger or a guest." An example of hospitality is used in Romans 12:13 where the phrase "given to hospitality" is included in the listing of character traits for a Christian. A second example is seen in Hebrews 13:2 and reminds us, "Do not forget to **entertain** strangers, for by so *doing* some have unwittingly entertained angels." The word "entertain" in that verse can be translated as "to show love to" and emphasizes the importance of not forgetting to be hospitable to strangers or guests and is used several times in Scripture. The Greek word for **hospitable** is *philoxenos*. Being "hospitable" is a requirement for church overseers (1 Tim. 3:2), elders (Titus 1:8), and Christians (1 Pet. 4:9).

Planning is the foundation of a Christ-honoring extension of hospitality. Consider beginning your planning time with a prayer of consecration. It is helpful to write out the prayer, review it each time you practice hospitality, and modify it as you mature in your spiritual life, as well as in your hospitality skills.

Pat Ennis

Prayer: *Thank your heavenly Father for His Word that challenges you to love both friends and strangers. Ask Him to help you to be excited about welcoming them into your home. Realizing that you cannot extend biblical hospitality without His strength, ask Him to empower you to be a useful woman for His Kingdom. Request that your guests would leave your home knowing more of Christ because they have spent time with you. Thank Him for His love. Ask for His help to model it as you extend biblical hospitality.*

Personal Reflection:

Why Obey the Government?

Romans 13:1–10

"Let every soul be subject to the governing authorities. For there is no authority except from God, and the authorities that exist are appointed by God." (v. 1)

Have you ever gotten a traffic ticket? How did you feel about the police officer who gave it to you? Do you view government authority as positive or negative? Protective or prying? Helpful or interfering? Your perspective may depend on your present mental state or on your political standpoint. Certain governments try to control their citizens, limit their freedoms, mismanage finances, manipulate the media, and punish all opposition. Yet, according to Romans 13:1, God allows even dictatorships to exist. Jesus told the Roman governor Pilate, who unjustly delivered Him over to be crucified, "You could have no power at all against Me unless it had been given you from above" (John 19:11). The Sovereign Lord reigns. Nobody governs unless God permits it.

Why should we submit to government authority? First, God established it. To disobey the government means to disobey God, for it acts as His representative. Second, the government punishes wrongdoing, so we will suffer the consequences if we disobey. Third, we should obey authority so that we will have a clean conscience, freeing us from guilt-causing anxiety and loss of joy. What would happen if we had no government? Crime would increase. The economy would collapse. Gangs would take over. Anarchy (lawlessness) would prevail. Everyone would begin to do what is right in her own eyes.

The fact that God establishes authorities does not mean that He approves of their sins. The Lord used the cruel Babylonians to discipline the Israelites by destroying their temple, capital, and exiling many. Yet, He later punished Babylon for its sins.

God must be obeyed. If government mandates conflict directly with His commands, He must be obeyed. Peter and John refused to stop preaching about Jesus when the religious authorities ordered them to stop. They affirmed, "We ought to obey God rather than men" (Acts 5:29). We can act to change government policies that violate God's laws by working within the law. For example, we can organize right-to-life prayer chains and letter-writing campaigns instead of bombing abortion clinics.

Are you submitting to the governing authorities in your life? Reflect on the following questions: Do you file your taxes every year honestly? Do you make copies illegally? Do you purchase or use pirated books or DVDs? Do you respect those whom God has placed in authority, or do you ridicule them? Do you pray for your government officials—even those you dislike? What actions can you take to become a better citizen?

Sharon Gritz

Prayer: *Ask God to reveal any bad attitudes you have toward government authorities and ways you are disobeying the laws of the land. Seek His forgiveness. Intercede for government leaders, asking the Lord to give them wisdom and moral courage to make God-honoring decisions. Pray also for their salvation.*

Personal Reflection:

Phoebe's Service to the Lord

Romans 16:1–2

∽

*"I commend to you Phoebe our sister, who is a servant of the church
in Cenchrea that you may receive her in the Lord in a manner worthy
of the saints, and assist her in whatever business she has need of you;
for indeed she has been a helper of many and of myself also." (vv. 1–2)*

In Romans 16, Paul sends greetings to specific people in the church in Rome, and several of the people found in the list are noteworthy women in the Roman church. However, before he begins giving "shout outs" to the believers in Rome, he instructs the church to receive his sister Phoebe. This remarkable woman probably was not Paul's biological sister; this term was an endearment, referring to Phoebe as a member of the family of God.

Phoebe lived in Cenchrea, a port city near Corinth, and was traveling to Rome, possibly on a business trip. She even could have been the carrier of Paul's letter to the Roman church. Paul commends her to the Christians in Rome for her character and her work for the Lord, encouraging the believers in Rome to help her in her work.

When Paul calls Phoebe a "helper" in Romans 16:2, this word can also be translated as "patron," hinting that Phoebe used her financial resources to help further the work of the Lord. Similar to the women in Luke 8:1–3 who served Jesus and supported His work from their own possessions or Lydia in Acts 16 who opened her home for Paul and the church in Philippi, Phoebe used her skills and resources for the Lord's work. Are their skills or possessions in your life that you could be using to contribute to the Lord's work?

Paul also refers to Phoebe as a "servant." Several scholars want to argue that this means that Phoebe was serving as an official leader over the church in Cenchrea, since the word for servant can be translated as "deacon" when referring to a specific office of the church or as "servant or slave" in other cases when the text is not talking about the church position.

Confusion has arisen about what to do with Phoebe. However, we know Phoebe was not teaching men or exercising authority over the church at Cenchrea because 1 Timothy 2:12 prohibits this type of ministry for women in the church. Paul would not prohibit something and then commend a believer for going against scriptural guidelines. What is abundantly clear in the text is that Phoebe used her time, talents, and resources to serve others—a significant example for believers today!

Candi Finch

Prayer: *Do you use your possessions to help God with His work? Would you spend some time today asking the Lord to help you be a good steward of your time, your skills, and your financial resources and reveal to you any changes you may need to make in order to support God's work?*

Personal Reflection: ....

....

....

....

....

....

....

Junia—Serving the Lord Even in Difficulty

Romans 16:3–11

"Greet Andronicus and Junia, my countrymen and my fellow prisoners, who are of note among the apostles, who also were in Christ before me." (v. 7)

You probably have not spent a lot of time poring over Romans 16:7! In fact, much like the genealogies with lists of unfamiliar names in portions of the Old and New Testament, a person could find herself racing through the "greetings" section in Romans 16 without spending a lot of thought on its significance. There is actually quite a disagreement over the person named Junia to whom Paul sends his greetings. Why the controversy? There are three reasons: Is the person named Junia (a woman) or Junias (a man); is the phrase following the names best translated "outstanding among the apostles" or "well-known to the apostles," and what is the meaning of the Greek word translated "apostles"?

The name in the Greek is *Iounian*, and because of the case of the word in the Greek text, possibly the name could be Junia or Junias. However, since Junia was a common woman's name in Latin and since Paul was writing to the church at Rome, Latin names would have been expected. So, it is best to understand the name as referring to a woman.

The "who" phrase after Andronicus and Junia, Paul's fellow countrymen and fellow prisoners, could be translated as "among the apostles" or "by/to the apostles." The question is whether or not this pair were counted as apostles or whether they were just well-known by the apostles. The most recent research in Greek grammar would lead one to understand the verse as "well-known to the apostles."

The word *apostolos* is used as a technical title when referring to the twelve apostles, or Paul. The word also means "messenger" or "one who is sent." For instance, the word is used in John 13:16 and translated as "he who is sent." Jesus uses the word here to refer to a messenger and not the official position of an apostle. In addition, the term *apostolos* could have the nuance of meaning a "traveling missionary" since a missionary is "one who is sent."

So, it is safe to conclude that Junia was most likely a woman and even that she was possibly married to Andronicus and that they served as missionaries—forerunners to the likes of Jim and Elisabeth Elliot or Adoniram and Ann Judson. Don't let this little trip through Greek grammar distract you from what Paul is actually saying about this believer. Junia spent time imprisoned for her faith, came to know Jesus even before Paul did, and she knew Paul so well that he wanted to send her greetings. Thank God that women and men like Junia stood strong even in the face of persecution in the early church!

Candi Finch

Prayer: *Pray for believers around the world today who may be imprisoned or persecuted because of their faith. Ask the Lord to protect and strengthen them.*

Personal Reflection: ....

....

....

....

....

....

....

How Would You Like to Be Remembered?

Romans 16:12–27

*"Greet Tryphena and Tryphosa, who have labored in the Lord.
Greet the beloved Persis, who labored much in the Lord." (v. 12)*

What would your obituary say if you were to die today? I know—what morbid thought! However, what do you really want your legacy to be? Would people remember your passion for Christ, your love for others, your heart for the outcasts? Or, would they remember a negative attitude, a short temper, or a sharp tongue? What would your family or your friends or your coworkers say about you? As Paul sent his greetings to the believers in Rome, he commended several women for their hard work and labor. The one defining characteristic of their lives was devotion and dedication to God. What a magnificent way to be remembered throughout the ages!

Though very little is known about these women, to read about sisters in Christ who gave their foremost energies to serve God is encouraging. Mary is commended for laboring hard (16:6). Tryphena, whose name means dainty, and Tryphosa, whose name means "delicate," are noted as women who labored for the Lord (v. 12). The woman Persis is described as "beloved," a dear friend of Paul's who labored much for the Lord (v. 12). Each of these ladies exemplified the admonition found in Colossians 3:23: "And whatever you do, do it heartily, as to the Lord and not to men."

Hebrews 11 is often called the Hall of Faith because one believer after another is noted for displaying incredible faith. Noah, Abraham, Sarah, Rahab, and others have an obituary of sorts in this chapter, and you can find one of the most remarkable phrases in all of the Bible in Hebrews 11:16: "God is not ashamed to be called their God." What an amazing thought! All those people in Hebrews lived in such a way that God was not ashamed to be called their God. Just like the hard-working women in Romans 16, the legacy of these believers was quite extraordinary. As one of my childhood softball coaches would have said, "They left it all on the field." They didn't hold back at all during the game. What a significant thing by which to be remembered!

Consider your own life and see if you are building a legacy of faith. Do you work hard for the Lord in your home, in your work, and at church, giving it your all—not so that people will notice you but so you honor the Lord with your effort? It is helpful to ask from time to time, "If today were my last, would the legacy of my life be one that honored the Lord?" If your answer is no, then start today!

Candi Finch

Prayer: *Ask the Lord to help you focus on important, eternal things. Even as you go about your day running errands, working, or possibly even doing laundry, would you ask the Lord to help you work heartily as unto Him?*

Personal Reflection: ....

....

....

....

....

....

....

We Are God's Temple

1 Corinthians 6:12–20

*"Or do you not know that your body is the temple of the Holy Spirit
who is in you, whom you have from God, and you are not your own?
For you were bought at a price; therefore glorify God in your body
and in your spirit, which are God's." (vv. 19–20)*

There's no such thing as a typical church building anymore. Oh, sure, there are the brick churches with white columns that dot the landscape throughout the Bible Belt. But there's also the CrossFit gym that doubles as a church meeting place when the workout facility isn't being used for weightlifting and cardio. In both places, despite the wide spectrum of interior design possibilities, the Word of God is preached and people draw near to know God and to make Him known.

What makes it possible to meet God in both types of places? Why isn't one building design more conducive to worship for all involved? Because we—not the building—are the temple of God.

The Corinthians had questions about how much a relationship with God was supposed to impact their lifestyle. They quizzed Paul on food issues, sexual matters, and much more. By emphasizing that the Holy Spirit resides within each believer, Paul wanted the Corinthians to consider more than just a list of do's and don'ts. He wanted them to go deeper for their motivation to live for Christ. Every place they went, every word they spoke, and every action they took was done with the Holy Spirit in residence.

Years ago, Robert Munger wrote "My Heart: Christ's Home," and in this essay, he described what it would be like for a believer literally to invite Jesus to come live in her home. He details the pride with which she might take Jesus into her well-decorated rooms, the concern when He inquires about certain closets, and the imposition it becomes to have to visit with Him every day when she is so busy. Munger challenged his readers to take seriously the responsibility and privilege of having such a special guest in their home and life.

What is your motivation for living a godly lifestyle? If it's all about getting someone else's approval or merely deferring to that list of do's and don'ts, you are missing out on the best part of all. Acknowledging that your body is a temple of the Holy Spirit and that you can grow in your relationship with Him is a huge step out of legalism and into freedom. And in freedom the Word of God is preached and people draw near to know God and to make Him known.

Judi Jackson

Prayer: *Walk through the rooms of your heart and home in a spirit of open submission. Ask God to show you areas that need to be cleaned up, polished, and/or overhauled. Thank Him for His sacrifice on the cross and seek to glorify Him in your thoughts, words, and deeds.*

Personal Reflection: ....

....

....

....

....

....

....

Divorce and Remarriage

1 Corinthians 7:10–16, 39

"Now to the married I command, yet not I but the Lord: A wife is not to depart from her husband. But even if she does depart, let her remain unmarried or be reconciled to her husband. And a husband is not to divorce his wife." (vv. 10–11)

Have you ever tried to peel something off a piece of paper that has been glued to it? Maybe you were working on a scrapbook, and the picture you glued was in the wrong place and needed to be adjusted? If so, you know how difficult it is to remove! I recently found a scrapbook that some of my students made for me in college, and I wanted to put one of the pictures they had glued to construction paper in a frame for my office. Unfortunately, the picture ended up ripping and having bits of red construction paper still attached. That picture and the red paper had been joined, bonded together—two separate elements had become one. Trying to separate them cleanly just was not possible because they had been united.

This visual is exactly what happens in a marriage. A man and a woman join together and become one flesh (Gen. 2:24). So, when a divorce occurs, it is never a simple, clean break. In 1 Corinthians 7:10–16 and 39, Paul is answering questions that the church at Corinth had sent to him about marriage, divorce, and remarriage (1 Cor. 7:1). When Paul tells them that husbands and wives should not divorce, he refers to the Lord's teaching about marriage (see Day 226 devotion on Matt. 19:1–11). If a couple does get a divorce, they are not to remarry. In fact, Paul teaches that if a person gets a divorce and then remarries while the first spouse is living, then it is adultery (Rom. 7:1–4). That may seem like a harsh word, but you see, even if a couple is legally divorced, they are still connected like that picture and red construction paper. God-designed marriage is a life-long union. However, if a person's spouse dies, then, and only then, does the Bible allow a person to be remarried (1 Cor. 7:39).

Marriage is not always easy because it involves two imperfect, sinful people. But don't forget, God is involved as well—He is the "glue" that binds marriages together! When it gets tough, our culture encourages us to move on to the next thing. You can even hear jokes about a "starter wife" on popular TV shows. God wants you to fight for your marriages. And, if hard times hit, He desires you to reconcile because this is how He deals with you. He does not give up on you when you are unfaithful to Him. He paid the price so you and I could be reconciled to Him (2 Cor. 5:19).

Candi Finch

Prayer: *Spend time praying for people who may be struggling in their marriages. Ask God to be the glue strengthening Christian marriages.*

Personal Reflection: ....

Don't Waste Your Singleness!

1 Corinthians 7:32–34

⌒

"The unmarried woman cares about the things of the Lord,
that she may be holy both in body and in spirit." (v. 34b)

The current cultural climate usually paints the single life as a time where you can do whatever you want, sow your wilds oats, and live with complete freedom. Or, if you have watched any romantic comedies lately, the single life is viewed as a time of misery and loneliness until you find that one person to "complete" you. However, God's Word describes the single season in a very different way. God wants us to use our time of singleness to get to know Him and serve Him with unhindered commitment. Singleness is not a time to live for self or wallow in despair!

Being single is a season of life that **every woman** will experience at some point in her life, whether it is for an entire lifetime, just the time before marriage, or possibly as a widow. Thus, to think of singleness from God's perspective is important. Singleness is not a sentence to be endured but an opportunity to live for the Lord with unfettered devotion (v. 32).

If you are single, you don't know how long your single season of life will be. Don't waste that time pining for what you don't have right now! First Corinthians 7:32–35 says that your time of singleness allows you to be devoted to the Lord in a unique way because He can be your focus. Spend this season (for however long it lasts) deepening your relationship with the Lord and learning how to be holy, both in body and spirit (v. 32). And if you never get married, you have spent your life pursuing God—not a bad deal!

Learning to cultivate a spirit of contentment while single will only help you if you do get married someday (Phil. 4:11). Let me hasten to add that wanting to be married is not a bad thing at all. I am pro-marriage (and so is God)! Unfortunately, far too many women make marriage an idol in their lives, often making really bad decisions because they think being married will somehow complete or fulfill them. If the desire to be married (or any other desire) becomes more important to you than the desire to be obedient to the Lord, you have a problem! Being married to the wrong man is far worse than not being married at all. Don't waste your season of singleness thinking the grass is greener on the other side of the fence (in marriage). Each woman's ultimate contentment must be found in God and not in any human relationship.

Candi Finch

Prayer: *If you are married, would you pray for single women you know to view this season of life as an opportunity to grow closer to the Lord? If you are single, pray the Lord would give you a hunger to get to know Him better and deepen your relationship with Him.*

Personal Reflection:

Who Is the Head and What Does That Mean?

1 Corinthians 11:1–3

⌒

"But I want you to know that the head of every man is Christ,
the head of woman is man, and the head of Christ is God." (v. 3)

Even though the first verse completes the preceding chapter in 1 Corinthians, it may also be a bridge into chapter 11. Especially in challenging situations, we are reminded that by imitating Paul, we have a pattern for imitating Christ, which is the ultimate goal (v. 1). All should be imitating Christ, and the Lord does aid those who seek Him, not only in giving them understanding but also in guiding them to accomplish His purposes. In this way, Paul wisely laid the groundwork for his theological argument.

Man is called **the head of woman,** which in no sense implies inferiority of the woman of superiority of the man. This statement affirms the difference in role assignments coming from God's order of creation, reminding readers that the creation order is irrevocable and inviolable. Paul uses the relationship between God the Father and God the Son as a model for husbands and wives— equality in personhood (John 14:9) and distinction in office (John 14:28). Men and women were created in the image of God, and yet each is given a distinctive and meaningful assignment. This order is not a reflection of personal worth or value but is a statement of God's plan for a purposeful and effective relationship between the man and woman and the backdrop from which they together will accomplish His plan.

Every worker wants a job description explaining his assignments and a flow chart explaining the pecking order. Any lack of clarity in the organizational structure causes confusion and perhaps mistrust and harm. An honest presentation of this vital information prepares all for better understanding and greater productivity. Such order and authority is part of every area of life, even within the godhead (1 Cor. 11:3).

Women should be encouraged by this truth. The three persons of the trinity are equal in value and importance. However, functionally, their individual roles vary. If the persons within the godhead can find contentment and satisfaction in their roles, then we as women can take comfort in following their example without question or hesitation. Therein we find the basis for role differentiation among men and women in the home and in the church.

Male headship in the home and church is necessary because of its reflection of the relationship between God the Father and Jesus the Son. Men and women are given unique roles on how to accomplish that assignment. They are both created to reflect the image of God.

Dorothy Kelley Patterson

Prayer: *Ask the Lord to give you peace and the will to be obedient to the assignment that He has given you. Be encouraged by the example He has given to you through His own outworking of the Father's will.*

Personal Reflection:

Head Coverings—Fashion Statement or Church Wear?

1 Corinthians 11:4–10

"But every woman who prays or prophesies with her head uncovered dishonors her head, for that is one and the same as if her head were shaved." (v. 5)

Men and women in the ancient world wore robes. Head coverings became a clear distinction of gender. There is a difference between a biblical principle (the husband as the head of his home) and practical application (head coverings). In biblical times, a woman covered her head as a sign of her submission to her husband and of her commitment to his leadership. On the other hand, for a man to wear a head covering or for a woman to refuse to wear a head covering appeared to be a role reversal. Such reversal in roles was a refusal to accept God's personal directives for men and women.

Paul had previously linked the order within the family and church to the trinity of the godhead (1 Cor. 11:1–3). The first role reversal occurred when Adam failed to fulfill his leadership responsibility by protecting his wife from the deception of Satan. Eve also refused to submit herself to her husband's leadership and made her own willful choice to disobey God. Women have a tendency to reject submission, and men are prone to abuse authority.

Paul gives a rationale for asking women in the church to cover their heads:

- The covered head was symbolic of a wife's submission to her husband (1 Cor. 11:3).
- Refusal on the part of a woman was equal to the disgrace of a shaven head (v. 5).
- God's order of creation was the foundation for practical application. The man was created first and vested with the unique task of authority, and the woman was created as his helper (Gen. 2:15–18).

Seldom do I attend church or leave my home without a hat. Does this make me a biblical literalist or holier than women who do not wear a head covering? Here is my "personal theology of head coverings":

- I love hats as the ultimate touch of fashion to my ensembles. They hide my poor skills as a hairdresser, provide warmth, and protect from high winds.
- Paul's admonition is the practical, cultural application for the early church, affirming the unchanging biblical principle of the headship of husbands in the home.
- Because my husband and I live public lives, perhaps God instilled in my heart this love of hats so that for a sister who might take offense to the absence of a hat, I would have my head covered!

Focus on the principle, which in this case is the headship of the husband in the home. The application will work itself out in every setting and is left for the individual to determine.

Dorothy Kelley Patterson

Prayer: *Consider how to order your life with the main thing as always the main thing. Focus on what is most important, while still keeping your heart tender so that you do not become a stumbling block to others.*

Personal Reflection: ....

....

....

....

Who Needs Whom?

1 Corinthians 11:11–16

"Nevertheless, neither is man independent of woman, nor woman independent of man, in the Lord. For as woman came from man, even so man also comes through woman, but all things are from God." (vv. 11–12)

Paul describes the Godhead and creation (1 Cor. 11:4–11). He poses a question: Is it right for a woman to forsake her role and abandon her responsibility to reflect God and her husband in the right way? He follows with another supportive argument. God created the woman with hair, and her hair points to the glory of her role, while also serving as her covering.

The passage is clear. Whereas the symbol of authority can vary according to time and culture, the bedrock principle cannot. The principle of the husband's headship in the home, based on Scripture, is universal, expressing the creation order. This principle is well understood by church leaders and churches committed to doing things according to divine design. Men should behave as men and women as women. Neither should shirk role or responsibility, seeking to fulfill the position each was created to fill. In a unisex culture, men and women are to display their obvious differences for the purpose of bringing glory to God and His creation order. Any role reversal is a serious violation of Scripture, which will result in tragic consequences.

The natural sense of this passage establishes that there are boundaries and guidelines, which are consistent and not contradictory with the whole of Scripture. There is a clear distinction between theological foundations (headship and submission) and how these principles work themselves out in practical application (covering the head). Interpreters in every generation must build a bridge from the theological truth to relevant and practical application. The man and the woman have been interconnected from the beginning. They cannot accomplish God's purpose alone. Both are needed in the church and in the home.

Whether or not women are to wear pants or hats or short haircuts is not nearly as important a question as the outcome of coming to church looking and behaving like a woman. The divinely assigned differences of the respective genders must be acted out and embraced with purpose. Even a symbol may remind you of what you ought to do. The head covering should be embraced with gratitude and not arbitrarily rejected. If some other symbol is better suited, then legalism should not cause disruption in the fellowship. The theological principle of God's creation order has remained unchanged even though its specific application, such as the head covering for women in Corinth, has differed from culture to culture and place to place.

Dorothy Kelley Patterson

Prayer: *Consider in your heart God's creative purpose in your life. Find direction for how you accomplish that purpose as you spend time with the Lord. Put aside what you consider your rights and be aware that even your giftedness must come under His direction.*

Personal Reflection: ....

....

....

....

....

....

Do Spiritual Gifts Trump Scripture?

1 Corinthians 12:1–11

"There are diversities of gifts, but the same Spirit. There are differences of ministries, but the same Lord. And there are diversities of activities, but it is the same God who works all in all. But the manifestation of the Spirit is given to each one for the profit of all." (vv. 4–7)

What guidelines do you use to determine the appropriate areas of service for women? God has given us guidelines for ministry in Scripture (see 1 Tim. 2:9–15; 1 Cor. 11:2–11; Titus 2:3–5). Even so, many reasons are offered today to justify why women should be allowed to serve as pastors or in some capacity in the church, teaching men or serving in authority over men. If you believe that God's Word gives boundaries for women as they serve in ministry, then any reason offered for dismissing or overruling God's directives to women needs to bow to Scripture.

One common objection people offer for overturning any boundaries for women in ministry is related to spiritual gifts. Paul mentions about 20 different gifts in his letters, arranged in four passages (Rom. 12:6–8; 1 Cor. 12:1–30; Eph. 4:7–13; 1 Pet. 4:10–11). These gifts are not merely natural talents or human gift-edness. The Holy Spirit gives one or more gifts to every believer (1 Cor. 12:7, 11), and clear purposes are noted for these gifts: the common good or "for the profit of all" (v. 7); edification and equipping of believers (14:3–12); affirmation of the preached word—the gospel (14:24; Acts 1:8; Heb. 2:3–4); and cooperation among believers (1 Cor. 12:14–26).

Some believers point out that the lists of spiritual gifts in Scripture aren't separated by gender, and that is correct. Women can have any of the spiritual gifts but must use them in biblically appropriate ways. What about women who have the spiritual gift of teaching (Rom. 12:7; 1 Cor. 12:28–29) or administration or leadership (Rom. 12:8; 1 Cor. 12:28)? As with any spiritual gift, each believer is responsible for exercising those spiritual gifts as God has directed.

Paul corrected some believers in Corinth because they were not using spiritual gifts appropriately (1 Cor. 12—14).

Because I believe one of my spiritual gifts is teaching, I use it to teach women. A woman with the gift of teaching or leadership can have a valuable impact on the church while still staying within biblical guidelines. **At the end of the day, we must each decide what, or who, is our ultimate authority.** Then we must submit to that authority, lining up our experiences, opinions, and abilities under it.

Candi Finch

Prayer: *Thank the Lord for the spiritual gifts He has given you and pray He would give you the opportunity to use your spiritual gifts today to encourage and edify fellow believers.*

Personal Reflection: ....

....

....

....

....

....

....

Love: The Motivation for Ministry

1 Corinthians 13:1–3

~

And though I bestow all my goods to feed the poor . . .
but have not love, it profits me nothing." (v. 3)

Have you ever ministered out of pride and selfishness? If you have been a Christian for any length of time, you are probably guilty of doing just that. Here are some examples: God has given you the gift of discernment, but you rebuke new Christians who are learning to hear God's voice. God has given you the gift of teaching, but you use that gift to manipulate others and bring glory to yourself. God has given you the gift of faith, but you tear down others because their faith is weak. Do you see what I mean?

In previous chapters of 1 Corinthians, believers were self-absorbed, selfish, and full of self-love. They enjoyed exercising their spiritual gifts in public and even boasted that certain gifts were above others. In 1 Corinthians 12, Paul rebukes them for their divisiveness and then gives them a better, more profitable way to minister—out of love.

There is an idiom that says, "People don't care how much you know until they know how much you care." In describing love to the Corinthians, Paul uses the word *agapē* (God-like concern and love) to help the Corinthian believers understand how they were to minister. God wants you to serve Him, follow Him, teach His Word, and die for Him because you **love** Him.

Ladies, God is not fooled by your outward "Christian" mask. In fact, Paul makes it very clear that you could be known as one who speaks in other tongues, helps the poor, adept in knowledge, and even willing to die for your faith and still do those deeds out of self-glory and not out of love and affection for Christ. How heartbreaking it would be for us to one day see Jesus and realize that every ministry we engaged, every mission trip we took, every hungry mouth we fed, and every church service we attended was to exalt self.

So, how can we protect ourselves from being caught up in serving God for our own glory and fame? We must realize that all ministries will one day end

(1 Cor. 13:8–10). The day is coming when the need for prophecy, knowledge, and soup kitchens is complete. But, God's love will *never* end. We only have one shot on this earth. We have only one opportunity to get it right. We cannot fall in love with Jesus and not fall in love with the hurting people who are made in His image. God is looking for women who will minister, first out of a deep love for Christ and then others. My prayer is that we would be consumed by Christ's love.

Amanda Walker

Prayer: *Ask God to reveal the motives of your heart. Do you serve for self-glory or for God's glory? Commit to minister out of a heart of love instead of pride.*

Personal Reflection:

Love: The Foundation for Marriage

1 Corinthians 13:4–7

"Love suffers long and is kind; love does not envy;
love does not parade itself, is not puffed up." (v. 4)

These verses are often posted in our homes, our offices, and our churches. Many of you, including me, even had them read at your wedding ceremony. We appreciate these verses and the meaning behind them. But, day in and day out, do we actually live out these truths in our homes and marriages?

"God is love" (1 John 4:8). Love is not a characteristic of God. Instead, love is the very nature of God. In this passage, John uses the same Greek word for love (*agapē*) that Paul uses in 1 Corinthians 13. However, Paul actually defines what *agapē* love encompasses. It is patient, kind, not envious, not puffed up, not rude, not self-seeking, not easily provoked, and not a keeper of wrongs (vv. 4–5).

Many times, in my marriage, I do not exemplify these qualities. I am actually impatient, unkind, envious, conceited, and rude. I demonstrate love to my husband only when I feel love in return. I give only when I receive. Why? Because there is a fundamental disconnect between knowledge of love and my obedience to love. And, somehow, I do not think I am alone in my sin.

Agapē love must be the foundation for marriage. When we refuse to allow the Holy Spirit to teach us how to love, our marriages will never be what God intended. God desires for marriage to reflect the gospel message to a lost and dying world (Eph. 5:22–32). Since Jesus is patient, kind, not self-seeking, and not rude to me, then I must also model those attributes to my husband. It is impossible **really** to love and serve Jesus and not love and serve my husband. If my overarching desire is to do what Jesus did, then I must love as Jesus loved.

Does your marriage reflect an accurate depiction of the gospel message? When others look at the love you have for your husband, are they drawn to God or repelled by your example? Sister, God wants His love to be the foundation of your marriage. And, thankfully, He has not left you alone in this pursuit. He has given you His Holy Spirit to love your husband through you. If you are struggling with patience, kindness, rudeness, or anger, then God is here to help. Turn to Him. Rely on Him. Trust Him. And, allow God to do in your marriage what only He can do. Never forget, God created marriage, and He wants your marriage to blossom in His love.

Amanda Walker

Prayer: *If you are not demonstrating God's love to your husband, pray that God would teach you how to love your mate. Ask Him to convict you of areas that need to reflect His love. And then thank God for your husband. Commit to loving him as Christ loves you.*

Personal Reflection:

Love: The Nature of the Church

1 Corinthians 13:8–13

"Love never fails. But whether there are prophecies, they will fail; whether there are tongues, they will cease; whether there is knowledge, it will vanish away." (v. 8)

Have you ever walked into a church building and sensed that something was wrong? The people were pleasant; the building was well maintained; the pastor was well-educated and versed in sermon delivery; and the programs were first class. But, there was something missing. The longer you engaged the people, the more you realized the missing piece . . . they did not love each other.

The Corinthian church was full of gifted people. Scripture suggests they had incredible knowledge, faith, insight into prophesies, and could speak in other languages. But, they were self-absorbed and full of self-love (1 Cor. 13:1–3). There was dissension and division among the body, and, sadly, they were not concerned about it. In their discord, they missed one key truth from Jesus. He says, "By this all will know that you are My disciples, if you have love for one another" (John 13:35).

Jesus expects His followers to show love to each other and then to the world. If we are honest, sometimes it is easier to love and serve the world than it is to love and serve your fellow sisters in Christ. We assume non-Christians will respond with contempt, but we do not expect that from fellow believers. Therefore, we go about our church life—teaching a class, going to Bible study, feeding the poor, and exercising our faith—yet harboring anger, envy, and even hatred in our hearts. We go to the early service because that person goes to the late service. We teach a Sunday school class because we do not want to learn beside that woman. After a while, we begin to realize that our whole attitude is focused on self and self-love. And, Christ's love is nowhere to be found. Ladies, may this not be so!

The time has come for Christian women to stand up and begin to show love toward each other. The world needs to see that Christ's love actually makes a difference in us. We respond to accusations differently because we have a different Spirit in us. We respond to gossip differently because we have God's truth residing in us. We respond to discord with unity because we have the Spirit of oneness living in us. God's love for us does not end—praise the Lord! And, our love for each other should not end.

Where are you on the love continuum? Does your love for others reflect the love of Jesus, or do you stir up discord and strife in your church? My prayer is we would seek the greatest thing . . . love.

Amanda Walker

Prayer: *Pray God would give you His love for others. If you are involved in disunity, seek God's forgiveness and then the forgiveness of others.*

Personal Reflection: ....

....

....

....

....

....

....

....

Do Women Have to Be Silent in the Church?

1 Corinthians 14:33b–36

∽

"Let your women keep silent in the churches, for they are not permitted to speak; but they are to be submissive, as the law also says." (v. 34)

This controversial verse in Scripture grabs the attention of most women. In 1 Corinthians 11, Paul affirms women praying or prophesying in church, which would certainly involve opening their mouths and speaking. Then three chapters later, he tells women to keep silent; the Greek word literally means to "close their mouths." Is Paul contradicting himself? Absolutely not! The key to understanding this passage is making sure you understand what is happening between chapters 11 and 14.

Paul had previously affirmed women, acknowledging that men and women would receive spiritual gifts (1 Cor. 12). He encouraged all believers, both male and female, to use their respective gifts in ministry within the body. However, women as well as men were required to follow guidelines in church meetings. Specifically in chapter 14, Paul addressed how the church should exercise the spiritual gifts of tongues, prophecy, interpreting tongues, and judging prophecies since the Corinthians were facing chaos in church meetings as believers exercised these particular gifts (14:1–40). Paul was warning against disorder and disobedience (vv. 33, 40).

There are three possible interpretations for verse 34:

- Women were not to speak at all, which would seem to contradict the earlier passages where Paul commended the women who prayed and prophesied under the headship of their respective husbands (1 Cor. 11:5).
- This verse was addressed only to the Corinthians and to no other church beyond them, which would seem to unravel the entire point of the letter since Paul's instructions have been carefully presented with clear theological foundations and as principles transcending time. In

addition, Paul frames this passage by stating these principles are for all the churches (1 Cor. 14:33).

- The final interpretation is that women are to "keep silent" with respect to the activity under discussion, which is the judging of prophecies since this is a task of governing and exercising authority (vv. 28–32).

This final option is the one that seems to best fit the context of the passage. Women speaking out of turn and critically evaluating teaching or interpretations would show a lack of submission and a rebellion against God's order. Therefore, Paul instructed the women to hold their tongues and refrain from speaking in order to judge prophecies in the meetings of the congregation, which would involve exercising authority over men.

This command to keep silent does not reflect a prejudice against women. Undoubtedly, God gifts women with intellect, leadership ability, and spiritual gifts. The restriction is not based on inherent value or ability but on order when the entire congregation gathers together.

Candi Finch

Prayer: *This passage reveals a command for women to obey when they gather for worship. Ask the Lord to help you to obey Him today with a glad heart in all things.*

Personal Reflection: ....

....

....

....

....

Struck Down, But Not Destroyed

2 Corinthians 4:7–18

*"But we have this treasure in earthen vessels, that the excellence
of the power may be of God and not of us. We are hard-pressed on every
side, yet not crushed; we are perplexed, but not in despair; persecuted,
but not forsaken; struck down, but not destroyed." (vv. 7–9)*

Mary Webb, at the age of 21, organized the first woman's missionary society in 1800. Her ministry was remarkable not only because she was a woman but also because she had a crippling disease that had confined her to a wheelchair since early childhood. Her physical challenges prevented her from traveling to speak face-to-face with women, and she did not have cell phones and e-mails. Instead, Mary wrote thousands of letters. Even when some opposed her efforts, she continued serving the Lord by helping others on His behalf. Mary Webb learned to focus on Jesus and rely on God's power in the midst of distress.

What causes you the most discouragement when you are trying to follow and serve the Lord? The apostle Paul encountered severe trials because of his commitment to proclaim Jesus. We can learn from him how to cope with difficult circumstances without despairing or feeling destroyed.

Like Paul, we can focus our ministry on Christ alone, not ourselves (2 Cor. 4:5). Some of us tend to promote our own agenda and position instead of remembering that we belong to Christ. We must tell others what Christ has done in our lives, not highlight our own achievements.

Paul described believers as earthen vessels, jars of clay. Despite our frailties, God uses us to spread His good news and empowers us to do His work. Like Paul, we may be hard-pressed on every side like a fighter whose opponent pushes her into a corner. However, God's all-surpassing power, keeps us from being crushed. We may be perplexed, not knowing what to do, but God's power keeps us from losing hope. We may feel persecuted—hunted down like an animal—but God will not abandon us to any enemy or leave us solely to our own resources. We may be knocked down by opponents, but God's power keeps our service for Him from being destroyed.

How can you serve Christ in the midst of your own discouraging crises without giving up? Follow the examples of Mary Webb and the apostle Paul. Keep your focus on Jesus. Recognize God as the source of enabling power and stay in constant fellowship with Him. God is inwardly renewing you every day. Your difficulties are getting you ready for an eternal glory that will make all your troubles seem like nothing (vv. 16–17).

Sharon Gritz

Prayer: *Share with the heavenly Father your personal struggles and hurts in ministry. Ask the Lord to help you to keep your focus on Christ and recognize Him as your source of power.*

Personal Reflection: ....

....

....

....

....

....

....

What Is Your Life's Purpose?

2 Corinthians 5:1–11

*"Therefore we make it our aim, whether present or absent,
to be well pleasing to Him." (v. 9)*

Businesses do it. Schools do it. Organizations do it. Churches do it. Individuals do it. Have you done it? Have you ever written a purpose statement for your life? Such an effort helps define who you are—your strengths and weaknesses—and how you will live your life. It gives you a goal to pursue. It guides you in making decisions. It provides you with a focus and keeps your life "on track."

The apostle Paul clearly stated his life's ambition: he wanted to be well pleasing to Jesus Christ. The image behind the word "aim" (v. 9) suggests one who devotes herself zealously to a cause. Followers of Christ should desire passionately to please the Lord at all times. This decision requires an intentional commitment.

None of us knows how long we will continue to live at home in the body or whether we will soon die and be away from the body. However, what we must decide is how we will live in the present. Paul provided a motivation for behavior that pleases the Lord: all of us one day must appear before the judgment seat of Christ (v. 10). Though we receive salvation and eternal life as free gifts based on God's grace through faith in His Son, Jesus will still judge our lives. This judgment will determine the rewards we receive for how we have lived. Faith does not excuse us from obedience.

Paul's life purpose challenges us to evaluate our own lives. Are we pleasing to God? Are you? Perhaps this aim will force you to turn away from movies, television, and best-selling books that flaunt immorality and promote godless values. Pleasing God may lead you to adopt a simpler lifestyle or to live within your income. Such a goal may require you to evaluate your speech: Do you gossip? Do you brag? Do you criticize fellow believers?

Pleasing the Lord may call for more kind words, patience, forgiveness, and self-sacrifice in your home. This goal may encourage you to put the needs and interests of your family above your own.

Pleasing the Lord may involve integrity in your place of employment. Do you take office supplies or make photocopies for personal use? Do you take credit for work you did not do or waste time looking at social media?

Only the Lord knows what changes your life requires before it matches Paul's purpose statement. When you appear before Christ's judgment seat to give an account for how you have lived, will your life reflect the aim of pleasing Him?

Sharon Gritz

Prayer: *Seek the Lord's forgiveness for wrong priorities, for goals that focus on the temporary (recognition, your house, money, education, "stuff"). Ask God to show you specific ways that you can please Him in actions and attitudes at home, at church, in your neighborhood, and at work.*

Personal Reflection: ....

....

....

....

....

....

New Creations in Christ

2 Corinthians 5:12–21

"Therefore, if anyone is in Christ, he is a new creation; old things have passed away; behold, all things have become new." (v. 17)

I confess that I like **new** things—new clothes, new school supplies, a new recipe, even a new tube of toothpaste. I delight in the fact that God's mercies and compassion toward us are **new** every morning! I rejoice in knowing that my life reflects God's **new** act of creation through my faith in His Son, Jesus. Are you a new creation in Christ?

To be **in Christ** means being in union with Him. Oneness with Jesus indicates we are no longer God's enemies but His children. Jesus' death and resurrection make possible this bringing together, that is, reconciliation. Reconciliation takes place when we confess our faith in Jesus as our Lord and Savior after admitting our sin and asking for forgiveness. We commit our lives to Him. A new life begins with a personal transformation. We become a *new creation*. This change is great and radical. Only God can do this. The Lord does not reform our old nature—the old has gone. Our reconciliation with God results in His creative act, making us new persons on the inside. We enter into a new state of being. The indwelling Holy Spirit creates God's life in us. We are not merely making a fresh start or behaving in a better way. We are beginning a new life under a new Master, the Lord Jesus Christ.

Newness in Christ does not mean we no longer sin. We may still have ungodly actions, speech, and attitudes. If we confess these sins, God faithfully forgives us. However, being a **new creation**, means we have the possibility and power to live following the example of Jesus with the help of God's Spirit.

When I think of becoming a new creation in Christ, the caterpillar comes to mind. This insect spins a cocoon around itself and eventually emerges as a beautiful butterfly. Commitment to Jesus creates a lovely person inside of us! This new life should result in continuing, inward growth. As we mature in Christ, our external behavior will increasingly reflect that newness. Other people will notice the difference.

Have you allowed God to transform your life? Let Him create a **new** you through Jesus Christ as you accept Him as your Savior and Lord. Are you already a **new** creation in Christ? Look at yourself in a "spiritual mirror." Where are you spiritually compared to the last year, the last five years, and beyond? In what areas have you grown? Where do you still need work?

Sharon Gritz

Prayer: *Thank God for His transformation of your life, making you a **new** creation. Ask Him to show you those parts of your life that do not reflect identity with Christ. Confess your sins and recommit yourself to Him. Ask God to show you someone who needs **new** life in Christ and commit to share the good news with her.*

Personal Reflection: ....

....

....

....

....

....

....

Lessons Learned from Giving

2 Corinthians 9:6–15

~

> "So let *each one* give *as he purposes in his heart, not grudgingly or of necessity; for God loves a cheerful giver. And God is able to make all grace abound toward you, that you, always having all sufficiency in all* things, *may have an abundance for every good work." (vv. 7–8)*

My family is not one of particular means, but my father instilled in me from a very young age the importance of giving. On Sundays, he left for church before my sister and I woke, but he always left two crisp dollar bills on the counter for us to take as our offerings. He wanted us to learn to be excited about placing something in the plate. As I have grown older, God has continued to give me models of joyful giving. They have blessed my life immensely, and my understanding of what it means to be a cheerful giver has expanded.

One of these models has impacted my life in such a profound way because they have given so generously to me. They see giving as an investment in the kingdom, and the joy they receive from anonymously blessing others is so evident. Many times they met my need before I ever even voiced it. Because of their generosity, I have been able to give to others and share in that joy with them. Once, they approached me with a specific gift that the Lord had impressed them to give me for someone else. I was only the conduit. I was amazed at how their commitment to giving drew them so close to the Lord's heart that they were sensitive to the unspoken needs of people they didn't even know.

When we focus on accumulating things for ourselves, our eyes turn inward, and our ability to impact others is extremely limited. Giving is not about the amount but rather about our focus. Giving shifts our eyes upward and outward—toward God and others. Giving sacrificially requires acknowledging that everything comes from Him. Focusing on others means to prioritize the expansion of His kingdom over our own. Giving opens the door for God's provision to flow into our own lives, but more importantly it equips the church for good works and enables it to grow (v. 8; Mal. 3:10).

The family I mentioned has been able to be a part of God's provision not only in their community and their country but all around the world. When you purpose in your heart to trust God and give, you cannot imagine how much He will multiply the reach of your sacrifice! Of course, God desires that we give monetarily, but a cheerful giver also sacrifices of their time, talents, and other resources. If you have a home, open the doors to those in need. If you have a talent, use it to serve others. May God's grace abound in your life as He supplies all the church needs for "good works!"

Laura Landry

Prayer: *Thank the Lord for His sufficiency in all things. Ask Him to help you become a cheerful giver.*

Personal Reflection: ....

....

....

....

....

....

....

Taking Thoughts Captive

2 Corinthians 10:4–5

*"For the weapons of our warfare are not carnal but mighty in God
for pulling down strongholds, casting down arguments and every high
thing that exalts itself against the knowledge of God, bringing every
thought into captivity to the obedience of Christ." (vv. 4–5)*

Part of the Japanese war strategy against the Allied troops during World War II
was to capture English-speaking females and force them to broadcast false propaganda over the public airwaves. The generic name given to these women by
the GI's was "Tokyo Rose," and the radio broadcast was called "The Zero Hour."
During the broadcast, the women were forced to call Americans humiliating
names and tell lies such as that their wives and girlfriends back home were
being unfaithful or that they could not win the war so they should just give up
and quit or kill themselves. The entire purpose of the broadcasts was allowing
the Japanese military leaders to work their way into their enemy's psyche, ultimately demoralizing and defeating the Allies.

I have a friend named Cosimo Santillo, a WWII veteran, who actually
fought in the Pacific Theatre and experienced "Tokyo Rose" and the "The Zero
Hour" firsthand. In his memoirs of the war, he wrote about being in the jungles
of New Guinea when the Japanese placed hidden speakers in the coconut trees
that surrounded their foxholes. Every night as they tried to sleep, the voice of
Tokyo Rose rang out loud and clear, so that there was no escaping her harrow-
ing messages. To survive this experience and come out victorious, the Allied
soldiers had to take action. Cosimo wrote, "We heard the broadcast, but did
not know where her voice was coming from. . . . It took several days to find the
speakers, but once they were found, they were destroyed."

This strategy wasn't new to the Japanese in the 1940s, but rather the original "Tokyo Rose" is God's enemy, Satan, who for ages has attempted to demor-
alize God's troops using this tactic of false propaganda. Paul clearly explains in
2 Corinthians that it is not **if**, but rather **when** thoughts and conflicts against

the believer's knowledge of Christ arise, for survival's sake, those voices must be destroyed. How can you defeat the voices? Not with weapons of the flesh, but with the same tactic used by Jesus against Satan in the wilderness—prayer and the Sword of the Spirit, the Word of God.

What is the "Tokyo Rose" in your life? Are any false truths present in your life, clouding your vision of Christ or combating your mission from God? If so, identify those voices as coming from the enemy, and begin taking them captive unto Christ, the eternal Commander-in-Chief.

Courtney Veasey

Prayer: *Acknowledge Christ as being the One who fights both with you and for you in every spiritual battle. Ask for His weapons of warfare to be your defense at all times. Claim your victory in the power of Jesus.*

Personal Reflection: ....

....

....

....

....

....

....

Strength in Weakness

2 Corinthians 12:1–13

"My grace is sufficient for you, for My strength is made perfect in weakness." (v. 9a)

Have you received a dreaded phone call? I can still remember sitting on my bed listening to the unwelcome news that our friend's cancer had returned. As a teenager, the same age as my two friends whose Dad is battling cancer, I can't imagine what it would be like to hear that news.

We don't typically enjoy hearing the word "weakness." The word "weakness" brings with it a very negative connotation. I don't know about you, but when I hear "weakness," I think of sickness, inability, and even fear. Weakness is not a word that we speak of lightly in casual conversations.

In 2 Corinthians 12:10, Paul encourages us with these words: "Therefore I take pleasure in infirmities, in reproaches, in needs, in persecutions, in distresses, for Christ's sake. For when I am weak, then I am strong." In this significant passage, Paul encourages us to use our times of weakness and sorrow as an opportunity to grow closer to the Lord. We must realize that God allows weakness in our lives as an opportunity for us to become more intimately related to Christ.

This passage causes us to reflect on God's faithfulness in our own lives. We should be reminded that God can see the entire picture while we may only see a mere piece. Even though we may not know what lies ahead, He is our shield and protector. He knows what will happen both now and in the future. We can rest in His everlasting love.

I am glad that I can share this promise with my friends as their dad battles cancer. They can encourage him and others with this biblical truth. As we live in God's grace, our lives give testimony to the strength only He can give.

Whether you're struggling with cancer or are simply feeling weak, rest in the fact that when you turn to God as the ultimate healer and encourager, your weakness will be made perfect in Him. Only He can take an ugly, broken heart and make it beautiful!

Abigail Howell

Prayer: *If you are feeling weak today, enter into a time of prayer and reflection. Reflect on God's faithfulness in your life and how He may choose to use this hurdle to grow you in your intimacy with Him. Last, ask Him to enable you to find strength in His Word.*

Personal Reflection: ....

....

....

....

....

....

....

....

....

....

Struggles of a People-Pleaser

Galatians 1:1–12

"For do I now persuade men, or God? Or do I seek to please men?
For if I still pleased men, I would not be a bondservant of Christ." (v. 10)

Have you ever met a woman who would do anything to make others happy? Anyone who falls under that description could be given the title of a "people-pleaser." Now, it doesn't sound like such a bad title, does it? However, what most women don't realize is that pleasing people is not God's ultimate desire. The Bible says that if we try to please men, we are not servants of Christ (Gal. 1:10). In other words, servants of Christ would do anything to please Christ. When we are trying to please people, our focus shifts away from God. Think about it this way: When we die and stand before God, are all the people we "pleased" going to matter? No! When we stand before God in heaven, all that is going to matter is how we served Him and if we surrendered our lives to Him and His glory.

Most of us who are "people-pleasers" don't think about this concept. We just think we are "keeping the peace." As a 15-year-old high school student and a pastor's kid, I am surrounded by many different people around the clock. Being a "people-pleaser" myself, I have tons of experience in the field. Through my experience, I have learned three basic struggles that come with being a "people-pleaser."

First, not everyone will be pleased. No matter how hard we try, there will always be a person who is not pleased with us. Second, people-pleasing is a full-time job. Our thoughts and our lives are consumed by how we can please others. Everyday there is a new person and a new goal. After a few days of this, we are worn out, bringing us to the third and final struggle. During all of this, we are making ourselves miserable. We can't enjoy anything we do because we don't want to make someone unhappy. When all is said and done, we are tired and miserable, and the people we tried so hard to please are still unsatisfied.

What we don't realize is that all of this work is really taking us away from the One whom we should be trying to please. I am not saying that we should go around making people angry, but I am saying that our purpose is not to please people; it is to please and bring glory to God. So I would challenge you to ask yourself: "Whom am I trying to please? God or people?"

Rebekah Howell

Prayer: *Ask the Lord to open your heart to see clearly whom you are trying to please or impress. Seek His guidance and strength in this area of your life. Use your energy to please Him and bring glory to His name instead praise from others.*

Personal Reflection: ....

....

....

....

....

....

....

Crucified with Christ

Galatians 2:11–21

"I have been crucified with Christ; it is no longer I who live, but Christ lives in me; and the life which I now live in the flesh I live by faith in the Son of God, who loved me and gave Himself for me." (v. 20)

I don't know much about electricity. When I flip the switch, the lamp comes on. But what if it doesn't? Maybe the bulb is burned out. Perhaps the power is off at the main electrical supply station. Possibly, somewhere between my house and that location, the circuit has been broken by a falling tree limb. I get aggravated when I realize I have failed to plug the power cord of my lamp into the power source available in the wall. Sometimes I imagine an available power outlet carved into the foot of the cross and an unplugged cord there with plenty of slack. Plug into the power!

Power may be available but unused, or adequate power may be unavailable. A hair dryer runs on a 110-volt circuit, but a clothes dryer runs on a 220-volt circuit. Some things require more power to operate at their proper capacity. The Scripture "address" of our verse (v. 20) reminds me that I must plug into the higher power of the cross so that I can let my little light shine for Jesus! His power is available and adequate for all.

Jesus freely gave Himself to be crucified. He died in our place. We have been crucified "with" Him though only He died physically. We must die to our sinful desires. Jesus stood again on the third day having conquered the power of death by His own resurrection from the grave. We stand as a living sacrifice pouring out ourselves for Him.

The death of Christ set all who choose to trust in Him, including those of us who were yet to be born, free. Now, because of faith in the Son of God, we have Christ living inside of us. His power is in us and with us. Our assignment is to share that power through our lives with others who need Jesus.

After Hurricane Katrina, I visited my Gentilly Baptist Church family in New Orleans. Pastor Ken Taylor was baptizing two new believers. Their sanctuary was being refurbished so they were meeting in the gym. They used a hose to fill their portable baptistery. The candidates used a step ladder to climb into the pool. When the first man lay back completely under the water and then stood up, he drew an unforgettable picture of dying and being raised with the resurrection power of Jesus. That baptistery looked just like a coffin, but its picture was not of death but new life in Christ.

Becky Brown

Prayer: *Pray asking God to help you stay plugged into the power of the cross and to be light in our dark world.*

Personal Reflection: ....

....

....

....

....

....

....

....

The Significance of Galatians 3:28

Galatians 3:26—4:7

⤚⤙

"There is neither Jew nor Greek, there is neither slave nor free,
there is neither male nor female; for you are all one in Christ Jesus." (v. 28)

Galatians 3:28 is one of the most debated verses concerning the role of women because people want to use it erroneously to argue that Christ abolished gender roles in the home and church. To understand this verse properly, you must consider its context within the book of Galatians. This verse is found in the midst of a discussion on how a person is saved—whether it is by keeping the law or through justification by faith. After Paul left, a group of people had infiltrated the churches in Galatia and were teaching salvation requires belief in Christ plus circumcision (Gal. 2:11–21). However, Paul rejects such a notion and boldly proclaims that these people were perverting the gospel of Christ (1:7).

Paul then builds a case for the Galatians to show them that even in the Old Testament a person was saved, not by keeping the law, but by faith in the promise to come (3:7). After Christ came, a person is still saved by faith, though his faith is in the work that Christ accomplished on the cross (3:11). Whether a man or a woman, a slave or a free person, a Jew or a Gentile, a person is saved the same way, by placing his faith in Christ.

Why is it so important to establish the context of this verse? As stated above, this verse has been used to argue that there are no longer distinctions in social relationships; specifically, there are no distinctions in gender roles between men and women. However, Paul was discussing the nature of salvation and not the proper social relationships of men and women in or out of the church and home. The interpretation of this passage cannot be separated from its context or from the other letters of Paul, which clearly set forth distinct responsibilities for husbands and wives (Eph. 5:22–33; Col. 3:18–19) and some distinct responsibilities for men and women in the church (1 Tim. 2:11–15; Titus 2:1–5). When studying Scripture, a verse should not be pulled out of context or used for another meaning that is not faithful to the text. The text must speak for itself.

Paul's assertion in Galatians 3:28 clearly does not obliterate social or role distinctions. Rather, the impartial nature of God's love is affirmed in salvation (Acts 10:34–35). At the foot of the cross, each person is the same–a sinner in need of salvation. Fully equal in essence and worth before God, women and men receive the same grace, must adhere to the same obedience, and experience the same blessing of being recipients of spiritual gifts, yet they still have some distinct functions in the family and church.

Candi Finch

Prayer: *Praise God for salvation that is available to every person because of Christ's perfect sacrifice on the cross.*

Personal Reflection: ....

....

....

....

....

....

....

....

Don't Feed the Flesh—Walk in the Spirit

Galatians 5:16–21

$\backsim$

"I say then: Walk in the Spirit, and you shall not fulfill the lust of the flesh." (v. 16)

When I was a young girl, the horror movie *Gremlins* hit theaters. You may not have seen the film (it was pretty scary when I was a kid—I am not recommending it!), but it tells the story of a dad who gave his son Billy a unique creature called a *mogwai* (imagine a weird-looking teddy bear/koala). There were three strict rules the son had to obey in order to take care of his new pet: (1) Don't get it wet; (2) Don't let it near bright light; and (3) Never ever feed it after midnight. As you may suspect, Billy doesn't follow the rules, and his new pet transforms into many evil gremlins that wreak havoc on the small town of Kingston Falls. The image of those gremlins has stayed with me for many years because the story took a decidedly frightening turn as soon as young Billy broke the rules and fed his pet after midnight.

When I became a Christian and read Galatians 5:16–21, I recalled the movie. You see, every believer is redeemed; we have been set free from being slaves to sin (5:1). However, until we get to heaven, we can still be tempted by our sinful desires. Our flesh wars against the Holy Spirit inside of us (v. 17), and too many times instead of walking in the Spirit, we make the mistake of feeding our flesh, which can lead to disaster in our lives, much more serious than anything portrayed in the movie *Gremlins*.

Our "flesh" does not simply refer to our physical body. It includes the mind, will, and emotions, which are all subject to sin. The works of the flesh (vv. 19–21) are sins that characterize all the unredeemed, though not every person manifests all these sins to the same degree. The flesh opposes the work of the Spirit and leads the believer toward sinful behavior. So, when a believer feeds and gives in to her sinful, fleshy desires, she ends up looking more like a lost person than a saved person. Believers do have a choice—they can be led by the Spirit, which results in righteous behavior and spiritual attitudes; or they can try to be good in their own strength, which does not have the power to help them resist the flesh (vv. 17–18).

The good news is that all believers have the presence of the indwelling Holy Spirit as the personal power for living to please God. Paul encourages believers to make it the habit of their lives to walk in the Spirit (v. 16). Walking implies progress; as a believer submits to the Holy Spirit's control, she will grow in her spiritual life.

Candi Finch

Prayer: *Ask the Lord to help you walk in the Spirit today and not feed your flesh or give into any sinful temptations.*

Personal Reflection: ....

....

....

....

....

....

....

The Fruit of the Spirit

Galatians 5:22–23

"But the fruit of the Spirit is love, joy, peace, longsuffering, kindness, goodness, faithfulness, gentleness, self-control. Against such there is no law." (vv. 22–23)

"The fruit of the Spirit" refers to behavior produced by the Spirit of God. These nine characteristics, attitudes, or behaviors are so inextricably linked that they are all commanded of believers throughout the New Testament. These traits are manifestations of the presence of the Holy Spirit at work in a believer and are the best evidences of the changed life brought about when a person accepts Jesus Christ. There is no law or need for one to prohibit them from being exercised in a person's life. Unlike speeding for cars, which need laws to regulate it, the fruit of the Spirit never needs restricting or limiting. There is no such thing as too much love or too much patience.

Love is a purposeful act of selfless giving for the good of others. Biblical love expects nothing in return (Luke 6:35); it enables us to love even our enemies. Jesus tells us that people will know whether or not we are Christians by the way we love each other (John 13:35). **Joy** refers to rejoicing, in spite of circumstances, because we know that God is in control. **Peace** is a sense of calm even in the midst of adversity because we trust God (Phil. 4:7). **Longsuffering** means patience; literally it is a willingness to suffer or be long-tempered versus being short-tempered.

Kindness was displayed by Jesus when He interacted with the woman caught in adultery (John 8:1–11). He treated her with compassion and fairness; while He did not condone her sin, He corrected her with love and kindness. **Goodness** refers to a quality of moral excellence or an uprightness of life; a person exhibiting goodness can be counted on to do the right thing in the right way. **Faithfulness** is a fruit displayed in a person who is trustworthy and dependable, and **gentleness** or meekness is strength under control because a person has genuine humility before God (Matt. 11:29). The final fruit, **self-control,** refers to what happens when a person allows her passions and appetites to be controlled by the Holy Spirit instead of by the flesh (Rom. 7:15–25).

The truth with each fruit of the Spirit is that all are most evident when it is most unnatural for us to exhibit them. Most people would expect a person to dislike an enemy, but a person controlled by the Holy Spirit will love an enemy. A person who displays joy even in trials (James 1:2–3) or peace in the face of adversity or kindness when people are unkind or patience in the midst of difficult days testifies to the power of the Holy Spirit in her life and is a wonderful witness for the gospel.

Candi Finch

Prayer: *Ask the Lord to cultivate the fruit of the Spirit in your life today.*

Personal Reflection: ....

....

....

....

....

....

....

Cultivating the Character of Christ

Galatians 5:24—6:5

~

*"And those who are Christ's have crucified the flesh
with its passions and desires." (5:24)*

Growing up in Florida, I couldn't escape a love for oranges because in certain parts of the state, there were orange groves as far as the eye could see. As the fruit developed from a fragrant blossom to a ripened fruit, a sweet smell infused the air, and anticipation rose as hopes for a delicious, refreshing crop grew alongside the budding fruit. The first bite of a ripe orange was so satisfying! The tang and sweetness was a delight and offered refreshment in the midst of the humid Florida spring and summers.

The fruit of the Spirit can be just as refreshing, if not more so, when demonstrated in our lives (Gal. 5:22–23). When we allow the crop of love, joy, peace, longsuffering, kindness, goodness, faithfulness, gentleness, and self-control to flourish in our own lives, people will be drawn to Christ. However, this fruit of the Holy Spirit is something that should be cultivated in our lives with even more care than a Florida orange.

Just as the farmers have to tend the trees in the groves, feed and water the soil, and protect the crop from insects and predators so the oranges can thrive, believers must take care to grow the right crop in their lives. This simple fact cannot be escaped: you cannot grow fruit if you are not being fed and nourished. Just as good soil and proper watering can allow an orange tree to produce its delicious fruit, believers must be fed and nourished on the Word of God—this is part of walking with the Spirit (v. 16). As you plant God's Word in your heart and meditate on it and allow it to pervade your thoughts, love, joy, and the other fruit of the Spirit can bloom in your life.

However, if you are instead feeding yourself on worldly thoughts, habits, and actions, then the "fruit" produced in your life will look more like the lusts of the flesh (vv. 19–21). What we sow and plant in our lives is what we will reap. A farmer cannot plant orange trees and expect to get apples. In the same way, we cannot plant the seeds of discord and sin in our lives and expect to produce patience and self-control. Just as Paul told the Galatians that those who are Christ's have "crucified the flesh with its passions and desires" (v. 24), believers today must stop feeding their flesh and instead feast on godly things.

Candi Finch

Prayer: *Are you nourishing your walk with Christ with godliness and protecting your life from enemies that would seek to stifle any growing fruit in your life? Pray that you would be on guard today, feeding and cultivating the right kind of characteristics in your life.*

Personal Reflection: ....

....

....

....

....

....

....

....

Don't Grow Weary in Doing Good

Galatians 6:6–18

⌇

"And let us not grow weary while doing good, for in due season we shall reap if we do not lose heart." (v. 9)

Have you seen the commercial in which a woman is in the waiting room of a doctor's office? The receptionist calls her name because the doctor is ready to see her. Instead of jumping up and heading into the examination room, the woman asks the receptionist to wait a few minutes while she completes a work assignment. Why? Because the wireless Internet is so fast in the doctor's office, she is getting a lot accomplished. The next frame of the commercial is of the doctor waiting for *her* and asking, "Is she ready yet?"

For many people who have endured lengthy wait times in a doctor's office, this commercial pokes fun at the reverse of the conventional. But, in a culture of instant gratification (thanks to smart phones, microwaves, and Google), waiting is not something most of us do well, no matter what side of the appointment we are on.

In this passage, the apostle Paul cautions the Galatian believers to hang in there for the long haul. He uses a sowing-and-reaping metaphor to describe the Christian life as a process that takes time. Instant results are not to be expected.

Farming is not for the impatient, especially when the hopeful planter starts with seeds. She has to prepare the soil by weeding, tilling, fertilizing, and **then** has to water and wait for the seed to germinate. And when sprouts begin to break through, she has to wait even longer for the actual fruit of her labor to be ready for harvest.

When the harvest begins, the farmer is assured of one thing: she will reap what she sowed. If she sowed corn, she'll have corn to show for it. The same goes for tomatoes, turnips, and tulips. "Do not be deceived, God is not mocked; for whatever a man sows, that he will also reap. For he who sows to his flesh will of the flesh reap corruption, but he who sows to the Spirit will of the Spirit reap everlasting life" (vv. 7–8). Oh, that we would be planting to the Spirit!

What if a farmer loses heart before the time to harvest? Perhaps he stops watering his crops or maybe he quits pulling weeds. Before long, the plants begin to wilt or get choked out by crabgrass and pigweed. No! The farmer needs to be aware that the growing season cannot be rushed just as believers need to wait on the Lord and "not grow weary in doing good."

Judi Jackson

Prayer: *Ask the Lord to give you patience to hang in there for the long haul. Thank Him for His constant presence and comforting peace. Pray for strength to push through the weariness so that you will be ready for the times of harvest.*

Personal Reflection:

The Work of the Holy Spirit

Ephesians 1:1–14

*"In Him you also trusted, after you heard the word of truth, the gospel
of your salvation; in whom also, having believed, you were sealed
with the Holy Spirit of promise, who is the guarantee of our inheritance until the
redemption of the purchased possession, to the praise of His glory." (vv. 13–14)*

If you are a follower of Jesus Christ, you can testify to certain events that have
taken place in the past:

- Around A.D. 33, Jesus Christ died on a cross, was buried, and rose from
  the grave (Matt. 27:45—28:8).
- As Christ promised, seven weeks later the Holy Spirit was sent on the
  Day of Pentecost (John 14:16–17, 26; 15:26–27).
- At some point in your life, you "heard . . . the gospel" and "believed"
  (Eph. 1:13).

Ephesians 1:1–12 elaborates on what God has done already for those who have
trusted in Christ. These past events, however, continue shaping the present and
secure your future.

Verses 13–14 utilize at least two vivid metaphors—using a seal and making a down payment—to demonstrate why your new life in Christ is absolutely
secure in both the present and the future. When you trusted Christ, "you were
sealed with the Holy Spirit." In the ancient world, a king or his official representative pressed a carved object, commonly a signet ring, into melted wax to
create a seal (see 1 Kin. 21:8; Esth. 8:8). The picture or design left in the wax
to close or mark a document served to authenticate, certify, and authorize its
words. A seal conveyed ownership and authority, as well as the unquestioned
security of both. Taking up residence in the life of a Christian, the Holy Spirit
likewise marks the believer as a child of God who belongs to the Lord (see

Rom. 8:16–17). The Spirit's presence proves you are "under new ownership" because Christ has paid the redemption price (cp. Col. 1:13).

In addition, the Holy Spirit is "the guarantee of our inheritance." His presence in the believer's life is compared to a **down payment**. When buying a house or car, for example, you give the seller a portion of the purchase price as a pledge or guarantee that the remainder will follow. The Spirit's residence ensures that Christ's promises of eternal life (John 3:16; 4:13–14) and of His return (John 14:1–3) are certainties.

You can count on Him to fulfill these promises. In fact, "all the promises of God in Him *are* Yes," and God "also has **sealed** us [who are in Christ] and given the Spirit in our hearts as a guarantee" (1 Cor. 3:20–22; cp. 5:5).

Tamra Hernandez

Prayer: *Thank the Lord that in Christ, your salvation is secure. Thank Him for the presence of His Holy Spirit in your life today—the indisputable proof of your salvation and the guarantee of eternal life for every tomorrow.*

Personal Reflection: ....

....

....

....

....

....

The Glory of the Gift

Ephesians 2:1–9

"For by grace you have been saved through faith, and that not of yourselves; it is the gift of God, not of works, lest anyone should boast." (vv. 8–9)

Many women in the strip clubs on Bourbon Street give a warm welcome to the church ladies of the Inward Ministry. But some of the ladies are offended by our visits to their workplace, seeing only judgment and condescension in our presence.

Sometimes the latter response is more about the Holy Spirit at work in them than anything in us. But sometimes we become a stumbling block to the gospel. Our hearts may be deceitful, and we may be vulnerable to the sin of pride in our salvation. It may not come out in a spoken word or even a conscious thought, but we can steal the glory that belongs only to God.

Self-examination is an important discipline in our preparation for sharing the gospel, whether in a strip club, a coffee shop, or our backyard. When we ask the Holy Spirit to search us, we are reminded that our salvation is a gift from which no work or worth of our own could obtain.

Even our faith is not our work. We could never conjure up the faith required to believe that Jesus Christ is the Son of God who died for our sins and rose on the third day in triumph over death. If we could on our own find those events credible, we would still fall short of "faithing" that His actions could have anything to do with us. It's all just too unbelievable. The faith through which we receive the gift of grace is itself a gift.

Humbled by this truth, we fall to our knees thanking God for the gift of salvation. We remember that we are the saved, not the Savior. We are the needy, not the philanthropist. We bring a gift that was given, not crafted or purchased by us.

The glory of a gift always belongs to the giver. We all are in desperate need for salvation because we all "fall short of the glory of God" (Rom. 3:23). The crazy thing is that when we believe this truth through the faith given by God, and we are sanctified by the Holy Spirit of God, we actually obtain that from which we fall short and are prone to steal—the "glory of our Lord Jesus Christ," the Son of God (2 Thess. 2:13–14). God accomplished our salvation in this way so that we cannot judge or be condescending because we cannot claim His glory as our own.

Christi Gibson

Prayer: *Ask the Holy Spirit to show you if there is any deceit in your heart causing you to take even a smidgen of credit for your salvation. Fall to your knees and give Him the glory for saving you by grace through faith.*

Personal Reflection:

Grace That Works and Works of Grace

Ephesians 2:10–22

"For we are His workmanship, created in Christ Jesus for good works, which God prepared beforehand that we should walk in them." (v. 10)

Becoming a work of art is not a painless experience. The potter kneads the clay. The editor marks through lines of the poem. The needle pierces the tapestry. Sometimes when God is working things together for our good, it feels more like He is working us over forever.

Being God's workmanship is of great and eternal value. The word here, *poiēma*, is translated in Romans 1:20 as "the things that are made." It is the means by which God's invisible attributes, including his eternal power and deity, are understood. If I am God's *poiēma*, created in Christ Jesus for good works, then my walking in those works may be the means by which someone comes to understand that God is God. That's powerful! Those works that God has prepared for me are much more than a simple "honey-do list."

God's beautiful and wonderful artistry and creativity in our workmanship serves a profoundly practical purpose. He prepares works for us beforehand, and He prepares us beforehand for those works. He works every single little detail about us into our design, and He uses it for His glory.

God formed us in our mother's womb. So everything in our nature—our personality, our natural abilities, our inherited traits—is a part of His workmanship. You are where you are on the introvert-extrovert scale because of the works that God prepared for you beforehand. You have the voice, the hands, the eye for color, the ear for music that you have because those things equip you to walk in His works.

God placed us into the surroundings and the lives in which we live. Our socio-economic status, family unit, country-of-origin, educational opportunities, personal abilities, and even the hardships we have endured, have built into us the perseverance, character, hope, and humility that we need to walk in a manner that is worthy of our calling.

But the "pièce de résistance" in our equipping for good works is our spiritual giftedness. Spiritual gifts are the supernatural icing on the cake, which manifests the Spirit and turns all glory to God in everything that we do, from making the bed to ministering healing to the person lying in it. In your giftedness, God has given you something to be, something to do, and plenty to show it's not about you! Your gift mix comes alongside your nature and life experiences to equip you in a unique masterpiece that bears the Father's signature. Seeing His hand in your design and His assignment in your works is what takes your life from daily grind to eternal glory.

Christi Gibson

Prayer: *Praise God for His unique workmanship in you. Ask Him to show you the works He has prepared for you today and to give you the strength to walk in them obediently and expectantly.*

Personal Reflection: ....

....

....

....

....

....

....

Corrupt Words or Edifying Grace

Ephesians 4:25–32

"Let no corrupt word proceed out of your mouth, but for what is good for necessary edification, that it may impart grace to the hearers." (v. 29)

Paul filled his letter to the church in Ephesus with guidelines for the Christian life and relationships with others. This passage focuses primarily on the role of the Holy Spirit in the believer's life. Three commands conclude the passage, two **do not's** and one **do**. **Do not** say anything that will hurt someone, and **do not** do anything that will hurt God (vv. 25–29). Christians are not to "grieve the Holy Spirit of God, by whom you were sealed for the day of redemption" (vv. 30–31). And, **do** be kind and forgiving to others as Christ has forgiven you (v. 32).

Are you surprised by the behaviors which grieve the Holy Spirit? The specific ones mentioned are: bitterness, wrath, anger, clamor, and evil speaking. Obviously these sins cause the Lord pain, and they also harm others. Evil speaking is addressed directly in verse 29: "Let no corrupt word proceed out of your mouth, but what is good for necessary edification, that it may impart grace to the hearers." Words are powerful! They can destroy the hearer or encourage her. One who is a true follower of Christ will imitate Him and speak words of love, concern, and comfort. In fact, we should never speak a word that would hurt or discourage anyone. That is difficult from a human perspective. With the help of the Holy Spirit, we can be kind and encouraging as we speak.

Think about the words you have spoken today. Have you spoken kind words in a loving way? Has your speech been pleasant and uplifting to others? Or have you spoken critical, negative words which hurt and discouraged them? Unfortunately, those we love the most often receive our harshest tones and cruelest words. The Bible is clear that our words to family, friends, and foes should be grace gifts of God's goodness. What a promise that our words can actually help and heal those we love!

Ephesians 4:29 is the theme of the book *Silver Boxes* by Florence Littauer. She writes that words should be gifts from the speaker to the listener, not just ordinary gifts but special: "Our words should be gifts to each other, little silver boxes with bows on top."* What an important truth for Christian women! Our carefully chosen words of encouragement can be a very special gift to others. On the other hand, words carelessly spoken can cause hurt and humiliation.

No money is required to be kind and speak with love. God's gift of grace freely given to you can be given freely through your speech. Do you want to be a gift giver or a gift taker?

Rhonda Harrington Kelley

Prayer: *Ask the Lord to help you speak only words that will encourage and edify others. Now wrap your silver box and put a bow on the top!*

Personal Reflection: ....

....

....

....

....

....

....

* Florence Littauer, *Silver Boxes: The Gift of Encouragement* (Dallas, TX: Word Publishing, 1989), 4.

Redeeming the Time

Ephesians 5:1–21

⌇

"See that you walk circumspectly, not as fools but as wise,
redeeming the time, because the days are evil." (vv. 15–16)

Christians have a responsibility to use our time wisely for the Lord; our time is actually entrusted to us by God to manage well. Our time is not our own; it belongs to Him. Whether you are a student, a business professional, a stay-at-home mom, or a senior saint, I imagine you can think of times when you have not made the most of your time. Consider the following steps to start REDEEM-ing your time:

Realize your purpose on earth. The first step is realizing that we are here to make Christ known to others and advance His kingdom. It is easy to get distracted with the "everyday-ness" of life and forget that God has a purpose for us here in this life. If we get so busy or distracted that we miss opportunities to share the gospel or serve someone in His name, then something needs to change.

Evaluate your priorities and how you spend your time. It is hard for me to tell people "no" when they ask me to do things, but then I end up over-committing myself. Does that happen to you? Instead of doing a few things with excellence, I end up doing a lot of things "just okay." It is important to consider all the things on your plates to evaluate if something really shouldn't be there.

Determine to change areas where you are not using your time wisely. It may seem simple, but this step is where many women drop the ball. After you have evaluated your priorities, if you do not make changes, then you have missed the mark.

Eliminate distractions. I don't know what your distractions are—Facebook, Pinterest, shopping, TV, sleeping—but I do know that you will never be able to accomplish all that you want if you allow distractions to rule your life.

Enlist help. Accountability is crucial! My sister has been a great help to me when I am trying to stay on task. I let her know what I am trying to get done and the steps I am taking to eliminate distractions, and then she checks in with me to make sure I am actually following through. Find people in your own life who will help you redeem your time.

Manage your time well. You must remain vigilant in guarding your time. That doesn't mean you never take a day to relax, but I think many of us have lost our urgency in being about the Father's business. I encourage you regularly to examine your life for ways to make the most of the time God has entrusted to you.

Candi Finch

Prayer: *Are there things that need to change in the way you manage your time or possible distractions that need to be eliminated? Pray the Lord will give you wisdom about how best to redeem the time He has given to you.*

Personal Reflection:

Marriage: A Visible Sign of an Invisible Reality

Ephesians 5:22–33

∽

"Wives, submit to your own husbands, as to the Lord. For the husband is head of the wife, as also Christ is head of the church; and He is the Savior of the body. . . . This is a great mystery, but I speak concerning Christ and the church." (vv. 22–23, 32)

Spiritual things are best understood through what we can see with our eyes, hear with our ears, taste with our tongues, smell with our noses, or hold in our hands. The Lord God, fully aware that our human limitations would keep us from knowing Him in all His glory, gives us all kinds of material evidence to show us what He and His kingdom are like. He knew we mere mortals would need help in order to "get it." If we pay attention, we can collect the evidence and find out more about Him—His creativity and omniscient omnipresence, His desire to save us from our sin, His ability to make us holy, and His eagerness to draw us to Himself. Such material evidence can be considered a *sacrament*, a word that means a visible sign of an invisible reality.

In the fifth chapter of Paul's letter to the Ephesians, we read a very specific example of how an earthly representation helps us understand an invisible reality. Paul writes about how the marriage of a man and a woman represents the mystery of the union between Jesus Christ and the church, a union between God and humankind.

We who are married become actors in a mystery play. In the Middle Ages, traveling troupes of actors went from village to village, setting up portable stages in the town squares. The people were illiterate and could not have read the Bible stories even if they had had Bibles (which they did not), so the players acted them out. The visible characters, props, and actions, and the audible dialogue portrayed the invisible truths of the Christian faith.

In the mystery play of marriage, the characters have already been cast, and they are not interchangeable. The husband has been given the role of the head. It is not by his choice (or the wife's), and it is not by his achievement or by popular vote. The wife has **not** been given the role of the head, anymore than the church has been given the position of Christ Himself. It has nothing to do with which partner in the marriage is smarter or more spiritual. (Nor does it have to do with Paul's personality quirks, by the way.) Human marriage represents an eternal reality. It's sacramental in the fullest sense of the word.

Elisabeth Elliot

Prayer: *Consider the truth God is trying to depict through Christian marriages. Spend some time praying today for married people you know (include yourself if you are married), praying specifically that those marriages would point people to the eternal reality of the way Christ loves the church.*

Personal Reflection:

An excerpt from Elisabeth Elliot's *Be Still My Soul* (pages 59–61).

Praying for Your People

Philippians 1:3–11

*"I thank my God upon every remembrance of you, always in every
prayer of mine making request for you all with joy . . . that He who has begun
a good work in you will complete it until the day of Jesus Christ." (vv. 3–6)*

Who are your people? Who holds your heart, fills it, and sometimes breaks it? Whose name makes it into every conversation you have with God? Who do you love so much it hurts?

Paul had the people in the church at Philippi in his heart (v. 7) and in every prayer (v. 4). He longed for them "with all the affection of Jesus Christ" (v. 8). The old King James translates "affection" more graphically as "bowels." Paul loved them "with all his guts" and let go of them in prayer. He thanked God for these "through-thick-and-thin" friends with whom he probably shared some not-so-pleasant memories. Paul was grateful every time they came to mind because he was confident that God was always at work in them—perfecting and completing them until the day of Christ.

Our instinct with those we love is to intervene and protect them, even if it means getting in God's way. We can inadvertently keep them from the good that the Father wants to do in them. Because of deep affection, we surrender our people to God's good training—even when it hurts.

Paul prayed joyfully that his people's love would abound—abundantly, beyond standard measure. He didn't ask for a naive love, but for one overflowing with knowledge and discernment. It's like the Father's love for us. He loves us knowing the good, the bad, and the ugly! This is the best kind of love—even though it hurts.

Finally, Paul prayed that his people would be filled with the fruits of righteousness, sincere and without offense. Are we diligent in asking God to keep our loved ones from being harmed, yet neglecting to ask Him to keep them from doing harm? Let's plead for our people's hearts to be pure and sincere—it is the divided heart that hurts others. We must pray for humility over ambition, self-sacrifice over gain, and willingness to be last, over eagerness to be first.

Paul prayed that his people would surrender to God. If we imitate his prayer for our people, we will let go of protecting them from growing, to sheltering them from knowing pain, and of dreaming for their best showing. Letting go is to the glory and praise of God (v. 11). What better prayer can we pray for our people—that their lives would be lived to give glory and praise to our almighty, most holy God?

Christi Gibson

Prayer: *Thank the Lord for your people and for always being faithful to finish your work in their lives even when you don't always understand what He is doing.*

Personal Reflection: ....

....

....

....

....

....

....

Esteem Others Better Than Yourselves

Philippians 1:12—2:4

*"Let nothing be done through selfish ambition or conceit, but in lowliness
of mind let each esteem others better than himself. Let each of you look out
not only for his own interests, but also for the interests of others." (2:3–4)*

During my second year of seminary, I took a course called "The Bible in the
Professional Counselor." My professor was convicted that we could become professionals who counseled with the power of Scripture if the Word of God dwelt
within us. The primary learning objective of the course was memorizing the
entire book of Philippians, a task which seemed impossible at the outset. As a
means of encouragement, our professor showed pre-recorded testimonies of
others who had already completed the course and successfully internalized the
text. Each one spoke of how God would bring to mind a relevant verse at just the
right time to convict, guide, or instruct.

As I began to memorize Philippians, God brought these verses in chapter
2 to my mind consistently. I could not escape His admonishment to put down
self ambition or His encouragement to consider the needs of others before my
own. I recall a time when standing in the check-out line at Walmart, I was
annoyed by how few cash registers were open during the superstore's rush hour.
I became more frustrated as the line inched along, thinking of all the better
things I could be doing with my valuable time. We've all been there, right?
Then, a woman with a screaming baby got in line behind me. As I glanced
back at what I sarcastically considered "the icing on the cake," I noticed the
exhausted mother.

A voice in my head began to whisper, "Esteem others better than yourself"
and then, "Look out not only for your own interests" (2:3–4). I only had a few
items in my basket, and the mother's cart was loaded down with everything
from bacon to toilet paper. I smiled at her, offering to let her take my place in
the line. Her face softened and tears filled the dark circles under her eyes. God

struck me with the reality that my conceited attitude almost caused me to miss out on the opportunity to minister to someone who needed His love.

As I loaded the woman's groceries onto the belt, she comforted her baby, and I pondered how insignificant my sacrifice was in view of Christ's sacrifice for me. He gave up a place in heaven, not a spot in the check-out line! As a church, we are called to put down our individual grievances and focus on ministry as a unified body. As individuals, we are called to unselfishly consider others for the sake of advancing the gospel.

Laura Landry

Prayer: *Ask the Lord to help you put on humility and become more focused on the interests of others. Thank Jesus for setting an example of selflessness by giving up His rightful place for you.*

Personal Reflection: ....

....

....

....

....

....

....

The Mind of Christ

Philippians 2:5–11

"Let this mind be in you which was also in Christ Jesus ..." (v. 5)

Human rights, animal rights, the right to life, the right to die, inalienable rights, the Bill of rights, the Equal Rights Amendment—you have heard about all of these and perhaps more. How many more rights could you add to the list? In our society, rights are highly valued.

Now think about what we do with our rights (other than talk about them). We exercise them, protect them, invoke them, defend them, fight for them. Our rights can be violated, contested, honored, forfeited, suspended, or upheld. However, one of the most challenging aspects of daily living for a Christian desiring to please God is surrendering to the Lord "**my** rights."

Those **rights**—areas you tend to withhold from the Spirit's inspection—include a perceived right to the privacy of your own thoughts. Yet God already knows your thoughts (see Ps. 139:1–12; Matt. 9:4). In order to grow in Christ-likeness, you must allow the Spirit to change the way you think (cp. Rom. 12:2).

Philippians 2:5–11 summarizes Jesus' pattern of thinking by describing the way He exercised His rights to be God. He never denied His identity as the incarnate Son of God. Instead, Jesus asserted and powerfully demonstrated His divine authority. However, Jesus denied Himself—i.e., chose not to exercise His rights as the Son of God—and took up our cross (cp. Luke 9:23). He "made Himself of no reputation" or, more literally, "emptied" Himself. A picture of the opposite is someone described as "full of himself" because of his pride or arrogance.

Jesus adopted the mind-set of "a bondservant," one who disregards personal interests in order to serve someone else. When a Roman soldier commanded Jesus to carry his equipment for a mile, Jesus carried it two miles (cp. Matt. 5:41). When the disciples neglected to arrange for the washing of feet before the Passover meal, Jesus laid aside His robe and took up a slave's garment to wash their feet (John 13:1–17). In the garden of Gethsemane, He "became obedient to *the point of* death," praying "Father, if it is Your will, take this cup away from Me; nevertheless not My will, but Yours, be done" (Phil. 2:8; Luke 22:42).

Today, if you allow the Lord to change your ways of thinking, substituting the mind of Christ for your thought patterns, what changes will result—in how you think about your rights, in your decision-making, in your relationships, in how you respond to others when they are inconsiderate?

Tamra Hernandez

Prayer: *Surrender your thoughts to the lordship of Christ. Ask the Lord to replace sinful thought patterns with Christ's mind-set marked by servanthood and humility. Ask Him to let you see at least one of the results that brings glory to His name.*

Personal Reflection:

Without Complaining

Philippians 2:12–16

"Do all things without complaining and disputing." (v. 14)

Sometimes I convince myself that I can do it all. I can work a full-time job and be a wife, a mother, a daughter, a friend, and a spiritual counselor. I can "bring home the turkey bacon and bake it up in the oven and serve it on a BLT with a butter lettuce bun." I am woman. I can do it. Sometimes.

But without complaining? I fail abysmally at this one again and again. I am not "blameless and harmless . . . in the midst of a crooked and perverse generation" (v. 15). I have not shone as a light in the world. Even when I do manage to bite my tongue and hold back the complaining words, God knows them before they form on my lips. He hears my complaining heart.

Philippians is full to overflowing with exhortations to rejoice and be joyful. Paul writes this affectionate letter from the midst of his own suffering to his dearly beloved brothers who are also suffering—and he offers joy. This reaction sheds some important light on his edict: "Do all things without complaining or disputing" (v. 14). There is no joy-stealer more effective than griping, grousing, and grumbling as we go.

"Complaining" does not refer to speaking out in truth against injustice or things that are not right. This complaining is a muttering under the breath with a secret discontent, the exact opposite of serving with a glad heart. The disputing doesn't have to be an open argument because the complainer sets her own heart against itself. Doing says "yes." Complaining says "no." It is an inward contradiction that is confusing and distressing.

Doing all things without complaining makes us "blameless and harmless" (v. 15). Our actions are to be pure and simple, without the defects of deceit and mixed motives. We cannot make a difference in this "crooked and perverse generation" if our hearts are not sincere. Do you believe Paul's words in 1 Corinthians 13? To do anything at all without love, which is the purest of motives, is to do more harm than good. Those murmurings under our breath are suddenly louder than a clanging gong or clashing cymbal.

So how do we bring peace to that inner argument? There's a great tool that will help you change the place where your thinking dwells (Phil. 4:8). Don't bother to pack your boxes, just move right on over to dwelling on what is true, noble, just, pure, lovely, of good report, virtuous, and praiseworthy. If you will practice "doing" from this new place, your heart will change. You will find rest from that inward battle. You will have joy in the doing.

Christi Gibson

Prayer: *Allow the Lord to tune your ear to hear the grumblings of your heart and replace them with rejoicing. Ask Him to make you blameless and harmless so that your doing is a song of praise instead of a clanging cymbal.*

Personal Reflection: ....

....

....

....

....

....

....

Euodia and Syntyche—Complaining Christians

Philippians 3:17—4:3

*"I implore Euodia and I implore Syntyche to be of the same mind
in the Lord. And I urge you also, true companion, help these women
who labored with me in the gospel, with Clement also, and the rest
of my fellow workers, whose names* are *in the Book of Life." (4:2–3)*

Conflicts and controversies in churches are not new. In fact, each of the letters of the New Testament was written at least in part because of some problems going on within the churches that was being addressed. Paul's letter to the Christian fellowship in Philippi demonstrates this truth. He first brings to light an issue of disunity taking place in the church,

> Therefore if *there is* any consolation in Christ, if any comfort of love, if any fellowship of the Spirit, if any affection and mercy, fulfill my joy by being like-minded, having the same love, *being* of one accord, of one mind. *Let* nothing *be done* through selfish ambition or conceit, but in lowliness of mind let each esteem others better than himself. Let each of you look out not only for his own interests, but also for the interests of others. (Phil. 2:1–4)

Later, in Philippians 4:2–3, Paul names three people in the congregation, particularly two women, who are involved in the conflict.

Who are Euodia and Syntyche? These two common first-century names are mentioned only in this brief reference. We know nothing more about these two women. Yet in what little Paul says about them, he actually speaks volumes to the church (then and now) about how to deal with interpersonal conflict. Notice that he doesn't bring up the specifics of the argument, and he doesn't take sides or make accusations. He simply acknowledges outright that a dispute has taken place and reconciliation is needed. Further Paul reminds the church of the support and aid these women gave to him in the past and demonstrates his respect for them in so doing. But most important, Paul reminds them that their names are written in the Book of Life, and thus God loves and accepts them, and so should the church.

Although it's easy to view those with whom we disagree as opponents rather than real people, we Christians seem to forget that the story is never over for anyone when God is the One writing the script. As you consider Paul's pastoral example in dealing with conflict at Philippi, let it be an encouragement to you to be a promoter of unity in your own church and to help your fellowship stay focused on the ultimate task of bringing the message of Christ to a lost and dying world.

Courtney Veasey

Prayer: *Praise God for the foundation of unity we have in Jesus Christ. Ask Him to help you to be an agent of peace both in the Christian church and in the pagan world.*

Personal Reflection:

Be Anxious for Nothing

Philippians 4:4–9

≈

"Be anxious for nothing, but in everything by prayer and supplication, with thanksgiving, let your requests be made known to God; and the peace of God, which surpasses all understanding, will guard your hearts and minds through Christ Jesus." (vv. 6–7)

Anxiety, or worry, is a daily struggle. We are constantly worrying about what is next. Recently, I began asking myself: What does the Bible say about worry? "Which of you by worrying can add one cubit to his stature?" (Matt. 6:27). This verse is simply saying: What good does worrying do? The answer to this question is commonly known—nothing. So, why worry if we know it does not accomplish anything?

I came upon one possible answer as I was evaluating my own life: We do not trust God. Most of us would deny this right away. In fact, I had a hard time admitting this was true in my life; but I kept thinking, if I totally trust God with each day and trust that He knows what is best for me, why do I still worry? The challenge for us is not how to avoid being anxious; it is a matter of complete trust in God.

In my dad's sermon a few weeks ago, he said, "Do not worry about tomorrow because God has already been there." This statement prompted me to think of the tests I take in school. I always look for a friend who took the test before me in order to ask her if it was hard or if she was unprepared for anything surprising. In my mind, this would ensure I was ready for everything. In our relationship with God, He has the knowledge of all, and we know that He is going to take care of His friends or, in this case, His children. We have nothing to worry about.

"In everything by prayer and supplication . . . let [our] requests be made known to God; and the peace of God . . . will guard [our] hearts and minds" (Phil. 4:5–7). This passage tells us to share our fears, thoughts, and questions with God through prayer. We are to tell Him our worries and anxieties. God already knows our thoughts. He knows what we are going to say before we say it (Ps. 139:1–4), so why not share it with Him? Telling God about our struggles and fears is a great release and one of the most revitalizing things we can do. An instant feeling of peace washes over us.

Next time you are anxious, or worrying about what is next, stop and make your worries and thoughts known to God. He is the only one capable of relieving you of your anxiety and providing the peace you need.

Rebekah Howell

Prayer: *Ask God to help you trust Him. Ask Him to give you peace in those times of worry and anxiety. Stop and share with Him your fears and thoughts and ask Him your questions.*

Personal Reflection: ....

....

....

....

....

....

....

True Contentment

Philippians 4:10–23

⌒

". . . For I have learned in whatever state I am, to be content." (v. 11b)

"Contentment" is a word most of us enjoy hearing. Perhaps the word has such a positive connotation because we associate contentment with being happy. However, the world's definition of contentment is backwards. The world says that contentment is a perfect combination of happiness and tranquility. If you listen to the world, you will be consumed with the lie that you can truly find contentment by exploring and pursuing material things and pleasant emotions.

Our world portrays contentment as being found in money, fame, sex, and alcohol. The world also implies that contentment cannot be found in the home or in a relationship with Jesus Christ alone. For women of God, the temptation to listen to the world's definition of contentment is a daily internal struggle. Ultimately, the devil and our own selfish desires create the struggle that we are left to fight.

As a pastor's daughter, there is always the possibility of moving. In my family, we have had the privilege of living in both places that we loved and places that we would not have chosen for ourselves. In difficult ministry circumstances, it was crucial for me to put my contentment in the Lord because if I were looking for contentment in my present circumstances, then I would have felt lost and empty.

The world's definition of contentment **is** backwards. True contentment is *not* found in material possessions or ever-changing emotions. Instead, Jesus Christ is the only one who can fulfill your longing for contentment.

True contentment comes from surrendering everything you have to the only One who can satisfy your need. True contentment is fully accepting where God has put you and committing to honor and glorify His name even in the midst of a storm. True contentment starts with your surrender of selfishness and pride. Only then will God open your eyes to the bountiful blessings He has already poured into your life. Only then will you be able to rejoice in hardships, confident that His plan is perfect and that His definition of contentment is true—"I have learned both to be full and to be hungry, both to abound and to suffer need" (v. 12). Only when your heart is fully surrendered to Him will you be able to accept with outstretched hands whatever He brings your way.

Abigail Howell

Prayer: *If you are desperately searching for contentment, surrender your life to Christ and His plan for your life. Thank the Lord throughout the day for what He has already done for you, for what you have (and do not have), for what you may have been taking for granted, and for His strength to choose His definition of contentment over that of the world.*

Personal Reflection: ....

....

....

....

....

....

....

....

What Do You Mean by Submission?

Colossians 3:18–21

~

"Wives, submit to your own husbands, as is fitting in the Lord. Husbands, love your wives and do not be bitter toward them." (vv. 18–19)

People are always asking me this. What **is** this business of **submission** you're always talking about? We're not really very comfortable with this. Seems kind of negative. Sounds as though women are not worth as much as men. Aren't women supposed to exercise their gifts? Can't they ever open their mouths?

I wouldn't be very comfortable with that kind of submission either. As a matter of fact, I'm not particularly comfortable with any kind, but since it was God's idea and not mine, I had better come to terms with what the Bible says about it and stop rejecting the whole thing just because it is so often misunderstood and wrongly defined. I came across a lucid example of what it means in 1 Chronicles 11:10: "Now these *were* the heads of the mighty men whom David had, who strengthened themselves with him in his kingdom." There it is. The recognition, first of all, of God-given authority. Recognizing it, accepting it, they then lent their full strength to it, and did everything in their power to make him—not them—**king**.

Christians—both men and women—recognize first the authority of Christ. They pray, "Thy will be done." They set about making an honest effort to cooperate with what He is doing, straightening out the kinks in their own lives according to His wishes. A Christian woman, then, in submission to *God,* recognizes the divinely assigned authority of her husband (he didn't earn it, remember, he received it by appointment). She then sets about lending her full strength to helping him do what he's supposed to do, be what he's supposed to be—her **head**. She's not always trying to get her own way. She's trying to make it easier for him to do his job. She seeks to contribute to **his** purpose, not to scheme how to accomplish her own.

If this sounds suspiciously like some worn-out traditionalist view, or (worse) like a typical Elisabeth Elliot opinion, test it with the straightedge of

Scripture. What does submission to Christ mean? "Wives, submit yourselves to your husbands, **as to the Lord**" (Eph. 5:22). Compare and connect.

Elisabeth Elliot

Prayer: *Do you struggle with the idea of submission—the idea that a wife is commanded to yield herself willingly in love to her husband's authority? Consider the other commands of "submission" in the Bible—the church submits to Christ (Eph. 5:24); believers should submit to God (Heb. 12:9), spiritual leaders (Heb. 13:7) and governing authorities (Rom. 13:1, 5); and children should submit to parents (Eph. 6:1–3). Ask the Lord to help you see this matter from His point of view and pray for Christian wives to honor the Lord through submission to their husbands.*

Personal Reflection: ....

....

....

....

....

....

....

An excerpt from Elisabeth Elliot's *Keep a Quiet Heart* (pages 85–86).

Whatever You Do, Do as unto the Lord

Colossians 3:22–25

"And whatever you do, do it heartily, as to the Lord and not to men." (v. 23)

Do you know women who feel inferior because they do not seem to have the kind of talents that make people gush? I often encounter women who minimize the giftedness that they have because it is not one of the "up-front" gifts like teaching or singing. I love to point them to this verse and its context for a source of encouragement.

Paul was primarily addressing these words to those who were slaves. He admonished them to obey their masters for all of the right reasons, including reverence for the Lord. He sums it up by the inclusive phrase from which we can all learn. No matter what our calling, talent, gender, aptitude, strength, or circumstance, we should strive to work with all of our hearts for one excellent reason. We are working for the approval of the Lord, who has placed us in our particular role and setting at this particular time in history for a very specific reason. We may not know on this side of heaven what all that entails. What we do know is that we must do the very best we can to work heartily—not sloppily or with a sense of drudgery.

This post-Christian society and interesting era are teeming with increasing pressure to jettison what the Bible clearly teaches about God's plan for the family. It serves us well to meditate on this verse and its context even as we seek to swim upstream against the prevailing opinion of our day. The timeless truth of God's Word reminds us of the joy and subsequent reward that is ours, not in fighting for the same roles and functions that men have, but in embracing the good work we have to do even as we thank God for giving us the strength and means to do it.

So, the next time you feel unnoticed or unappreciated in the work that you are so diligently doing, take heart! The Lord knows if your motivation is for the praise of others, and you are thus often disappointed. He made you to fulfill a specific purpose. Be "all in"! Work as unto the Lord!

Mary K. Mohler

Prayer: *Think about what it must have been like to be owned by a master who could order you around day and night. Would these words from Paul have been welcome to them? Take time now to thank the Lord that you are not under bondage and that slavery in this country has been abolished. As you think about your long "to-do" list and its seeming monotony or maybe its difficulty, will you ask the Lord to enable you to work as unto Him, even in the little things, and to do so with a happy heart? Remember, you were bought with a price that can never be repaid.*

Personal Reflection: ....

....

....

....

....

....

....

....

Does Prayer Matter?

1 Thessalonians 3:6–13

∽

"For what thanks can we render to God for you, for all the joy with which
we rejoice for your sake before our God, night and day praying exceedingly
that we may see your face and perfect what is lacking in your faith?" (vv. 9–10)

Does prayer matter? The apostle Paul thought so. In nearly every one of the Holy Spirit-inspired personal letters penned by Paul in the New Testament, he specifically mentions praying for others and being prayed for by his readers.

Around A.D. 51, Paul embarked on his second missionary journey with Silas (Acts 16—17). First, they traveled through Lystra and Derbe (towns in Asia Minor, modern-day Turkey). They chose a young believer named Timothy as a ministry companion. Timothy would become Paul's **son in the faith** as they journeyed together. Next, during a time of prayer, God spoke to Paul through a vision to relocate this team to Macedonia (modern-day Greece). After major victories in Philippi, they traveled to Thessalonica. Our Scripture passage for today was a prayer written for the Thessalonians.

These prayers of Paul were proof of his deep, abiding relationship with God through Jesus Christ. Prayers were his anchor to the Rock of Ages in the vast ocean of his ministry life. His letters were written to individuals, to churches, and to geographical ministry points. Paul recorded deeply personal prayers of gratitude as well as requests for guidance and growth. Along the way, Paul was also teaching Timothy the eternal value of prayer, establishing his relationship with God as a young pastor.

Does prayer matter? Jesus the Messiah thought so. The gospels describe how Jesus regularly withdrew from the crowds, often spending entire nights alone in prayer and communion with His Father. Jesus offered blessings at mealtimes. He prayed for healings. He prayed as He was dying on the cross. He taught His disciples to pray using a model we have named "The Lord's Prayer." I treasure what I call "MY Lord's Prayer" as recorded in John 17. In verse 20, Jesus prays specifically for me . . . and YOU!

Does prayer matter? Missionaries today think so. Many are prayed for specifically on their birthdays. They wait to make major life decisions on their birthdays, knowing they are being prayed for by believers all over the world. Prayer connects believers with each other as they hold the hand of God.

Does prayer matter? In July 2014, NBC News reported that people spend an average of 40 minutes per day on Facebook. In October 2014, Ed Stetzer, executive director for LifeWay Research, said, "Most people pray when they need the 'red phone' for help, but their prayer life isn't a habit rooted in a relationship with God." Ask God to keep your "face" in His "book" as you bow the knees of your heart in His presence. Prayer matters. God is listening.

Becky Brown

Prayer: *Does prayer matter to you? I hope so. Spend time in prayer now, renewing your commitment to a daily quiet time with the Father.*

Personal Reflection: ....

....

....

....

....

....

....

Whetted Appetites

1 Thessalonians 4:1–8

*"For this is the will of God, your sanctification: that you should abstain
from sexual immorality . . . that no one should take advantage of and
defraud his brother in this matter, because the Lord is the avenger of all such...
For God did not call us to uncleanness, but in holiness." (vv. 3, 6–7)*

Elisabeth received a letter from Jim Elliot while they were dating:

> Since you left it has been as if a film has been over my soul. My
> genuine fervor in prayer was gone for two days. Too much rubble so
> that I couldn't get to building the wall. I must confess to you, Bett,
> that I have had regrets about going even as far as we did in physical
> contact, and that was very little as most judge. We must guard
> against this if we are ever together again, for it gave me a whetted
> appetite for your body that I have found to be "rubble" in getting to
> the work.

Elisabeth, reflecting upon Jim's letter, wrote:

> That "film over my soul" that Jim wrote about, those "regrets about
> going even as far as we did in physical contact," that "whetted appe-
> tite," that "rubble"—what about all that?

A question of chasity. An outmoded word, the world says, but the truth
is it's a Christian obligation. It means abstention from sexual activity. For the
Christian, there is one rule and one rule only: total abstention from sexual
activity outside of marriage and total faithfulness inside marriage. Period. No
ifs, ands, or buts.

The physical contact Jim referred to was my taking his arm when we
walked, our sitting with shoulders tightly pressed together, and on one occasion

as we sat on a park bench his suddenly stretching out on his back with his head in my lap. My fingers entwined his hair.

Chaste means "not indulging in unlawful sexual activity." Who would accuse us of having done so? We were trying to live honestly before God, not before any worldly tribunal. . . . We recognized that we were strongly drawn toward each other. There were "butterflies" when we were near. Those perfectly human, natural appetites were being whetted with every slightest touch, and the idea of even a single short kiss seemed like heaven itself.

Honesty required us to admit that we could not be sure precisely where the "line" **should** be drawn, and it was a potentially unmanageable force we were dealing with. Chasity meant for us not to take lightly any least act or thought that was not appropriate to the kind of commitment we had to God. For God called us to holiness, not to impurity.

Elisabeth Elliott

Prayer: *Ask the Lord to help you identify and repent of any areas in your life where you are toying with sexual immorality. Pray for strength to resist temptation and to pursue holiness.*

Personal Reflection: ....

....

....

....

....

An excerpt from Elisabeth Elliot's *Passion and Purity* (pages 122–26).

Keep Praying

1 Thessalonians 5:12–22

༄

"Pray without ceasing." (v. 17)

The church of Thessalonica, although a new church, remained faithful to God in the absence of Paul and those who mentored them. What a positive imitation of Christ and the apostle Paul. "Faith is the substance of things hoped for, the evidence of things not seen. For by it the elders obtained a *good* testimony" (Heb. 11:1–2).

"We give thanks to God always for you all, making mention of you in our prayers, remembering without ceasing your work of faith" (1 Thess. 1:2–3). Paul complimented the Thessalonians, who testified of their strong faith in the midst of persecution, to those in the surrounding regions.

Paul shows concern for the church as the challenges become more difficult. Timothy is commissioned to go strengthen and encourage their faith. Paul shares his joy over Timothy's great report regarding their steadfast faith in God. His greater concern included the ability of the enemy of the faith to divide and conquer them, leaving no evidence of the work invested by Paul's ministry.

The Thessalonian church received more encouragement from Paul to add to their faith. They were reminded that we will take part in the resurrection and live with Christ forever. Jesus our Lord and Savior encouraged Martha, Lazarus's sister, accordingly: "I am the resurrection and the life (John 11:25–26).

The return of Christ serves as our greatest source of comfort (1 Thess. 4:18; 5:11). In chapter 5, the conversation shifts to when Christ would return. They were assured of their position as saints. They were instructed to stay alert, watching and waiting for the return of Christ, wearing the breastplate of faith and the helmet of salvation, completely adorned and protected. Until Christ returns, the perfect survival kit is included: "Rejoice always, pray without ceasing, in everything give thanks" (vv. 16–18).

Since entering my senior season, my walk with the Lord is more challenging—with limitations and adjustments, I am moving toward a mental state of retirement. Overwhelming odds and a spirit of exhaustion are trying to replace my grit and tenacity to finish strong for Christ. My source of strength is my present discipline of journaling prayers, for more than 500 days consistently. Spending longer hours on my knees, and a 5 o'clock morning meeting with the Lord, changes my daily perspective. As trials surmount and confusion ensues, my entering into His gates with thanksgiving and His courts with praise transforms my finite outlook (Ps. 100:4). My mind moves from daily cares to heavenly desires. I release my mountaintop view to serve fully the saints in the valley. Each day the process starts all over again. Prayer consistency is my necessity to preserve a thankful heart and a sustained relationship with the Savior of my soul. Jesus Christ is the hope of my salvation.

Elizabeth W. Luter

Prayer: *If your faith is wavering back and forth during trying times, you may consider a greater prayer life. Spend time now with the Author of Life who can bring stability and strength.*

Personal Reflection: ....

....

....

....

....

....

Is It Judgmental to Tell Someone She Is Wrong?

2 Thessalonians 2:5–12

"And with all unrighteous deception among those who perish, because they did not receive the love of the truth, that they might be saved." (v. 10)

I have three daughters and a baby boy. I was told that each child would have a unique personality but am just now beginning to see the depth of their distinctiveness. My oldest daughter is eight years old; she has a strong sense of justice coupled with a great desire to see people come to Christ. Not long ago she asked Laura, one of the girls in our neighborhood, if she knew about Jesus. Laura replied, "Not really. My family isn't religious." Mary Grace sat down and began to read aloud from her Bible with the hopes that Laura would want to know more about Jesus. A week later the girls were playing again, and Mary Grace posed the same question to Laura: "Do you know about Jesus?" Laura's response came quick: "My dad said that we don't believe in that and that this is private. I don't have to talk to you about Jesus any more."

Mary Grace's little heart was crushed because she knows the result of not having a relationship with Jesus: "For the wages of sin *is* death, but the gift of God *is* eternal like in Christ Jesus our Lord" (Rom. 6:23). This doesn't sound very nice or kind, does it? The culture in which we live promotes ideas like acceptance and tolerance, allowing everyone to believe anything as long as we are all getting along! And yet we know that Jesus said: "I am the way, the truth, and the life. No one comes to the Father except through Me" (John 14:6).

The heart-wrenching reality is that many with whom we cross paths each day live in a state of deception. They do not know the truth of Christ or the message of the Gospel. We often shy away from speaking the truth out of fear of hurting their feelings, though 2 Thessalonians 2:10 gives us the truth. The question is this: Am I more concerned about momentary emotional discomfort or eternal damnation and separation from God?

Jesus is the way of salvation! To truly love another is to share this message with every breath we breathe until we have none left. This love is of the greatest kind, that they too may "receive the love of the truth and may be saved" (v. 10).

Kristin Yeldell

Prayer: *Do you have someone in your life like young Laura who does not know Jesus? Pray today that God would so fill your heart with His love that you would be unable to remain silent with the message of the Gospel. Ask that God would give that person eyes to see Christ's sacrifice for him on the cross, ears to hear His love, and a heart to receive His truth.*

Personal Reflection: ....

....

....

....

....

....

....

....

Woman-to-Woman Mentoring

2 Thessalonians 3:6–9

⌒

"For you yourselves know how you ought to follow us,
for we were not disorderly among you." (v. 7)

Are you a woman who can say to other believers, "Follow me?" Paul said exactly that! It was a bold statement, but Paul was a bold Christian. He was reminding the believers at Thessalonica to remember how he lived above reproach while he was with them in order that he might make himself an example to them (v. 9). This teaching was not new from Paul but a reminder of his previous encouragement that they were to imitate the lives of the apostles (1 Thess. 1:6).

The word "follow" (Gk. *mimeisthai*—from *mimos*, a "mimic") means to "follow an example, or imitate." Paul never claimed to be perfect, but he knew he had to show congruence between what he said he believed and how he lived his life. Paul didn't just expect this of himself, but he calls us to the same standard (1 Thess. 2:14; 1 Tim. 4:12; Titus 2:7). He expects us to strive to live lives that can be emulated. The context of the lives of women often suggests the word "mentorship."

In Titus 2:3–5, Paul speaks specifically to older women, encouraging them to live their lives so that they may have the credibility and platform to impact the women of the next generation. They were to do this through their own example and by their teaching.

Can you also say, "Imitate me, just as I also *imitate* Christ" (1 Cor. 11:1)? This is truly the essence of mentorship. Is it possible that women make mentorship too complicated? (Probably not, because we never do that, right?) Mentorship is really just one woman following after Christ who invites another woman to come on the journey with her. This journey may take the two of them to a cozy coffee shop or it may consist of a chat over heaping piles of laundry accompanied by several "little helpers."

When examining mentorship, we need to examine the "how" and the "who." The "how" of mentorship can vary depending on your season of life.

Look for opportunities to invite women into your everyday life so they can see how you follow Jesus.

Then consider the "who" in your life. The Lord is faithful to guide as we seek Him in each season and identify who we are to bring on this journey of faith. Sometimes this may be many women. Other times this may be one. For young moms, there may be seasons where your only disciples are your children. Remember, your children are your first priority for discipleship. Pouring into anyone else is just a bonus during this season!

Meredith Bone Floyd

Prayer: *Ask the Lord if you are living your life worthy of being imitated. What are the areas in which you are not following after Him? Ask the Lord to use you in the lives of your children and with other women as He allows.*

Personal Reflection: ....

....

....

....

....

....

....

Modesty Is a Choice

1 Timothy 2:9–10

"... That the women adorn themselves in modest apparel." (v. 2:9a)

Modesty is a difficult subject to discuss. Unfortunately, the number of people who oppose modesty far outweigh the number of people who support it. My own high school generation has generally ignored modesty and considered it insignificant.

The world tells us that we should wear what makes us feel confident and sexy with no concern for what honors the Lord. However, Scripture teaches that the way in which we dress should be a reflection of Christ in us and not a distraction. What we choose to wear can either bring honor or disgrace to God. Women who wear immodest clothing miss out on three things. Let's look at these more closely.

First, women who wear immodest clothing are stealing. It is no secret that God made men and women differently. God designed men as visual human beings. Therefore, when you walk past a gentleman in your tight pencil skirt and he lusts after you—you have taken his purity, stolen his godliness.

Second, you are not representing the One you profess to worship. If you have asked Christ into your heart, then parade yourself around the beach in a skimpy swimsuit, you are causing others to gaze at you, not Christ in you. First Timothy 2:9 strictly informs us to adorn ourselves in respectable apparel with modesty and self-control. Self-control is choosing clothing that will demand the respect you deserve as a daughter of the King, not subject yourself to the lusts of the flesh.

Third, when you choose to dress immodestly, you are not seeking to attract a godly man. I know many girls who choose to wear skimpy clothing simply to attract a male. The fact of the matter is that wearing poorly chosen clothing will attract a male, not a man of God, worthy of your time or energy.

Choosing modesty is a difficult daily decision. It is not the popular decision in our culture nor is it the default. Modesty is not about a set list of rules and regulations. It is a question of what your heart is clinging to—a love for Jesus or a love for things in the world. Modesty is rather a daily question in which you ask yourself first, "Does this piece of clothing honor Jesus?" and second, "Does this piece of clothing draw attention to my countenance rather than my body?"

While modesty is not easy, it is rewarding to know that you are glorifying God in what you wear. As women in Christ, we are called to represent Him and to make the hard decisions in order to do so. Let's bind together and support one another in the quest for modesty.

Abigail Howell

Prayer: *Ask the Lord to reveal to you His standards for modesty. Reflect over your life, and ask the Lord to help you choose clothing that will bring honor to His name.*

Personal Reflection: ....

....

....

....

....

....

The Best Mind-set for Learning

1 Timothy 2:1–15

༄

"Let a woman learn in silence with all submission." (v. 11)

In this passage, Paul addresses worship in the public assembly. He speaks of the significance and content of public prayers (vv. 1–7), of the need for men to pray with a clean conscience (v. 8), of the appropriate attire for women (vv. 9–10), and of the importance of women to be submissive to the teaching of God's Word in the assembly.

Paul realized the importance of prayer in the worship assembly. He included in his words the scope of that prayer, mentioning that God wanted everyone "to be saved" and that He had made provision through giving His Son to be a "Mediator" (v. 5) and "a ransom for all" (v. 6). The truth of the gospel is set forth in a straightforward way. Paul concluded with a word of personal testimony about his own calling to bring the gospel to both Jews and Gentiles (v. 7).

The apostle addressed appropriate attire and demeanor for women in the worship assembly, first admonishing the women to adorn themselves in an honorable and modest way and then noting some inappropriate adornments ("braided hair or gold or pearls or costly clothing," v. 9). His emphasis is not to prohibit tasteful accessories but to embrace modesty and propriety. Some women were dressing in a sensual manner; others were flaunting their superior social status with conspicuous accessories and clothing. Most important is his emphasis on attitude and demeanor (v. 10).

Paul assumed that women could and would learn (v. 11). He wanted women to be grounded thoroughly in sound doctrine. He gives his attention to the appropriate attitude—quiet submissiveness. He mentions two criteria for learning:

- Since women did speak during the worship assembly (1 Cor. 11:5; 14:26), the apostle here was referring to a demeanor of quietness rather than to absolute silence or the absence of speech (Gk. *hēsuchia*).

- Closely akin to this instruction is his admonition to learn "with all submission," suggesting that the instruction was to be received respectfully, which is a measure beyond obedience to include a heart-felt and determined receptivity. This attitude suggests serenity, contentment, the absence of chaos. Women were to submit themselves to those pastors who taught sound doctrine.

Charlotte von Kirschbaum said it well: "Women in silence are the listening church, which the teaching church must again and again become."* The desire to learn should not be viewed as a mere stepping stone to the privilege. Learning is not an excuse for overturning divine order. Rather learning is the opportunity to equip ourselves with the truth of God's Word. How better to learn than not to speak but to listen!

Dorothy Kelley Patterson

Prayer: *Listen to God speak to your heart. Hear what He wants you to do and then submit your heart and will to do it.*

Personal Reflection: ....

....

....

....

....

* See *The Questions of Woman: The Collected Writings of Charlotte von Kirschbaum*, trans. John Shepherd (Grand Rapids, MI: Eerdmans, 1996), 112.

God's Crowning Touch to the Creation Order

1 Timothy 2:11–12

*"And I do not permit a woman to teach or to have authority
over a man, but to be in silence." (v. 12)*

Boundaries in every area of life not only mark something off limits, but they also define an area with expectations. This apostolic directive is more than the personal preference of the apostle Paul. Rather, he used his apostolic influence to affirm the divine mandate based on the creation order clearly recorded in Genesis.

Paul presents two boundaries for women in their service to the church:

- First, a woman is not "to teach" (Gk. *didaskein*) a man in the worship assembly. A teacher gives systematic explanation of truth to others, emphasizing its application for daily living. The context is instruction within the worship assembly. The most natural understanding of the very clear statement would be that women are forbidden to teach Scripture to men.
- Second, a woman is not "to have authority over a man" (Gk. *authentein*) in the worship assembly. This Greek word appears only here in the New Testament and is used rarely in Greek literature.

Since the prohibitions are joined by the conjunction "or," it is logical to assume two separate activities. Evidently some women were violating God's pattern of authority and submission through their teaching in the assembly.

The apostle adds a postscript to his notation of these boundaries by reiterating again that a woman is "to be in silence," the same phrase (and the same word in the Greek text) used in verse 11. Again the emphasis is **quietness**. Of interest is that the phrase is used at the beginning as well as at the end of this prohibition to women. Yet the prohibition is introduced with Paul's positive directive that women are to receive instruction. He carefully describes the process for their receiving instruction—with an inner attitude of quietness and submission to the truth of Scripture.

There is no hint in these verses that a woman should not teach in the church. There is no suggestion that a woman has no authority or leadership in the church. Rather the prohibition is very specific. A woman is not to teach or exercise authority over a man. In other words, women are encouraged to teach other women—a model clearly set forth by Paul in Titus 2:3–5. Women are expected to have leaders among themselves, for that leadership is a tool for building up women into an effective ministering group. Yes, boundaries define limits, but they also identify areas of concentration so that we can work efficiently and effectively.

Dorothy Kelley Patterson

Prayer: *Ask the Lord to help you set boundaries in your life, including in the arena of responsibilities you have in the church. Do not ignore clear biblical mandates in favor of cultural trends or even needs arising in the church. Allow the Lord to place you strategically where He wants you to be.*

Personal Reflection: ....

....

....

....

....

....

Who Is in Charge and Why?

1 Timothy 2:11–14

*"For Adam was formed first, then Eve. And Adam was not deceived,
but the woman being deceived, fell into transgression." (vv. 13–14)*

Paul offers two reasons why women were not to teach or to exercise authority over men. The theological reasons were not derived from a survey of giftedness or prompted by opportunities in the church body. His reference is to the creation and the fall (vv. 13–14; see also Gen. 2—3).

The apostle was well trained in rabbinic exegetical methods of his day. Accordingly he used the rabbinic method of summary citation. This tool was commonly used for helping the people to understand God's words. The summary statement in verse 13 refers to the setting forth of the creation order (Gen. 2:4–24) and then to the account of the fall (Gen. 3:1–15).

The chronological priority in creation is clear. Adam was created first, which, according to the Old Testament concept of primogeniture (i.e., the firstborn son succeeded his father as the leader of the family, Deut. 21:15–17), included the assignment of spiritual leadership. Paul was demonstrating how his instruction, authoritative because it came from God through inspiration of the Holy Spirit, harmonized with God's creation order. The man's leadership in the church was in harmony with the Creator's design for the home.

The same line of argumentation is used in verse 14. History supports what is found in Scripture: Both men and women are easily deceived and vulnerable to making wrong choices. Believers are repeatedly warned about false teachers (see Rom. 16:17–18; Eph. 5:6; Col. 2:8; 2 Thess. 2:3). Paul's message is that the reversal of roles described in Genesis 3 was devastating. God gave His instruction about the forbidden fruit directly to Adam. The text does not say that Eve was present (Gen. 2:17). The Lord placed the ultimate responsibility for this mandate with Adam (cp. Rom. 5:12). The serpent deceived Eve and encouraged her to eat the forbidden fruit. She ate it herself and then offered the fruit to

Adam; he, too, ate the fruit; they both fell into sin (Gen. 3:7). Yet Scripture notes that God held Adam ultimately responsible for their fall into sin (Rom. 5:12).

Reversing what God has ordained is not acceptable. Paul's application to the matter of leadership in the church is supported by the fact that the role reversal, which caused much trouble in the beginning, should not be repeated in the worship assembly. However, the apostle does not forbid women to teach in the church. He admonishes women to teach other women and even gives a curriculum to be taught (Titus 2:3–5). He does not suggest that women have no opportunity for leadership in the church since women did exercise leadership within biblical boundaries. Spiritually mature women functioned as teachers and as leaders of women who were new to the faith (vv. 3–5).

Dorothy Kelley Patterson

Prayer: *Submit yourself to the Lord for work in the church, according to biblical guidelines. Ask the Lord to protect you from being deceived or pulled away from God's purposes for your life.*

Personal Reflection: ....

....

....

....

....

....

How Can a Woman Be Saved by Bearing a Child?

1 Timothy 2:1–15

⌒

*"Nevertheless she will be saved in childbearing if they continue
in faith, love, and holiness, with self-control." (v. 15)*

Paul concludes this passage on women and church order with some shocking but carefully chosen words in which women find both a reward worthy of their best efforts and a challenge demanding their full energies. Many interpretations for this difficult verse have been made, but the best explanation is consistent with and not contradictory to the whole of Scripture. The salvation that awaits women who turn to Christ is expressed here with an eschatological (future) reward. By faithfulness to her proper role as assigned by the Creator (i.e., motherhood), a woman will receive heavenly rewards (2 Cor. 5:10).

The apostle sometimes presented salvation as a whole, but on other occasions he focused on its respective component, as here on the future aspect of salvation through his use of the future tense. A holy and obedient lifestyle will lead to future rewards, which will come when salvation is consummated in heaven (see Col. 1:22–23; 1 Thess. 5:8–9).

Childbearing is one of the good works that are typically part of the life of a godly woman. This figure of speech is a synecdoche, in which a part represents the whole. For example, childbearing is representative of the many activities in a woman's life. In the first century, a woman spent most of her adult years focused on her marriage and the rearing of her children. Paul seems to embrace the importance of this responsibility and its ensuing rewards to women as he rounds out his argument. Certainly this great work would be a part of the "good works" with which she is admonished to clothe herself (1 Tim. 2:10).

Note the qualities that should characterize a woman's lifestyle as a prelude to future, heavenly rewards:

- **Faith** is a reference to your relationship to Christ.
- **Love** is the impetus for serving others.

- **Holiness** describes the daily process of becoming conformed to the image of Christ.
- **Self-control** is a reference to reasonableness, good sense, and perhaps most accurately, discretion. The ideas of moderation and good judgment round out the character of this godly woman.

One of the ways women who find themselves on the front lines in this fallen world can influence the world is through their investment in the next generation, bearing and nurturing children in the Lord. Even if they themselves do not marry and bear children, they can invest spiritual guidance in the lives of children and young people. How exciting to be a part of introducing God's redemptive plan to the next generation!

Dorothy Kelley Patterson

Prayer: *Examine your heart before the Lord. How are you investing in the next generation? Are you taking seriously the responsibility for nurturing and pouring into children and young people biblical truth and spiritual goals?*

Personal Reflection: ....

....

....

....

....

....

Worthy of Honor

1 Timothy 5:3–16

"Do not let a widow under sixty years old be taken into the number, and not unless she has been the wife of one man, well reported for good works: if she has brought up children, if she has lodged strangers, if she has washed the saints' feet, if she has relieved the afflicted, if she has diligently followed every good work." (vv. 9–10)

In this passage, Paul writes to Timothy about the care and treatment of widows. He makes the statement that widows should be cared for by their children or grandchildren (v. 4). These words sound foreign to a society where the first thought is nursing home or assisted living. Some elderly make this decision in an effort not to be a burden. Others encourage such thoughts to rid themselves of inconvenience or obligation to care for parents. This passage presents the counter-cultural idea of caring for those who once cared for you when needed. While not possible for all, more should consider the blessing of spending time with aging parents or grandparents.

In reading this passage, the characteristics Paul gives of a widow worthy of honor should strike us as characteristics to which we should all aspire. First, Paul describes her as "the wife of one man" who has "brought up children" (vv. 9–10). Here Paul exalts the wife's role at home. She should be a one-man woman, living out her marriage in a lifelong covenant relationship and fulfilling the command to be fruitful and multiply. The home should be her priority. Other than her relationship with the Lord, nothing should be more important than her husband and children.

Next, Paul writes "if she has lodged strangers" (v. 10). He describes a woman who uses her home for biblical hospitality to minister to others. When missionaries, evangelists, and fellow believers travel through town, she offers a meal or a place to stay. Paul continues this theme when he writes, ". . . if she has washed the saints' feet and relieved the afflicted," indicating she has a servant's heart (v. 10). In modern times, it would be someone who provides meals for those in surgery, provides a listening ear, or volunteers to help wherever needed. The widow worthy of honor described here by Paul is a godly woman, one who places others before herself and seeks to glorify God through ministering to the least of these people.

Although you might not be a widow, would you be described as a woman worthy of honor? If God has blessed you with a husband and children are they your earthly priority? Do you use your home as a venue to bless others? Are you willing to serve those in need? Strive to be a woman worthy of honor.

Joy Martin White

Prayer: *Ask God to show you ways that you can be a blessing to others. What can you do to bless your family, friends, fellow church members, or strangers? Ask God to help you become a woman worthy of honor.*

Personal Reflection:

Lois and Eunice—Nurturing Women

2 Timothy 1:3–7

*"I thank God, whom I serve with a pure conscience, as my forefathers did,
as without ceasing. I remember you in my prayers night and day, greatly desiring
to see you, being mindful of your tears, that I may be filled with joy, when I call to
remembrance the genuine faith that is in you, which dwelt first in your grandmother
Lois and your mother Eunice, and I am persuaded is in you also." (vv. 3–5)*

Second Timothy is the last letter the apostle Paul wrote from his Roman imprisonment, and it bears the name of the young man to whom it was addressed. Timothy is first introduced in Acts 16:1 as being from Lystra where he had become a follower of Christ and where he later joined Paul as a co-laborer in his missionary endeavors. He was raised primarily by the two women noted in Paul's opening prayer, His grandmother Lois and his mother Eunice. Paul addressed Timothy as "a beloved **son**," which in Paul's day was not a culturally acceptable thing to do if a boy's father was still alive and in the picture (2 Tim. 1:2). Paul adopted Timothy as a spiritual son, but he constantly pointed him back to his greater root system, to the legacy of Timothy's faith, beginning with his mother and grandmother.

Cut flowers are no good when the going gets tough! When the wind grows strong and the rains pour down, only those flowers which have not been severed from their root system can endure tough times. Paul demonstrates in this letter to Timothy that the same is true for people. Timothy had been appointed as the leader of the church at Ephesus, a transient port city that was the provincial capital of the Roman Empire. It was a windy landscape. For Timothy to be able to persevere in his ministry in Ephesus, Paul knew he needed to have a good memory, recalling the genuine faith that was nurtured in his life from the beginning by these two incredible women.

Are there people in your life to whom you can point back as being a part of your spiritual heritage? The answer is most likely yes. But a more challenging question to consider is: Are there people who can point back to YOU as being a part of THEIR spiritual heritage? Timothy had the spiritual legacy of his grandmother and mother, but he was also building a spiritual heritage as he ministered to others. True legacies are not bequeathed at the reading of a will. No, true legacies are made through a lifetime of nurturing relationships of faith that will continue on through the ages.

Courtney Veasey

Prayer: *Praise God for your spiritual heritage. Remember those who influenced you in the faith and thank God for each one by name. Humbly ask that your life also be used to nurture faith in the lives of others.*

Personal Reflection: ....

....

....

....

....

....

....

....

Rightly Dividing the Word of Truth

2 Timothy 2:14–26

"Be diligent to present yourself approved to God, a worker who does not need to be ashamed, rightly dividing the word of truth." (v. 15)

Second Timothy is sometimes called Paul's last will and testament since he wrote this letter to his son in the faith in full acceptance of his probable impending death. The letter gives us a glimpse into the heart and mind of a man who made it his goal to bring glory to God and who at the end of life could say that he had fulfilled his ministry (2 Tim. 4:7). That should be the goal of every believer, and this letter offers insight into how to run the race of life with endurance, how to keep the faith in the midst of difficulties, and how to fulfill your life's purpose with a clear conscience before God.

One of Paul's final encouragements to Timothy was to be a diligent man of integrity who correctly handled God's Word. Paul wanted Timothy to stand before God as one who had lived and proclaimed the gospel message as unadulterated, undistorted truth. Unlike the false teachers who were causing trouble in the church at Ephesus and twisting the Scripture for their own purposes, Paul called Timothy to be "a worker who does not need to be ashamed" before God because of faulty craftsmanship in regard to the Bible.

So what does "rightly divide" or "correctly handle" God's Word mean? In order to understand God's Word, we need to learn how to study and interpret it correctly. Therefore, we must study each book, passage, or verse in context to understand what it meant when it was written before we try to apply it to contemporary situations. When we come across a word or thought that doesn't make sense, we are diligent and work to grasp the meaning. We don't manipulate or twist Scripture to mean something it does not say, but we let the Scripture speak for itself.

In studying God's Word, we also gladly submit to what it teaches and apply it to our lives so that we are doers of what it says (James 1:22). Then, we can stand before God one day unashamed because we know that we have not been deceptive or lazy in the way we treated His Word.

Knowing how to handle God's Word is the safest way for believers to protect themselves from being led astray with the latest fad, gimmick, or quick spiritual fix that cannot fulfill its empty promise (2 Tim. 2:13). Believers will face difficult days (3:1), but the Lord stands with His children, strengthening them in the midst of trials (4:17). Let His Word strengthen you today by digging in and studying it!

Candi Finch

Prayer: *Thank the Lord for giving us His Word. Pray the Holy Spirit would give you discernment as you study the Bible, and pray that you would be diligent in working to understand it.*

Personal Reflection: ....

....

....

....

....

....

....

Gullible Women of the World or Godly Women of the Word

2 Timothy 3:1–7

～

*"For of this sort [hypocrites] are those who creep into households and make
captives of gullible women loaded down with sins, led away by various lusts,
always learning and never able to come to the knowledge of the truth." (vv. 6–7)*

Do you know someone who is gullible? We have several gullible family members. My husband has a knack for tricking his gullible mother and sister. He once told his mother that there were no calories in donut holes, so she bought donut holes for the family. (Of course, he meant the missing holes had no calories not the donut made in the shape of the hole.) He often tricks his sister Kathy into believing there are absolutely no shrimp in the city of New Orleans. (Our city always has an abundance of the shrimp she so loves.) These innocent people are easily misled or tricked by someone they love.

Paul begins 2 Timothy 3 with a sound of alarm concerning perilous times and perilous people. In the difficult times of the last days, he warns that false teachers and their erroneous doctrine will prevail. "Men will be lovers of themselves, lovers of money, boasters, proud, blasphemers, disobedient to parents, unthankful, unholy, unloving, unforgiving, slanderers, without self-control, brutal, despisers of good, traitors, headstrong, haughty, lovers of pleasure rather than lovers of God" (vv. 2–4). Oh my! What a dismal prediction!

Perilous people (or hypocrites) will pervade the world and creep into the church. Gullible women are described in 2 Timothy 2:6–7 as captives who are "loaded down with sins, led away by various lusts, always learning and never able to come to the knowledge of the truth." This description of first-century women sounds like women of the world today who are sinful and searching. The hope for women then and now is found in the verses that follow. We must carefully follow true doctrine, live godly lives, and seek God's divine purpose (3:10–11).

Like he writes in other New Testament letters, Paul makes clear comparisons. He contrasts the perilous times and perilous men with men of God and the Word of God, gullible women of the world with godly women of the Word. Then, Paul gives guidelines for godliness:

- "continue in the things you have learned" (3:14);
- be instructed in righteousness (3:16);
- be "equipped for every good work" (3:17).

Only then will Christian women be prepared for every good work, be ready to speak and teach the gospel, endure afflictions, and fulfill their ministry (4:1–5).

What about you? Do you want to be a gullible woman of the world or a godly woman of the Word? God needs His children to be firm in their faith, resisting false teaching and folly.

Rhonda Harrington Kelley

Prayer: *Confess your sins to God if you have allowed yourself to be tricked by the world. Pray for God to strengthen your faith for the perilous times ahead.*

Personal Reflection: ....

....

....

....

....

The Unparalleled Bible

2 Timothy 3:10–17

"All Scripture is given by inspiration of God, and is profitable for doctrine, for reproof, for correction, for instruction in righteousness, that the man of God may be complete, thoroughly equipped for every good work." (vv. 16–17)

Charles Spurgeon, the famous English preacher, once said, "Oh, to be bathed in a text of Scripture, and to let it be sucked up in your very soul, till it saturates your heart!" By his exuberant exclamation, this preacher of old was pointing his listeners to the matchless nature and vital importance of the Bible. God's Word is different than any other book. While Jane Austen's *Pride and Prejudice,* Homer's *The Iliad,* and Charles Dickens' *A Tale of Two Cities* are impressive works of literature, the Bible surpasses them all with the very words of the Creator of the universe.

The Bible will never fade or pass away (Is. 40:8; Matt. 24:35), doesn't return void (Is. 55:11), is living and active (Heb. 4:12), and can be trusted because it is perfect, right, and true (Ps. 19:7–11). This Book helps us stay pure and can keep us from sin (Ps. 119:9, 11). Unlike any other book that has ever been penned, Scripture can actually bring us life (v. 93).

In 2 Timothy 3:16–17, Paul reflects on the true character of the Scripture and its value for every believer. The fact that all Scripture **is** given by inspiration of God emphasizes God's initiation and control of the process of communicating His thoughts to human beings. The Holy Spirit orchestrated this process, so the original writings are without error (2 Pet. 1:21). God's written Word is authoritative and infallible simply because it is **God's** Word. What God says will come to pass. As Paul explains, Scripture is profitable:

- For **doctrine** (God's truth to others)—the Bible lets us know what God has said about how to live and think (1 Tim. 4:3, 6, 13, 16; Titus 1:9; 2:1, 7, 10);

- For **reproof** (Gk., "proof, conviction")— the Bible exposes and brings to light the errors of ungodly living and thinking (1 Tim. 5:20; 2 Tim. 4:2);
- For **correction** (Gk., "restoring to an upright position, making straight again")—for people who are in error, the Bible can set them on a path of restoration (John 17:17; 2 Tim. 2:25); and
- For **instruction in righteousness**—the Scripture is aimed at the cultivation of both knowledge and character; it provides wisdom in how to develop an intimate relationship with the Lord.

The question we must ask ourselves since the Bible is God's Word: Do we live in a way that affirms that truth? As Spurgeon proclaimed, we must let this unparalleled Word be sucked up into our very souls so that we are saturated by it and can then live it out.

Candi Finch

Prayer: *Are there any areas of your life that need reproof or correction? Confess that to the Lord, and thank Him for His Word that shows us how to live life.*

Personal Reflection: ....

....

....

....

....

Who Are the Spiritual Mothers?

Titus 2:1–10

*"The older women likewise, that they be reverent in behavior,
not slanderers, not given to much wine, teachers of good things—
that they admonish the young women . . ." (vv. 3–4)*

Mentoring relationships among women were ordained by God as a profoundly effective way to transfer from generation to generation biblical instruction and spiritual applications. Paul describes the character of the spiritually mature women who will be teaching the women who are new and fresh to the faith. These qualities are similar to those assigned to the wives of deacons (1 Tim. 3:11). All women in leadership in the local church should be expected to meet high standards in character and lifestyle.

The word used to describe these teachers (Gk. *presbutidas*, which is a *hapax legomenon*, a word used only once in the Greek New Testament) is usually translated "older women." In considering the contrast between the "older women" who are teaching and the "young women" who are being taught, the sense of the passage seems more accurate to consider this gap as being not so much in years as in spiritual maturity—"spiritually mature women" and "women who are new to the faith" (Titus 2:3–4).

Women who are immersed in faith and saturated with His wisdom would be responsible to equip women who have not yet been equipped with the knowledge of God's Word and with the discerning wisdom that comes from time in studying Scripture. Of course, older women who have been studying biblical truth for years will have the advantage of experience in applying the truths of God's Word to their lives, but a young woman who has paid the price in preparation and study is not excluded from being a spiritually mature teacher any more than an older woman who does not know the Scripture herself is bereft without the benefit of teaching from a spiritually mature woman.

Paul presents qualities characterizing such a spiritually mature woman:

- **Reverent in behavior,** living as one engaged in sacred duties, marked by holiness in her daily life;
- **Not slanderers** (Gk. *diabolous*, lit. "devils" or "those who cast through"), no gossip but using words that encourage and lift up;
- **Not addicted to wine,** a quality holding them to the highest standard of restraint from anything that could generate a bad influence;
- **Teachers of good things,** incorporating what is Christlike into lives that are an example of spiritual maturity.

Character is intertwined with instruction. Habits and lifestyle exhibit the heart of who you are. The emphasis is not on formal instruction; rather these spiritually mature teachers teach through private counsel and encouragement as well as through the example of their own lives.

Dorothy Kelley Patterson

Prayer: *Ask the Lord to make you a spiritually mature woman. Sit at His feet by reading and meditating upon His Word. Bring into your life godly women who can teach you spiritual lessons. Be willing to continue that mentoring in the lives of women the Lord brings into your life.*

Personal Reflection: ....

....

....

....

Divinely Assigned Curriculum for Women

Titus 2:3–5

"The older women likewise, that they be reverent in behavior, not slanderers, not given to much wine, teachers of good things—that they admonish the young women to love their husbands, to love their children, to be discreet, chaste, homemakers, good, obedient to their own husbands, that the word of God may not be blasphemed." (vv. 3–5)

The apostle Paul presents the curriculum for teaching women the things of the Lord. Missing from the list are skills in evangelism, methods for Bible study, strategies for helping the poor and needy, etc. These are important and come in due course as the fruit of spiritual life development. Paul, however, sets his focus on priorities from the creation order. What is to be taught is not left to personal discernment or emotional whim or natural impulse. Rather this curriculum begins with the basic foundations for living the Christian life.

In addition to the character qualities set forth, there are three primary areas of instruction:

- **Lovers of husbands** (Gk. *philandrous*) refers to a woman whose God-given nature and assignment from creation has a unique bent to love unconditionally and to be willing to make sacrifices in behalf of her husband. However, her challenge comes in daily life, respecting her husband through her words and actions.
- **Lovers of their children** (Gk. *philoteknous*) puts the focus of a woman on going beyond a willingness to die for her children but loving them enough to live for them—treating children with respect, not releasing on them angry words or retaliatory punishment.
- **Homemakers** (Gk. *oikourous*) puts an emphasis on the efficient management of your household. There are no churches or communities or governments without families. This homemaker is to be hard-working and passionately devoted to her husband and children. What she does

in providing an orderly household is not mere duty but is offered as joyful service ultimately unto the Lord.

Woven into this master curriculum are reminders of character qualities that are necessary to do the tasks taught. They are to be **discreet,** using good sense, being wise, understanding the importance of the home and relationships therein; they are to be **chaste,** sexually pure; they are to be **good,** a word that encompasses character and life. Paul concludes his list with a reminder of the importance of a wife's submission to her husband, a choice she makes to line up under the authority and protection of her husband. This link connects the passage in Titus with the household codes found elsewhere in the New Testament (Eph. 5:22–33; Col. 3:18; 1 Pet. 3:1).

This unique curriculum links Christlike character with God-honoring curriculum to prepare women—not so much through a formal and structured classroom approach but rather through nurturing spiritual mothering.

Dorothy Kelley Patterson

Prayer: *Consider spiritual mothering in your life. Do you need a spiritual mother—a mentor to guide you to spiritual truths and enrich your life? Are you prepared spiritually to become a mentor to another woman who is new to the faith?*

Personal Reflection: ....

....

....

....

....

The Task of Spiritual Mothering

Titus 2:11–15

⌒

"Speak these things, exhort, and rebuke with all authority.
Let no one despise you." (v. 15)

Why is spiritual mothering important? With the many Bible study groups available in churches and neighborhoods, is there a need for this woman-to-woman mentoring, or can a woman grow spiritually solely through the preaching of a godly pastor and the purposeful study of passages throughout the Bible? Why focus on this curriculum and why woman-to-woman teaching?

Because the Lord created you as a woman, He knows everything about you. He knows how you learn; He is aware of the special bond that can be forged between women. And He knows what curriculum is most basic to your spiritual growth. To underscore the importance of this method and curriculum, Paul endorses a woman-to-woman teaching so "that the word of God may not be blasphemed" (Gk. *blasphēmētai*, 2:5). In other words, this method and curriculum serve as a guard against tarnishing the reputation of God's word.

To use the strong word "blasphemed," carrying the nuance of "slander," seems a bit over the top since blasphemy is a sin not to be taken lightly. However, the emphasis here is especially to the damage done by speaking lightly of holy things or speaking against the instruction of God so that you cast through or make null and void His truth. Disobedience, even in the management of your household and in your relationships with husband and with children, can bring the gospel itself into disrepute and cause reproach against God's Word.

God's Word is honorable whatever you may do in your personal lifestyle; but as His creation, women can bring honor and glory to the Lord by obedience to His Word. In addition to keeping us from bringing dishonor to the Lord and His Word (v. 5), this instruction will help to guard the sanctity of the home (vv. 4–5). Spiritual mothering can also cast a vision for spiritual ministry to family and others through the impact of woman-to-woman teaching for women who are new to the faith (vv. 12–15).

Nothing brings as much credit to Christ and the truths of Christianity as the set-apart qualities of character a believer's faith produces in her life. As you pursue this way of excellence, you do well to keep "looking for the blessed hope and glorious appearing of our great God and Savior Jesus Christ" (v. 13).

Dorothy Kelley Patterson

Prayer: *Ask the Lord to protect your testimony and keep you from doing anything to dishonor His Word. Enlist His help to give you understanding of what He expects from you—in your personal life and in the influence you wield in the lives of others.*

Personal Reflection: ....

....

....

....

....

....

....

Apphia—Hostess for God's People

Philemon 1–3

"To Philemon our beloved friend and fellow laborer, to the beloved Apphia, Archippus our fellow soldier, and to the church in your house." (vv. 1–2)

There is nothing sweeter than a selfless serving saint! You know her—someone who is willing to work hard behind the scenes to accomplish kingdom ministry. She cooks, decorates, arranges, washes, sweeps, and her work is never done. The spiritual gift of serving is necessary for the work of the body of Christ and is demonstrated graciously through many Christian women.

Apphia is mentioned in the Bible in only one verse, commended by Paul for her service alongside Philemon (v. 2). Little is known about her personally, though her work for the Lord has been remembered through the ages. She was possibly the wife of Philemon and probably the hostess for the church meeting in his home. Tradition suggests she was martyred with Onesimus, Philemon, and Archippus during the persecution of Nero. Her active faith impacted her life and the lives of others.

The short book of Philemon was written by Paul to Philemon, who opened his home as a place of worship in Colosse. Its message is about Christian fellowship, the special relationships among believers in the church and unbelievers in the world. Hospitality is essential to fellowship, and women are key to hospitality. Apphia played a crucial role in the body of Christ—she was a hostess for God's people

Kingdom ministry today places a great emphasis on church planting in America and around the world. Missionaries or ministers gather other believers together to form a new church congregation, taking the gospel to a targeted area to reach unbelievers. These new churches begin meeting in homes and often build around the spiritual needs of women. Worship services and Bible studies draw people to God's Word and the support of likeminded people. Fellowship is a natural and needed expression of the church. And, of course, that means food—coffee and donuts, chips and dip—provides the opportunity for personal interaction and connection. It has been said that Christian's spell fellowship F–O–O–D! We like to feed ourselves spiritually and physically, especially churches in New Orleans where I live.

If there is fellowship and food, there must be a hostess. Someone is needed to prepare the details and preside over the event. Are you a beloved hostess like Apphia (v. 2)? Do you have the spiritual gift of hospitality? Whether or not you are bent toward hospitality, Christians must be willing to open their hearts and homes to others in Jesus' name. Let Apphia be an example to you of a selfless saint who served the Lord and His people faithfully.

Rhonda Harrington Kelley

Prayer: *Take a few moments to thank the Lord for gracious hostesses who have served you. Now ask Him to work His gift of hospitality in you. Seek to be a beloved hostess for God's people.*

Personal Reflection:

Refreshing the Saints

Philemon 4–7

"For we have great joy and consolation in your love, because the hearts of the saints have been refreshed by you, brother." (v. 7)

In this passage, Paul is writing to his dear friend and co-worker Philemon. He thanks God for Philemon because of his love and faith in Christ Jesus and care for all the Christians. Philemon was the kind of person who brought joy and encouragement to others. He was like a fresh ocean breeze that blew in people's hearts.

What a great compliment for Philemon! What did he do that caused such a response? First, Philemon was joyful. When my children were in school they participated in a speech contest sponsored by the Optimist Club. What a wonderful experience for my children. I was impressed by the positive attitude of the people in this club. They were not denying the negative the world, but deciding to focus on the positive.

Part of being joyful is understanding how God uses bad circumstances for good. The Bible says God can work all things together for good (Rom. 8:28). God uses the imperfections to cause us to humbly depend on Him. We need difficulties in our lives for our own personal growth. James tells us we should count it all joy when we fall into trials, because we learn patience (James 1:2–3). Philemon was able to have joy in the midst of the challenges of life, and he inspired others with that joy.

Second, Philemon was encouraging to others. At some time, everyone gets discouraged from the struggles of life. We cannot see a way out of our problems. We need a person who can give us a fresh perspective. Philemon was that kind of person.

How can we be more like Philemon? One way to be joyful is to give thanks to God. I am not a morning person, but when I wake up, I try to thank God for His blessings. My attitude of gratitude helps shake off my morning blues and gets me off to a good start in the day. Joy is a natural byproduct of gratitude.

Morning, noon, and night remember to give thanks to God for the wonderful things He is doing in your life, in spite of the troubles.

Another way to be more like Philemon is to remember to be encouraging. People get negative feedback everywhere they go. Parents are often angry with their children. Workers are angry with their bosses. Even when people are trying to do what is right, they are criticized due to misunderstandings, unrealistic expectations, and personality differences. A word of encouragement can be a drink of water in the desert, refreshing the soul and giving a will to go on in life.

Ann Iorg

Prayer: *Ask God to help you to remember to be grateful for all the blessings He pours out in your life. Seek His help to refresh people with joy and encouragement so they can continue to serve Him.*

Personal Reflection: ....

....

....

....

....

....

....

Spiritual Peter Pans

Hebrews 5:12—6:12

*"For though by this time you ought to be teachers, you need someone
to teach you again the first principles of the oracles of God; and you have
come to need milk and not solid food. For everyone who partakes only
of milk is unskilled in the word of righteousness, for he is a babe. But solid
food belongs to those who are of full age, that is, those who by reason
of use have their senses exercised to discern both good and evil." (5:12–14)*

Growing up is a good and natural part of life, yet there is a section of our society that clings to the Peter Pan-like spirit that declares, "I don't wanna to grow up!" Unfortunately, some Christians are satisfied with "never growing up" when it comes to their relationship with God. If your relationship with God looks exactly the same way it did 30 years ago, 10 years ago, or even two years ago when you came into a relationship with Jesus, something is amiss. You are not growing. Just as human parents would get concerned if their children stopped growing and developing, God does not want us to be spiritual infants for the rest of our lives.

Fortunately, the Bible does give us some signs of a person who struggles with being a spiritual Peter Pan so we can examine our own lives in this regard:

- **Her behavior isn't any different than that of a person who doesn't know God.** Once a person becomes a Christian, she doesn't instantly become perfect. However, sinful behavior should start to change as a person matures in her faith (see 1 Cor. 3:1–3; 1 Pet. 2:1–3).
- **Her understanding and knowledge of God aren't deepening.** First Corinthians 14:20 says: "Do not be children in understanding; however in malice by babes, but in understanding be mature." God wants all of us to progress in our understanding of Him, to be able to move from baby food to solid food in spiritual matters (Heb. 5:12–14).

- **Her heart is easily led astray.** A childish believer doesn't know her Bible well and, as a result, can fall prey to false teaching. A person who says things like "Well, I don't know what the Bible says about that," and is content to leave it there, is childish (see Eph. 4:14–15).

Christians start their spiritual journey as spiritual babies. The key is that we should not be content to remain spiritual babies for the rest of our lives (Heb. 6:1)! Can you imagine a 50-year-old who would be content to have baby formula for every meal? Think about all the wonderful culinary delights she would be missing out on—bacon-wrapped filet mignon and homemade pot roast come immediately to mind! Ladies, in the same way, we have delights awaiting us as we progress in the maturity of our faith.

Candi Finch

Prayer: *Ask the Lord to help you grow in maturity in your faith today and each day after that.*

Personal Reflection: ....

....

....

....

....

....

A Woman's Hall of Faith

Hebrews 11:11–31

*"By faith Sarah herself also received strength to conceive seed, and she bore
a child when she was past the age, because she judged Him faithful who
had promised. . . . By faith the harlot Rahab did not perish with those who
did not believe, when she had received the spies with peace." (vv. 11, 31)*

People love to honor those who show exemplary skill or character. There is a hall of fame for most sports and many other areas of interest. In the Bible, there is a "Hall of Faith." This passage lists the great people of faith in the Bible. Two women are mentioned. Both women were flawed, but each showed great faith as she lived out her life.

Sarah was the wife of Abraham. God promised to give her a son even though she and Abraham were both past the childbearing years. Sarah was 90 and Abraham was 100 years old when their son Isaac was born. However, Sarah believed God and received His promise (v. 11; Gen. 17).

Rahab was a prostitute in Jericho. She hid the Israelite spies in her house and told them what she had heard and believed about their God. She asked them to spare her family when they came to destroy the city where she lived. She kept her word to the spies and helped them escape. They kept their word to her and rescued her and her family when they conquered Jericho (Heb. 11:31; Josh. 2; 6)

Both Sarah and Rahab showed courageous faith when they believed in what God was doing. Both were willing to reject their past lives and trust God for a new future. Sarah rejected her barrenness at God's promise of a son, and Rahab rejected her past prostitution for a new life of following God and His people. Rahab married Salmon, became the mother of the godly man Boaz, who married Ruth and was included in the ancestry line of Jesus (Matt. 1:5).

How can we be more like Sarah and Rahab? If we refuse to let the past dictate our future, we show faith like these great women. Whether we are waiting on a promise from God or rejecting a past life of sin, we can have a better future.

The old is forgotten when the new arrives. Sarah no longer felt the pain of her barrenness when Isaac was born. Rahab no longer followed her sinful lifestyle when she accepted a new life with a new people. The Bible says we are a new creation in Christ; the old is past and the new has come (2 Cor. 5:17).

Are you still struggling with the past? If so, by faith receive God's promise of a new future. Follow the examples of these women of faith.

Ann Iorg

Prayer: *Allow God to help you see the past as past and receive the future He has for you. Commit to study the Bible so you can know what God promised and live by faith in His promises.*

Personal Reflection:

Run with Endurance

Hebrews 12:1–29

*"Let us lay aside every weight, and the sin which so easily ensnares us,
and let us run with endurance the race that is set before us,
looking unto Jesus, the author and finisher of our faith." (vv. 1b–2a)*

Have you ever thought to yourself, "If I can just hang on?" Many times when a woman thinks of **endurance,** she considers the act of hanging on by a thread in an effort to survive a difficult task. In these verses, the writer of Hebrews wants his readers to envision a race where the runner is not merely hanging on but is moving on purposefully in the direction of the finish line with full intent to complete the course, no matter the obstacles.

How does a woman muster up the endurance needed to run the race of life set before her? She builds strength by staying in the race, pushing through the pain, and celebrating the mile markers. In exercise science, the term **progressive overload** is used to describe how a muscle gets stronger with use. By applying resistance repeatedly, a muscle builds strength and endurance.

The writer of Hebrews points out that the runner needs to be aware of what may be affecting her endurance negatively. What are "weights" that may slow down a runner? In ancient days, competitive runners ran without clothes because they didn't want to be weighted down by garments blowing in the wind. They laid aside what got in the way so they could focus more freely on the race at hand.

A key ingredient for succeeding in the race is one's focus. There is nothing wrong with enjoying the scenery, but that is not the purpose of the race. Watching other people at the race can be quite entertaining, but that is not the point of the race. The race of life is about Jesus, the Author and Finisher of our faith. He started the race; He runs alongside each runner; and He is indeed waiting at the finish line. The runner should focus on Jesus.

In the Crescent City Classic 10K, many runners are fooled as they are running the final mile and see an apparatus over the road that appears to be the finish line banner. They begin to sprint toward it and quickly figure out that it is merely the photo truck in place for photographers to catch action shots of the participants. The finish line is still a quarter of a mile away which feels like an eternity for those who blew their last burst of energy prematurely.

Endurance is not merely an act of the will. It is the expression of purpose-filled training. To improve at running, a person must run . . . and run . . . and run.

Judi Jackson

Prayer: *Ask the Lord to show you a training plan that will keep you in the race of life. Consider what needs to be laid aside so that you can run your race with your focus on the Author and Finisher of your faith, Jesus Christ.*

Personal Reflection: ....

....

....

....

....

....

....

Marriage, Contentment, and Adultery

Hebrews 13:3–6

*"Marriage is honorable among all, and the bed undefiled;
but fornicators and adulterers God will judge. Let your conduct
be without covetousness; be content with such things as you have.
For He himself has said, 'I will never leave you nor forsake you.'" (vv. 4–5)*

Marriage. Fornication. Coveting. Contentment. Abandonment. At first glance, these words seem to have nothing in common. How do contentment and fornication relate? Why does God want to protect us from coveting by promising His faithfulness? The answers to these questions start at the beginning in Genesis and continue throughout the Old Testament. As a reminder of the thread of redemption weaving throughout all of Scripture, the writer of Hebrews brings these concepts back to the forefront.

First, marriage is a picture of God's covenantal relationship to His people, showing His pure love and unrelenting pursuit of His children. Marriage is honorable and pure because it is not a creation of man but of God Himself. Therefore, when sin enters what God created to be pure and holy, God will judge it. Sexual sins are very dangerous because they encroach upon the holy territory of marriage.

God gave the Israelites judges as leaders, but the people wanted a king: "No, but we will have a king over us, that we also may be like all the nations" (1 Sam. 8:20). They coveted other nations who led them away from God's plans and adopted the false gods of those nations. God had provided His people with everything they needed, His very presence. However, they wanted what they did not have, a king to rule over them. As the Israelites began to follow after false gods, God likened it to adultery, even calling them harlots.

The major mistake of the Israelites was their discontentment, which led to covetousness, seeking after things that were not of God, committing adultery in their hearts. The writer of Hebrews lays out this pattern as a warning. Why should we not follow this path? Because God Himself has promised that He will never leave us or forsake us. Even in our sin, even in our adultery, even when we have turned our backs on God, He will never leave us. Through this passage, we can see the link between God's holiness and His passionate, unrelenting love for His people. His passion should prompt us to forsake our sins and follow after God.

Think about your own life. Has discontentment led you down paths that you did not want to go? Has coveting ever tethered your heart to other sins? If so, remember God has not abandoned you. He is always pursuing a relationship with you, offering freedom from those sins.

Melanie Lenow

Prayer: *Reflect on ways your heart has been unfaithful to God. How have you not trusted Him but sought after things you coveted? Ask God to forgive you of your discontentment. Thank Him for His continued faithfulness, and praise Him for His relentless pursuit of you.*

Personal Reflection: ....

....

....

....

....

....

Count It All Joy

James 1:1–4

"My brethren, count it all joy when you fall into various trials, knowing
that the testing of your faith produces patience. But let patience have its
perfect work, that you may be perfect and complete, lacking nothing." (vv. 2–4)

As you read the words "count it all joy," you are doubtlessly thinking this is a biblical command, which is a little far-fetched for those who have walked difficult and heartbreaking paths. However, these words apply to both the small hurdles and the deep valleys through which we walk in the journey of life.

James is speaking to a group of believers who are under serious persecution from the leaders and people of their day, just like many are today. Believers are being persecuted and martyred for their faith. James is being very practical, reminding all believers who walk with Jesus that life will not be easy for anyone. We will all face difficulties as a result of our sin (James 1:13–15). It is not "if" but "when" trials will come (v. 2). Also, he is clear that the trials will be "various."

Trials will not be the same in type or intensity. Trials are defined as something bringing distress, pain, grief, or trouble into our lives, hence disrupting our peace and comfort. It may be an accident, an intense battle with a life-threatening disease, personal depression, or a seemingly impossible relationship with a spouse, child, or parent. Trials are common to all. We learn from verses 13–15 that trials are not caused by God but by our own sinful "desires." While God is not the author of them, He is the Provider through them.

Our God loves us so much that He takes our selfish desires, which can lead us to sin, and provides a way for them to lead us to Him. Trusting His heart of love through the trials and temptations is what enables us to "count them all joy" even when we cannot see the purpose and the plan.

God's transforming power, love, and light are revealed to us in the darkness. You cannot see the difference a light makes unless you are in complete darkness. A light illuminated in a bright room does not make nearly the impact of a light revealed in complete darkness.

Carmen Howell

Prayer: *Recognize the trial you are walking through today and ask God to help you see His light more brightly than ever before. See the joy in knowing you have a purpose for this trial (Rom. 8:29). Count your trials as joy because they are what enables you to see how God can illuminate complete darkness when nothing else can!*

Personal Reflection:

Give Me Wisdom or Give Me Death

James 1:5–11

*"If any of you lacks wisdom, let him ask of God, who gives to
all liberally and without reproach, and it will be given to him." (v. 5)*

While James states that we will all face many conflicts, heartaches, sorrow, and pain in our lives every day, he doesn't leave us in desperation without hope. Although he proclaims with certainty the difficulties, James has also given us clear direction about how to survive and even thrive in the midst of these struggles. One of the greatest blessings of our heartache and anguish is that it causes us to recognize that we are not self-sufficient. We do not actually know it all. No matter how strong, gifted, and talented we are, there are circumstances in our lives from which we cannot claw, climb, or maneuver our way out.

James is clear that we will need counsel (wisdom) in our desperation. Our instinct (flesh) will tell us to run to pastors, parents, teachers, friends, and counselors for direction and help. How ironic that James makes no mention of these in this passage. For while some may give us good words for the moment, there is only One who can give us wisdom, comfort, and strength to equip us to "count it all joy" (James 1:2) and "ask in faith, with no doubting" (v. 6). We need counsel based on God's truth and His plans.

Every human counselor is bound by what he can see, hear, touch, and feel. God is bound by nothing! He sees all, knows all, understands all, and has the power over everyone and everything in this world. When our feelings and pain overwhelm us, we need Him—His Word, His strength, His peace, His perspective. Even the most spiritual among us is not capable of seeing, knowing, and understanding all. Therefore, no one among us is able to give us all the wisdom we need for each day. I firmly believe that one of the many reasons God allows us to suffer and struggle is so that we will come to Him for guidance and direction. Typically we do not ask for help unless we are desperate for it.

If you are like me, you have sought help from someone in your life at a point of desperation. Yet that person was unable to do anything or his counsel failed at some level. We have a promise from God that, if we will ask with confidence, He will give us the wisdom and insight we need. Further, He will not just give it, but He gives it "liberally and without reproach." He gives it freely, generously, without any condemnation! Many counselors and people we turn to for help in this world, give us counsel, but have been known to condemn us in the process. There is only one "Wonderful Counselor" (Is. 9:6).

Carmen Howell

Prayer: *Acknowledge God's provision in your struggles. Thank Him for His sufficiency to meet every need and desire of your heart. Allow Him to speak to you faithfully as you read His Word today.*

Personal Reflection:

Does God Tempt Us to Sin?

James 1:12–18

"Let no one say when he is tempted, 'I am tempted by God'; for God cannot be tempted by evil, nor does He Himself tempt anyone. But each one is tempted when he is drawn away by his own desires and enticed. Then, when desire has conceived, it gives birth to sin; and sin, when it is full-grown, brings forth death." (vv. 13–15)

Have you ever heard someone joke, "The devil made me do it"? Or, as a kid, did you ever try to shift blame to one of your siblings or a friend when you knew you were guilty of something? You may be like Adam and Eve, who shifted the blame after they were tempted—Adam blamed Eve, and Eve blamed the serpent (Gen. 3:12–13). We often want to blame someone else or the circumstances when we sin. However, James cautioned believers against casting blame on God when they are tempted and give into sin because it goes against God's very nature to try to tempt or cause His children to stumble.

James pinpoints the true cause of temptation— it happens when we are drawn away and enticed by our own desires. "Drawn away" is actually a hunting term used to describe a trap designed to lure and catch an unsuspecting animal, and "enticed" is a term suggesting luring prey from safety to capture and even death. Our desires can lure and trap us if we are not careful. Satan knows just how to catch us in his trap, so we must be on guard.

"Desire" or lust, although long associated exclusively with evil deeds and especially sexual promiscuity, actually describes a strong, deep-seated longing for anything—good or bad. When a desire grows out of control and becomes a governing habit, the bent toward sinning takes charge. The human desire becomes so overwhelming that the person ignores the trap until she cannot turn back.

There is a difference between what God **allows** to happen and what He **causes** to happen. God's purposes are always pure because He is pure. Because God will not allow you to be tempted beyond what you can bear, the only attack against your faith that the enemy has permission to launch is that for which

God has given you the grace and power to overcome (1 Cor. 10:13). What Satan uses to destroy your faith, God uses to reveal your faith. And if any believer does sin, she has an "Advocate . . . Jesus Christ the righteous" (1 John 2:1). Remember, "If we confess our sins, He is faithful and just to forgive us *our* sins and to cleanse us from all unrighteousness" (1 John 1:9).

Candi Finch

Prayer: *Do you have any desire in your life that is drawing you away from God? If so, confess that to the Lord, and ask Him to give you the strength to resist that temptation. Then, spend a few moments thanking God for His forgiveness.*

Personal Reflection: ....

....

....

....

....

....

....

....

To Speak or Not to Speak

James 1:19–25

*"So then, my beloved brethren, let every man be swift
to hear, slow to speak, slow to wrath." (v. 19)*

James intentionally follows his discussion of maneuvering through trials and temptations by addressing our hearing and speaking skills. In the midst of a trial when we are hurting, vulnerable, or frustrated, we tend to close our ears and hearts and open our mouths! In light of the wisdom, grace, and love God gives to us liberally, He has issued some commands regarding how we should respond to His truth and to others.

James gives three simple and clear commands. He prefaces these by again making it clear that they are for "every man" and for all "brethren." Anyone who claims to have a personal relationship with Jesus, no exceptions, must adhere to them. When His Spirit lives within us, we are given the capacity to choose to follow these principles. We must be "swift to hear" (listen). Listening must happen quickly and continue until we understand. We must go the extra mile and listen until we understand God's truth as well as how it should be used in the circumstance or relationship.

Proverbs 10:14 states we are to "store up knowledge." If we are truly focused on listening, we will follow the second command more readily, be "slow to speak." Our tongue is repeatedly addressed throughout Scripture. James gives it more attention in chapter 3. Proverbs 10:19 proclaims, "In the multitude of words sin is not lacking, But he who restrains his lips *is* wise." Proverbs 13:3 states, "He who guards his mouth preserves his life, *But* he who opens wide his lips shall have destruction." Rarely do we regret speaking carefully and thoughtfully. However, many regrets follow in speaking quickly and emotionally.

The last command by James will likely follow if the first two are practiced. We must be "slow to wrath" (anger). There is a much higher chance of our anger not festering if we are listening to understand and holding our tongues. Wrath is defined as an inner deep resentment that seethes and smolders. Focusing on our feelings instead of God's truth will be a breeding ground for anger and will not produce words, responses, and attitudes that testify to our faithful righteous God (James 1:20).

In the midst of trials we are squeezed and perplexed. Choosing to follow God's commands allows God to show His protection, love, and provision. His message will more likely be heard clearly if we learn when to speak and when to listen.

Carmen Howell

Prayer: *Ask the Lord to help you listen to Him and to others in order to understand. Try to apply His truth while sympathizing with the hurts and struggles around you. Silence your tongue when you desire to be right or fix something. Do not allow trials, hurts, and misunderstandings to fester and become anger. God will help you learn when to speak and when not to speak!*

Personal Reflection:

Pure and Undefiled Religion

James 1:26—2:13

"Pure and undefiled religion before God and the Father is this: to visit orphans and widows in their trouble, and to keep oneself unspotted from the world." (v. 27)

Have you ever had the opportunity to observe someone from another religion practicing his religion? I had the chance to visit a country in South Asia and observe men and women practicing Hinduism, and my heart broke for these people who are blinded by this false religion. Several times during my trip, traffic would come to an absolute standstill as a cow lazily meandered its way through the city. Cows are honored and respected among Hindus—if a car struck a cow, the result would be disastrous for the person who caused the harm. Because Hindus believe in reincarnation, a cow could be someone's reincarnated ancestor so the people treat the animal with great respect. The problem, though, is that the life of a cow is treated with greater dignity than the life of a young girl.

Though banned by South Asian governments, the *devadasi* system (a Hindu practice of temple prostitution) is still practiced today. Parents dedicate girl babies to the goddess Yellamma, and once the girl reaches the age of 11 or 12, she begins a life of prostitution. The only hope offered to this young girl is the chance that she will one day be reincarnated in a better life. When the life of a girl is less valuable than a cow, something is terribly wrong!

James explained that true religion is displayed by the way we treat other people (1:27). We aren't saved by performing works; but if we are saved, it should impact how we live (1:22). We show evidence of what God has done in our heart and lives by caring for people like He would care for them (Matt. 25:31–46). In ancient society, orphans and widows were among the most vulnerable, needing protection. By extending compassionate care and provision for the defenseless and refusing the world's values ("keeping oneself unspotted from the world"), Christians point people to the one true God and the message of hope found in the gospel.

My trip to South Asia gave me the opportunity to watch just a handful of Hindus and how their religion impacted them. Since coming back, I have often wondered what people would think of Christianity by observing my life. Does the way I live out my faith point to the hope and joy people can experience by knowing Christ? Would someone watching me for a few minutes in my day see any difference in me? Would someone watching you? I pray that each of us would live in a way that points people to the hope found only in Christ.

Candi Finch

Prayer: *Would you spend a few moments praying for people you know who may be suffering or vulnerable to exploitation? Then, pray that you demonstrate the genuineness of the gospel as you live out your faith today.*

Personal Reflection: ....

....

....

....

....

....

....

Taming the Tongue

James 3:1–12

"But no man can tame the tongue. It is an unruly evil, full of deadly poison. With it we bless our God and Father, and with it we curse men." (vv. 8–9)

James challenges us to be very careful in our use of one of the tiniest, yet most powerful muscles in the body—the tongue. He begins by giving a picture of its power. He compares the tongue to a bit in a horse's mouth, a small rudder that guides a large ship, and a small spark that can quickly grow to a powerful flame. Each of these devices may seem to be very small and unimpressive, yet they are capable of much!

Our tongues seem unimpressive, yet we can all quickly recall instances when someone's words have changed the course of history. Personally, we have all had times when our words or the words of those we love have changed the temperature, direction, and relationships within our homes. This fact brings me to James' next truth.

The tongue is not evil in and of itself. We have power to use it to "bless our God" and "curse men." In Matthew 12:34, Jesus says: "For out of the abundance of the heart the mouth speaks." The words that come out of our mouths are an accurate picture of our hearts. In my house of teenagers, I often hear harsh words spoken to one another or about someone else. I always respond, "That was cruel, unkind, and a bit extreme." They say, "Mom, that is not what I meant." This verse has been useful a thousand times to remind them that what they said is exactly what is in their hearts. I usually get the eye roll, but it is true.

The words that we utter are what are actually in our hearts. So, how do we overcome? "No man can tame the tongue" (James 3:8). We need Jesus and His Holy Spirit to change our hearts and direct our speech. Since we know our hearts are "deceitful" and "desperately wicked" (Jer. 17:9), we need Jesus to change our hearts. Without His transformation of our hearts, our mouths will be used for evil instead of good. The tongue is a muscle that is capable of destroying all people in its path if not relinquished to the control of our Savior.

As a young married mom, I cannot tell you how many times I was bitter, frustrated, tired, or angry, and words flew off my tongue to prove it. The arguments and sorrows that resulted from those times caused much anguish for many. As I have grown older and hopefully a bit wiser, I seek to use my tongue to praise, encourage, build up, and count it all joy. It has made such a difference in the atmosphere of our home and lives.

Carmen Howell

Prayer: *Allow the Lord to change your heart! Let your words be a reflection of a heart that is completely His, that trusts in Him to right the wrongs, heal the hurts, and navigate the struggles. May your words bless the Lord and not curse others.*

Personal Reflection: ....

Patience

James 5:1–11

◡◠

"You also be patient. Establish your hearts,
for the coming of the Lord is at hand." (v. 8)

Believers must be righteous in our responses to others. Following a discussion of how the rich are oppressing the righteous (vv. 1–6), James issues the command imploring believers to "be patient." In this passage, it is important to note that he is not referencing our circumstances or trials as he was in chapter one. He is referring to our dealings with people, more specifically, the people who are treating us poorly. How difficult!

Patience is translated as having a long fuse or being longsuffering. Practically, it means that we repeatedly forgive and love without condition or expectation, even when it is spurned and not appreciated in the slightest. Yes, even when we do not receive the thank you or the courtesy nod, we must exercise the same patience with others that God has exercised with us.

James is clear once again about how this is accomplished. We must "establish our hearts." Our hearts must be grounded in God's love for us and in the truth of His Word. We must establish our hearts not just for the moment but until "the coming of the Lord." There is no possibility of exercising this kind of patience if our love for Jesus is not the most important thing in the world to us. If we truly love Jesus with all our heart, soul, mind and strength (Deut. 6:5), we will love others as He has commanded and will enable us to do. Don't get me wrong . . . this is not an easy task.

In my strong-willed, obsessive-compulsive world, a daily surrender is required, pleading with my God to control my heart and use it for His glory. As a pastor's wife, patience with all (the good, the bad, and the hateful), if you know what I mean, is never easy. However, I have learned continually as James says that as I am patient and as I establish my heart in His truth, "the Lord is very compassionate and merciful" (James 5:11). He will bless in His time. He will right the wrongs in His time. He will give the ability to persevere and forgive in His time. He will hold my tongue.

The Bible is replete with examples of those who were patient when others mistreated them or made life difficult for them (Joseph, Moses, Job . . . just to name a few). Allow God to give you patience and resist taking matters into your own hands. Remember—His ways, not our ways; His time, not our time!

Carmen Howell

Prayer: *Do you see others as God sees them? Ask Him to convict you when you are not patient with the difficult people in your life. He will teach your heart how to respond with His compassion, mercy, and forgiveness.*

Personal Reflection:

Not "If " But "When" You Suffer

1 Peter 1:1–9

∽

"In this you greatly rejoice, though now for a little while, if need be, you have been grieved by various trials, that the genuineness of your faith, being much more precious than gold that perishes, though it is tested by fire, may be found to praise, honor, and glory at the revelation of Jesus Christ." (vv. 6–7)

The first 60 seconds after a baby is born are critical. The newborn infant must begin breathing on his own, so he must cry. The baby's first cry signals a successful transition to life outside the womb where the baby's own lungs must work to sustain respiration.

Verse 3 of today's passage refers to the Christian reader's experience of conversion—turning from sin to receive, by faith, forgiveness in Christ—in terms of a new birth: "Blessed *be* the God and Father of our Lord Jesus Christ, who . . . has begotten us again." Like a newborn baby who must be able to inhale and exhale in order to survive, a newborn Christian must quickly begin living by faith nurtured by the Holy Spirit, who empowers obedience and produces the fruit of holy living (Gal. 5:22–23). However, the infant's cry in the delivery room is audible proof of life, but how is the genuine faith of a true follower of Jesus distinguished from the piety of an impostor (especially one who is sincerely mistaken about her own identity)?

1 Peter 1:6–7 provide a partial answer in the little phrase "if need be" (Gk. *ei deon estin*), which conveys the idea of necessity. Typically, the verb *deō* denotes "binding" or "putting under obligation." Although your own lifetime and whatever length of time remains until "the revelation of Jesus Christ" seem to last longer than "a little while," for now trials are necessary. "Trials" (Gk. *periasmois*) are "tests" that prove your fidelity to the Lord, that your faith is genuine.

This idea of testing, examining, proving something to be genuine after intense scrutiny is central to the message of 1 Peter. In Greek, the word translated "genuineness" is *dokimion*, literally a "test" or "that by which something is tried or proved" to be authentic. If you have been born again in Christ, you can expect that "the genuineness of your faith" will, like gold, be "tested" (Gk. *dokimazomenou*, from the same Greek root as *dokimion*).

The faith of many Christians has been tested and proved genuine literally "by fire," but all Christians will be tried through one form of suffering or another. Every Christian's faith must undergo the refining process—not only to eliminate impurities, as extreme heat would do for gold, but to put the truth of the gospel on display. Therefore, "in this you greatly rejoice."

Tamra Hernandez

Prayer: *Ask the Lord to help you see His purposes for whatever trials you or your loved ones are experiencing as believers in Christ. Thank Him for bringing glory to His name through your suffering in ways you cannot see at this time.*

Personal Reflection: ....

....

....

....

....

....

....

Me? Obey Him?

1 Peter 2:1—3:2

"Wives, likewise, be submissive to your own husbands, that even if some do not obey the word, they, without a word, may be won by the conduct of their wives, when they observe your chaste conduct accompanied by fear." (3:1–2)

Jesus, in His life and especially through His atonement for our sins, is the most powerful example of submission. He provides the pattern for how His children—women and men—should live.

A wife is to be submissive to her husband, not because of any merit on his part but as an act of obedience to the Lord. Submission becomes an act of worship motivated by your love for the Lord and your desire to follow the example of Christ. Genuine biblical submission represents a wife's response to God in light of His love for her. It demonstrates the importance and uniqueness of the marriage relationship through which God has chosen to display His power and glory. Wives are created in the image of God just as their husbands; they are equally valuable to Him and stand before Him on level ground. Nevertheless wives are to submit themselves voluntarily to their husbands because God commands that they do so.

This submission calls for an inward disposition as well as outward actions. Peter begins from the outside and works in by noting that it is the wife's demeanor and lifestyle—the way she relates to an unbelieving husband—that will be her best evangelistic tool in reaching him with the gospel. Peter anticipated that wives who were believers might question the relevance of their submission to unbelieving husbands. Yet Peter reminds these wives that the purity of the life of a godly woman who is submissive even to a difficult husband can soften his heart without a word of testimony.

Chapter 2 prepares the way for understanding submission in chapter 3. There Peter notes that craving the Word of God, living holy lives, and drawing attention to the grace of God by the way you treat other believers, citizens, and employees—these will mark believers and set them apart.

Submission (Gk. *hupotassō*, lit "lining up under authority") does not mean that a wife should subject herself to abusive tyranny. Biblical submission is willingly choosing to obey, voluntarily placing yourself under the authority of another. It means equality in personhood but does not call for the same role assignment. You do not choose when to obey but determine to obey God's mandate in all situations and circumstances. Your will is void of personal stubbornness as you voluntarily commit yourself to service to others and ultimately to the Lord.

Dorothy Kelley Patterson

Prayer: *Ask the Lord to give you a submissive spirit, reflecting Jesus' example of submission to God the Father. Let your marriage be a testimony to your humble obedience to Christ.*

Personal Reflection: ....

....

....

....

....

....

....

Bejeweled by God

1 Peter 3:3–6

⌒

"Do not let your adornment be merely outward—arranging the hair, wearing gold, or putting on fine apparel—rather let it be the hidden person of the heart, with the incorruptible beauty of a gentle and quiet spirit, which is very precious in the sight of God." (vv. 3–4)

Peter in these focal verses turns to the inward attitude that characterizes a godly woman. Some misinterpret this passage by suggesting that women are not to wear certain things or even care for their appearance, which is not what Peter is saying. Elsewhere Scripture refers to the attractive dress of godly women as noted in the description of Queen Esther in the court of Persia. Peter does not stop with a prohibition but rather continues with his teaching point (v. 4). He is not setting forth a legal code of what can and cannot be worn, but he is reminding women that the outward appearance is not what matters most to God (see 1 Sam. 16:7).

Peter records three aspects of biblical beauty as being:

- **hidden**—internal and not external, not ostentatious but modest and humble;
- **incorruptible,** not fading away, timeless;
- **precious,** of great value to God.

This failsafe combination is described as **a gentle and quiet spirit**. To be "gentle" (Gk. *praeos,* "meek, humble") is a mark of strength rather than weakness. It is not a natural quality; it is acquired painstakingly. Gentleness is included as a character quality in the Beatitudes (Matt. 5:5) and as a fruit of the Spirit (Gal. 5:23).

Being "quiet" (Gk. *hēsuchiou*) does not allude to total silence, nor does it suggest the absence of joy or a bland personality. Rather the idea expressed is self-control—or better, God-control—not so much a reference to what you do as to how you do it. There is no chaos or confusion but an overall calm spirit even in challenging circumstances.

In contrast to gold, jewels, and other ornamentation—all of which eventually fade—the woman with **a gentle and quiet spirit** will catch the attention of others in a very positive way. Not only her husband, but others as well, will observe her behavior. This godly demeanor carries the divine seal of approval and brings glory to the Lord and a calming peace to all in her household.

Dorothy Kelley Patterson

Prayer: *Ask the Lord to create in your heart this gentle and quiet spirit—to give you humility and God-control so that your life is governed by a peace that sets you apart from all others.*

Personal Reflection: ....

....

....

....

....

....

....

The Reciprocity of God's Plan for Marriage

1 Peter 3:7–14

*"Husbands, likewise, dwell with them with understanding,
giving honor to the wife, as to the weaker vessel, and as being heirs
together of the grace of life, that your prayers may not be hindered." (v. 7)*

Husbands, as well as wives, are admonished to follow the divinely established pattern for marriage. This focal verse exhorts husbands to pursue the assignment of servant leadership with two gifts of love: **understanding** and **honor**.

Is there any man who truly understands women? Yet, the challenge remains for a husband to study his wife, to take note of what she likes to do and of what brings delight to her soul. No other person in her life has the opportunity to know her in such an intimate setting—emotionally (what makes her happy or sad), intellectually (what does she read; what draws her listening ear; what are her interests in learning), physically (what does she like to do; what keeps her healthy), and spiritually (what are her deepest hurts; what draws her to God and His disciplines).

The **weaker vessel** could simply be a reference to the biological differences between women and men. As the bearer of life, a woman's body is fashioned to protect life, which means that she must avoid some of the heavy physical labor that has been traditionally pursued by men. A woman is fully equal to a man in bearing the image of God. She possesses intellectual and moral virtues just as he does, but she is generally physically weaker. However, there is much more to this analogy. In my home, after decades of travel and collecting, I have beautiful, rare, AND fragile porcelain. Each is definitely a "weaker vessel" and must be treated accordingly—with honor and respect to avoid accidental damage or destruction. So a husband is reminded to treat his wife with respect and honor because they are **heirs together** before God with the same spiritual standing.

As with many mandates of importance, this encouragement to a husband comes with a warning that to ignore this command concerning his responsibility to his wife will affect his own relationship to God. To ignore this divine directive will interrupt his own intimacy with the Lord, i.e., his **prayers** will be **hindered** or, more literally, "chopped off."

Without doubt, God takes the roles of husbands and wives seriously. A wife is to demonstrate her submissiveness to her husband before the Lord, and a husband is to live out meaningful leadership and gracious care of his wife. Both illustrate thereby that their hearts are committed to obedience before the Lord and a determination to follow his plan for their lives and home.

Dorothy Kelley Patterson

Prayer: *Ask the Lord to help your husband understand you and place before the Lord your own willingness to respond graciously to your husband's efforts to understand and honor you.*

Personal Reflection:

The Heart of Your Witness

1 Peter 3:15–22

*"But sanctify the Lord God in your hearts, and always be ready
to give a defense to everyone who asks you a reason for the hope
that is in you, with meekness and fear." (v. 15)*

Throughout chapter 3 of 1 Peter, you have been reminded of the difference between the inside and outside of your witness—the "in and out" of life! Unless you have the inward reverence for Christ and honor Him as the Lord of your life, your outward manifestation of the faith within will falter and lose its effectiveness.

Peter uses Jesus as the ultimate example for his directives to wives and husbands. He does so because Jesus is the innocent, sinless man who suffered and died in submission to the Father; He provides the ultimate model for submission. In this chapter, Peter also gives guidelines for living in a hostile culture, including the importance of attitudes that should mark the lives of all believers:

- **Unity.** Jesus Himself prayed that His disciples would be united together (John 17:11). Peter echoes that call for likemindedness (1 Pet. 3:8).
- **Compassion.** Jesus is the primary example of this Christian virtue. Peter calls for believers to be sympathetic with each other (v. 8).
- **Love.** Believers do not suffer with one another by default or because it is the right thing to do; rather they are admonished to genuinely love one another (v. 8).
- **Tenderheartedness.** The love and affection among believers is so ingrained that they respond with tenderness and concern (v. 8).
- **Courtesy.** They actually do the acts of love in deferring to one another with humble graciousness (v. 8).

As believers respond to one another in these loving ways, they are developing an inward reverence for Christ as Lord, which, in turn, prepares them to demonstrate that commitment in an outward readiness to bear testimony to the world of what has happened in their hearts. The word "defense" (Gk. *apologian*) describes how you are to make your case or to provide reasoned argument to support your position.

When someone recognizes your changed life and asks how such a change could happen, you should be ready to provide with joy and enthusiasm the reason for your **hope**. If someone comments on the sense of peace and calm, the smile of confident joy that seems to mark your demeanor, you then have the opportunity to testify to the source and motivation for the differences that have been observed in your life.

Dorothy Kelley Patterson

Prayer: *Seek the Lord's help in the midst of your life challenges to bring into play unity, compassion, love, tenderheartedness, and courtesy as you relate to believers. Then move a step forward to work toward developing the inward strength that will work itself out into a countenance of hope. Ask the Lord for the opportunity to share your testimony.*

Personal Reflection: ....

....

....

....

....

Does My Behavior as a Guest Cause My Hostess to Grumble?

1 Peter 4:1–11

"And above all things have fervent love for one another, for 'love will cover a multitude of sins.' Be hospitable to one another without grumbling." (vv. 8–9)

During the holiday season, invitations to a wide variety of activities are often extended by and to us. We know how we would like our guests to respond to our invitations. Frequently, in our haste, we don't take the time to consider how to biblically respond to the invitations offered to us so that we will be known as a gracious guest. While it is important for both men and women to be gracious, I chose to focus on women since, according to Solomon: "A gracious woman retains honor" (Prov. 11:16).

"Gracious" is a word that is not heard very often anymore. Even in Christian circles, it is often linked with the Victorian lifestyle rather than a behavior practiced by a twenty-first-century woman. "Etiquette" is a formal word for simple kindness that helps us put graciousness into action.

A woman's graciousness is a mirror in which she reveals her character. The apostle Paul shows his willingness to be considerate of others when he states in 1 Corinthians 9:19–22: "For though I am free from all *men*, I have made myself a servant to all, that I might win the more. . . . I have become all things to all *men* that I may by all means save some." Sadly, Christian women are often most guilty of failing to practice common courtesy.

A gracious woman, though not inflexible in her behavior, displays courtesy by adopting some simple etiquette guidelines:

- **Receiving an invitation is a special privilege.** Failing to respond to it within the stated time period is an ungracious action that demonstrates a lack of discretion, maturity, and responsibility. Proverbs 11:22 provides a poignant description of such a woman: "As a ring of gold in a swine's snout, *So is* a lovely woman who lacks discretion."

- **Arrive for the function fashionably on time.** The standard rule is no more than 15 minutes before or after the stated time for the function begins. Punctuality shows consideration of the host and hostess.
- **Select a suitable hostess gift**. The gift reflects your appreciation for your hostess's kindness. However, it is not a substitute for a thank-you note.
- **Send a warm, gracious, handwritten thank-you no later than one week after the event.** Whenever possible, refrain from using electronic communication.

Keeping these simple guidelines in mind will assist you in retaining the character and reputation of a gracious woman and remove any reason for your hostess to grumble about your behavior as a guest!

Pat Ennis

Prayer: *Ask the Lord to help you to choose to extend hospitality without grumbling and to learn to be a gracious guest. Pray that He will help you to learn simple etiquette skills so that your reputation as a guest brings honor to Him.*

Personal Reflection: ....

....

....

....

....

The Dividends of Suffering

1 Peter 5:1–14

"But may the God of all grace, who called us to His eternal glory by Christ Jesus, after you have suffered a while, perfect, establish, strengthen, and settle you." (v. 10)

In the midst of his discussion on the suffering God's children must endure, Peter focused again on the **grace** of God. He reminded his readers that God will use trials and difficulties to **perfect** and **strengthen them**—as a refining fire.

Only believers have the peace of God, for they alone have met and accepted the Prince of Peace. Peter called for believers to continue to hope in the Lord regardless of the difficulties they faced, for in the end they will be witnesses to others of God's marvelous grace and peace in their own lives (see 1 Pet. 1:2).

Never has there been a day when the body of Christ has experienced any more suffering. Modern-day martyrs for the Christian faith are continually before us as a reminder of what it costs to follow Christ faithfully even unto death. Believers know that God is in control; He cares for His children; He hears their prayers; they can entrust themselves to His protection.

Yet believers must remain alert and on guard at all times. We have an **adversary** who **walks about like a roaring lion** (1 Pet. 5:8). He is no ordinary opponent; he is dangerous. Taking a stand against Satan and protecting yourself from his attack calls for standing firmly in your faith. Peter admonishes us to resist him, which calls for a proactive approach, not just passively ignoring his attempts (v. 9).

What a comforting word to know that even in the midst of persecution, when left to your own devices, **the mighty hand of God** is ready to lift you up. Peter calls for you to cast your cares upon Him, intentionally moving your worries and concerns to God.

The poetry of Annie Johnson Flint (1866–1932), who suffered from debilitating arthritis, testifies to God's faithfulness in her life:

He giveth more grace when the burdens grow greater,
He sendeth more strength when the labors increase;
To added affliction He addeth His mercy;
To multiplied trials, His multiplied peace. . . .

His love has no limit; His grace has no measure.
His pow'r has no boundary known unto men;
For out of His infinite riches in Jesus,
He giveth, and giveth, and giveth again!

(from "He Giveth More Grace")*

Dorothy Kelley Patterson

Prayer: *Ask the Lord to give you strength to walk through the challenges and difficulties you face. Allow Him to carry the burden. Seek His help in resisting the devil, who offers a quick fix that is really no solution. Put your trust in the Lord, who brings ultimate victory.*

Personal Reflection: ....

....

....

....

....

* See http://www.hymnary.org/text/he_giveth_more_grace_as_our_burdens.

Precious Promises

2 Peter 1:1–4

". . . Have been given to us exceedingly great and precious promises." (v. 4a)

God's Word is full of promises. Perhaps one of the most exciting things about following Christ is learning about His precious promises. Throughout God's Word, He makes promises to His children, which He will fulfill at the appropriate times.

God's promises vary from daily assurances to the end times and everything else in between. For example, in Psalm 50, God assures us that when we call on His name He will answer. In Ezekiel 37, God promises that He will one day return and collect to Himself those who have put their faith in Him. God's promises are found all throughout the Bible in many shapes and sizes.

Each of God's promises has a special meaning. They are applicable both to me as a high school student and to women in all ages and stages of life. His promises serve as encouragement to the oppressed, food to the hungry, and confidence to the weak.

Second Peter 1:4 is a reminder that God's promises are given to us as a defense mechanism to equip us for fighting off the temptations and struggles of the flesh. Everyone needs God's strength to combat spiritual warfare. The promises that we find throughout the Bible are possibly one of the greatest forms of encouragement we have available to us in this life.

In 2 Peter, God's promises are described as "precious" and "exceedingly great." The dictionary defines the word "precious" in this way: "of high price or great value." God's promises in the sacred Word of God are to be hidden in our hearts, serving as reminders and encouragement in the daily battle we all know as life.

I love to think of God's promises as His gift to us. When I receive a gift, I treasure it. It means something special to me. The same should be true of God's promises. We ought to value them as His gifts to us, the greatest gifts we will ever receive. His promises serve as a reflection of His love for us, which was ultimately on display when He died for us on the cross.

As Christian women striving to grow in our knowledge of God, we should be memorizing His promises and treasuring them in our hearts. I challenge you to dig deeper into God's Word and memorize some of His unfailing promises. They will be the ultimate resting place for you to lay the foundation of your life.

Abigail Howell

Prayer: *Ask the Lord to reveal His precious promises to you. In your quiet time, ask the Lord to help you to grasp a deep understanding of His promises and how they are applicable to your life.*

Personal Reflection: ....

....

....

....

....

....

....

The Ladder of Faith

2 Peter 1:5–11

". . . Add to your faith virtue, to virtue knowledge, to knowledge self-control, to self-control perseverance, to perseverance godliness, to godliness brotherly kindness, and to brotherly kindness love." (vv. 5–7)

Some have called these focal verses a "symphony of faith" because when blended together they are as a memorable melody to be played again and again, yet always pleasing to the ear! Peter is describing the qualities that should be evident and ever increasing in the life of a believer as she grows in her knowledge of God and in understanding His purposes for her life. Because believers belong to Christ, they must reflect Him by exhibiting the virtues that are pleasing to Him. As they become more like Him, this growing maturity in faith not only brings glory to the Lord but also helps the believer to escape the **corruption** of the world (2 Pet. 1:4).

Henry Ward Beecher made an astute observation on the difference between perseverance (i.e., continuing faithfully on the journey despite obstacles in the way) and obstinacy (i.e., stopping and diverting from the path of the journey because of difficulties). He noted that perseverance comes from "a strong will" and obstinacy from "a strong won't."

Too many woman today rebel against the "wait" our Lord demands as we make our journey through life. They expect instant gratification and instant results. Waiting is tough—and not for the faint-hearted. It carries uncertainty and challenges; yet for the believer waiting often gives time for God to work. If you try to bypass the divine timing, you may well miss some blessings along the way as well as some lessons to be learned. You begin the climb of this ladder from a foundation of **faith** (v. 5) and culminate your ascent with **love**. The emphasis is not on the order in which these character traits come into your heart and guide your life but rather that every believer must be diligent to cultivate these virtues. Faith indeed is the springboard for all, and love is the crown for perseverance in the journey.

The first six qualities (faith, virtue, knowledge, self-control, perseverance, godliness) primarily address your relationship with God, and the final two (fellowship and love) represent the overflow of that relationship into how you relate to others (v. 7). All these qualities should set apart a believer who is growing in grace and understanding of what it means to follow Christ. This zealous pursuit of holiness is rooted in the active grace of God in a woman's life. Godly character comes only through an active, personal walk with the Lord.

Dorothy Kelley Patterson

Prayer: *Ask the Lord to give you strength for the journey, perseverance and not obstinacy. As you meet challenges along the way, place them before Him and call upon Him to help you overcome and move forward.*

Personal Reflection: ....

....

....

....

....

....

What Is True?

1 John 1:1–10

*"That which was from the beginning, which we have heard,
which we have seen with our eyes, which we have looked upon,
and our hands have handled, concerning the Word of life." (v. 1)*

How do we know that Jesus was who He claimed to be? John begins his epistle attempting to settle the controversy over how the historical man called Jesus truly was the Christ (vv. 1–3). This topic was and still is important because the truth surrounding the life of Christ determines all other truth. To say it another way, if the claims and life of Jesus are really true, it carries implications that impact every aspect of our lives. The gospel is the ultimate domino effect. No area of our life is left untouched.

Here John is giving a clear progression of the gospel. It "was from the beginning" (v. 1); it was revealed (v. 2); it was proclaimed by the apostles (v. 3) and shared with others to complete their joy (v. 4). John could speak with authority regarding the life of Christ because he was a witness to the life, teachings, and actions of Jesus during His earthly ministry (vv. 1–3). John saw Jesus, touched Him, and experienced the truth of Jesus' nature (vv. 1–3).

The word "declare" is found in verse 3, meaning "report, announce, or tell." What he had personally experienced, John wanted to share with others so that they too could know the truth regarding Jesus: He is the Christ. He didn't just see Jesus as one who spoke the truth but as one who is the Truth. In other words, Jesus was not just the messenger, but He is the actual Message (John 14:6).

John provided two reasons for writing this historical account—fellowship and joy (1 John 1:3–4). First, believers enter into eternal fellowship with God at the time of salvation. Because of this reality, they also enter into fellowship with other believers being co-heirs of heaven with one another. Second, John shared that it would bring him great joy as a pastor, if they were able to participate in this fellowship along with him.

If we want to know the truth, we must actually know Jesus! We don't just need to know about Christ; we actually need to know Christ Himself personally. Even though we can't walk beside Jesus like John did, God has given us His Word along with the Holy Spirit living inside of us to know Him better. Are you daily seeking to know Christ better?

Meredith Bone Floyd

Prayer: *Have you ever received for the first time the truth in the Bible about Jesus? If not, why don't you act on the truth of the gospel and willingly choose to repent of your sin and put your faith in Christ? Jesus said in John 14:6, "I am the way, the truth, and the life. No one comes to the Father except through Me."*

Personal Reflection: ....

....

....

....

....

....

....

....

Fellowship = Most Intimate Kind of Relationship

1 John 1:1–10

"That which we have seen and heard we declare to you,
that you also may have fellowship with us; and truly our fellowship
is with the Father and with His Son Jesus Christ." (v. 3)

Have you entered into the fellowship of which John speaks? If you are in Christ, the answer is yes. You too, like every other believer enter into fellowship with God and His Son Jesus Christ at the moment of salvation (v. 3).

John provides two reasons for writing—fellowship and joy (vv. 3–4). Fellowship, from the Greek word *koinōnia*, means "close relationship or participation." This word suggests that a group, corporately or with each possessing an equal part, has joint ownership of something. What is this something? In this case, believers are all co-heirs of heaven. The fellowship that believers share together can only be a reality after each person first has her own individual fellowship with God. This fellowship is eternal and will be perfected one day in the presence of God. Therefore, we can have fellowship with one another because first we each have personal fellowship with God.

The second purpose for his letter is joy (v. 4). John, as their pastor and spiritual shepherd, explained that he could not experience complete joy until those under his care experienced this same fellowship he himself had experienced (v. 3). John could testify to the truth of Christ as the embodiment of the Gospel because he saw Him, touched Him, and witnessed His miracles (vv. 1–2). John felt responsible for his flock and desired for them to share in eternal life through Christ (v. 3).

Have you ever crossed paths with another Christian woman and with one conversation felt like you have known her for a lifetime? What fellowship and joy! As believers, we forget what a blessing this intimate connection is, often taking it for granted. As Christ followers, we have so much we share in common, not just the hope of heaven. We connect because we both share in His love, His goodness, His faithfulness, His grace, His supernatural power, His life-changing abilities, His powerful Word, His healing, His Holiness, and the list goes on and on.

God often uses the fellowship that believers share to minister to one another. We weep together, we rejoice together. In other words, we do life together. May we never fail to be thankful for the reality of fellowship with our Father, with Christ, and with other believers. Fellowship is a spiritual reality, ours to treasure and enjoy.

Meredith Bone Floyd

Prayer: *Spend some time thanking God for the opportunity to enjoy fellowship with Him, with Christ, and with other believers now and for eternity. Thank Jesus for bringing this blessing to us through His sacrificial death on the cross. Ask the Lord to allow you to understand and experience fellowship fully, as He intends, with Him and with other believers.*

Personal Reflection: ....

....

....

....

....

....

The Christian's Response to the World

1 John 2:12–17

"If anyone loves the world, the love of the Father is not in him." (v. 15b)

What is your primary loyalty? Who do you love? In this passage, John writes to three groups of people in the church and highlights their various spiritual characteristics. He thinks of the church as a family and addresses the three groups accordingly as "children," "fathers," and "young men." The "children" might be new believers who have experienced forgiveness of sins and have entered into a relationship with the Father. The "fathers" in the church are older, more mature believers who have a firmly established relationship with God. The "young men" are characterized as strong and victorious over the evil one. These young men are clearly strengthened to vanquish Satan by the "word" (Gk. *logos*) that abides in them (v. 14).

Sometimes John uses the term "Word" or "His Word" (Gk. *logos*) to refer to the Son but in this verse, "Word" refers back to His commandments (John 1:1–3). Overcoming evil and temptation in our personal spiritual walk will only happen after forgiveness of sin, knowledge of God, and regular study of the Scriptures. In His human state, Jesus also overcame temptation by being strong in the Word (Matt. 4:1–11; Luke 4:1–13).

John moves to an issue of great concern to Christians even today. He admonishes his readers not to "love the world," a dark and demonic power producing a set of attractions, priorities, and loyalties that human beings experience in this life and that comprise an outlook and attitude that stands in rebellion against God. We "love the world" whenever selfish priorities and attractions to things that please our bodies, eyes, and egos squeeze out God's eternal agenda, in effect blinding us and making us insensitive to God's will for us and to the world's negative effect on us.

Christians must beware of allowing cultural definitions of body image, beauty, sensuality, or pride in an affluent lifestyle to determine how we use our time, resources, and energy. John states clearly that the world and its desires or lusts stand in opposition to God. Indeed, they are unlike God, temporary and passing away. God is the Eternal One, "Him who is from the beginning" (1 John 2:13–14).

Christians who love the world cannot love God (v. 15b): Those whose life priorities line up under the eternal God, who has forgiven their sin and empowers them to overcome the evil one, will always stand in conflict with the world, for the believer who fulfills God's will "abides forever" (v. 17).

Stefana Dan Laing

Prayer: *Hold fast to God our Savior and view your world with eyes that are unblinded by a selfish and rebellious agenda. Seek to reflect God's holy and eternal priorities, living a godly life in this ungodly world.*

Personal Reflection: ....

....

....

....

....

....

....

God's Idea of Love

1 John 4:7–12

⁓

"Everyone who loves is born of God and knows God . . . for God is love." (vv. 7–8)

In this passage, John urges believers in the church to love one another, a basic command given by Jesus Himself to His disciples before His death (John 13:34–35). John, who had been present as a young man with Jesus at that time, reiterates it many years later to the church, the Christian disciples of his own time. In 1 John 4, John addresses the problem of false teachers in the church, and in this context, he focuses on how one can know that she is a true believer. For John, the test is love (*agape*) shown within the Christian communion. But what kind of love?

First, love originates in God's very nature: "God is love" (4:8). It does not occur naturally in human beings but comes in response to God's gift of love (v. 10). We must first know and experience God's love in order then to love others.

Second, love is active, manifesting itself in self-sacrifice for the other: "He loved us and sent His Son *to be* the propitiation for our sins" (v. 10). In sending His most beloved and unique, only-begotten Son (v. 9), God met our deepest need and solved our greatest problem. By atoning for our sins, He cleansed us and spared us from the death-dealing wrath we deserved. This sacrifice leads to the third characteristic of God's love: its life-giving nature (v. 9).

The parallels between this passage and John 3 and 13 are stunning, with equally powerful implications for the church. As God gave an example of true love manifested in sacrifice of the best He had (John 3:16), Jesus gave an example of true love as sacrificial service (John 13:15). John calls upon believers to follow those examples and love one another since "God so loved us" (1 John 4:11). As the pinnacle of expressing God's love in serving, loving, and self-sacrificial action, John writes: "His love has been perfected in us" if we love as God loves us (v. 12).

Jesus told His followers that their love for one another in sacrificial service is the evidence of their discipleship and faith in Jesus (John 13:35). John passes on the lesson he learned at the farewell supper with Jesus, writing to believers that when they love one another, they manifest the presence of God Himself, whom "no one has seen" (1 John 4:12). How amazing: We make the invisible God visible by our love for one another in a community of sacrificial service!

Stefana Dan Laing

Prayer: *Express your gratitude for God's love for you, shown in sending the unique Son. Ask Him to give you godly, sacrificial love to reflect the invisible God.*

Personal Reflection: ....

....

....

....

....

....

....

....

Prayer as a Divine Conduit

1 John 5:14–17

"Now this is the confidence that we have in Him, that if we ask anything according to His will, He hears us. And if we know that He hears us, whatever we ask, we know that we have the petitions that we have asked of Him." (vv. 14–15)

"Mom, I just want you to listen to me!" my daughter often says, especially when she wants something already refused. She believes I said "no" because I didn't fully understand her request. Some approach our heavenly Father the same way, asking for something, then if we don't get it when we want it, assuming God was not listening to our request. As I love my daughter and want the best for her, God loves His children in a more perfect way and desires only the best for us.

John challenges us to come to God with confidence. David reminds us there is nothing that deserves our confidence more than God Himself: *"It is better to trust in the Lord than put confidence in man"* (Ps. 118:8). When we have a burden, only God is trustworthy to handle it. So if we are confident in anyone's help, we should turn first to God, asking anything according to God's will. His will is found in His Word.

Because God is our heavenly Father and loves us with the perfect love of a parent, we can confidently come to Him with the requests that we know are important to Him. Then, He hears us. When I can reassure my daughter that I have heard her and understand her request, she becomes more content. She may or may not get what she is wanting, but the knowledge of being heard satisfies her striving soul.

God not only hears us, He will give us our petitions. If prayer is a divine conduit, then the act of bringing our requests to God is a two-faceted process. First, we confidently make our requests known to the Lord who hears. Second, as the Lord hears those requests, He responds to our petitions. Because God is sovereign, omnipotent, and all together good, the granting of our petitions might look different from what we imagine. The answers to our prayers could be like looking into a mirror dimly lit (1 Cor. 13:12). We might not understand fully now, but one day, in the perfect completion of time, we will understand completely.

Now we must choose to step out in faith and trust God with our requests. As we step out boldly and with confidence, seeking God's perfect will, God hears. Knowing that God hears, we find peace in His perfect answer.

Melanie Lenow

Prayer: *Meditate on the fact that the God who loves you and created you will hear your requests. Thank Him and open your heart to Him with requests and petitions. You can be honest with God about what is on your heart. Confidently trust that He hears and He will answer you.*

Personal Reflection: ....

....

....

....

....

....

....

Elect Lady and Her Children

2 John 1–3

"The Elder, To the elect lady and her children, whom I love in truth, and not only I, but also all those who have known the truth." (v. 1)

"The elect lady" is a term of endearment and respect. Actually, the word "lady" (Gk. *kuria*) is the feminine form of the word "lord." In this verse, we discover that this woman has not only been chosen by God, but she has also chosen Him. A woman chosen by God is a blessed woman indeed. Clearly when God chose her, she became aware of His selection; and she made a choice to serve the one true God. As a result, she has many responsibilities and many blessings. Women chosen by God have great influence on others. He has sketched out our days before even one of them began (Ps. 139:16).

Scholars differ greatly about the nature of "the elect lady," whether the Bride of Christ or a literal lady. Let's consider both. The Bride of Christ and the special lady of the church both have an opportunity to live the truth and be the truth in the community where they reside. Though it is a challenge for us totally to submit our lives as women to be truth, we must live truth and produce spiritual children along the way. Many times we get busy doing many good deeds, but if we are to act as the bride and be the "elect lady," then we must learn to have "grace, mercy, and peace" (v. 3), all of which we receive from our Lord.

As a young child, the idea of a mighty God choosing me seemed foreign and unbelievable. I am a mostly unlikely "elect lady." Today, years after my conversion, I stand in awe at the profound grace, mercy, and peace God has shown me through His love (v. 3). He plucked me out of the grey miry clay, and God chose me. Out of my family of origin, a family marked by secrets and dysfunction, God chose me.

Can you relate? Have you been plucked out of your crazy world? Christians have been chosen by God, and have chosen to follow Him. How are we reproducing ourselves as the "elect lady," the Bride of Christ? Women should be intentionally investing their time, energy, influence, and resources in reproducing spiritual children.

Diane Nix

Prayer: *Praise the Father for choosing you and allowing you to choose Him. Pray that you will live the truth and be the truth in the world He created for you. Ask Him to help you always to be aware of the people in your path and the responsibility you have for producing spiritual children. Pray for yourself and other Christians to produce growing, healthy spiritual children.*

Personal Reflection: ....

....

....

....

....

....

....

....

This is Love, That We Keep His Commandments

2 John 4–6

"This is love, that we walk according to His commandments. This is the command-ment, that as you have heard from the beginning, you should walk in it." (v. 6)

Love and acceptance are two of the greatest needs of people today. Women have, as one of their greatest desires, to love and to be loved. John reminds Christians that we are to love one another. The question to answer today is: How am I loving? Do I love others as I am instructed in 2 John? Do I speak the truth in love (Eph. 4:15)?

God's children are to keep all His commandments. Knowing the truth allows us to be on guard for deceivers (2 John 7–8). Scripture says that we will know the truth, and the truth shall make us free (John 8:32). Let's be challenged and dig deeper into His Word.

John pleads for us to love one another (2 John 5). As we love one another, we are fortified in our faith and the truth. This reference is to *agapē* love. We can only love in this way if we are walking in truth (1 John 3:23).

Since the beginning of Christ's earthly ministry, He instructed us to love one another, not a sensual or selfish but unconditional and limitless love. This type of love is forgiving and empowering; it seeks the best for others and is sacrificing. This love is not about legalistically following rules but is about sacrifice of time, service, and heart–rending intercession for others. This love is costly as it cost our Savior His life. Our love for one another is first expressed in how we live our lives, obeying the commandments of our Lord. Vance Havner, a Baptist preacher, once said: "What we live is what we believe. Everything else is just religious talk."

Love as Christ loved; walk in love. Love sacrificially. Love intentionally. Love when you are understood and when you are misunderstood by others. Love when you are falsely accused or trusted. Love when no one is watching or when everyone is watching. Love when you are accepted or when you are rejected. Love when there is approval or when there is disapproval. Love when you are hated or when you are loved. Love when it's hard and when it's easy. Love. *Agapē* love! The world in which you live will take notice if you love like Christ.

Diane Nix

Prayer: *Through prayer, examine your walk. Are you walking in love? Pray and seek forgiveness for your lack of love. Forgive others for not loving as they should? Ask God to help you to express His love in every aspect of your life. Ask God to help you to walk in His truth, protecting you from any deceivers or false teachers.*

Personal Reflection: ....

....

....

....

....

....

....

....

The Ultimate Satisfaction for Every Mother

3 John 1–8

"I have no greater joy than to hear that my children walk in truth." (v. 4)

The greatest mission field for a mother is her children. Fathers and mothers have the high calling and high privilege of pointing their children to Christ. The most powerful way of leading your children to truth is by imitating Christ daily. Nothing can be more challenging, but it is possible, as we gain our strength from Christ and are renewed daily from His Word, to be the mothers He desires us to be.

Known as the "beloved disciple," the apostle John wrote 3 John to Gaius, his spiritual child. He speaks of his love toward him in the first verse of 3 John: "To the beloved Gaius, whom I love in truth." John had heard reports from others that Gaius was walking in truth. John's entire life was surrendered to being a testimony for Christ, and he rejoiced in this friend's reputation for love and faithfulness to Christ.

Mothers must also surrender their lives to the Lord. They cannot, nor should they, depend on the church, the school, or the babysitter to teach their beloved children given to them to nurture for His glory. Mothers must enter into their prayer closets, praying daily for their children. John prayed that Gaius would prosper in all things and be in good health. He also prayed that he would walk in truth.

Nothing is more grievous to a mother than to discover that her little one is sick. It hurts her heart to see a precious child suffering in any way. Naturally, mothers begin to pray for the health of their little children at a very young age.

Dear sister, let us not neglect to pray for the spiritual health of our children on a daily basis. John prayed for soul of Gaius. We are called to pray for our children spiritually and be examples of Christ to them daily in all we say and do. May we point their little hearts toward eternity by being living examples of the truth to them as we lean on Christ daily for guidance and endurance to be godly mothers.

May our children's spiritual growth and maturity be our greatest concern and mission! May we be filled with joy as we anticipate the fruit that will result as they respond to Christ! Our ultimate satisfaction as mothers is seeing our children walk with the Lord.

Monica Rose Brennan

Prayer: *Ask the Lord to place a specific prayer on your heart for your children. Begin to pray this prayer over them daily. Pray that they will respond to truth and that you will be the example of Christ to them. Ask the Lord for strength to be the mother He desires you to be for His glory.*

Personal Reflection: ....

....

....

....

....

....

....

....

He Is Able

Jude 20–25

"Now to Him who is able to keep you from stumbling,
And to present you faultless
Before the presence of His glory with exceeding joy,
To God our Savior,
Who alone is wise,
Be glory and majesty,
Dominion and power, both now and forever.
Amen." (vv. 24–25)

One of my all-time favorite movies is *The Sound of Music*. The lead character, Maria, is a postulant at Nonnberg Abbey. To say she was a challenge to the nuns, who had charge over her, is an understatement! The song "Maria" describes their frustration as they try to keep her out of trouble, develop her spiritually, and prepare her to take her final vows as a nun. They asked questions like, "How do you keep a wave upon the sand?" and "How do you hold a moonbeam in your hand?"

Maria was being prepared to live at Nonnberg Abbey. Those of us who believe in Jesus Christ as Lord and Savior are being prepared to live in Heaven for all eternity (John 3:16). The nuns were quite befuddled about how they were going to meet their challenge. Our text today assures us that Jesus is not challenged in preparing us to stand one day in the presence of God (2 Cor. 5:21). He is not wringing His hands and asking, "How am I going to protect this one?" or "How am I going to keep this one until the time of presenting her before the heavenly Father?" No, in fact, the text tells us that "He is able" to keep us pure and holy. The death of Jesus on the cross assures that believers are faultless and filled with great joy. He will present us to our heavenly Father one day.

Maria had to do her part in the preparation as well. What is our part in the preparation for eternal life with God? Jude 20–23 sheds light on this question:

- We are to build upon our faith by hearing God as we read His Word and committing to a body of believers (i.e., the church).
- We are to continue in prayer, simply talking to God.
- We are to keep loving Him.

As Jude tells us, our preparation for eternity is fueled by a constant reminder of His character—glorious, majestic, and powerful—as well as by the constant reminder of His love for us. He gave His only Son, "who is able" to present us faultless. If He can do that, He is able to do anything.

Denise O'Donoghue

Prayer: *Worship the Father as glorious, majestic, powerful, and all-loving. Thank Him for the work Jesus did on the cross and the work that He continues to do as He keeps you from stumbling, ever preparing you to meet your heavenly Father. Thank God for His Word, and ask Him to give you motivation as well as the practical skills to manage your time well, as you study His Word.*

Personal Reflection:

Reviving Your Marriage

Revelation 2:1–7

*"Remember therefore from where you have fallen; repent and do
the first works, or else I will come to you quickly and remove your
lampstand from its place—unless you repent." (v. 5)*

Paul used Ephesus as a center for evangelizing the entire region. Jesus reminded the church at Ephesus that He is walking among the churches and observing their actions as well as discerning their motives, something only God can do (v. 1).

The Ephesian believers were praised for their "works . . . labor . . . and patience" in their pursuit of Christ (v. 2). They were intent on ridding the church of evil, especially the false teachers in their midst (vv. 2, 6). In addition to zeal for truth and purity, the Ephesians did not become weary in their labor for Christ (v. 3).

Despite all this good, the Ephesians abandoned their "first love," which is a reference to their love for Christ (v. 4). They had moved away from their all-consuming love for their Savior or perhaps lost their love for one another.

John's message may also be applicable to any situation in which you fall away from your first love and from the joy and commitment of a new and fresh relationship. Here is his pattern for revival and renewal:

- **Remember**—In marriage, the honeymoon and days immediately thereafter are usually full of unconditional love and of patience with mistakes or omissions. However, when challenges come—taking one another for granted, overlooking praise and gratitude for what is good, harping on what is wrong—affections begin to wane and bitterness takes root.
- **Repent**—Until you recognize that things are not right and accept responsibility for your part in the deterioration of your relationship, you cannot move forward. You must literally change your thinking,

turn around, and go another way. This spirit of repentance will be marked by sorrow for wrong-doing and the desire to go a different way.

- **Do the first works**—It is not enough to remember how it was when you were loving and serving one another, nor does it solve the problem to recognize wrong and turn away from a destructive path. You must set your course again on the divine plan for exclusive loyalty to one another and inclusive commitment in all areas of life.

The message is clear—to the church at Ephesus and, by extension, to wives and husbands in marriage: A relationship without God-anointed love, pure and undefiled, is no longer a Christ-honoring marriage. The Lord will always reward obedience—in the church and in marriage or in any other relationship.

Dorothy Kelley Patterson

Prayer: *Allow the Lord to bring to your heart and mind a memory of the new and fresh and God-anointed relationship from which you have strayed. Ask Him to give you courage to turn around and go back to what you know you should do to honor Him in that relationship. Then do it!*

Personal Reflection: ....

....

....

....

....

Opening the Door

Revelation 2:12–17

". . . These things says He who has the sharp two-edged sword: 'I know your works, and where you dwell, where Satan's throne is. *And you hold fast to My name, and did not deny My faith even in the days in which Antipas* was *My faithful martyr, who was killed among you, where Satan dwells.'"* (vv. 12–13)

In the first century A.D., the city of Pergamos was the leading religious center of Asia Minor and thus full of temples, shrines, and altars. It was also a center for emperor worship, and Christians were persecuted harshly for their refusal to participate in this expression of civic loyalty and patriotism. For this reason, Jesus called Pergamos the place "where Satan's throne *is*" (v. 13).

Jesus reminded the Christians in Pergamos that Christ, not the Roman government, is the true and ultimate judge. He transformed Rome's symbol of their might and power to turn their attention of Christ and His **"sharp two-edged sword,"** which Charles Haddon Spurgeon described in this way: "God's sword is all blade!"

In light of the heresy infecting the church at Pergamos, Jesus called them to repent of their immorality and antinomianism immediately (vv. 14–15). If they refused to repent, Jesus warned that He would "fight against them" (literally "carry on a war," v. 16). Jesus promised to execute swift judgment upon the heretics and their followers as well as on the church for harboring them (v. 16).

When false doctrine arises within a local congregation, the church is responsible to root out the heresy, correct those who are teaching it, and exercise discipline upon those who refuse to repent. If the church refuses to accept this responsibility, Jesus Himself will deal with those inflicting damage.

Jesus chose to use the **sword** for this fight. John uses this vivid language as bookends for the passage—first in verse 12 and then again in verse 16, the "sword" is mentioned. There is no doubt that God's word is a powerful tool for fighting the enemy.

Paul refers to the "sword of the Spirit, which is the word of God" (Eph. 6:17). Believers are admonished throughout Scripture to study and commit to memory the word of God because this tool can be a devastating weapon against Satan and a healing balm for wounds you suffer in the battles of life. Setting aside time every day to read His word, meditate upon it, consider its application to life—such discipline sets you on a path to victory in the battles of life.

Dorothy Kelley Patterson

Prayer: *Ask the Lord to use His powerful sword to give you the best weapon to use against Satan. Take the verses of Scripture, and pray them from your heart. Find the victorious life through sitting at His feet.*

Personal Reflection: ....

....

....

....

....

....

....

....

Jezebel—A False Prophetess

Revelation 2:18–29

"Nevertheless I have a few things against you because you allow that woman Jezebel, who calls herself a prophetess, to teach and seduce My servants to commit sexual immorality and eat things sacrificed to idols." (v. 20)

The Old Testament introduces the vicious Queen Jezebel (1 Kin. 16—19; see Day 82), and the New Testament reflects on her wickedness (Rev. 2:18–20). Unfortunately, she is remembered for all the wrong reasons. Jezebel was the daughter of the King of Sidon and wife of King Ahab, who reigned in the northern kingdom of Israel during the ninth century B.C. (1 Kin. 16:31). She was a zealous worshipper of Baal and opponent of the one true God who ordered the prophets of God to be murdered (1 Kin. 18:4, 13). She threatened to kill the prophet Elijah and goaded her husband into evil acts (1 Kin. 19:2; 21:25). Jezebel met her tragic fate as prophesied by Elijah—she was eaten by dogs (21:23).

Jezebel's wicked life and gruesome death provide an illustration for the apostle John's message to the church at Thyatira (Rev. 2:18–29). In his messages to the seven churches, Paul gives a compliment for service, criticism of unfaithfulness, and a command for obedience. The church at Thyatira was full of good works, but many believers also participated in the idolatrous rituals and immoral lifestyles of the society. Paul harshly criticized them for following the practices of Jezebel in worshipping idols and committing sexual sins (vv. 20–23). Though Jezebel had been dead for nearly a thousand years, a false prophetess with the same evil spirit had arisen in the first-century church. Some professed Christians were serving the Lord while practicing idolatry; they were following the teaching of Jezebel, living idolatrous and immoral lives.

Does Thyatira sound like our world today? Do those church members seem like some of ours? Christians in the twenty-first century must look like Christ in this sinful world, serving Him and living sanctified lives. Only godly believers will receive God's blessings and be witnesses.

The warning to the church at Thyatira is our warning today—be faithful to the Lord, resisting the influence of the world. Jesus promises that those who keep His works until the end will receive "power over the nations," sharing authority with Jesus Christ Himself (vv. 24–28). What a great reward for a lifetime of faithfulness!

Rhonda Harrington Kelley

Prayer: *Evaluate your own heart and life in light of this Scripture. Are you living like the world or like Christ? Ask God to strengthen you to be faithful in your service and sanctification.*

Personal Reflection: ....

....

....

....

....

....

....

....

Opening the Door

Revelation 3:14–22

⚮

"Behold, I stand at the door and knock. If anyone hears My voice and opens the door, I will come in to him and dine with him, and he with Me." (v. 20)

Laodicea was an important city for both trade and communications in the eastern region of Asia Minor. It was famous as an administrative and judicial center, as a banking center for the region, and for its school of medicine. To the Laodicean Christians, Jesus called Himself "the Faithful and True Witness." This identification put Him in stark contrast to the Laodiceans, who were not faithful to Christ and whose witness consequently was meaningless.

Jesus had no words of commendation for the Laodiceans. He described them as **"neither cold nor hot,"** but **"lukewarm"** (vv. 15–16). The Laodiceans did not have a water supply; they had to pipe their water from a hot springs four miles away. By the time the water reached the city, it was lukewarm in contrast to the water from nearby Colosse, on one hand—its waters were famously cold, pure, and refreshing to drink—and, on the other hand, Hierapolis, whose hot springs were well known for their healing and therapeutic effect on the body. In both of these cities, respectively, the cold or hot water would be useful for something. However, lukewarm water was distasteful and useless.

Have you ever been served a tepid cup of coffee or tea? You were expected it to be piping hot or cooled down with ice cubes, but instead it is lukewarm. The drink is worthless—not refreshing to taste but depressing to your palate. Christ was saying that their deeds were worthless to Him. He had no use for a church that is not serving its proper purpose (v. 16). Jesus further exposed them as "wretched, miserable, poor, blind, and naked" (v. 17). This description was indicative of shame and degradation in the ancient world.

Christ had this advice (v. 18):

- They needed spiritual riches instead of earthly wealth ("gold refined in the fire");
- They should seek to get clothing of righteousness instead of worldly attire ("white garments");
- They should be looking for spiritual discernment to replace earthly vision ("eye salve").

The passage concludes with another rich metaphor. Jesus is standing "at the door" of the church—this is a group of believers. He is announcing His presence and sharing His eagerness to join them in fellowship (v. 20). The person who "hears" has a personal responsibility to open the door. The verse is not a reference to an appeal to an unbeliever but rather an admonition to believers to invite Christ in to share an intimate meal and time of fellowship.

Dorothy Kelley Patterson

Prayer: *Invite the Lord into your heart for a time of intimate fellowship. Let Him clean out the cobwebs and sweep out what should not be there so He can accomplish His purposes through you.*

Personal Reflection:

Come Up Here

Revelation 4:1–11

*"After these things I looked, and behold, a door standing open in heaven.
And the first voice which I heard was like a trumpet speaking with me, saying,
'Come up here, and I will show you things which must take place after this.'" (v. 1)*

Every woman understands the feeling of a door slammed in her face. Maybe literally, maybe figuratively, but it does not take many years of living to understand the feelings of rejection. Maybe it's a friend who has turned her back on you. Maybe it's a marriage where hurt is often felt. Maybe it's being overlooked for a promotion after many hours of hard work. Sometimes, with the best of intentions, we can strive to help, serve, and please others only to have the door of rejection closed on us.

Jesus Himself is standing before us, knocking for us to open the door of our heart and allow Him to come fill us with His divine fellowship (Rev. 3:20). John, the writer of Revelation, looks up and sees an open door welcoming him to come inside. Along with the open door, he hears a voice like a trumpet saying, "Come up here, and I will show you things which must take place after this" (4:1).

In comparison to the disappointment that we often find in the world around us, today's verse is a beautiful picture of what we find in a relationship with Christ. He is forever opening the door, not closing it. He is constantly welcoming us into His fellowship, not excluding us. Even when we hide because of hurt or shame, Christ comes to seek us out with forgiveness and acceptance.

The world around you might shut you out. You might feel alone and rejected, but notice the first thing John did, he looked up. God is forever standing before you with an open door beckoning to you, inviting you into His presence. Look up. Seek His face. Dig into His Word, and you will see Christ standing before you with open arms.

Is there one area in which you have been hurt by rejection? Write it down, and pray to God about it. Only He can take away that hurt and replace it with contentment and love. Allow Him to heal your heart. As you study Scripture, write down verses where you feel God beckoning you into fellowship with Him. Next time you feel disappointment, meditate on those verses to remind yourself that the God of the universe wants fellowship with you.

Melanie Lenow

Prayer: *Ask the Lord to forgive you for looking to the world for acceptance and love. Thank Him for always loving, always seeking, and always welcoming you. Ask Him to guide you into forgiveness for those who have rejected you.*

Personal Reflection: ....

....

....

....

....

....

....

....

Breaking News: "Babylon Has Fallen!"

Revelation 14:6–13

*"And another angel followed, saying, 'Babylon is fallen, is fallen,
that great city, because she has made all nations drink of the wine
of the wrath of her fornication.'" (v. 8)*

The nation of Babylon comes on the scene during the times of the kings. While the nation ended up being the instrument of judgment God used against Judah, the first king that welcomed Babylon into the gates of Jerusalem was not a wicked king, but Hezekiah, one of the more righteous kings of Judah. In a moment of pride, Hezekiah welcomed them into the gates to show them the acquired wealth of the nation of Judah. Later, Isaiah prophesied saying: "'Behold, the days are coming when all that *is* in your house, and what your fathers have accumulated until this day, shall be carried to Babylon; nothing shall be left,' says the LORD" (Is. 39:6). Thus began the important relationship that God orchestrated between His people and Babylon. Because of Judah's continued disobedience, God made Babylon His instrument of judgment toward His people. Just as Isaiah prophesied, the people of Judah were eventually swept away into captivity in Babylon.

God was still at work among His people, though. He did not leave them orphaned in Babylon. Through prophets like Jeremiah, the Lord still spoke to His people. He placed bold men like Ezra, Nehemiah, and Daniel who spoke up about the one true God in places of influence. However, over the vast span of time, Babylon remained a wicked nation. Its wretched worship of false gods paired with its incredible influence over the known biblical world led to its description as a harlot leading her followers to drink the wine of wrath (Rev. 17:5). Because of her own wickedness, Isaiah also prophesied Babylon's destruction in Isaiah 13:19.

Babylon was the world leader of her day. She was great, beautiful, and rich. However, she was godless. There are in the world many modern nations that are great, beautiful, and rich. They may seem untouchable even by God. However, the story of Babylon, which ends with the proclamation in Revelation, reminds us that God will not be mocked. Ultimately, He will judge the hearts of wicked and godless people and nations.

Is your heart turned to God, or are you following godless ways that lead to "drinking the wine of wrath?" Even among the wicked people of Babylon, God raised up leaders to point the way to the one true God. Could you be bolder in your areas of influence to point others to Christ? Could you be your city's Ezra or your nation's Daniel?

Melanie Lenow

Prayer: *Ask the Lord to forgive you when your heart has been wicked just like the people of Babylon. Thank God that He is faithful, promising to redeem the righteous as well as judge the wicked.*

Personal Reflection: ....

....

....

....

....

....

....

The Bride of the Lamb Readies Herself

Revelation 19:1–10

"'... His wife has made herself ready.' And to her it was granted to be arrayed in fine linen, clean and bright." (vv. 7b-8a)

Becoming a bride is one of the most exciting seasons in a woman's life. When the Lord in Scripture calls believers the "church" or His "bride," He is speaking a language we understand and talking directly to our hearts as women. A few facts about our preparation process as His bride are particularly interesting.

First, **the anticipation is palpable** (v. 7). With words like "glad," "rejoice," and "glory," intense and rightful merriment leaps off the pages of Scripture as Christians expectantly await the marriage of the Lamb to His bride, the church. It is going to happen, and it is will be the best wedding party imaginable.

Second, **she readies herself** (v. 7). The bride is clothed in the most beautiful dress, ready to meet her Husband. What bride-to-be do you know who, after she receives a proposal, does not immediately go on a strict diet and exercise program because she has only months to look the best she has ever looked? It is her wedding day, which means bridal photographs are going to be hung on the walls of their homes for the rest of their lives. The bride must look her best!

Third, **the fine linen she wears is given to her** (v. 8). She did not take it from any other person, make it with her own sewing skills, or purchase it with any money that she had earned. No, it was freely given, "clean and bright."

What a perfect picture of our own sanctification. Paul wrote something similar to the Colossians: "To this *end* I also labor, striving according to His working which works in me mightily" (Col. 1:29). This description is the perfect melding together of both "working out your own salvation" and "God working in you both to will and do of His good pleasure" (Phil. 2:12–13). We are to work toward maturity in Christ, actively disciplining ourselves to spend time in His Word and with His people, adding to our faith as we grow in our knowledge of Him (2 Pet. 1:5–9). But our work should never be about becoming better people and should never come from our flesh trying to be holy. We grow with the strength that He provides.

As the bride of Christ, we actively ready ourselves for the marriage of the Lamb with the fine linen we are given. We are not making ourselves pure; we are pure by way of Christ's redemptive work on the cross. Then, in response to being made pure, we conduct our lives in purity as the betrothed of Christ—the church.

Sarah Bubar

Prayer: *In what ways are you working toward growth in your relationship with Christ? Can you be doing more? If you are practicing these Christian disciplines in the strength of your flesh, stop. Confess that to God, and operate under His strength working through you.*

Personal Reflection: ....

....

....

....

....

....

....

Victory in Jesus

Revelation 21:1–8

"'God Himself will be with them and be *their God. And God will wipe away every tear from their eyes; there shall be no more death, nor sorrow, nor crying. There shall be no more pain, for the former things have passed away.'" (vv. 3b–4)*

The resurrection is the anchor of our hope. We know that heaven is not **here**, it's **there**. If we were given all we wanted here, our hearts would settle for this world rather than the next. Through myriad variations of "soap in the eyes," God is forever luring us up and away from this kingdom of pain, wooing us to Himself and His still invisible Kingdom where what we so keenly long for we shall, if we stoop to enter the small gate, most certainly find.

Read Revelation 21:3b–4 above. The Bible begins with perfection and ends with perfection, but in between is the saga of man's sin and God's mercy, the mercy that endures forever, reaching down to loved sinners. The story is faithful to the dark side and the bright side, to blatant disobedience and heroic obedience, chaos and order, suffering and joy—it's all in there, with God the Father standing always within the shadows, keeping watch above His own.

All that the world so desperately seeks the Lamb won, not by aggression but by surrender. That is the principle of the cross. It takes the weak and makes them strong. It takes our sin and bestows Christ's righteousness. Out of bondage we are made free. Darkness is overcome by light. Loss turns to gain.

Long before John wrote the Book of Revelation, the prophets had written of wonderful exchanges—Isaiah wrote of pine trees and myrtles replacing camel thorns and briars; of God's giving garlands instead of ashes, oil instead of mourners' tears, a garment of splendor for a heavy heart (Is. 61:3). Nehemiah wrote of blessings where there had been cursing; the psalmist of dancing and joy where there had been laments of pasture instead of wilderness. Were these mere visions of unreality?

Jesus spoke of transformations. The poor, the sorrowful, the hungry and thirsty, the persecuted would be happy, would inherit the Kingdom of Heaven, find consolation, be satisfied, have rich rewards.

Jesus, for the joy that was set before Him, accepted, embraced, and endured the cross. And for all who follow hard after Him, faces set as His was, "like a flint," refusing to be pushed backward, that same joy is in store, for He prayed, "that they may have my joy within them in full measure" (John 17:13).

Elisabeth Elliot

Prayer: *Thank God for the victory you have because of Christ's sacrifice on the cross. Thank Him that there will be a day in the future where every tear will be wiped away and where sorrow, death, pain, and crying will be exchanged for joy forevermore because of that victory!*

Personal Reflection: ....

....

....

....

....

....

....

An excerpt from Elisabeth Elliot's *A Path Through Suffering* (pages 188, 192–93).

No Adding or Taking Away the Words of This Book

Revelation 22:1–19

"If anyone adds to these things, God will add to him the plagues that are written in this book; and if anyone takes away from the words of the book of this prophecy, God shall take away his part from the Book of Life." (vv. 18b–19a)

At the very end of the book of Revelation, John issues a final warning to "everyone who hears the words of the prophecy of this book" (v. 18). All hearers and readers of Revelation from biblical times until forevermore needed to know not to add or take away from this book. God's perfect words written through John needed no improvement.

Other places in Scripture echo this sentiment. "You shall not add to the word which I command you, nor take from it, that you may keep the commandments of the Lord your God which I command you" (Deut. 4:2). It is imperative that God's Word remains as He intended so that God's commandments may be kept. In the fall of mankind (Gen. 3) is an example of both taking away and adding to God's Word. The serpent took away from God's Word by questioning things that God said. Eve added to God's Word by adding the prohibition that she could not even touch the fruit. Both of these mistakes are made frequently.

Some cults, such as Mormonism, add to God's Word by holding other writings on the same level with Scripture. Legalism also adds to God's Word. Some people today are like the Pharisees, adding rules not found in Scripture and creating a religion that relies on works more than grace. On the other side, some people seek to take away from God's Word. Some suggest that parts are not relevant today. Others question the authenticity of God's Word or diminish its importance by their disobedience. They do not want to live their lives according to God's Word, so they dismiss parts they don't like.

By adding to or taking away from God's Word, we place ourselves in judgment over Scripture when in reality, Scripture judges us. The Holy Spirit led the apostle John to write that no one should add to or take away from the words he had written. We would do well to heed this command and to apply it to the entire canon of Scripture. God breathed His Word through the inspiration of the Holy Spirit working in human authors to create the Bible—God's Words as He speaks. We need to read, study, memorize, and obey it. All of it is important and relevant to our lives.

How important is God's Word in your life? Do you seek daily to know God better through studying the Bible? God wants to work in your life, and He will use His Word to do so.

Joy Martin White

Prayer: *Pray that God would speak to you through His Word. Pray that you would be consistent in spending time with God in prayer and Bible study each day.*

Personal Reflection: ....

....

....

....

....

....

....

....

Even So, Come, Lord Jesus!

Revelation 22:20–21

*"He who testifies to these things says, 'Surely I am coming quickly.'
Amen. Even so, come, Lord Jesus!" (v. 20)*

As we come to the end of the New Testament, Christ's last words are recorded, emphasizing His imminent return: "Surely I am coming quickly" (v. 20). Jesus came to earth to save those who trust His deliverance from the penalty of their sins, and His return to take His followers to heaven with Him. These words promise a blessed hope found only in Jesus Christ.

Although these words promise a blessed hope for believers, they also deliver a harsh warning for unbelievers. Christ is coming again, and you need to be ready. At the end of this life, only two destinies await—heaven or hell. Every person who has ever lived or who will ever live ends up in one place or the other. The only way to get to heaven is through faith in Jesus Christ. Have you ever come to the place where you have recognized that you are a sinner, repented of your sins, and placed your faith and trust in the atoning work of Christ?

Jesus came to this earth as a baby born of a virgin. He did something that no one else has ever done. He lived a sinless life. When He died on the cross, He took upon Himself all the sins of the world. Three days later, He rose from the dead, conquering death and defeating the devil. Now He sits at the right hand of the Father making intercession for you and me. If you have never trusted Christ to be your Savior, will you do so now?

You may have trusted Christ as your Savior, but you must have some friends and family members who are not saved. Be bold, and share the blessed hope that is found only in Christ. With eternity in the balance, make sure you have done all that you can to tell others about Jesus. You will never regret your witness, but you very well may regret not sharing your faith. The most important decision anyone can ever make is trusting Christ. It is eternally important for us to proclaim Him faithfully.

The apostle John affirmed Jesus' promise that He is coming again: "Amen. Even so, come, Lord Jesus!" John knew Jesus and was anxiously awaiting His return. Having been exiled to the island of Patmos, John was the last surviving apostle. He loved Christ and longed to spend eternity with God in heaven.

Are you anxiously awaiting heaven? Do you long for Christ's return? Are you living as if Christ could return at any moment? If you knew Christ were returning tomorrow, how would you live differently?

Joy Martin White

Prayer: *Ask God to give you a longing for heaven. Ask Him to help you live today, as if He is returning tomorrow. Pray and ask God to show you with whom you should share Christ and be faithful to do it.*

Personal Reflection: ....

....

....

....

....

....

....

Co-Editors

Rhonda Harrington Kelley is the president's wife and adjunct professor of women's ministry at New Orleans Baptist Theological Seminary. She is also a Christian author and speaker. Formerly the director of speech pathology at Ochsner Medical Center, Dr. Kelley has a Master of Arts in Speech Pathology from Baylor University, a Doctor of Philosophy in Special Education from University of New Orleans, and additional studies in Women's Ministry from New Orleans Baptist Theological Seminary. She lives in New Orleans, Louisiana, with her husband Chuck, who has been president of New Orleans Baptist Theological Seminary since 1996.

Dorothy Kelley Patterson, a homemaker, helps her husband Paige Patterson, president of Southwestern Baptist Theological Seminary, by serving as professor of theology in women's studies. With graduate and post-graduate degrees in theology, Dr. Patterson teaches, speaks, and writes for women. She is a member of the Evangelical Theological Society, serves on the Advisory Board for the Council for Biblical Manhood and Womanhood, and attends Birchman Baptist Church. The Pattersons reside in Fort Worth, Texas, but travel extensively throughout the world. Their children Armour and Rachel Patterson live in Texas; Carmen and Mark Howell, with their daughters Abigail and Rebekah, live in Florida.

Special Contributor

Elisabeth Elliot, born in Belgium, moved to the United States as an infant with her missionary parents. She was called to missions, serving in Ecuador where Jim Elliot, who would later become her husband, also served. They were missionaries together to the Auca of eastern Ecuador. Jim was killed by tribe members in 1956 when their daughter Valerie was one year old. Elisabeth continued her work there for several years before returning to the States. She is the author of more than 20 books and has been a popular Christian speaker around the world. She married Lars Gren, a hospital chaplain, in 1977. The Grens now live in Magnolia, Massachusetts. For more information: www.elisabethelliot.org.

Contributing Authors

Chris Adams is senior lead women's ministry specialist at LifeWay Christian Resources. She is also an adjunct professor in the Women's Ministry Program at New Orleans Baptist Theological Seminary, where she received her undergraduate degree in Christian Ministry from the seminary's Leavell College. She is executive editor of *Journey,* a women's devotional magazine, and has compiled several Women's Ministry resources for LifeWay. She and her husband Pat live in Nashville, Tennessee.

Karen B. Allen is wife to Midwestern Baptist Theological Seminary President Jason Allen. In addition to her responsibilities as the president's wife, she also oversees the Midwestern Women's Institute. She received her undergraduate degree from the University of Mobile. She is the mother of five children: Anne-Marie, Caroline, William, Alden, and Elizabeth. The Allens live in Kansas City, Missouri.

Monica Rose Brennan is associate professor of women's leadership in the Department of Church Ministries and Christian Leadership as well as the director of the Center for Women's Leadership at Liberty University. She holds an advanced women's studies certificate from Southeastern Baptist Theological Seminary plus a Master of Arts in Religion and a Doctor of Ministry from Liberty Theological Seminary. Dr. Brennan and her husband Michael, parents to two-year old Elizabeth, are expecting their second child. They live in Madison Heights, Virginia, and serve with a church plant, Oasis Church.

Becky Brown is an author and composer through her ministry Little Brown Light. She has a Bachelor of Arts in History and English from Louisiana College, a Master of Arts in Student Personnel Administration from Northwestern State University, and a Master of Arts in Christian Education from New Orleans Baptist Theological Seminary, where she served in administration for a number of years. She enjoys writing devotionals and teaching women in retreat and conference settings. She lives in Richland, Mississippi.

Sarah Bubar is the dean of women for Word of Life Bible Institute at their extension campus in Hudson, Florida, overseeing the spiritual needs and discipleship of the women. She received a Master of Divinity with concentrations in Women's Studies and Biblical Languages from Southwestern Baptist Theological Seminary. She teaches a biblical womanhood class and is actively involved in the college ministry at her church.

Pat Ennis is distinguished professor and director of homemaking programs at Southwestern Baptist Theological Seminary. Dr. Ennis has authored and co-authored several books, including *The Christian Homemaker's Handbook* with Dorothy Patterson. Her life's mission is to love her Lord with ALL of her heart (Matt. 22:37), walk worthy of her calling (Eph. 4:1–3), and train the younger women to fulfill the Titus 2 mandate so that God's Word will not be discredited (Titus 2:3–5). She lives and serves the Lord in Fort Worth, Texas.

Candi Finch serves as an assistant professor of theology in women's studies at Southwestern Baptist Theological Seminary where she received a Master of Divinity with a concentration in Women's Studies and a Doctor of Philosophy in Systematic Theology and Church History. She has a heart to see young women come to know the Lord and become mature disciples of Christ. Dr. Finch lives in Fort Worth, Texas.

Meredith Bone Floyd is a pastor's wife in Fayetteville, Arkansas, where her husband Nick Floyd is one of the teaching pastors at Cross Church. She is mother to three children: Reese, Beckham, and Norah. She received a Biblical Studies degree from Liberty University with a concentration in Women's Ministry. Her desire is to encourage women toward the high calling of biblical womanhood.

Donna Gaines is a teacher/speaker to women at conferences and Bible studies. She has authored three books, gives leadership to the SBC Pastors' Wives Conference, and serves on the Executive Committee of the Ministers Wives Luncheon. She is married to Dr. Steve Gaines, pastor of Bellevue Baptist Church, Memphis, Tennessee. They have four children and nine grandchildren. Donna has a Bachelor of Science from Union University and a Master of Education from Texas Woman's University. She is passionate about missions and discipleship.

Christi Gibson serves in the Missions and Discipleship Ministry at First Baptist New Orleans and teaches in the women's ministry and student wives programs at New Orleans Baptist Theological Seminary as well as at the Louisiana Correctional Institution for Women. She received her Master of Divinity in Biblical Studies from New Orleans Baptist Theological Seminary, where her husband John is professor of communication. She is also a part of Inward—a ministry to the Bourbon Street sex industry in New Orleans. Her adult children, Callie and Trey, are a delight to her heart.

Sharon Gritz has written Bible study curriculum for LifeWay Christian Resources and enjoys teaching Bible studies to all ages in many settings as well as leading prayer groups. She has advanced degrees from and has taught at Southwestern Baptist Theological Seminary, where her recently-retired husband, Paul, taught for 32 years. Her daughter Lydia and son-in-law Taylor Whitley serve in an English-speaking church in Germany. She and her husband live in Fort Worth, Texas.

Susie Hawkins received her Master of Arts in Christian Leadership as well as a Master of Arts in Theology from Criswell College. She is married to O. S. Hawkins, president of GuideStone Financial Resources of the Southern Baptist Convention, They have two married daughters and six grandchildren. She has been actively involved in teaching, speaking, and writing for women's ministry and ministry wives. The Hawkins family lives in Dallas, Texas.

Tamra Hernandez has a Master of Divinity with Biblical Languages and a Doctor of Philosophy in Systematic Theology from Southwestern Baptist Theological Seminary. She has one son David, who is a long-term survivor of pediatric cancer, and a wonderful daughter-in-law Katie. Dr. Hernandez lives in Fort Worth, Texas, where she serves on staff at Southwestern Seminary and is a member of Wedgwood Baptist Church.

Abigail Howell is a pastor's daughter and a high school student living in Daytona Beach, Florida. In her free time, she enjoys writing her *Counting It All Joy* blog, traveling, and doing anything and everything with her family.

Carmen Howell is a pastor's wife and mother to two beautiful girls. Her favorite pastime is her family, and her passions are God's Word and her home. She loves to teach, mentor, and write. The Howell family lives in Daytona Beach, Florida, where her husband Mark is pastor of First Baptist Church Daytona Beach.

Rebekah Howell is a pastor's daughter and a high school student. She enjoys playing her guitar, writing her *Me . . . Plain and Simple* blog, and serving in the children's ministry at church. She lives with her family in Daytona Beach, Florida.

Ann Iorg is the wife of President Jeff Iorg of Golden Gate Baptist Theological Seminary. They have been married for more than 30 years and have three children and one grandchild. She has a Bachelor of Behavioral Science from Hardin Simmons University and a Master of Arts in Educational Leadership from Golden Gate Baptist Theological Seminary. She has also served as a pre-school director and teacher at various churches for more than 30 years. At the seminary, she enjoys being a hostess and teaching women about the practical aspects of life and ministry.

Judi Jackson currently serves as associate dean of students, coordinator of women's programs, and adjunct faculty member at New Orleans Baptist Theological Seminary where she received her Master of Religious Education as well as a Doctor of Philosophy in Christian Education. Dr. Jackson teaches and writes in the areas of women's ministry, ministerial wellness, and recreation/sports ministry. She is married to Dr. Allen Jackson, professor of youth ministry at NOBTS. They have two young adult children, Aaron and Sarah.

Stefana Dan Laing is assistant librarian for the Houston campus of Southwestern Baptist Theological Seminary and adjunct professor at Houston Graduate School of Theology. She received a Master of Divinity and Doctor of Philosophy in Patristics/Historical Theology from Southern Baptist Theological Seminary. She and her husband Dr. John Laing have three children. They teach an adult Sunday school class and are involved in discipleship training at Nassau Bay Baptist Church. They are also a military family—John has had two recent deployments as a chaplain in the Texas Army National Guard.

Laura Landry is nearing the completion of her Master of Arts in Counseling at New Orleans Baptist Theological Seminary. She is a research assistant with Dr. Rhonda Kelley, serves as a counselor intern for two ministries in New Orleans, and is a worship leader for a local church plant. She is also a birth doula, passionate about empowering women to honor God in their bodies. She has spent much of her young adult life traveling and serving Jesus overseas, where she hopes to return in the future as a counselor to abused women.

Melanie Lenow is the wife of Dr. Evan Lenow and mother of four precious children ranging in age from three to ten. She received an undergraduate degree in psychology and Christian studies as well as a Master of Biblical Counseling from Southeastern Baptist Theological Seminary. God has called her first to minister to her family and, second, to serve the ladies of her local church and Southwestern Baptist Theological Seminary. She has a passion for teaching God's Word as she leads Bible studies and writes for the *Biblical Woman* website. The Lenows live in Fort Worth, Texas.

Elizabeth W. Luter is a pastor's wife and retired pharmacist with a passion for women in the areas of spiritual growth and divine calling. She graduated from Xavier University College of Pharmacy and has also taken courses at the New Orleans Baptist Theological Seminary. She is director of women's ministry at Franklin Avenue Baptist Church and annually teaches women at the LifeWay Conference Center in Ridgecrest, North Carolina. She and her husband, Pastor Fred Luter Jr., have two married children—Kimberly (son-in-law Howard) and Fred, III, "Chip" (daughter-in-law Jasmine)—as well as one grandson, Fred Luter, IV, "Drew." They live in New Orleans, Louisiana.

Jaye Martin serves as president of Jaye Martin Ministries, whose mission is equipping leaders to share Christ and mobilizing believers through resources, training, and partnerships. She has earned two master's degrees from Southwestern Seminary and a Master of Theology from Southern Seminary. She has served in the Ministry of Evangelism, Women and Prayer at Houston's First Baptist Church, as women's evangelism strategist at North American Mission Board, and as director of women's leadership at Southern Seminary. She writes and equips leaders at numerous seminaries, state convention and church events and is a trustee of the International Mission Board. Jaye is married to Dana, an attorney, deacon, and Bible study teacher, and they have a daughter Kelli. The Martins live in Houston, Texas.

Katie McCoy is the editor of *Biblical Woman,* a women's issues website from the Women's Programs at Southwestern Baptist Theological Seminary. She received her Master of Divinity with a concentration in Women's Studies from Southwestern Baptist Theological Seminary and is pursuing her Doctor of Philosophy in Systematic Theology from Southwestern. She has a passion for connecting God's Word to contemporary culture.

Erika N. Mercer is pursuing a Master of Divinity at Southwestern Baptist Theological Seminary, where she works as administrative assistant to the first lady. She enjoys serving through the music and children's ministries in her local church, Cana Baptist Church, and in ministry to international students in Arlington, Texas. She resides in Fort Worth, Texas, with her Jack Russell Junia and is a devoted "Aunt E" to her six nieces and nephews. She has a passion for disciple-making and hopes to serve the Lord on the international mission field after she graduates.

Mary K. Mohler serves in ministry as the president's wife at Southern Baptist Theological Seminary in Louisville, Kentucky, and as the founder and director of the Seminary Wives Institute, an academic program for student wives. A native of Michigan, she graduated from Samford University with a Bachelor of Science in Biology. She enjoys serving as a women's conference speaker and contributing author. She and her husband Dr. R. Albert Mohler Jr. have two children, Katie (Mrs. Riley Barnes) of Washington, D.C., and Christopher of Louisville.

Diane Nix is the director and founder of *Contagious Joy 4 Him,* a network of encouragement to ministry wives around the globe, as well as an author, speaker, and blogger. Her husband, Dr. Preston Nix, is professor of evangelism and evangelistic preaching at New Orleans Baptist Theological Seminary. Serving in ministry together for 31 years, they have two biological daughters and two grown spiritual daughters. She lives in Abita Springs, Louisiana.

Barbara O'Chester loved being a pastor's wife, during which time she mentored and encouraged other ministry wives and founded the Great Hills Women's Retreat Ministry. Barbara received a Bachelor of Church Music from New Orleans Baptist Theological Seminary. She has been the recipient of awards acknowledging her contribution to the lives of ministry wives. She and her husband continue serving the Lord in retirement in Cedar Park, Texas.

Denise O'Donoghue is the director of women's life and an assistant professor at Southeastern Baptist Theological Seminary, where she earned her Master of Arts in Biblical Counseling and Doctor of Education. Dr. O'Donoghue has served as the women's ministry coordinator at Bay Leaf Baptist Church, where she loves discipling women in the Word. She has two married daughters and six grandchildren. Denise and her husband Rod live in Raleigh, North Carolina.

Jessica Pigg is a contributing writer for the *Biblical Woman* website and enjoys serving in ministry alongside her husband Timothy, who is the pastor of First Baptist Church Immokalee. She received her Bachelor of Science in Biblical Studies from Southwestern Baptist Theological Seminary, where she is currently pursuing her master's degree. Her passion is sharing biblical advice about the home and hospitality. She lives in Immokalee, Florida.

Terri Stovall is the dean of women's programs at Southwestern Baptist Theological Seminary where she oversees the academic programs for women as well as the various women's organizations on campus. She has earned two master's degrees and a doctorate from Southwestern Seminary. Dr. Stovall has also served in several churches in women's ministry and has co-authored books about women's ministry. She and her husband Jay live in Arlington, Texas.

Courtney Veasey is the Director of Women's Academic Programs at New Orleans Baptist Theological Seminary as well as a blogger and speaker. She holds a Master of Theology in New Testament from Golden Gate Baptist Theological Seminary and a Master of Divinity in Biblical Languages from New Orleans Baptist Theological Seminary, where she is currently pursuing her Doctor of Philosophy in Biblical Interpretation. She lives in New Orleans, Louisiana, and loves walking with Jesus, seeing Him do the impossible in her life every day.

Amanda Walker is an author and a contributing writer for the *Biblical Woman* website and enjoys serving alongside her husband Chris, who is a college and missions pastor. She has a Master of Arts in Christian Education with a concentration in Women's Studies and Biblical Counseling and a Doctor of Educational Ministry in Educational Leadership from Southwestern Baptist Theological Seminary. She has two daughters and is passionate about training women to fulfill God's calling in their lives. She lives with her family in Ruston, Louisiana.

Joy Martin White is an adjunct professor and Bible study leader as well as the president's wife at Cedarville University. She has a Master of Divinity in Women's Studies and a Master of Theology from Southeastern Baptist Theological Seminary. She enjoys serving alongside her husband Thomas and homeschooling their two children, Rachel and Samuel. She lives in Cedarville, Ohio.

Janet Wicker is the women's ministry leader and pastor's wife at First Baptist Church Naples, where she and her husband have served for 23 years. She enjoys mentoring and teaching women at her church on a weekly basis. She has three children who love the Lord and four grandchildren. She lives and serves the Lord in Naples, Florida.

Karen Yarnell is a Bible study leader and ministers to women through teaching. She has a Master of Divinity from Southeastern Baptist Theological Seminary and is pursuing a Master of Theology at Southwestern Baptist Theological Seminary. She enjoys homeschooling her five children and serving alongside her husband Malcolm. The Yarnell family lives in Fort Worth, Texas.

Kristin Yeldell teaches women about the transforming power of the Word of God and serves alongside her husband Eric, who is a worship pastor at First Baptist Church Naples. She has a Master of Divinity with a concentration in Women's Ministry from Southern Baptist Theological Seminary. Kristin and Eric have four children and live in Naples, Florida.

Acknowledgments

Sincere gratitude is expressed to many people who have labored diligently "behind the scenes." Appreciation is conveyed to Laura Landry and Julie Stewart of the New Orleans Baptist Theological Seminary for their support and encouragement. Special thanks are extended to the Southwestern Baptist Theological Seminary team—Tamra Hernandez, Erika Mercer, and Candi Finch, who have provided excellent skills and expertise.

Working with Kim Stanford, managing editor of book production, B&H Publishing Group, has been a joy. We are also thankful for the continued support of the entire B&H Publishing team, especially Jennifer Lyell.

Our families have provided overwhelming encouragement in our commitment to develop excellent Bible study resources for women. We are especially grateful for our parents, who have prayed for us and taught us to love God's Word. Rhonda is grateful to her husband Chuck Kelley, who encourages her in the pursuit of her ministry calling and lovingly supports her personally, while maintaining the many responsibilities as president of the New Orleans Baptist Theological Seminary. Dorothy is grateful for her children Armour and Rachel Patterson; Mark and Carmen Howell (and her granddaughters Abigail and Rebekah); and most of all her husband Paige Patterson, who generously offers guidance and wisdom and the loving support that made such a project possible, while serving as president of the Southwestern Baptist Theological Seminary.

Daily Bible Reading Plan

Daily Bible reading plans have been developed to familiarize readers with God's Word through a systematic reading of portions of Scripture every day. Many different daily Bible reading plans are available to assist Christians in developing the spiritual discipline of Bible study. This unique plan follows these devotional readings from Genesis to Revelation providing the broader biblical context and insight into the whole counsel of truth.